STOP ME IF YOU CAN

How The Capture Of The Criminal Justice System In South Africa Was Disrupted And Reversed

PAUL O'SULLIVAN CFE

ACFE®
Association of Certified Fraud Examiners
Together, Reducing Fraud Worldwide

100% of the proceeds of sale of this book will be donated to www.forensicsforjustice.org to assist in the fight against corruption.

Irish for O'Sullivan is *"O'Suileabhain"*,meaning *"Son of Hawk-Eye"* or son of the one-eyed giant.

The family motto is *"Lamh foistenach abu"*,

meaning ***"The Steady Hand to Victory"***

"The only thing necessary for the triumph

of evil is for good men to do nothing. "

- Edmund Burke

"When bad people rise up, it's up to the rest of us to drag them back

down. A simple enough solution I suppose, but one that works.

- Paul O'Sullivan – April 2022"

First published by Paul O'Sullivan

978-0-620-97328-1 (print)
978-0-620-97329-8 (e-book)

Edited by Phillipa Mitchell

Cover and interior crafted with love by the team at:

www.myebook.online

MYEBOOK
WE EMPOWER AUTHORS

This book is dedicated to:

My wife, Viktoria.

My seven children.

Sarah-Jane Trent.

Melissa Naidu.

Kim Marriott

The brave men and women of IPID.

All the good prosecutors in South Africa.

All the good police officers in South Africa.

My friends who stood by me in difficult times.

Mandla Mahlangu, who made the ultimate sacrifice.

Kallie Kriel and his team at AfriForum for their faith in me.

All the hard-working Certified Fraud Examiners in the world.

All the staff at Forensics for Justice & Paul O'Sullivan & Associates. All the honest and hardworking civil servants who do the right thing.

All the whistle-blowers who risked their lives or livelihoods by blowing the whistle on corruption.

The good and decent citizens of South Africa who took a stand – and continue to take a stand – against corruption. We're all in this together!

CONTENTS

THE CAST

(IN ALPHABETICAL ORDER)

Abrahams, Shaun	Ex-unlawfully appointed National Director of Public Prosecutions (NDPP)
Abramjee, Yusuf	Prior journalist and chairman of the Pretoria Press Club
Africa, Mzilikazi wa	Pen name of controversial journalist Leonard Vusi Ndzhukula
Agrizzi, Angelo	Self-confessed corruptor and Bosasa whistleblower
Baloyi, George	Flexible prosecutor
Batohi, Shamila	National Director of Public Prosecutions
Beamish, Anthony	Controversial self-styled journalist
Beukman, Francois	ANC member of Parliament; Ally of Police Minister
Bhana, Solly	Alleged Controversial mine looter
Bhana, Faizal	Alleged Controversial mine looter
Binang, Temane Abram	Fearless Special Investigator at IPID
Bobroff, Darren	Controversial personal injury lawyer
Bobroff, Ronald	Controversial personal injury lawyer
Bokaba, Selby	Jackie Selebi's spin-doctor

Bolhuis, Mike	Convicted Fraudster and private investigator
Booysen, Johan	Retired general and KZN head of DPCI
Booysen, Rean	Business partner of Neil Diamond
Botha, Colonel	Sidekick of General Vineshkumar Moonoo
Brauns, Jerome	Zuma Lawyer and business partner of Judge Leona Theron
Breytenbach, Glynnis (Advocate)	Democratic Alliance (DA) member of parliament; Ex-Prosecutor of Commercial Crimes
Brown, Lynne	Zuma loyalist member of Parliament
Cele, Bheki	Minister of Police; Formerly disgraced Chief of Police
Coetzee, Gysbert	Detective Warrant Officer in the Police
Coetzee, Candice	Lieutenant Colonel in Crime Intelligence
Cronje, Hermione (Advocate)	Ex Special Director of Public Prosecutions
Daniel, Frederick	Victim of unlawful land grabs in Mpumalanga
De Beer, Sally	Spin Doctor for Khomotso Phahlane
De Lange, Deliwe	Disgraced co-accused of Khomotso Phahlane
De Nysschen, Gareth	Accused in stolen military ammunition case
Deale, John Henry	Alleged corruptor of Phahlane
Diamond, Neil	Disgraced ex-ANC councillor
Dramat, Anwar	Ex-Lieutenant General National and head of DPCI
Du Plessis, Piet	Controversial criminal defence lawyer
Els, Hennie	Aka Nicolas, professional forensic investigator
Epstein, Lance	Private investigator and WO Kobus Vlok's friend
Ferreira, Mario	Shareholder and director of Siyangena; Corruption suspect
Fliess, Douglas	Alleged abusive ex-husband of Lynn Fliess

Fliess, Lynn	Victim of Vlok extortion attempts
Fraser Arthur	Controversial ex-head of National Intelligence
Furman Darryl	Attorney, part of O'Sullivan legal team
Gigaba, Malusi	Zuma loyalist and controversial ex-ANC Minister
Gininda, Lieutenant (Colonel)	Now Brigadier; Head of Krejcir investigation team
Gordhan, Pravin	Controversial ex-ANC Finance Minister
Grobler, Wynand	Managing Editor of Carte Blanche
Guptas	Controversial immigrant family that fled South Africa
Hain, Peter (Lord)	Member of UK House of Lords and ex-anti-apartheid campaigner
Hartley, Ray	Controversial ex-Sunday Times editor
Hartman, Suzette	Whistle-blower on Phahlane corruption
Hathorn, Moray	Head of pro bono department at Webber Wentzel Attorneys
Hathurani, Edrees	Controversial director of Africa Cash & Carry
Hlahla, Monhla	Controversial ex-director of Airports Company South Africa
Hlakudi, Mangope Frans	Corrupt senior Eskom manager
Hlongwane, Fana	Friend of the family to Jacob Zuma and Dudu Myeni
Hodes, Laurance	Controversial criminal defence counsel
Hofstatter, Stephan	Disgraced former Sunday Times journalist
Hogg, Alec	Owner of Biznews
Holzen, Stephen (Magistrate)	Kempton Park magistrate who unlawfully stopped Krejcir deportation
Hoosen, Amod (Colonel)	Corrupt friend of General Vineshkumar Moonoo

Huang, Jen Chi	Convicted murderer and business associate of General Vineshkumar Moonoo and Khulubuse Zuma
Hulley, Michael	Zuma lawyer; Business partner of Judge Leona Theron
Issa, Sam	Murder victim of Radovan Krejcir
Jackson, Lolly	Murder victim of Radovan Krejcir
Jasat, Yusuf	Controversial lawyer of Yusuf Kajee
Jiba, Nomgcobo (Advocate)	Dismissed Deputy National Director of Public Prosecutions
Johnston, Alice	Convicted fraudster used as a pawn against O'Sullivan
Jooste, Chris	Dishonest estate manager at Phahlane's luxury development
Kajee, Yusuf	Controversial tobacco baron
Kalawe, Monwabisi	Ex-CEO of South Africa Airways; Victim of Myeni purges
Kanarak, Robert	Controversial lawyer for corrupt persons
Karamitsos, Efthimios Demis	Co-accused of Gareth de Nysschen
Keating, Keith	Owner of FDA; Alleged corruptor of Khomotso Phahlane
Kebble, Brett	Murdered mining tycoon
Kgamanyane, Israel	Disgraced ex-Acting Director of IPID
Kgorane, Clifford (Brigadier)	Part of Phahlane's unlawful Northwest Province team
Khana, Alfred (Major General)	Ineffective head of DPCI's Commercial Crimes Unit
Khuba, Ngogodlo (Lieutenant)	Part of the police squad that harassed O'Sullivan
Khuba, Innocent	Limpopo provincial head of IPID
Klatzow, David	Forensic specialist
Komodolowicz, Jolanta	Alleged corruptor of Khomotso Phahlane

Krejcir, Radovan	Convicted underworld criminal
Krejcir, Denis	Wanted person; Son of Radovan Krejcir
Kriel, Kallie	Founder of Afriforum
Lackay, Adrian	Ex-spokesperson of South African Revenue Service
Laganin, Veslin	Murder victim of Radovan Krejcir
Lamont, Justice	Trial judge of Radovan Krejcir
Lebeya, Godfrey (General)	National head of DPCI
Linnell, Nick	"Mr Fixit" of Dudu Myeni
Luca, George	Now deceased witness against Radovan Krejcir
Mabandla, Brigitte	Mbeki government Justice Minister
Mabasa, Joey Mabula	Corrupt ex-head of Crime Intelligence in Gauteng
Mabula, Ntebo 'Jan'	Kidnapping and torture accused; Phahlane Protector
Mabuza, David	Controversial Deputy President
Madonsela, Thuli	Ex-Public Protector
Maema, Sello (Advocate)	Controversial prosecutor
Magashula, Ace	Suspended Secretary-General of the ANC; Corruption accused
Mahlangu, William (Colonel)	Crime intelligence friend of Richard Mdluli
Mahlangu, Mandlakayise	Senior IPID investigator, murdered at his home in 2020
Mahlobo, David	Disgraced Ex Minister of Intelligence
Malema, Julius	Commander-in-chief of Economic Freedom Fighters
Malima, Colonel	Accomplice of Mokotedi
Manthatha, Vimpie	Self-styled blue light prince; Co-accused of Khomotso Phahlane
Manzini, Manala	Disgraced head of National Intelligence
Marriot, Kim	Fearless ex-colleague

Masango, Abram	Corrupt senior Eskom manager
Mashaba, Herman	Politician and friend of Paul O'Sullivan
Mavundla, Philane	Jacob Zuma benefactor and accomplice to Paulo Porcelli
Mbalula, Fikile	Current Minister of Transport a.k.a. 'Fear Fok All'
Mbangwa, Leon Abednigo	Imposter and illegal immigrant with fake identity documents
Mbulawa, Abednego	Fabricator of fake Myeni bank documents
Mcbride, Robert	Ex-Executive Director of IPID
Mccarthy, Leonard	Controversial former head of Scorpions
Mdluli, Richard (General)	Convicted former head of Crime Intelligence
Millar, Anthony	Competitor to Ronald Bobroff attorneys
Miya, Sibonisa	Krejcir co-accused, convicted murderer
Mkhwebane, Busisiwe	Controversial Public Protector
Mlotshwa, Jabulani	Prosecutor who masqueraded as an advocate
Modise, Lavery	Controversial head of Hogan Lovells in South Africa
Mokovhi, Captain	Unwilling member of Mokotedi squad
Mokotedi, Prince	Unlawfully appointed head of DPCI in Gauteng
Molefe, Popo	Ex-chair of PRASA, now chair of Transnet
Molefe, Brian	Disgraced former chair of Eskom
Montana, Lucky	Disgraced former CEO of PRASA
Moodley, Chockalingam (Roy)	Friend and benefactor of Jacob Zuma
Moonoo, Vineshkumar	Disgraced former Divisional Commissioner of Police
Moonoo, Manitha	Daughter of General Vineshkumar Moonoo and ex-employee of Jen Chi Huang
Moonsamy, Sandragasen	Brigadier; Brave police whistle-blower

Morema, Dan	Useless investigator at IPID
Movshovich, Vlad	Fearless lawyer at Webber Wentzel
Moyane, Tom	Disgraced head of SARS
Mrwebi, Lawrence (Advocate)	Disgraced and dismissed senior Prosecutor
Mulaudzi, Hangwani	Brigadier, disgraced and dismissed spin doctor
Mullon, Paul	Victim of Beamish fraud and harassment
Mundie, Yegan	Disgraced SARS investigator
Murray, James	Victim of Alice Johnston fraud and attempted murder
Myburgh, Peter-Louis	Fearless investigative journalist
Myeni, Thalente	Dudu Myeni and Jacob Zuma's alleged "love child"
Myeni, Cynthia Duduzile	a.k.a. 'Dudu', disgraced former chair of SAA
Naidu, Melissa	Fearless ex-colleague and victim of various attacks
Nare, Jacob	Pseudonym of witness against Krejcir and others
Ncube, Daniel	Member of the infamous Northwest Police Squad
Nel, Gerrie Advocate	Ex-Scorpions provincial head; Prosecutor of Jackie Selebi
Nel, Wynand	Magistrate, Kempton Park
Nhleko, Nkosinathi	Useless ANC Minister of Police
Nkabinde, Cedrick	Dishonest traitor and snitch
Ntlemeza, Berning	Disgraced and dismissed head of DPCI
Ntlemeza, Anele	Criminally convicted daughter of Berning Ntlemeza
Ohanes, Agopyan Hovig	Thailand crime victim of Vuyo Mkhize
Padayachee, Preggy	Associate of General Vineshkumar Moonoo
Phahlane, Khomotso Johannes	Corrupt Chief of Police
Phiyega, Mangwasi Victoria	Disgraced and dismissed Chief of Police

Porcelli, Paulo	Corruption accused and fugitive from justice
Potgieter, De Wet	Journalist 'friend' of Radovan Krejcir
Potiska, Milosh	Radovan Krejcir associate-turned-witness
Pretorius, Tori	Disgraced prosecutor who aided State Capture
Ramuhala, Freddy	Lieutenant Colonel; Part of the Radovan Krejcir investigation team
Ramahlaha, Boitumelo	Captain; Fearless whistleblowing cop
Ramaphosa, Cyril	President of the Republic of South Africa
Ramaphosa, Andile	Son of Cyril Ramaphosa
Rampedi, Piet	Disgraced journalist
Raphesu, Mantsha	Fearless IPID investigator
Roux, Barry	Senior Counsel; Part of O'Sullivan legal team
Sales, Mike	Colonel; Alleged Keith Keating beneficiary
Sarjoo, Charles	Tenderpreneur
Satchwell, Kathleen	Judge, SANEF panel
Selebi, Jackie	Disgraced convicted ex-Chief of Police (deceased)
Serrao, Angelique	Fearless investigative journalist
Sesoko, Mathews	Fearless National Investigative head of IPID
Shongwe Jeremiah	Judge; Recused from Zuma rape trial
Sitole, Khehla (General)	National Police Commissioner, 2017 -
Smith, Vincent	Corruption accused, ANC member of Parliament
Snyman, Durand	Corruption accused; Used car dealer
Sole, Sam	Fearless investigative journalist
Spies, Willie	Lawyer; Part of O'Sullivan's legal team
Stimpel, Cynthia	Courageous SAA whistle-blower
Swart, Werner	Investigative journalist
Symington, Vlok	SARS employee; Police kidnap victim

Taioe, Norman (Major General)	Retired senior police officer
Taljaard, Louis	Counsel; Part of O' Sullivan's legal team
Tau, Poloko	Captured ex-Sunday Times journalist
Taute, Monique	Fearless Afriforum anti-corruption campaigner
Terblanche, Frederik	Contractor who built Phahlane's mansion
Thamm, Marianne	Fearless investigative journalist
Theron, Hennie	Controversial private investigator
Theron, Leona	Judge; Previous business partner of Zuma legal team
Trindade, Antonio	Corrupt owner of company that bribed Eskom officials
Lindi, Nkosi-Thomas	Controversial Advocate and friend of Dudu Myeni
Thomas, Chad	Controversial private investigator
Trent, Sarah-Jane	Fearless attorney; Director of Forensics for Justice
Tsotsi, Zola	Disgraced former Eskom Chair who admitted perjuring himself
Van der Merwe, Cornelia	Girlfriend of Tony Beamish and bringer of fake charges
Van der Merwe, Michelle	Daughter of Cornelia van der Merwe
Van Loggerenberg, Johann	Former SARS Special Investigator
Van Niekerk, George	Dudu Myeni's attorney at ENS Africa
Van Rooyen, Des	Gupta/Zuma puppet and ANC MP
Viljoen, Peet	Disbarred Pretoria attorney
Vlok, Kobus	Warrant officer awaiting trial for crimes against O'Sullivan
Zuma, Jacob	Disgraced corrupt former President of South Africa
Zuma, Edward	Son of Jacob Zuma; Yusuf Kajee's business partner

Zuma, Khulubuse	Nephew of Jacob Zuma
Zuma, Nkosazana Dlamini	Ex-wife of Jacob Zuma and stepmother of Edward Zuma
Zuptas	Term coined by Julius Malema in reference to the Zuma and Gupta crime syndicate
Zuptoid	Any person loyal to (or an accomplice of) the Zuptas

ENTITIES

(IN ALPHABETICAL ORDER)

Absa	Absa Group Limited, financial services group in South Africa
ACSA	Airports Company South Africa Limited
AfriForum	Afrikaans civil rights movement
AmaBhungane	Investigative journalism NGO
ANN7	Gupta media empire
BDK Attorneys	Criminal defence attorneys in Johannesburg
Biznews	Online business news service
BNP Capital Pty Limited	Almost a beneficiary of Dudu Myeni's unlawful conduct
BNP Parabis	French bank
Bosasa	Corrupt company owned and run by the Watson family
CIG	Crime Intelligence Gathering, a division of Police Crime Intelligence
Crime Intelligence	Intelligence gathering division of the police
Dave Sheer Guns	Firearm dealer previously owned by Dave Sheer

DPCI	Directorate for Priority Crime Investigation a.k.a. 'Hawks'
DSO	Disbanded Directorate of Special Operations a.k.a. 'Scorpions'
EFF	Economic Freedom Fighters, a political party led by Julius Malema
ENS Forensics	A division of ENS Africa (attorneys)
EOH	Public information technology company
EOH Abantu	BEE subsidiary of EOH that acquired and then dumped FDA
Eskom	South African national electrical producer and distributor
EY	Auditing firm previously called Ernst and Young
FDA	Acronym for Forensic Data Analysts; Information technology firm owned by Keith Keating
FNB	First National Bank
Forensics for Justice	Not-for-profit entity fighting corruption
Freedom Under Law	Not-for-profit entity fighting legal wrong-doing
Hawks	Catch name for DPCI
Helen Suzman Foundation	Not-for-profit entity guarding the Constitution
Hogan Lovells	UK-based law firm that set up a South African office
IPID	Independent Police Investigative Directorate
Jacob Zuma Foundation	(So-called) non-profit used by Dudu Myeni for money laundering
JMPD	Johannesburg Metropolitan Police Department
Mpisi Group (Pty) Limited	Company owned by convicted murderer Jen Chi Huang
New Age	Now defunct Gupta newspaper
NIA	National Intelligence Agency

NPA	National Prosecuting Authority
OUTA	Organisation Undoing Tax Abuse – membership-based NPC
PCLU	Priority Crime Litigation Unit – a division of the NPA
POPCRU	Police and Prison Civil Rights Union
PRASA	Passenger Rail Agency of South Africa
RICA	Regulation of Interception of Communications Act
SAA	South African Airways
SAA Voyager	SAA's frequent flyer program
SAB	South African Breweries
SABC	South African Broadcasting Corporation
SANEF	South African National Editors Forum
SAPS	South African Police Service
SARS	South African Revenue Service
SCOPA	Parliamentary Standing Committee on Public Accounts
Scorpions	Catch-name for now-disbanded Directorate of Special Operations
SITA	State Information Technology Agency
Siyangena Technologies	Company awarded corrupt contracts by PRASA
TMM Holdings	Holding company of Siyangena
Transnet	State-owned transport and logistics infrastructure company
Tubular Construction Projects	Private company used by Antonio Trindade for corruption

AUTHOR'S NOTE

Some parts of this book include written extracts of transcripts of people whose first language might be something other than English. For reasons of accuracy, I have not interfered with these extracts and have reproduced them exactly as I found them, including any errors they may contain.

WHO IS PAUL O'SULLIVAN?

Although an engineer by profession, Paul O'Sullivan is recognised as one of South Africa's leading crime fighters, having given up engineering in the 1990s. With more than forty-five years experience in law enforcement – including diverse areas such as counter-espionage, counter-terrorism, counter-trafficking (drugs, weapons and human) – and local law enforcement – including syndicated crime, such as fraud, robbery and murder.

Paul O'Sullivan was the subject of multiple unlawful searches, arrests and torture between 2015 to 2018 as criminal cops sought to stop him from exposing systemic corruption in South Africa – which formed the backbone of state capture. He still exposed it and worked closely with others to stop it.

Apart from being an electronics engineer, Paul O'Sullivan is also a:

- Certified Fraud Examiner (CFE)
- US Department of Justice Certified Document Examiner
- Certified Voice Stress Analyst
- Certified Aviation Security Specialist
- Fellow of the Institute of Directors

He was involved in Law Enforcement Operations in the UK, Cyprus, the USA, Zimbabwe and South Africa between 1973 and 2002.

Notable Recent South African Cases Investigated:

- Jackie Selebi — Corrupt Head of Interpol/South African Police
- Radovan Krejcir — Transnational Organised Crime
- Lucky Montana — Corrupt CEO of Passenger Rail Agency of South Africa (PRASA)
- Khomotso Phahlane — Corrupt Chief of Police
- Berning Ntlemeza — Corrupt Head of Directorate for Priority Crime Investigation (DPCI)(Hawks)
- Dudu Myeni — Corrupt Chair of South African Airways (SAA), mistress of Zuma
- Tony Trindade — Owner of Tubular Steel, bribed senior ESKOM employees
- Jacob Zuma — Corrupt President of South Africa

Commendations Relating to Law Enforcement:

1978	Commendation from Scotland Yard: Preventing a kidnapping/murder
1994	Cop of the Year – Johannesburg
2002	Commendation from the Canadian government for work in the field of reducing human trafficking
2003	Commendation from the Australian government for work in the field of reducing human trafficking
2011	Named a 'Paul Harris Fellow' by Rotary Club International
2014	Certified Fraud Examiner of the year – Africa
2015	Founded Forensics for Justice www.forensicsforjustice.org

CHAPTER 1
INCARCERATION

1 April 2016 - A SPEEDING CAR

I had just been dragged off a plane, my two young daughters beside me.

I was furious, but I was more worried about my children.

I knew what these criminals with badges were capable of.

Sitting in the back of a white Hawks' branded VW Golf GTI, I was jostled from side to side. The car hurtled at high speed, its blue lights flashing and siren blaring. The speedometer quivered between 200kph and 220kph.

We were surrounded by five other cars, all of them recklessly speeding, sirens blaring. I was being treated like a high-profile criminal. I might as well have been mafia boss Radovan Krejcir, who by now was on trial for a whole raft of crimes, including several attempts to assassinate me, having already been sentenced to 35 years in prison.

I always knew there was a good chance this day would come. You don't mess with powerful criminals with police badges and not expect them to retaliate in some way. And yet, in that moment, I still couldn't quite comprehend why I was in this car, my hands cuffed behind my back, being thrown around the rear seat like a rag doll. After all,

I was a crime fighter, having made many personal sacrifices in the name of justice. I was the one who watched the many villains I had recently laid charges against, being seized by the country's supposedly elite police force, the Directorate for Priority Crimes Investigation, or DPCI (often referred to as the Hawks). I was the person who *put* offenders in police cars, their hands bound by the cold, smooth steel of handcuffs. Now that person was me.

At the first turn onto the freeway, the car in front slammed on brakes. We nearly sped into it. Swerving at the last moment, we narrowly avoided hitting the crash barrier. I don't know how long it took us to get to Pretoria Central Police Station, but my relief at being able to get out of that speeding car was immense. I would soon learn that the nightmare was only about to begin.

I was led into a room and searched from head to toe. The officers rifled through my suitcase, searching for who knows what. I watched a policeman in civilian clothes take my two phones and begin downloading information off them. When I asked him why he was doing that, he casually replied:

"Because you used the phones to make interceptions."

What was this man talking about? What charges were the police trying to cook up against me?

I asked to see my warrant of arrest. I needed to know why I was there. I was told I would be shown it later. I would subsequently find out that there wasn't one.

In contrast to the mad rush to get me to the station, the police now seemed to have all the time in the world. It took several hours for them to process me. They took a set of my fingerprints and then repeated the exercise a further five times. I was searched again. I was read my constitutional rights. Colonel AK Hoosen from Durban's Organised Crime Unit, the policeman who had arrested me, examined my three passports and made a sarcastic comment about me carrying so many of them.

"So what?" I said. "There's no law against it."

A second official looked at the documents while typing onto a computer. It appeared the police's investigation was being carried out right in front of me. The following day, at half an hour past midnight, I signed a form acknowledging my arrest.

I would later discover that a private investigator, a convicted fraudster by the name of Mike Bolhuis, had tweeted just after midnight that I had been arrested. He quoted the exact serial number on my constitutional rights form. How had Bolhuis obtained this information twenty-eight minutes before I had even signed the form, I wondered? Later, I found out that he had been recruited as part of a team to "take down Paul O'Sullivan". I was taken to a general cell block full of men who had been incarcerated in the habitual Friday-night mayhem. The cell they led me to was overcrowded. I didn't know where to stand. Sitting on the ground was out of the question. The little space there was available was filthy. Every inch was covered in human excrement and rat droppings.

Dead rats had been pushed into the corners of the cells, while others lay where they had been killed. Those still alive ran around brazenly – even up the bars of the cells – chasing each other and copulating. After observing them for a while, I discovered that it took them less than three seconds. I imagined Sir David Attenborough commenting on this mating ritual.

As if the filth wasn't enough, raw sewage seeped out of the ground, running across the floor, mingling with the faeces and dead animals. The toilets didn't work, adding to the sewage ooze. There was no toilet paper – the men simply wiped themselves with their hands, rubbing whatever excrement they could salvage onto the wall alongside the toilet. The smell was indescribably nauseating. There was no escape from its putridness.

I was still wearing my smart casual clothes. What had been the perfect outfit for a Business Class flight was now glaringly out of place in this hellish place. Furthermore, I had a fractured heel and other complications with my right foot, which needed surgery. I usually wore a moon boot and kept one in both London and Johannesburg. I had travelled without the moon boot so as not to draw attention to my vulnerability. One of my cellmates kindly offered me a grey blanket to lie down on. As I took it from him, I saw insects crawling around in it. I chose to suffer the hot and humid conditions standing up.

Leaning against the wall, unable to sleep and or rest, I listened to the sounds of human abuse emanating from somewhere in the building. I had never been in such a hellish place. My human rights were deleted the minute I was shut inside that cell. Every man had been stripped of his dignity. We were being treated worse than some humans treat animals. No person, not even society's most hated, the murderers and rapists, should be held in such disgusting conditions.

There was no doubt in my mind that this treatment was a deliberate attempt to torture or punish me for me exposing corruption in the highest corners of the justice system and government. Clearly, it was revenge, but by who?

Finding the evidence would occupy the next few years of my life. I knew that the project to silence me was being driven by those I had exposed, men in the top leadership positions of the police. I was determined to make these crooked cops and prosecutors pay for what they were doing to me. But first, I had to get out of this hell-hole. I knew that turning the tide against them would be a long slog and would require all my stealth and persistence. Failure was not an option.

12 HOURS EARLIER

1 April 2016 - 20:45. On board SA237 JNB to LHR

"Good evening, Mr O'Sullivan. As a Lifetime Platinum member, I would like to welcome you on board. Can I offer you Champagne? Orange juice? Water?"

I recognised the South African Airways air hostess from my regular trips between Johannesburg and London.

"Champagne, please," I replied, reaching out and taking a flute. Normally, I took the water, but I was in high spirits, thinking that a small relaxation of my habits was in order. I was on my way to London. There was an important mission I was determined to accomplish. I took a sip of the cold bubbly. It seemed to melt on my tongue.

I was in seat 5A, one row back from the second door of the aircraft. I always booked this seat as it meant I would be the first off the plane when it landed in London. As a Lifetime Platinum member of SAA's voyager rewards programme, I often managed to bag my seat of choice. God had blessed me with five girls and two boys. I was always happy to have them with me. However, the complicated life I led – through my own choice, having taken on some of South Africa's most vicious gangsters – meant we did not spend much time together. This was for their own safety. This time, Anna and Mary, my two youngest daughters, were travelling with me. Seated three rows behind me, they were heading back to school, having spent their Easter holidays with me.

I had made sure they were given the usual activity packs presented to young children on SAA's long-haul flights. Although Anna was only nine years old and Mary eight, they often travelled alone. This was a special trip, as we would all be together – at least that was the plan.

It was Friday, so I would have ample time to get them home, settled in and off to school that Monday, before attending a media conference in London that same day. I was planning on exposing the depths of the evil, corrupt regime that had taken hold of my beloved country, South Africa.

Anna was born in South Africa in 2006, but Mary was born in Europe while I was in temporary exile after exposing former police chief and Interpol Head, Jackie Selebi. He had not yet been criminally charged at that stage, and I had moved to Europe for a while after finding out he had plans to murder my family.

My two older daughters lived in different corners of the world. My eldest was the lead casualty doctor at Hamilton Hospital, two hours south of Auckland in rural New Zealand. Her younger sister was a scientist working for NASA. Fortunately for me, NASA had covered the cost of all her post-graduate tertiary education, and she worked on combined NASA and US Navy projects in one form or another. Her biggest claim to fame was being one of the eighty or so persons in Houston's Mission Control when Curiosity landed on the surface of Mars. Having a rocket scientist for a daughter always made for interesting dinner table conversation.

As I sipped on the champagne, I thought about the media conference I had called to take place on the 4th of April 2016 in London's Whitehall. I was going to expose the links between the mafia, al-Qaeda and one of the most senior cops in the South African Police. I had already notified the US and British governments about the threat to regional stability posed by al-Qaeda's links to certain members of the Zuptas – a term coined by Economic Freedom Fighter's leader Julius Malema to describe the corrupt relationship between Zuma and the Indian immigrant Gupta family – and their accomplices within the criminal justice system.

I also had plans to meet my old friend Herman Mashaba. We have been friends for many years, and Herman had recently found a new home in the Democratic Alliance, or DA, the official opposition to the

ANC. At that time, he had just been announced as the DA candidate for Mayor of Johannesburg, and I was keen to see him get the job. He was going to London to meet its then-mayor, now Prime Minister, Boris Johnson, and we were all going to hook up for lunch on the Sunday.

Herman, like me, was another of the many loyal ANC members who had simply had enough of the systemic corruption that had flourished under the dictatorial control of Zuma and his many criminal accomplices. Unbeknownst to me then, the entrenched corruption of the governing party was so bad that they would only control one major city after the 2016 municipal elections, with Johannesburg, Pretoria, Port Elizabeth and Cape Town governed by the DA or DA-led coalitions. I thought about the rot I had uncovered since embarking on a clean-up of the South African Police in 2001. It was clear to me that the Zuma and Gupta associates who had taken over the criminal justice system were being protected. I had realised, by that stage, that the Zupta Empire was the largest organised crime syndicate that South Africa had ever seen.

The captain's voice interrupted my thoughts as he announced that we would soon be ready for take-off.

My attention was drawn to the aircraft door. The crew were closing the door so that the ground crew could pull back the air-bridge and we could be on our way. Just as they were pulling the door in towards the aircraft, I heard a male voice shouting, "Stop! Stop! There's an emergency! I need to come on board."

The door opened, and a male supervisor, wearing the traditional red-jacket of SAA management, walked over to my seat.

"Are you Mr O'Sullivan?" he asked.

"I am," I said. "What's the problem?"

"Sir, I have to ask you to step off the plane right away. There are some police officers here, and they will not let the plane go unless you step off first. You also have to bring your two minor children with you."

We never travelled with anything other than carry-on baggage, so I went straight to Anna and Mary, who were by now engrossed in colouring in pictures in their activity books.

"Come on, girls," I said. "There's a problem. We need to get off the plane."

"What's wrong, Daddy? Why do we have to get off?' Anna asked.

"I don't know, my darling. We just need to, so let's go and find out."

I led my two girls off the plane. They wanted to bring along their colouring-in books, but I told them to leave them on the seats, thinking they would soon go back to them.

At the top of the air bridge, I was met by an Indian male in a flashy suit and shoes, who introduced himself to me as Colonel Hoosen from the Hawks in Durban. I wondered how a police officer on a Colonel's salary could afford such expensive attire. I immediately recognised his name. This guy was no ordinary police officer – he was a close friend of Lieutenant-General Vineshkumar Moonoo, the alleged corrupt Head of the police's Detective Unit. He was also the country's so-called top detective. He was the Divisional Commander of the Detective Services and, as such, had dotted line control over every detective in the country. Moonoo wielded massive power and influence and allegedly abused this power to protect many criminals. There were also plenty of rumours about him spending time at casinos blowing money.

Hoosen, known as one of Moonoo's accomplices, had been involved in a secret meeting that had taken place in November 2015. I had been investigating him and his connections to organised crime for some time. The intelligence I got back from that meeting was that they had been discussing ways to stop my investigations. They had even allegedly discussed allowing – or encouraging – Radovan Krejcir to kill me. More evidence corroborating this would come out during the next three years.

"I know who you are, and I know everything about you," I said tersely to Hoosen. "I even know where you live. You are one of Moonoo's accomplices. What do you want with me?"

Hoosen angrily kicked me on the ankle. "You'd better watch your tongue. You are already in big trouble."

"Don't you touch my daddy!" Anna screamed. "He will arrest you!"

I laughed. "Don't worry, my darling," I said calmly. We are just joking." I did not want the girls to be traumatised by whatever was happening.

Hoosen was with other cops who I had never seen before. I later identified them as Zuptoid cops who were under the control of the corrupt Hawks Head Lieutenant General Berning Ntlemeza. Prince Mokotedi, who had recently surfaced as a Major General in the Directorate of Priority Crime Investigation, also known as the DPCI, or Hawks, was also there. Mokotedi had previously resigned ahead of his disciplinary enquiry at the NPA for dishonesty, which was ironic since he was the Head of 'Ethics' at the country's National Prosecuting Authority. He was also a self-confessed Zuma supporter. I suspected he'd been appointed to his current post for what he would *not* do, rather than what he *could* do – or what he would be prepared to do like harassing Zuma detractors like me. As soon as I saw Mokotedi, I knew trouble was coming and that I would not be getting back on that plane to London.

Hoosen turned to me and instructed one of his accomplices to read a pre-prepared note:

"Paul O'Sullivan, you have been arrested for breaching Section 26B of the South African Citizenship Act. You do not have to say anything, but anything you do say will be taken down in writing and used as evidence against you."

"Is that a serious offence?" I asked. I had no idea what he was talking about.

"It *is* for you," Hoosen replied sarcastically. "We are arresting you, and you will be detained."

I promptly asked for a copy of the arrest warrant and was told I would get it as soon as we got back to the station. I would later discover there never was one – the prosecutor had refused to request a magistrate to issue one, as he did not believe the charges were genuine.

"Which station?" I asked.

"Wait and see."

Hoosen told me he was the head of a 'special task team' that had been set up to investigate my actions and bring me down. Of course, I already knew he was busy with that.

I phoned Anna and Mary's mother in the UK and told her we had just been taken off the flight because I had been arrested, although I had no idea why. She laughed and accused me of playing an April Fool's prank on her. It took me several minutes to convince her this was no joke.

Arrangements were then made for my two little girls to be taken from the airport. My wife, Viktoria, would drive through and collect them. They still needed to be flown back to the UK so they would not miss school that Monday, but, as it turned out, they would have to miss school, as there were no seats on the next day's flight. I have since vowed to make every single one of those thugs pay for what they did to me and my girls.

Anna and Mary at OR Tambo Airport, on their way to the UK whilst I was in prison.

I called my attorney, Darryl Furman, and told him I had been arrested and would be taken to Kempton Park Police Station. Having been a police officer for many years – which included a three-year stint in the Border Police at Johannesburg's international airport – I knew that all persons detained at the airport, for any offence, had to first be taken to Kempton Park Police Station for processing. Hoosen then took my phone away and told me I would no longer be needing it.

We walked to SAA's roadside check-in office to wait for Viktoria to fetch the girls. As soon as she arrived, the police handcuffed me tightly, my hands behind my back, and marched me away in front of my two little girls, who were crying with fear. I was bundled into a Golf GTi. As we passed the Kempton Park turn-off on the freeway, I asked the two cops in the front of the car where we were going.

"Pretoria," they said.

15 DAYS EARLIER

I had already begun turning up the heat on the police. I now had proof that not only Moonoo but also Ntlemeza were involved in the corrupt state capture Zupta regime. I had also started looking at a mansion that General Khomotso Phahlane, the Acting Police Commissioner, had purchased in an exclusive residential estate in the North of Pretoria. How could a police general afford an R8-million house, I wondered? It didn't take a genius to figure out that something wasn't right. I had opened a corruption docket against Phahlane that February and was pursuing it vigorously since I knew that corrupt cops had the potential to bring my country to its knees. My docket contained prima facie evidence of bribes paid to Phahlane, so I knew I had the high moral ground.

At 6 p.m. on the 15th of March 2016, I sent out an email to the dishonest Hawks' spin doctor, Brigadier Hangwani Mulaudzi. I copied Phahlane and Moonoo in, as well as several other senior police and Independent Police Investigative Directorate (IPID) officials. I also blind copied many journalists, one of whom later described the email as a trap that these crooks walked straight into.

> **From:** *Paul O'Sullivan*
>
> **Sent:** *15 March 2016 06:01 PM*
>
> **To:** *'MulaudziH@saps.gov.za'*
>
> **Cc:** *PhahlaneK@saps.gov.za; 'tshikat@saps.gov.za'; taioeno@saps.gov.za; Ikgamanyane@ipid.gov.za; moonoov@saps.gov.za; 'Tom Winnifrith'*
>
> **Subject:** *FW: PRAVIN GORDAN'S NO-KNOWLEDGE OF LETTER IS MISLEADING*
>
> *Mulaudzi,*
>
> *I would have hoped that Bokaba's replacement would have been an ethical person.*

I'm going to cut straight to the chase. After reading the disgusting diatribe replete with invective, lies and spin-doctoring, that you have set out below, my hopes are dashed. First of all, we all know that it's a witch-hunt at the taxpayers' expense and distracting the real police from the real job of putting crooks behind bars. The criminal cases of defeating the ends of justice in the IPID cases will follow just as soon as I can get the docket prepared. That will also be lodged with IPID for them to hide in a dark room somewhere.

You should be ashamed of yourself for producing such unadulterated garbage aimed at intimidating a respectable Minister.

I have today started a process that will see Ntlemeza go to prison and spend a very long time there. There will be a lot of other dirty cops joining him there. Of this, I am 100% certain.

A lot of good people paid the ultimate sacrifice for our country to be free and democratic, and I (along with 45 million other South Africans) do not take kindly to rubbish like Ntlemeza, Zuma and the Gupta's (collectively Zuptas) destroying that democracy, to keep a crooked president out of prison. Namely Zuma. And you, you choose to propagate their disgraceful crimes by helping them.

And I, a considerable taxpayer, do not appreciate that my taxes are being wasted on the rubbish being produced by low-ethics people like you to prop up a criminal assault on Treasury, NPA, SAPS, SAA, Dube Tradeport, and, and, and..... Where the Zuptas have all but taken over.

I shall leave no stone unturned (and no cost will be spared) to put those who are busy criminalising the criminal justice system (to protect corrupt politicians and their lackeys) behind bars where they so rightfully belong.

*All the appointments that are criminalising the criminal justice system **WILL** be set aside.*

STOP ME IF YOU CAN!

I then went on, in the same email, to directly accuse South Africa's Chief of Police, Lieutenant General Johannes Phahlane, of corruption.

Phahlane,

Before you start taking sides, remember that you are the one that has worked so hard to protect the crooked cop Moonoo, who is on the payroll of Krejcir and many other mafia king-pins, many of them with Zupta connections. You are also the one that has forced me to spend over R100k per month to protect a key state witness that dirty cops on your payroll, led by Moonoo, are trying to have murdered so that Krejcir can get a leg-up.

Before I forget, Phahlane, I wanted to ask you where the money came from to build this mansion in Sables Hills Waterfront Estate? I've got a copy of the title deeds and bond details. As I see it, you had spare cash of between R3m and R5m. Did you win the lottery?

Picture of Phahlane's mansion. Source: Paul O'Sullivan

I opened a case about this house with IPID, but to date, they have not even acknowledged my complaint and have refused to return my emails enquiring on the progress. No doubt also nobbled by the Zuptas, just like SAA, Treasury, SARS, NPA, Hawks and SAPS. If you've got nothing to hide, tell me who built it and where the cash came from, as a R2.2m bond did NOT buy the land and build that house.

Guess what you cannot do? You cannot stop freedom of speech. People died for that, and dirty cops cannot stop it.

If it takes a ratings downgrade for South Africa to kick things into gear, then I guess we better take the downgrade.

One thing's for sure, I'm meeting in Whitehall on 2016-04-04, and I will hand a detailed report of the levels of corruption that this country has sunk to, with a request that it be shared globally, and this rot can be brought to a halt, by targeting the Zupta's and his dirty generals.

Remember, DON'T even dream of sending dirty cops to raid me like was done by Moonoo last year. I will tear into you all like a rabid dog.

My methods may be unorthodox, but given I am fighting corrupt state machinery with deep pockets, I will resort to tactics designed to win rather than make friends.

Watch this space!

TAKING AIM AT GORDHAN

At the time, the Hawks had taken aim at then Finance Minister Pravin Gordhan in an attempt to implicate him in the fake SARS (South African Revenue Service) 'rogue unit' saga. SARS is the state body responsible for the collection of taxes and excise. I had worked with senior SARS members for many years in taking down some significant criminal enterprises. However, Zuma and his Gupta family associates had become very wary that they were also in the sights of the SARS criminal investigation department and had started a process to taint the department. Zuma eventually appointed a crooked Head of SARS, who completely shut down the criminal investigation department, claiming that they had acted illegally by 'spying' on citizens, including

Zuma. It was an all-out attempt to tarnish the name of good, hard-working civil servants to capture the tax body and a further assault on a well-run institution, whose negative financial ramifications are still being felt in the country today. The Zuptoid battle axes were now being aimed at Treasury through Gordhan, which, if successful, would topple the country into chaos. I was intent on letting these crooks with badges know that I was onto them and would stop them in any way that I could.

South Africa was at a critical point in its democracy. The criminal Zupta empire had successfully taken over most of the country's key state institutions, with only a few left uncompromised. Only a small number of people seemed willing to stand up and fight against what was happening. . I knew how dangerous the situation was that we were in. The other South Africans who stood up against corruption were career police officials and prosecutors – or opposition members of parliament, who did what they were paid to do without fear or favour. I was the only one mounting the fight out of my own pocket and initiative, and I had adopted a very hard and radical approach to exposing them all. I was taking the fight right to their doorstep, even going so far as enquiring at the private school that Phahlane's children attended and how he paid their school fees.

TRAPPING SELEBI

Writing and publishing hard-hitting emails was just one such approach. I would also send these criminals WhatsApp messages and then delete the message as soon as I saw it had been read. On other days, I would talk to known contacts and drop some vital – but false – information about my activities, leading them up the garden path. I had developed one such ploy during my efforts to take down the world's top cop, Jackie Selebi. While he was out and about collecting brown envelopes, he also had an eye over his shoulder for me since I was knocking on the doors of the people who were paying him off. His paid spin doctors Sally de Beer and Selby Bokaba had insinuated that they knew who was behind the 'malicious media leaks' behind Selebi's dealings with the underworld and that the person would soon be arrested. I knew they were referring to me, and I also knew that Selebi's goons had set out to have my family murdered. That's when I decided to take my family into exile for two years while I carried on my work.

When my family was safe, I decided to ramp up the heat on Selebi. I decided to ruin Selebi's 2007 Christmas by setting up an elaborate hoax. I contacted one of Selebi's police colleagues, who did not like Selebi, and told them that the Directorate of Special Operations, also known as the Scorpions, or DSO (now absorbed into the Police as the Hawks), would be arresting Selebi at his home early the following morning. I also tipped off a few journalists. It was the only time I ever planted false data in the media. I received calls from two separate journalists asking me if I knew anything about an arrest warrant for Jackie Selebi. Of course, I knew one had been issued, but after the unlawful suspension of then-National Director of Public Prosecutions, Vusi Pikoli, steps had been taken to cancel it. I told the journalists that I had also heard that something would happen early the next day at his house in Pretoria and that he would appear in court soon thereafter.

The results were far better than I could have hoped for. That morning, at least twenty journalists were gathered outside Selebi's house and the police headquarters, with their long lenses, hoping for a shot of Selebi being taken away in handcuffs. It had a tremendous effect. The crooked chief of police must have felt so exposed while he wrung his hands with worry, wondering whether or not his arrest was imminent.[1]

1 Simon Nare and Siphi Masombuka, Selebi 'in his office working', Sowetan Live, 13 December 2007, https://sowetanlive.co.za/amp/news/2007-12-13-selebi-in-his-office-working/

Dealing with General Khomotso Phahlane and his accomplices was déjà vu – but ten years on from Jackie Selebi. I knew that I had to turn up the heat so that the members of the Zupta cabal in the criminal justice system wouldn't get away with what they were doing. If they did, South Africa would be on a downward spiral to ruination from which it might never recover. My email was intended to make the crooks squirm, and it did. The picture I had taken outside the front of his mansion was intended to unsettle him.

Now under arrest, I sensed that I had angered far too many powerful people. I believe that telling them about the planned 4th of April meeting in Whitehall, London, to inform the world of the corrupt regime that had taken over South Africa was a tipping point for my unlawful arrest. By telling them that I was onto them and would not take my foot off the gas in exposing their corrupt conduct, I had exposed myself for retaliation

CHAPTER 2
THE BEGINNING

BACK IN TIME

To understand how I got arrested on the 1st of April 2016, it is necessary to go back in time and explain the events of the prior twenty years. It's a long story. Some of what I will relate here has been covered in much more detail in well known *Daily Maverick* journalist Marianne Thamm's best-selling book *To Catch a Cop – The Paul O'Sullivan Story*. I have no wish to repeat everything here, so I will merely give an outline for the benefit of those who have not read that book.

In 1996, I was a director of Tourism Johannesburg, the City's tourism marketing entity. I had just been appointed the managing director of the company that owned the Randburg Waterfront. I was also the founder and Chairman of Johannesburg's Big Five Tourist Destinations, carefully chosen by me: the Randburg Waterfront, Gold Reef City, Soweto, the Rhino and Lion Nature Reserve, and the Johannesburg Zoo.

I persuaded the City Council of Johannesburg to get involved with what would become the 'Johannesburg City Slicker', the City's first hop-on hop-off tourism bus. Johannesburg Metro bus provided the busses and the crew to operate them, as well as the purpose-built bus stops and necessary ticketing service. The busses – I think there were about five of them – had their roofs removed and were painted bright green with the words 'Johannesburg City Slicker' emblazoned along the sides.

In the mid-1990s, getting tourists into Soweto was almost unheard of. However, the project took off like wildfire. I got many of the potential tourism product owners on board, and together, we paid for the formation of a not-for-profit company, which we called Soweto Tourism Development Association or SOTODA for short. The Hector Pieterson Square, the seat of the infamous Soweto uprising on 16 June 1976 (where thirteen-year-old Hector Pieterson was one of the first to be murdered by the apartheid police), needed a serious face-lift if it was to be worthy of receiving tourists.

Not far away from Hector Pieterson Square was Vilikazi Street, the only street in the world where two Nobel Peace Laureates – Nelson Mandela and Archbishop Desmond Tutu – once lived. Tutu won the Nobel Peace Prize in 1984, and Mandela won it nine years later, along with his oppressor, then President of South Africa, Willem de Klerk. Mandela's old house, like the Hector Pieterson Square, was also in a terribly run-down condition and in dire need of a face-lift. I joined others in raising a chorus of voices, requesting funds from the government. We were all delighted when the Poverty Relief Fund granted sixteen million rands for the development of Hector Pieterson Square. A purpose-built visitor's centre and memorial was the result.

In the early days of the tourism project in Soweto, I focussed on domestic tourists. The thought dawned on me that there were about one million or so whites and Indians within a fifty to seventy-five-kilometre radius of Soweto who had never stepped foot there. Using local media and the brightly painted busses, we decided to promote Soweto as a fun weekend activity. We doubled the number of busses running for the weekend and published that the busses would be free.

I had signs made up to place on the City Slicker bus stop that read *Whites Only*. This certainly got tongues wagging. We were only a few years out of the apartheid regime's oppressive years, but the tongue-in-cheek trick paid off. If you were white, you got a free ride to Soweto, with return trips every half hour.

The busses were soon flowing, and for the first time ever, busloads of white people were visiting Soweto. The busses always ended up at Wandies Place, a traditional themed restaurant where its new white patrons were made to feel welcome. Soweto was now firmly on the domestic tourism map. Soweto has become one of the must-see and must-do calendar items for local and international tourists alike. Local Africans see it as a return to their roots, and many of them spend late nights and long afternoons in its many trendy restaurants.

My time promoting tourism in Soweto made me many solid friends, such as Wandy Ndala, the entrepreneurial owner of Wandies Place and Tebogo Motswai of The Rock. When The Rock burnt down due to an electrical over-load in 1997, Tebogo lost everything. He had full insurance cover with Auto & General, but they refused to pay out, stating that the fire had been started deliberately. What some insurance companies disrespectfully referred to as 'Jewish Stocktakes' was now being used to stop the pay-out. Yet, there was no evidence of arson. South African Breweries' Museum of Beer, was on the City-Slicker's route. A quick call to Meyer Khan, SAB's CEO, saw a huge marquee erected in the parking lot in front of the burnt-out building, fully equipped with fridges and furniture. The Rock was back in business, but it was not sustainable. It would cost millions to rebuild.

At the time of the disaster, I was a part-time detective in the police and had undergone multiple forensic training courses. I carried out my own investigation of the fire, produced a report, and had it hand-delivered to Douw Steyn at Auto & General (who were, coincidently, also my insurers). My report found that an electrical overload in one of the rented shops had started the fire, caused by the tenant shopkeeper plugging too many items into an extension cable socket outlet, making it a high-resistive, heat-producing connection.

I wasn't going to let an insurance company put my friend out of business on false grounds, so another finding in the report was that Auto & General might be found to be biased by trying to insinuate that the fire had been started deliberately and was merely using this as an excuse to avoid paying out. I telephoned Douw Steyn and made sure he was aware of the report. He called me two days later, saying the claim had been 'approved' and that they would settle in full, despite a small degree of under-insurance.

CHANGING A PAINFUL PAST

I started my time with the police as a reservist at Booysens and then the notorious John Vorster Square. In 1996, I filed a petition with the Gauteng Legislature to change the name to Johannesburg Central Police Station and set up an official name-changing ceremony, which took place on Heritage Day in September 1997. I was the Master of Ceremonies and invited special guests, including Winnie Mandela, Jessie Duarte, and the family of the late Ahmed Timol, who had died after being detained at the station. The then Mayor of Johannesburg unveiled a memorial plaque to all those who had suffered at the hands of the apartheid Security Police.

I was hopeful that closing the chapter on John Vorster Square would result in the cops on duty performing their jobs with dignity and pride. I quickly came to realise that crime was one of South Africa's biggest challenges, which slowly started to occupy more of my time.

I started developing an inner-city security project aimed at reducing crime in the city centre of Johannesburg and had persuaded Standard Bank to donate R3-million to help fund the CCTV infrastructure. I also got bank executives involved in Soweto. They agreed to provide free banking facilities to SOTODA and later appointed their Properties Division to project manage the development of the Hector Pieterson Square at no cost. Standard Bank delegated one of their senior executives, Lyndon Barends, to head up the projects on their behalf and, by 2000, Soweto was well and truly on the "must-do" map for tourists visiting South Africa.

LACK OF SECURITY AT JOHANNESBURG INTERNATIONAL AIRPORT

In March 1999, I attended ITB in Berlin, one of the world's leading travel trade shows. My suitcase was full of glossy tourism brochures. I had seen with disgust how other exhibitors left their surplus brochures on the floor at the convention centre in Berlin. I could not do this, knowing how much money had been spent to produce them. I knew they could be used in other ways, so I brought about twenty kilograms of these brochures back with me. SAA was helpful in waiving excess baggage fees.

After picking up my suitcase from the carousel in the airport terminal, I called Jan to fetch me at the curb side. Jan was the Security Manager at the Randburg Waterfront and had helped me clean up its previous bad image. At 1.86 metres and about one hundred kilograms, Jan was not a guy to be messed with. He said he would look out for me at the front of the terminal building, and, as I saw him driving towards me, I stepped out into the road to signal to him. I had my shoulder bag with my computer on me, but I had to leave the big suitcase full of brochures on the curb side. When I turned back to get the suitcase, I saw a guy making off with it. Not a good choice, I thought. The case weighed in at just over thirty kilograms. As Jan pulled up, I threw my shoulder bag to him and took off after the suitcase thief. I brought him down with a tackle that would have made any Springbok rugby player proud.

It was then that I saw first-hand just how shocking the levels of police incompetence and corruption were at Johannesburg International Airport. I had to move mountains to ensure that this common criminal, who was part of a syndicate targeting tourists, was eventually jailed. I realised that South Africa was wasting its time and resources promoting the country as a tourist destination. If we could not prevent visitors from stepping off the plane and becoming victims of crime before the ink had dried on their passport stamps, we should not be promoting the country as a destination. By this stage, I was also a director of the Tourism Business Council of South Africa, or TBCSA. I raised the lack of security at the airport at the next board meeting and was horrified to discover that each board member had an equally damaging story to tell. The TBCSA resolved to make tourism safety and security one of its key projects in the ensuing years, mindful of the potential damage to brand South Africa. I was appointed to champion the project, which I did to the best of my ability. I transferred from Johannesburg Central Police Station to Johannesburg International Airport (now OR Tambo) as a reservist. What better way to get a deep understanding of how to fix crime against tourists than to be at the coalface of the action?

A FAILED WORLD CUP BID

My trip back from Berlin a year later in 2000 had another dark story to add to South Africa's woes. At the time, South Africa had just bid for the Soccer World Cup to take place in 2006. Joining us on the plane were five members of FIFA, who were visiting South Africa on a fact-finding tour. There would be a further thirty FIFA members arriving the following month. As is customary, the host bidding country pulls out all the stops to make sure the FIFA members see the best the country has to offer in an effort to prove that they are a worthy host.

In those days, the staple fleet of SAA was its Boeing 747-400s. I was in First Class with some of the FIFA members. This was before the advent of onboard LCD TV screens, where there is a screen per seat. In first-class, there was a drop-down screen with a projector. They put a movie on while supper was being served and again during breakfast when they screened a couple of TV shorts. One of the TV shorts being screened that morning was a programme called *Foods Around the World*. Some bright spark at SAA's in-flight entertainment division had thought it a good idea to purchase a thirty-minute programme that showed viewers how to buy and cook Cape Salmon. It showed a middle-aged to semi-retired white male going to the fish market in Cape Town, buying his choice of fish, and driving home. Approaching his home on the slopes of Table Mountain, the gentleman whipped out a remote control and pressed a button. The camera zoomed in on the sliding gate with an electric fence running across the top. The presenter's English accent could be heard saying, "Wow, you have good security". "You need it in South Africa," the gentleman replied. "The crime here is terrible." As if to take the edge off what he had just said, he added, "But this is nothing compared to Johannesburg. There, they will kill you in the street." I was gob-smacked. I turned to look at the five FIFA representatives, who were all staring at the screen with their mouths hanging open.

As soon as we got off the plane, I phoned then SAA CEO Coleman Andrews. To put it mildly, he was a hands-off CEO who knew nothing about running an airline. His wife was a senior employee with Bain and Co, who, curiously, were appointed by Andrews to manage the domestic fleet-replacement process underway at that time. Bain and Co also counted Boeing amongst its clients, so it was no surprise that the domestic fleet replacement took the form of Boeing 737-800s. When I told Coleman what I had seen on the TV, he seemed surprised. He didn't understand why I was so bothered. I then called the board members of TBCSA and gave them Coleman's number. They all called him and, after five more days, the video was finally pulled from the airline's entertainment line-up. The 2006 soccer World Cup went to Germany, courtesy of SAA and a Cape Salmon chef.

SECURITY FOR TOURISTS

Working with various stakeholders, we convened multiple workshops. By April 2000, I had written the government's draft policy on the safety and security of tourists, which was presented to Vali Moosa, the Minister of Tourism, at a TBCSA board meeting held at the Randburg Waterfront. During the same period, I was a member of the South African Council for Shopping Centres and had raised security issues at their meetings. I was then invited to put a module together for the University of Pretoria's course on Retail Management, which I did – and presented it too. If I was being paid for all this work in enhancing security at tourism spots and shopping malls, I am sure I would have made a healthy living, but that was not the case. I was more concerned with increasing tourist numbers. I had seen the potential economic benefits to the country, not to mention the job-creation potential.

Within weeks of joining the Border Police Unit of the South African Police, I started to plot the main issues that would need to be resolved if we were to turn the corner on crime at the airport. I had pretty much uncovered all the factors that enabled crime. I put a project plan together – a coordinated approach to overall security that would involve all the role players, including the police, customs, immigration, airport security, baggage handlers, airlines and their staff, cleaners and, last but by no means least, the airport owners.

The ten busiest airports in South Africa are owned and managed by Airports Company South Africa, or ACSA. ACSA is a monopolistic state-owned company that does not have to compete with other airport operators. They had their own narrow views on how their airports should be run and who should be involved in what. Security lapses at the airports were quickly moving up on their radar. After attempting and failing to get certain ACSA managers to make some fundamental changes to the way they did things in terms of security, I decided to escalate the discussion to the board of directors.

In early 2001, after much badgering and many telephone calls, I was invited to give a presentation on my security project proposal to the directors. I attended an ACSA board meeting at their head office in Bedfordview, where I was told I was limited to half an hour to make my presentation and deal with queries. I left an hour and a half later, with the whole board showing genuine enthusiasm for my project plan, particularly the Chairman, Mashudu Ramano.

WORKING FOR ACSA

A few weeks later, I got a call from Mashudu. He asked me to meet him at the airport, which I did. He wanted me to show him some of the weaknesses I had identified in my project plan. I spent the next two hours showing him parts of the airport he did not even know existed. We even saw crimes in progress. He thanked me for my time and boarded a plane for Cape Town.

The owners of the Randburg Waterfront had decided to sell their property as a going concern to Alan Gray Investments in Cape Town. I'd spent the last three years fixing up the broken shoppertainment centre and getting it back onto a profitable footing. The sale would realise a small fortune, for me anyway, as I had a minority share in the development. I assisted in pushing the sale through and decided the time had come for a career change.

Two weeks later, Mashudu called me and told me to buy the next week's *Sunday Times*. ACSA was advertising a position, and he wanted me to apply for it. The advert was for a Group Executive: Aviation

Security for the ten airports under ACSA's control. The timing could not have been better.

During my time working on high-profile fraud cases (and with the border police at the airport), I became known for my ability to investigate and get to the bottom of some complex cases. I was also head-hunted and offered the position of Director of Forensics at Grant Thornton in South Africa. While I had been told the job at Grant Thornton was mine, I did not have anything in writing. They also wanted me to take a cut on the salary I was earning as MD of the Randburg Waterfront but supplement it with a portion of the profits they hoped I would make. During the final negotiations with Grant Thornton, I was invited for my first interview with ACSA. The position would likely require a lot more work and be a bigger challenge, but it came with a much higher salary. A week after the first interview, I was invited back for a final interview at ACSA on Tuesday afternoon on the 24th of July, 2001.

On the morning of my final ACSA interview, I made a turn past the offices of Grant Thornton in Sandton to pick up my letter of appointment, which I was supposed to counter-sign and return before the end of the week, thereby allowing me to start on the 1st of September 2001. I started to think about the 16th-century proverb concerning the value of a bird in the hand as opposed to two in the bush. I was tempted to sign the Grant Thornton letter and be done with it, but I also thought that if I could make a difference to aviation security across the country, particularly in Johannesburg, I would be contributing to the well-being of all South Africans – with the exception of criminals, of course. I left with the letter, unsigned.

When I arrived for the final interview at ACSA, I discovered that the then Head of Security for ACSA, Andre Olivier, was being interviewed for the same position. His position was two notches below the position he had applied for, as Group Executive, which was a position on the executive board of ACSA. I thought that if Andre had not fixed the security issues in all his years as Head of security, he would be unlikely to fix it by being promoted two levels up to the company's executive board.

During the interview, I was asked a barrage of questions, all of which I confidently answered, demonstrating that I knew what was broken at the country's airports and what would need to be done to get it fixed. After the interview, Mashudu asked me to wait as he wanted to have a further discussion with me. I took a chair in the lobby area and waited about an hour. Mashudu eventually came out and told me that the job was mine if I could start the next day – subject to Ministerial approval. I asked how I could possibly start if it needed Ministerial approval. Mashudu said he had Dullah Omar, the then Minister of Transport, under whose umbrella ACSA fell, on telephonic standby.

Dullah and I knew each other quite well. We had interacted quite a bit whilst he was Minister of Justice, and I had set up a pilot project in the Johannesburg CBD to fast-track simple prosecutions in the Johannesburg Magistrates Court. I asked Mashudu why the Minister had to be involved. He told me that when Dullah Omar had appointed him the Chairman of ACSA, he had undertaken to ensure transformation by making sure that every executive board appointment going forward would be a person of colour. I was *very* white and approaching my forty-sixth birthday, almost fitting the bill for 'pale, male, and fifty'.

Mashudu made the phone call, and Dullah Omar had no problem endorsing my appointment. The Minister even released a media statement, saying he hoped I would bring positive change to the security and safety at ACSA's ten airports.

My arrival at ACSA was an unsettling affair. I had no office, no PA, and no computer. I started working out of the empty CEO's office since the CEO had recently resigned and ACSA was still looking for a replacement. Mashudu was doubling up as the Acting CEO, but he did not need an office. I was told that an office would be ready for me by the time the new CEO was appointed, which it was.

SECURITY ISSUES AT ACSA

My first day at ACSA turned out to be a baptism of fire. At around 10 p.m. on the 25th of July 2001, an armed robbery took place at Johannesburg International Airport. The security contractors to Swiss Air were relieved of around USD16-million, which at the time was worth a staggering one hundred and R60-million. ACSA's Head of Security and the Head of Security at Johannesburg International airport jointly decided *not* to tell me about the robbery, so I only found out the following morning when I received a phone call from a journalist. I was livid for being kept in the dark.

I called an urgent meeting with Andre Olivier, Johannesburg Airport's Head of Security, the General Manager, and the Assistant General Manager. I met with the security heads first, as they reported to the airport manager and me. It immediately became apparent that they were not being honest with me and were keeping details of the robbery and how it happened secret. When we met an hour later with the management of the airport, I insisted on an *in-situ* inspection of the incident. This quickly revealed that none of them had even visited the crime scene, nor had any of the senior managers at the airport. Within an hour, I quickly worked out how the crime had taken place and the very clear weaknesses in security, which included a missing section of the perimeter fence that had not been completed by contractors a few weeks earlier. I also figured out that the guards who were supposed to be at that location were not on duty and were missing altogether. When I asked the senior managers assembled before me why they had not visited the crime scene, they could not answer me. The fact that they could not even show me where the crime had taken place proved they were incompetent – or worse.

I then discovered that Andre Olivier, the 'head' of security, had been involved in all sorts of suspicious activities, including the award of the security contract to a company called Khuselani Security, the owner of which was a personal friend and financial sponsor of then Commissioner of Police, Jackie Selebi. I later obtained solid evidence of cash payments not only to the Head of Security at ACSA and the chief of police but also to the person who was supposed to be monitoring quality and compliance on the contract with the security company. The contract was dirty from the get-go.

Khuselani Security was run by a somewhat overbearing and politically connected businessman by the name of Noel Ngwenya. Khuselani supplied the security to all ten airports, which equated to more than five thousand personnel. Ngwenya had allegedly benefited from the millions of rands being poured into Khuselani's coffers on a monthly basis. At the time I joined ACSA, the contract had been in place for about a year and had a further two years to run. Strangely, it also contained a one-sided three-year renewal clause that could *only* be invoked by the contractor. I had never seen anything like it in all my years of contract management, and I immediately smelt a rather large rat. My nose was, as usual, bang on the mark. The rat I smelt turned out to be none other than Noel Ngwenya. When I first met him, I did not know that I was the one who would eventually send him to jail, but that's what happened.

One bad incident after another led to a complete breakdown of trust between myself, my respective heads of security, and Khuselani Security. Between the end of July and the end of August 2001, I had written no fewer than twenty-three letters placing Khuselani on terms to fix contract defects. These defects included hiring criminals, giving them security uniforms with no training, and then deploying them at the continent's largest commercial airport. They also rendered fraudulent tax invoices for ghost workers – security staff who did not appear for work. I met with Mashudu Ramano and told him I planned to cancel the contract and split the ten airports between different security companies so that we did not have all our eggs in one basket. He agreed with my suggestion, and I put the wheels in motion.

AUDITING JOHANNESBURG INTERNATIONAL AIRPORT

In September 2001, I was in the USA as part of an Aviation Security Audit on the three airports of New York's JFK, New Jersey's Newark, and Chicago's O'Hare. Before going to the United States, I hosted an audit of Johannesburg International Airport by AVSEC Auditors from the UK.

On the New York leg of the audit, I was accompanied by Johannesburg Airport's Border Police officer, Captain Vusi Maseko. My host for the visit and audit was Inspector Tony Infante of the Port Authority of New York and New Jersey Police Department (PAPD). Newark and JFK were among the airports owned by the PAPD, which also owned the World Trade Centre. Tony Infante was a twenty-year veteran and was Commander of the Police at JFK and La Guardia airports. Although we were on the job when we saw the first plane go into the North Tower, Tony Infante selflessly chose to return to his office at the World Trade Centre to assist with the evacuation. He was last seen on the stairwell of the North Tower shortly before it collapsed.

We were shocked and horrified to witness the planes fly into the World Trade Centre Twin Towers and the subsequent collapse of the towers and the buildings around them. One of the buildings that collapsed was my hotel, New York's Trade Centre Marriott, a twenty-two-floor, eight-hundred-room hotel known as World Trade Centre Three.

The following Thursday, I attended Tony Infante's funeral in what had become a month of funerals in New York. New York's mayor, Rudi Giuliani, was also present and was tight-lipped about his recent attempts to take over the policing at New York's JFK. He did, however, pay tribute to the fallen heroes and made a special mention of Tony Infante.

I saw with my own eyes what could happen when Aviation Security systems failed. I was determined that nothing remotely like a 9/11 would ever take place on South African soil. Being in charge of Aviation Security at South Africa's ten major airports, I became an IATA Aviation Security Auditor. AVSEC Auditors, as we had become known, would audit aviation security in different airports around the world.

When I departed on the first SAA flight back to Johannesburg after the September 11 attacks, I was already planning how to get rid of the incompetent and corrupt Khuselani Security.

Ngwenya, realising that Khuselani's days at ACSA were numbered, demanded an urgent meeting with me. He levelled threats at me, saying I did not know who I was messing with and that he would not be subject to a cancellation of his contract. A few weeks later, the final notice of cancellation was served on his company. A week or so after this, murder attempts on myself and Mashudu Ramano took place. I was left with bullet holes in my car on the second attempt, and Mashudu had bullet holes on the side of his family home. Fortunately, neither of us was injured.

Photo taken by Sunday Times journalist Jessica Bezuidenhout in November 2001

Ngwenya took us to court to overturn the cancellation of the contract and lost.

SELEBI AND HLAHLA PLAN MY ACSA EXIT

I then started receiving pressure from then-Commissioner of Police Jackie Selebi, who had teamed up with new ACSA CEO, Monhla Hlahla. Hlahla had scant idea how to run a business, let alone a business that included ten airports. I quickly realised she had been 'persuaded' by Jackie Selebi to get me out of ACSA. It took her eighteen months to finally terminate my contract with three months' notice, having tried and failed already. By this stage, Ngwenya was in prison, serving out a five-year term for fraud, with me as the complainant. Hlahla went on to allegedly make millions through her lucrative deals with Imperial and Sun International, both of whom were ACSA stakeholders.

If Hlahla and Selebi thought they had silenced me through my dismissal, they were wrong. From April 2003, and for the next seven years, I mounted a relentless civil court and media campaign against the pair. Hlahla eventually vanished into obscurity and Selebi was convicted of corruption and sentenced to fifteen years in prison. He passed away in late 2014 after being released from prison hospital on full medical parole, never having served a single day in an actual prison.

Much has been written about my seven-year fight to win justice by ensuring that Selebi was sent to prison. By the time Marianne Thamm had written *To Catch a Cop – The Paul O'Sullivan Story,* I was just getting my teeth into the next bunch of public servants who believed they were entitled to bring South Africa to its knees. As they would also discover, I would not let that happen. Not on my watch, anyway.

CHAPTER 3

THE SEEDS OF STATE CAPTURE

AFTER THE BEGINNING

The capture of the criminal justice system was really the beginning of the entire state capture project. It began with the collapse of the Scorpions, with Richard Mdluli pulling strings at Crime Intelligence and Zuma placing captured cadres at the National Prosecuting Authority. Once those key positions were in place, the state-owned agencies were taken over one by one. It was like a deck of cards slowly collapsing and then coming down so fast that you could barely see what was happening.

I knew something was wrong from the start as all the warning signs were fl ashing a dangerous red during the Selebi saga. In late 2012, the Supreme Court of Appeal dismissed Selebi's appeal against his conviction and sentence. A few weeks later, I set my sights on those who had helped Selebi stay out of prison since they were no longer of any use to him. These were people on the public payroll and included Advocate Lawrence Mrwebi, a senior prosecutor in the NPA, who had been the KwaZulu Natal Head of the Directorate for Special Operations (DSO), otherwise known as the Scorpions. Then there was an advocate by the name of Nomgcobo Jiba (one of Mrwebi's alleged sidekicks) and the National Prosecuting Authority's purported "ethics" manager, Prince Mokotedi. Others included the then Justice Minister Brigitte Mabandla, the then-President of South Africa, Thabo Mbeki and Manala Manzini, the Head of the National Intelligence Agency, as well as a handful of other corrupt senior policemen and women.

I opened a case against them all – Silverton CAS 369/10/2012 – where I named and shamed the corrupt remnants of Selebi's eight-year rule as the Commissioner of Police. I did not really believe that anyone would seriously investigate and prosecute any of the suspects in the Silverton case since, by that stage, the criminal justice system in South Africa had quite literally been penetrated and taken over by criminals, loyal first to Selebi and, after Selebi, to Zuma. However, I was adamant that the case docket be opened as I intended to point to it later as evidence that the system was rotten to the core, an allegation I would repeat many times over the next eight years.

It's worth mentioning the suspects and the charges I levelled at them insofar as these charges should have led to at least a handful of criminal prosecutions. I shall also include some detail about each person, as contained in my October 2012 sworn statement:

> *As I closed in on Selebi, I became aware of a criminal conspiracy to simply let him off the hook. This conspiracy included creating a red herring by Selebi, pretending that there was a 'turf war' between him and the DSO (Scorpions). Selebi did this for no other reason than to shake the Scorpions off his tail, as I had supplied them with all the evidence I had managed to uncover over a period of many years. This included Selebi using his 'power' as a member of the National Executive Committee of the ANC (which was unlawful in terms of the Police Services Act). Selebi used his political connections not only to poison the case against him but to create political rifts within the NPA, to eventually cause bitter infighting. He was working on the basis that he would create havoc and thereby walk free of his crimes...*

Those responsible for Selebi's failed bid to avoid prosecution and conviction were never brought to book. Many, strangely enough, rose to positions of power where (as I presciently noted in 2012) they would cause irreversible damage to the criminal justice system unless they were stopped.

From the NPA, the two main suspects were Lawrence Mrwebi and Nomgcobo Jiba, who would land up doing the most damage at the prosecuting authority. Prince Mokotedi, who was also at the NPA at the time, would later come to play a large part in the years of persecution that followed my 2016 arrest. Leonard McCarthy and Bulelani Ngcuka were also on the list, although they disappeared from public life after the so-called "Zuma tapes" emerged.

From the police force, I named Lieutenant General Richard Mdluli, who, despite his suspension as the Head of the police's Crime Intelligence division, where he served between 2009 and 2012, I believe he continued running the unit from behind the scenes. Prior to 2009, Mdluli was a Major General and served as the Provincial Head of Crime Intelligence in Gauteng under then National Head Lieutenant General Mulangi Mphego. Mphego and Mdluli appeared joined at the hip. From the National Intelligence Agency, I named Arthur Fraser and agency head Manala Manzini. Fraser would move up the ladder to become the Deputy Head of the State Security Agency during Zuma's rule – in my opinion, a well-chosen 'plant' on Zuma's part.

I believe Justice Minister Brigitte Mabandla and then President Thabo Mbeki (whose names were both in the docket) had both conspired to prevent Selebi from being criminally charged.

In my docket, I laid out why these nine officials should have been charged with obstruction of justice, perjury and breaching Section 32 of the NPA Act. My statement described how Mrwebi conspired to interfere in the investigation and prosecution of Selebi unlawfully and intentionally. He had written an affidavit on the same day an arrest warrant against Selebi was unlawfully cancelled (and three days after

Mbeki had unlawfully suspended the Director of Prosecutions, Vusi Pikoli) to get Selebi off the hook. Mrwebi then lied under oath while giving evidence in the High Court during Selebi's trial.

Mokotedi followed Mrwebi into the witness stand, where he too lied under oath. He falsely tried to bolster Selebi's defence by claiming that he had enlisted Selebi's help in bringing criminal charges against Advocate Gerrie Nel. I made it clear in the docket that Mokotedi was promoted following his false testimony:

> *It is interesting to note that Mokotedi, far from being dismissed from the NPA, has now been promoted to the position of Executive in Charge of Integrity. How such a person ended up in charge of integrity should be the subject of a Judicial Inquiry. Apart from comparing it to allowing the mice to guard the cheese, it is worrying that the NPA, now so riddled with criminals, is a dwindling spiral of low ethics and corruption that all steps **MUST** be taken **URGENTLY** to stop the rot.*
>
> *Notwithstanding the fact that Mrwebi was caught red-handed helping Selebi try and avoid the criminal justice system, he then subsequently decided, for reasons best known to himself, to help out some of the rotten cops left after Selebi's removal from office. One of these cops is a criminal by the name of Richard Mdluli. Mdluli was himself very active in helping to (unlawfully) protect Selebi as part of a pre-conceived plan.*

I then listed a number of what I considered to be criminal activities that had been linked to Mdluli, which included:

- Finding and 'persuading' witnesses to give false evidence against Adv Gerrie Nel.
- Having me, and certain State witnesses I was working on, followed, and harassed.
- Having potential State witnesses against Selebi arrested and then brought to Mdluli's office in Braamfontein, where they were threatened to stay away from me.

The attempts to have the case against Selebi squashed would come to have serious political ramifications in the country.

After the NDPP was unlawfully suspended by President Mbeki in September 2007, Selebi and his accomplices (including Mdluli) held a meeting to discuss matters. Selebi considered it a risk that honest elements within the DSO would simply ignore the suspension of the NDPP and execute the search and arrest warrants they had lawfully obtained against him. This was something that neither Selebi nor Mbeki could afford for differing reasons – Selebi because he feared prison and Mbeki because he wanted to nail Jacob Zuma and remain the President of the ANC – and possibly the country. I believe Mbeki was hoping Selebi would be the man to take Zuma down.

In any event, a decision was taken at that meeting to fabricate a case against Adv Gerrie Nel, who was leading the prosecutorial-led investigation into Selebi, so that they (Mdluli and Mphego) could obtain an illegal wiretap warrant. The wire-tap warrant was duly obtained, and unlawful eavesdropping of the phone of (at least) Leonard McCarthy (the Head of the Scorpions) began. As previously stated, the intention was to ensure that none of the suspended NDPP's colleagues would move forward and arrest Selebi.

A completely unexpected result of this illegal wiretap was that, apart from ensuring that McCarthy would not move ahead and have Selebi arrested, the eavesdroppers picked up some tit-bits that might be of some (political) use in the future. What they effectively got was McCarthy, being dictated to by the erstwhile NDPP, Bulelani Ngcuka. From the tone and inflection in the calls, as well as the content, it was evident that Ngcuka was still very close to the then President Thabo Mbeki and that all the stops were being pulled out in an attempt to (unlawfully) hasten the prosecution of Jacob Zuma, on various charges. Mbeki had obviously realised that Zuma was dangerous and would bring the country to its knees if given a chance.

I noted in my 2012 statement that I had no knowledge of the validity (or otherwise) of such charges against Jacob Zuma, but could easily see (as would anyone else who read the transcripts of those tapes) that the conduct of McCarthy and Ngcuka was unconstitutional and, therefore, in breach of Section 32 of the NPA Act.

> *Finally, with regard to the telephone intercepts, I should mention that same clearly provided evidence of serious criminal activity on the part of the current Acting NDPP, Nomgcobo Jiba. Despite the overwhelming evidence, no (criminal) steps have been taken against Jiba, and she was re-appointed to her position at the NPA, then promoted, then appointed by Zuma as Acting NDPP.* ***CLEARLY NONE OF THIS IS RIGHT*** *– as Jiba and Mrwebi then decided to return the favours of Mdluli in the past by letting him off very serious criminal offences. She, Mrwebi and Mokotedi are a* ***danger to the well-being of the Republic*** *and* ***MUST be taken out of active duties URGENTLY if crime in South Africa is to be brought under control.*** *The NPA is put to prove to me and the country as a whole that it has taken steps to stop the rot.*
>
> *If the NPA does not put a stop to what is going on, then it is clear that* ***these three will become a threat to national security.***

How prophetic my 2012 statement would turn out to be.

In respect of the subsequent alleged crimes linked to Mrwebi and Jiba, I went on to say that Mrwebi and Jiba had tried to get Mdluli off the hook for plundering the Crime Intelligence secret accounts. I mentioned in the docket that the only reason they would have done this was because Mdluli had allegedly done Zuma a big favour with the illegal wiretaps, which were delivered to Zuma's lawyer, Michael Hulley, who used them to bamboozle Advocate Mokotedi Mpshe into dropping the 783 corruption charges against Zuma. Jiba and Mrwebi, and in return, prevented Mdluli's prosecution – at least until civil society stepped in. Of course, the other wiretaps provided were handed over by Arthur Fraser. Between Fraser and Mdluli, Zuma remained a free man – free to become President and free to bring South Africa to its knees.

I summarised it all in the docket:

In the conspiracy between Jiba, Mrwebi and Mdluli, the following facts are pertinent:

- A (failed) conspiracy involving many persons (nearly all of them ANC Cadres) took place to try and get ANC NEC member Jackie Selebi off the hook.
- That conspiracy, amongst other criminal conduct, included having Adv Gerrie Nel arrested.
- Amongst certain members of that conspiracy that have not yet been adequately neutralised (let alone punished – as most of them have not been) are Richard Mdluli, Nomgcombo Jiba and Lawrence Mrwebi.
- *These three, apart from being exposed, have charmed lives and even get rewarded for their conduct by being appointed to high office so that they can wreak havoc, but be in place as 'sleepers' to repay their political leaders when the time is right.*
- *This leaves the only conclusion that they were really rewarded for finding evidence that would assist Jacob Zuma in beating back a politically motivated prosecution by persons loyal to Thabo Mbeki in clear breach of their oath of office.*
- *I repeat that I have no knowledge of the charges facing Zuma, other than what I have seen in the media. I am therefore unable to and do not wish to comment on same. However, various media attribute the appointments of Jiba and Mrwebi to Zuma and, if that is true, it is* ***WRONG as they are not fit and proper persons.***
- *Accordingly, the rot within the NPA is cancerous and goes deep into its ranks. It* ***MUST*** *be removed at all costs, and I pledge to keep up my campaign of harassing the criminals that are embedded within the NPA until they are gone.*

The 2012 threat of decisive action against any 'retribution' by the criminals was ignored. As would later be seen, the fightback from them was as merciless as it was criminal. The fortuitous irony in my sworn statement of October 2012 will not be lost on any of today's readers who are up to speed with what ultimately happened to the individuals concerned and how they became crucial in the capture of the criminal justice system of South Africa by criminals. It is a big part of why I would be mercilessly and unlawfully targeted four years later, in April 2016.

As it turned out, what happened in 2012 wouldn't be the first time Zuma would owe his freedom to Fraser. Twelve years later, in August 2021, whilst Zuma was serving out a prison sentence for 'Contempt of Court' for refusing to attend the Zondo Commission of Inquiry, Arthur Fraser unlawfully released him on so-called 'Medical Parole', in a move that would show the middle finger to the whole country. This would be the final corrupt act by Fraser. A month later, his fixed-term contract expired, and he was gone.

THE CRIMINAL EMPIRE STRIKES BACK

One of the biggest problems faced by any country with high crime levels is the penetration of the criminal justice system – by criminals. South Africa is no exception. While not (yet) on a par with Mexico or Columbia, South Africa is certainly headed in that direction. I knew that if I was to have any impact on the crime levels in South Africa – and I was determined that I would – then I would first have to clean up the rot in the management of the criminal justice system.

Back in 2012 and 2013, I was certain that the NPA, South African Police and the Hawks had been penetrated and that South Africa was moving towards becoming a Police State. A Police State is a government that exercises repressive control through the police. It is controlled by a politicised police force that secretly supervises its citizens' activities. For a criminal justice system to be effective, it must be controlled by the rule of law. A Police State rules through totalitarian power that does not tolerate scrutiny, so if someone like me came along and exposed its dark underbelly to public scrutiny, that person would – and *must* – be dealt with. The system cannot be exposed. If it is, it will become unstable because the public will suddenly realise that 'something can be done about it'. Although most people do not personally want to roll up their sleeves and get stuck in, they will happily lend moral support to anyone willing to do so.

With the South African criminal justice system being controlled by criminals, a Police State was inevitable. With or without support, I decided that I would *not* allow a bunch of criminals with badges and gowns to run my country into the ground.

I spent the next four years investigating the NPA and the police and, while some of the key players like Mdluli, Mrwebi and Jiba cemented their positions of power, new criminals were being brought in. A new tactic in the state capture enterprise was being deployed: certain media were used to publicly accuse loyal public servants of falsified crimes so that they could be forced out and replaced by Zuptoids. These newly appointed criminals would do anything to protect their political masters.

I was on to them from the start – and they knew it.

THE HAWKS – THE NEXT TARGET?

Once the Scorpions were gone, it was necessary to make sure the leaders in its replacement body, the Hawks, had corrupt pigeons leading the charge against crime.

In 2011, a secret campaign to get rid of decent, hard-working police in leadership positions at the Hawks was well underway. Some of the key players in the state capture project had already been placed in key positions at the NPA through their joint efforts to defend Selebi and protect the much-feared Crime Intelligence head, Lieutenant General Richard Mdluli. Later, the project morphed into one aimed at protecting a whole grouping of underworld figures who would come to be linked to state capture, which, by 2014, was well underway.

It was in May 2012 when I first realised that there was a concerted effort to capture the criminal justice system by using media smear campaigns against leaders in the Hawks. The *Sunday Times* ran a series of now-discredited investigative articles on the Cato Manor death squad and the illegal deportation of Zimbabweans to face execution. Later, the same *modus operandi* was used to peddle the fake SARS Rogue Spy Unit stories. I knew the articles were false from the start, but it was only in 2012 that I realised that what was happening was a well-constructed campaign being led on multiple fronts across various government sectors.

Back in 2011 and 2012, articles on so-called Zimbabwe renditions and Cato Manor death-squads were being planted to discredit the Kwa-Zulu Natal Hawks' head, Major General Johan Booysen, National Head of Hawks, Lieutenant General Anwa Dramat and Gauteng Head of the Hawks, Major General Shadrack Sibiya, amongst others. All three of them just happened to be busy with investigations, which, if allowed to follow their logical conclusion, would have implicated underworld figures who were working closely with members of the Zuma family in fleecing the public purse.

The false public allegations were then used to suspend, dismiss and lay fake charges against them. They were replaced by Jacob Zuma sycophants – Major General Ntlemeza and Major General Mokotedi – whose sole purpose appeared to be to protect Zuma whilst lining their own pockets. I was later able to prove that both Mokotedi and Ntlemeza's appointments were illegal.

At that stage, an investigative report by Colonel Kobus Roelofse of the SAPS anti-corruption team for the Directorate of the SAPS anti-corruption task team, dated 2 March 2012, became public. It formed part of an urgent High Court application by Freedom Under Law to suspend Mdluli.

It revealed that members of Crime Intelligence and the NPA, particularly Major General Solomon Lazarus, who was the Chief Financial Officer of the police's Secret Services Account (Crime Intelligence) and Lawrence Mrwebi, were going all out to protect Mdluli from facing criminal charges.

Mdluli was accused of murdering his ex-wife's lover Oupa Ramogibe. When Mdluli was first arrested for this case, believing they were finally free of his clutches, honest Crime Intelligence officers started to come forward to reveal how Mdluli had used the secret service account to fund his own lifestyle and those of his family and friends. Crime Intelligence had become nothing more than a family business for Mdluli.

The Hawks had been put in charge of these investigations, but there was interference from the start. Members of the investigating team were threatened, the case was dropped numerous times, and it took the dedication of committed, uncaptured members of the NPA to ensure a prosecution. It would only be in July 2019, and only once Zuma was out of the picture, that Mdluli was found guilty of the crime. He had dodged justice for years and, during that time, was one of the most feared men in the country.

Aside from details on how Mdluli looted state resources, the anti-corruption report revealed how the Zimbabwean rendition stories appeared in the media. A witness from Crime Intelligence came forward to say that in 2011 he overheard Lazarus telling a colleague that at a key moment in the Mdluli investigation, an article would be placed in the *Sunday Times,* which would focus on Sibiya and Dramat in order to take attention away from Mdluli. The report of the witness stated:

> *He stated that Major General Lazarus wanted to use sources within the media (journalists paid by CI) to write a story in order to take the focus away from them. This, according to the member, is a strategy employed to cast suspicion on those they perceived to be a threat.*
>
> *This newspaper article was published in the Sunday Times on 23 October 2011. Lieutenant General Mdluli has made representations to the National Prosecuting Authority earlier that month and uses the above-mentioned article to cast suspicion on Lieutenant General Dramat and the investigating team.*

The *Sunday Times* story was titled "Sent to Die. Shocking Fate of Suspects in Alleged Rendition Deal with Zim Cops", and instead of a by-line, the story ran as a special report by the (at that stage, anonymous) 'investigation staff'. In my mind, this added weight to the allegation that they had indeed been bribed and probably told the editor they wanted to remain anonymous because they were afraid of revenge. What they were afraid of was being 'outed' as corrupt.

It's my take that what started as a red herring to protect Mdluli and his accomplices from arrest and prison for robbing the Crime Intelligence funds blind and turning the Crime Intelligence Gathering (CIG) into a family business, then took on a more sinister role of enabling state capture by eviscerating the criminal justice system so that the coast would be clear for the wholescale looting of state coffers and SOEs.

The *Sunday Times* later ran a fake story with the narrative of the Cato Manor Death Squad, which falsely accused KZN Hawks of running a hit squad.

The article led to Kwa-Zulu Natal Hawks Head Major General Johan Booysen being unlawfully suspended and having false charges brought against him. It took him seven years to clear his name and prove his innocence. Dramat and Sibiya were suspended and criminally charged for their alleged role in so-called Zimbabwe Renditions. It was only in

2018 that the charges against the Hawks' leaders were dropped. In the meantime, they had all been unlawfully dismissed.

On the 16th of May 2012, I wrote to Yusuf Abramjee – who was then the Head of News and Current Affairs at Primedia Broadcasting, the head of Crime Line and the chairperson of the Pretoria Press Club – as well as Werner Swart of the *Sunday Times*:

> *Look at paragraphs 85 and 86. This is horrifying, but something I've well and truly suspected for years. These cheque-book journalists can bring the country to its knees by being on the payroll of the 3rd force, a.k.a. SAPS Crime Intelligence.*
>
> *We must find these journos and, if they are culpable, make sure they* ***NEVER*** *work in journalism again, ever! Naturally, we must make sure they are properly investigated first, as even a journalist is entitled to give his/her version of events.*
>
> *It shouldn't be too hard, as all we have to do is get hold of the Sunday Times and ask them who wrote the story. Why do journo's hide behind 'investigative staff'? Surely this fact alone makes their conduct suspicious. If they were straight and above board, why do they write anonymous stories? In fact, I'm copying Werner Swart of Sunday Times on this email. I've put both stories below for your (and Werner's) information purposes. (Jeez-like Werner, I hope it wasn't you that wrote those stories!)*
>
> *By the way, this is the same Mdluli that ran a campaign, using 'flexible' journalists to try and nail me and others that were working on the Selebi case. He had me followed; he had people whom I had met with dragged into his office and warned them against speaking to me. He was the architect of the false charges against Gerrie Nel. He was the one that tapped the phones of McCarthy and others, including myself. He did all of this to try and save Selebi. His reward was that he got Mphego's job after Mphego was charged and quietly jumped ship. It was one of Selebi's last activities to make sure they left a 'sleeper' in place, to keep the wheels of corruption greased. One*

could almost say that Selebi was still screwing the police from behind prison walls.

Then we must look at the dirty NPA staff, Mrwebi and Jiba, who also have many, many questions to answer, not only about their role in (unlawfully) trying to get Mduli off the hook but also their role in trying to get Selebi off the hook. They both supplied documents for Selebi. They were both instrumental in trying to nail the Selebi team at the Scorpions, and Mdluli was their 'assistant' or was he their 'guide'?

After Mdluli has been neutralised, all efforts must be focussed on nailing them, as they are filthy through and through. Mdluli is Prime-Evil and must be stopped, ***whatever it takes****.*

These dirty NPA senior staffers must also follow him into jail.

Werner,

Please let's get the author of the two stories below identified ASAP. I'm prepared to offer, free of charge, a polygraph for the journos in question. Media have to be seen to want to clean their house up. This would be a good place to start. of course, no one can blame the Sunday Times, per se, as they would not have known that the journos in question were dirty. However, if they (ST) take the relevant steps, which in my opinion should include a review of the cellular phone accounts and the seizing of their laptops and email accounts, then we might prevent a repeat of this tragedy. Naturally, in view of the shocking revelations, the journo/s in question should be suspended pending the investigation.

These sure are interesting times in which we live.

In late 2014, Dramat's replacement was quickly brought in. Berning Ntlemeza became the Head of the Hawks through a process that was later declared unlawful by the courts. He was an out and out self-centred criminal, and his appointment was an absolute disaster. I had opened dockets against him in early 2015, alleging corruption and obstructing criminal justice. He hated me like a dog hates fleas and would do anything to get at me – I believed he might even kill me if he thought he could get away with it – because I stood in the way of him and his dreams of corrupt power. Trained by the apartheid regime, he knew all their dirty tricks. I would later prove that he was one of the ringleaders of the criminal empire that had been built in the criminal justice system of South Africa for the sole purpose of protecting the Zuptas and their Zuptoids.

It took longer to find someone who would replace Sibiya but, in 2016, they found their man. Prince Mokotedi emerged from obscurity as the Gauteng head of the Hawks. He had resigned from the NPA in 2014, the day before his disciplinary hearing, having been charged for gross insubordination and bringing the NPA into disrepute after he allegedly leaked his own fake report relating to the NPA's battle with Prosecutor Glynnis Breytenbach.[2] A publicly acknowledged Zuma fan, I believe Mokotedi has had a grudge against me since Selebi's prosecution. His main beef, I guess, is that I am white and honest. He regularly displayed his racist rants on Twitter, which ultimately led to his downfall.

In June 2012, a new National Police Commissioner entered the picture. Mangwashi Victoria Phiyega, better known as Riah Phiyega, was appointed by President Jacob Zuma to much fanfare. She had no experience in the police but had been successful in the private sector. As the first woman to hold the post, it was hoped Phiyega would turn the police service around after the disaster that was Jackie Selebi.

Instead, her time turned out to be a monumental blunder. She was suspended from her position in October 2015, following a recommendation by the Farlam Commission of Inquiry into the tragic

2 Staff Reporter, No NPA disciplinary hearing for outgoing Prince Mokotedi, Mail & Guardian, 12 August 2014, https://mg.co.za/article/2014-08-12-no-npa-disciplinary-hearing-for-prince-mokotedi

platinum belt massacre at Marikana. This gave Zuma the window of opportunity he was seeking – to put someone more 'flexible' in charge.

I was willing to give Phiyega the benefit of the doubt until I realised that, like Selebi, she appeared more interested in protecting corrupt police officers than she was in solving crimes. Her suspension paved the way for the final appointment to the Head of the Police, Lieutenant-General Khomotso Phahlane, fully completing the conspiracy to capture the criminal justice system.

I knew it was vital for the country that we fight back. Between 2015 and 2019, my not-for-profit organisation, Forensics for Justice, opened no fewer than thirty criminal dockets implicating Zuma and his cronies in serious crimes, including corruption, fraud, defeating the ends of justice, and state capture. I did not only go for Zuma. I went for those near and dear to him, including family members.

CHAPTER 4
ENTER THE ZUPTOIDS

MOONOO, A KEY FIGURE

Before these Zuptoids started ploughing their way through the Hawks' leadership, I had already discovered that a key viper in the police's nest was Lieutenant General Vinesh Moonoo, the country's so-called top detective. Moonoo wielded massive power and influence and abused this power to protect many criminals. He established, within his own offices and without any protocol whatsoever, a stand-alone detective service that he called the National Intervention Unit, or 'NINU' as it later became known. NINU became Moonoo's own private fiefdom. One part of this unit was being led by Colonel Botha, a retired police officer brought back in as a contractor on assignment to Moonoo. This unit did not report to any police station or geographical area. It was its own police unit within the police force, and its members were able to handpick whatever cases they wanted. I believe that Moonoo 'selected' cases so that he could neutralise valid criminal complaints against his own criminal associates. He also used this method to target me.

By 2013, I had been able to link Moonoo to some crooked crime networks in the country that seemed to be flourishing under his 'protection'.

Moonoo realised I was onto him when I leaked to the media an investigation I was working on dealing with a contract the police had unlawfully signed with well-known car tracking company Tracker Connect. Moonoo and Phiyega had signed off on an extension of this contract, but the problem was that the original contract, which was purportedly signed in 2008, never actually existed. Tracker Connect (Pty) Limited had only been formed in 2011, three years afterwards. This was a clear case of fraud.

It also appeared that this private company had managed to build themselves up using police resources and the public purse, costing taxpayers hundreds of millions of rands. It pushed Tracker up from a start-up company in 1996 to a company – forty percent of whose shareholders was an Indian based consortium called Actis Trace, located in the tax haven of Mauritius – worth over R11-billion in 2014.

I opened a case of fraud, bribery and corruption against SAPS and Tracker in February 2014.

In my statement, I set out how, in 1996, Tracker was purportedly awarded their first so-called tender by SAPS. SAPS claimed to have created a tender process but then 'lost' or 'misplaced' the original tender documents. I did not believe that any tender was created at all, but rather a memorandum of understanding binding SAPS to extremely high amounts of fruitless and wasteful expenditure. I understood this 'contract' was created for the sole purpose of utilising a vehicle tracking company's technology to help SAPS recover stolen vehicles. Since 1996, Tracker had been re-awarded this so-called 'contract' every five years.

A 2013 press release explained that the relationship had resulted in one thousand four hundred SAPS vehicles and fifty SAPS aircraft fitted with Tracker equipment. SAPS created dedicated radio channels used solely for communication between SAPS and Tracker operational personnel at the taxpayer's expense. Tracker employees were given police radios and were placed at the 10111 control room in Midrand. Annually, Tracker 'rewarded' police officers who had recovered the greatest number of vehicles, which I argued could be viewed as a gratification. It had the net effect of police officers spending more time recovering vehicles fitted with Tracker devices than attending to other serious crimes like rape, murder and housebreaking. But because police did not give the same service to other vehicle tracking companies, their dent into car theft crime turned out to be not as successful as it could have been. It also resulted in SAPS resources being unlawfully utilised by Tracker to recover stolen vehicles. I estimated this to have cost up to R212-million per month, or R2.5-billion per year, which Tracker benefitted from at the time through hundreds of thousands of monthly subscriptions. These are resources that other private vehicle recovery companies were denied any chance of having access to since no competitive tender process had ever been allowed to take place.

During my investigation, I was able to obtain a copy of a letter that was issued by Phiyega to Tracker in June 2013 that extended the alleged contract between Tracker Connect and the SAPS. The letter stated that it was an extension of an agreement signed between SAPS and Tracker Connect in 2008. The 2008 agreement was, however, not with Tracker Connect (which did not exist at the time), but with a completely separate entity called Tracker Network, which had since ceased trading.

Phiyega stated in the letter that it was upon the advice of the Divisional Commissioner of Detective Services (Moonoo) that she authorised the extension of the 'contract'. Both Moonoo and Phiyega signed the document, but at the time of opening the case, I wasn't sure who had deceived them into fraudulently signing the extension to a non-existent contract. As time went on, I strongly suspected that the person who had misled Phiyega was Moonoo himself.

When my Tracker investigation appeared in the media, it infuriated Moonoo.[3] He behaved as if he had been caught out, and I can only assume Phiyega, who now had egg on her face, must have called him in to ask what was going on. I wish I could have been a fly on the wall to have seen his reaction. Whatever his response, it seemed to have won Phiyega over, as she chose to defend him and attack me whenever I sent her information on his alleged criminal dealings in the months that followed.

After the Tracker investigation went public, information on Moonoo started pouring in. Whistle-blowers came forward and painted a picture of a deeply tainted man whose corruption had seriously dented investigations into dangerous criminals he had associated with. It would also emerge that, through some of these connections, he had formed powerful ties with family members of the President. I had not realised it when investigating the Tracker contract, but, in naming Moonoo, I had made a dangerous enemy who was a key player in the state capture network that was thriving.

THE UNDERWORLD

Cigarette baron Yusuf Kajee was a key figure in the suspicious cigarette business. In underworld circles, it was alleged that Kajee was a tobacco smuggler. He had opened a cigarette factory in Pietermaritzburg called Amalgamated Tobacco Manufacturers (ATM) and was business partners with (former) President Jacob Zuma's son, Edward Zuma. The on-record director of ATM was a ghost – a person who did not exist. This way, if the proverbial mess hit the fan, Kajee could simply claim he had no knowledge, which is precisely what he later did when special investigators from Customs and Excise came knocking at his door.

3 EWN, O'Sullivan: Tracker, SAPS deal unlawful, 18 March 2014, https://ewn.co.za/2014/03/18/OSullivan-slams-Tracker-SAPS-deal

I had a photo in my possession of Moonoo posing with Kajee at a function hosted by Kajee in Pietermaritzburg. My informants told me that Kajee had paid for Moonoo's flights, cars and accommodation. Conveniently, Kajee's lawyer, subsequent to the event, sent a letter to Phiyega demanding that all the cases against his client be investigated out of Moonoo's office. I also learnt that Moonoo and his wife visited India in February 2011, with a stopover in Dubai. Kajee had allegedly upgraded their airplane tickets and paid for the Dubai hotel through a friend of his, Iqbal Ganchi.

Lt General Moonoo (left) with Yusuf Kajee (right) in Pietermaritzburg, at Kajee's cigarette factory. Picture sent by me to then-chief of police, General Phiyega

A picture was emerging of a *modus operandi* being used by criminals who were being investigated by SARS, which was now fighting back by laying false charges against SARS employees. This would often stall the legitimate cases opened against them. Kajee had numerous run-ins with SARS and allegedly employed the same tactics. I discovered that these dockets were sent to Moonoo's own (unlawful) investigation unit, where they sat gathering dust. SARS was forced to delay any action against Kajee while the police "investigations" against them were 'ongoing'.

These same tactics were allegedly being used by a convicted murderer, Jen Chi Huang. Huang was deported to China after being released from prison, yet mysteriously re-appeared in South Africa sometime later. He was also allegedly part of the Chinese mafia and an associate of Jacob Zuma's nephew, Khulubuse Zuma. I then discovered that Moonoo's daughter, Manitha, worked as a legal advisor for Huang at his company Mpisi Trading 74 (Pty) Limited. Moonoo, it seemed, was intervening to stop SARS from acting against Huang by investigating fake criminal charges against SARS members in the same manner Kajee employed.

As mentioned earlier, in October 2014, I decided it was time to alert Phiyega to what Moonoo was up to. I emailed her, making it clear that my email was private and confidential. I attached the photograph of Kajee with Moonoo and told Phiyega I had information that Kajee used his air miles to upgrade a flight ticket for Moonoo from Economy to Business class:

> *There have been a few things that have been worrying me this year.*
>
> *Corruption at the highest levels within SAPS.*
>
> *When the country's purported top detective is seen hobnobbing with unsavoury characters, it leaves an uneasy feeling in the air. It was precisely this type of conduct that enabled me to build a solid case against Selebi and take him down.*

Instead of doing something about these allegations, Phiyega forwarded my email to Moonoo. Why would she do this other than to deliberately defeat the ends of justice, I wondered? Now that Moonoo had solid proof I was onto him, I believe he started to concoct a plan to have me arrested or otherwise 'dealt with'.

On the 25th of October 2014, I told Phiyega that by sending Moonoo my email, she had made a costly mistake:

> *I have reliably learnt that he has given instructions to find anything that can be found in order to have me arrested. I hear that he has stated that I am guilty of the offence of defeating the ends of justice and that trumped-up charges in that regard will be used...*

Moonoo had also made out a false case for interception of my phone calls. I told Phiyega:

> *Corruption is the single biggest reason why the police fail to tackle the real issues of crime. Since that corruption stems from Wachthuis (police headquarters in Pretoria) to station level, you will never achieve your mandate until you clean the mess up around you. The problem you face is that you have the mice guarding the cheese.*

Phiyega responded by saying that she was concerned that I did not want my emails forwarded to the Detective's Unit.

> *Your view that "I think forwarding [your] email to head of detectives may have been a costly mistake" bothers me as it borders on you suggesting that as National Commissioner, I must take instructions from you, which is a more than condescending attitude.*
>
> *I am also concerned by the continued threatening attitude that laces your communication. It is definitely unfortunate and to be direct, intolerable.*

How was it unreasonable to ask the Police Commissioner not to forward the emails of a complainant to the person they were accusing, I wondered?

FURTHER PROOF OF WRONGDOING

As my investigations into Moonoo intensified, I discovered more gangsters with whom he was in regular contact. I learnt that Moonoo was also involved with Solly and Fazil Bhana, notorious gold mine strippers most famous for their Amlac oil scam. They stripped all the value from the Aurora and Blyvooruitzicht mines and, like Huang, were also connected to Zuma, through his nephew Khulubuse Zuma. The two were being investigated for a range of racketeering cases and openly boasted that they also were being protected by Moonoo. Yaseen, a source I was in contact with, called Solly after I told him that the Hawks were investigating them.

A recording of the phone call states:

> ***Solly***: *Then I spoke to General Moonoo.*
>
> ***Yaseen***: *Ja.*
>
> ***Solly***: *You know he's in charge now. He's second in charge.*
>
> ***Yaseen***: *Moonoo, ja.*
>
> ***Solly***: *He says he'll set it up in the morning, and he'll call me straight away.*
>
> ***Yaseen***: *Okay, okay.*
>
> ***Solly***: *So, don't worry.*

Why were key criminals in the Indian community bandying Moonoo's name around as the person in the police they could go to, to make their criminal allegations disappear? It was clear to me that Moonoo was no angel.

Again, I emailed Phiyega. By now, I was fed up. Despite the mounting evidence I had against Moonoo, she was ignoring it:

> *Despite multiple communications to you over the last few months requesting you to intervene in the disgraceful corrupt state of the police under your command, you have done nothing other than to complain to me about using your private email address and arrogantly complaining about my tone with you. What you have completely failed to see is that dirty cops on your payroll are assisting with my planned murder, not your murder, mine, so any tone I might take with you is a tone of anguish because of your complete and utter failure to carry out your constitutional mandate, thereby leaving me to take the law into my own hands. In short, I'm now taking the gloves off because I see you as part of the problem and no longer part of the solution...*

Whilst you are dilly-dallying around, dirty cops, people in your employ, are conspiring with criminals to have me murdered. Other dirty police in your employ have been handing my cellular phone records to criminals, and yet others have given undertakings to criminals that they will get me arrested on trumped-up charges in order to protect their criminal paymasters...

During your time in office, crime levels have increased like never before. I believe this is because you are too busy in the creation of a politically corrupt and back-biting service, which completely lacks credible leadership. Where Generals are rewarded for spying on Generals and heads are shuffled without regard for their constitutional rights.

You have created a climate where people like Moonoo have busied themselves with turf wars against colleagues in the Hawks for no other reason than he himself has questionable conduct to explain... The end result is the inevitable collapse of law and order in this country.

In February 2014, I sent Moonoo a letter asking him questions about the criminals I had discovered he was associated with. I asked him why he had attended a party with Kajee and who had paid for his flights, meals and accommodation. I asked him how it was that the Bhanas could remain above the law and readily call him when in trouble? I also asked why it was that the criminal elements in the Indian community saw him as their go-to man when they faced serious criminal charges? Needless to say, I received no response.

MOONOO AND THE KREJCIR CONNECTION

I subsequently learnt that Moonoo was allegedly assisting Radovan Krejcir through his connection to Paddayachee. Paddayachee had allegedly been heard bragging that he was going to get Krejcir off the serious charges he was facing.

In 2015, Krejcir was in custody, facing numerous charges, including one of plotting to kill me, and Crime Intelligence member Colonel Nkosana Ximba, with the help of corrupt police. He was thwarted before he was able to carry out his evil intent because of an important informer in his camp who kept the police abreast of what was happening every step of the way.

This informer, Jacob Nare – a crucial witness to the case – had initially been whisked off to England as part of the country's witness protection programme.[4] There, he was safe from Krejcir's murderous reach. But then, suddenly, Nare was brought back to South Africa to be interviewed by Moonoo. Instead of returning him to a place of safety, Nare was unceremoniously dumped from the witness protection programme. He had no place to go and, without help, would surely be killed. He had literally been left out in the cold and brought to my doorstep. The move made no sense. Why would the police leave a key witness in two key cases against Krejcir – who was arguably one of the most evil murderers in South Africa – in a position where he would be assassinated?

Who was the person behind the decision to move Nare back from the UK? I believed it was Moonoo. He had engaged in a campaign of intimidation against Nare by calling him and telling him that one of the other witnesses in the case, Colonel Ximba, was on Krejcir's payroll. The intention was to instil fear in the man, making him believe the case against Krejcir was hopeless. I believe Moonoo was desperate to destabilise the case against Krejcir.

Moonoo didn't stop there. In late 2014, a police officer who worked under Moonoo, Lieutenant Colonel Romeo (from Vosloorus), commissioned a sworn statement by Krejcir where Krejcir laid false charges against Captain (now Lt Colonel) Freddy Ramuhala, one of

---

4 Angelique Serrao, 'I was part of Krejcir's evil world, IOL, 19 February 2016, https://www.iol.co.za/news/i-was-part-of-krejcirs-evil-world-1986739

the investigating officers in the Krejcir cases. Another officer who worked in Moonoo's office, Colonel Botha, went to the High Court to try to arrest Ramuhala when he was giving evidence against Krejcir. This forced the judge in the case, Justice Lamont, to intervene and stop what would have been a travesty of justice.

I sent Moonoo a text message:

> *In a nutshell, everything you are doing is under scrutiny, and your abuse of power and hobnobbing with criminals has not gone unnoticed by me or the country as a whole. I consider your conduct to be, quite frankly, nothing more than the last desperate acts of a very desperate man.*

He must have been furious. He thought he was untouchable, and here I was, reaching out and slapping him in the face.

I had also discovered that in 2014, a warrant had been applied for Moonoo's arrest, and Nomgcobo Jiba at the NPA learnt about it. Since Jiba was being politically protected from what should have been her own arrest, she decided to capitalise on her knowledge of Moonoo's impending arrest. She allegedly had secret meetings with Moonoo and, between them, allegedly arranged that the case against her would not be investigated by Moonoo's team. It looked like a *quid pro quo.* They could help each other avoid prosecution. I believe Moonoo then instructed the investigating officer on the case to hand the docket against Jiba to him, where it joined the many other dockets gathering dust in Moonoo's office.

I opened multiple cases against Moonoo detailing these allegations in 2014 and again in 2016, but with his connections in high places, it was clear that they were never going to be properly investigated.

Moonoo publicly denied all the allegations I made against him, but I had enough proof to know he wasn't being transparent.[5]

---

5 Angelique Serrao, Former top cop denies corrupt dealings with Krejcir, News24, 19 October 2016, https://www.news24.com/SouthAfrica/News/former-top-cop-denies-corrupt-dealings-with-krejcir-20161019

My sources warned me that Moonoo was planning my downfall. He had instructed the staff in his office to find anything they could to shut me down. A plan was hatched to search my premises, where they aimed to find incriminating evidence against me. They were hoping to find classified police documents to have me arrested and humiliated in the media.

My lawyers wrote to Phiyega in advance:

> *Our client is of the opinion that any such arrest would be unlawful and would be motivated as either an act of revenge for the fact that our client had exposed the conduct of General Moonoo, which appears to have been condoned by General Phiyega, alternatively that our client's arrest would be as the result of a further attempt to defeat the ends of justice, by drawing 'first blood' with a public and humiliating arrest of our client, on trumped-up charges.*

The letter asked that I not be arrested by any officers reporting to Moonoo and that if I needed to appear in court, that it be done through an indictment or summons. The letter was ignored, and another dirty cop who worked in Moonoo's office under Colonel Botha entered the picture – an unimpressive, short and overweight policeman by the name of Warrant Officer Kobus Vlok.

Vlok, a typical underachiever in the police, appeared to lack the skills or intelligence required to rise up the ranks. And yet, probably as a result of this, he was a useful tool to criminals with badges at a higher rank. He was ready, willing, and able to put his name to anything if it pleased his masters.

It came to my attention that Vlok had unlawfully approached some of my clients and told them that he was investigating me on numerous different charges. He had also collected the dockets on cases I had opened, thereby becoming the 'investigating officer'. One could be sure that no investigation would take place on any of them. Moonoo, through his blunt instrument, Vlok, turned up the heat.

On the 15th of April 2015, my doorbell rang. It was Vlok, accompanied by about thirty police offers. They arrived in thirteen police cars, but only two of them were marked. They raided my offices using an unlawfully obtained search warrant. The Police spokesman was there, along with numerous journalists. Stories appeared in the press, making me out to be a criminal whom the police would soon arrest. Moonoo was going all out to ensure he humiliated me publicly – exactly what my lawyer had told Phiyega would happen four months earlier. Certain elements in the media were only too glad to lap it up and give it credence. One journalist sent the police spokesman a message asking, "Is Paul O'Sullivan being arrested?" The response, which the journalist showed to me, was: "Unfortunately not". The criminals with badges were going all out to nail me.

The warrant stated they were looking for any official SAPS document or one bearing the SAPS insignia. Clearly, they were on a fishing expedition with no case they could use to search me. What they were really trying to find was any intelligence or information I might have and any proof of wrongdoing I might have against the police's hierarchy. All my computers and other electronic equipment were taken.

On my instructions, my attorney, Darryl Furman, launched an urgent application to have the search warrant overturned. An interim order I obtained stated that my lawyers had to be present when mirror images of the items were taken and that they had to be sealed and be kept safely with the Registrar at the Johannesburg High Court. This was to ensure that these corrupt officers did not obtain any of my private information based on an illegal search warrant. I would later prove that Vlok had lied to a Magistrate to obtain the search warrant and that this was, therefore, fraud.

However, Vlok breached the court order and refused to allow my lawyers to be present on the dishonest excuse that the location had to be kept secret.

In October, my High Court application was successful. The judge ordered that the search warrants be reviewed and set aside, that all the equipment be returned, the mirror images be destroyed and that the police pay all my legal costs on a punitive scale.

It was a victory for me. But unsurprisingly, I would learn that for Vlok and the other members of Moonoo's team, a judge's order meant nothing to them. They would do anything to bring me down – and that included breaking the law in any way necessary. They unlawfully kept a copy of my computer's hard drive and data-mined it to drive an unlawful campaign against me. I believe that having me murdered was not entirely off the menu and evidence of this conspiracy was later given to me.

CHAPTER 5

EXPOSING DUDU MYENI

THE LOOTING AT SAA BEGINS

In January 2014, a private investigator by the name of Hennie Theron walked into my office. He said he urgently needed to speak to me as he needed help with an investigation, he was busy with. Theron proceeded to ask me if I could obtain the bank statements and telephone records of three directors of South African Airways (SAA). I was immediately on my guard. It is illegal to obtain somebody's bank statements and telephone records without their knowledge unless a Section 205 *ex-parte* subpoena is first obtained. It is a huge invasion of privacy and carries heavy sentences. Only the police are authorised to do this when pursuing an investigation, and then only with a justifiably obtained subpoena. In terms of the so-called Regulation of Interception of Communications Act, or RICA, unlawfully obtaining someone's cellular records carries a ten-year prison sentence.

I immediately wondered who had hired Theron. I decided to string the PI along to see if I could get evidence of who had given him the instructions. He told me a woman by the name of Advocate Lindi Nkosi-Thomas had hired him but that she had been instructed to do so by the chairman of SAA, Dudu Myeni. He also left the file laying in front of me with her telephone number clearly visible. I memorised it so that I could run checks on her.

By early 2014, information was just starting to come out about Myeni – a former primary school teacher who would come to be known as the wrecking ball of SAA. She had been made a non-executive director of the board of SAA in September 2009. By December 2012, she was made the Acting Chairperson of the board, a position that was made permanent in January 2015. As the Head of the Jacob Zuma Foundation, Myeni was known to be remarkably close to the President. Later, we would find out just how close she was when pictures of the President cosying up to her came into the public space on social media. With so many wives and girlfriends, it wasn't always easy to tell who the President was in a relationship with, but the pictures hinted that Myeni was more than just a friend of Number One. We would later learn of rumours that her son, Thalente, was staying at Zuma's Forrest Town mansion and that Zuma was his father.

One of the directors Theron was asked to target was the CEO of SAA, Monwabisi Kalawe. I had known him since my days on the board of ACSA, when MK, as we all knew him, was the General Manager of Cape Town Airport and won several international awards for his diligent work there. I considered him to be a trustworthy, hard-working man with a no-nonsense approach to ethics. I immediately alerted him to what Theron was searching for and provided him with an affidavit.

At the time, a tender involving wide-bodied aircraft was being discussed with the Board. SAA reportedly intended to procure twenty-three of these new wide-bodied aircraft, estimated to cost R60-billion for the whole package.[6] At the time, SAA was reporting a R990-million loss that was attributed to its loss-making long-haul

6 Londiwe Buthelezi, SAA looks for fuel efficiency from Airbus, Business Report, 28 May 2014, https://www.iol.co.za/business-report/economy/saa-looks-for-fuel-efficiency-from-airbus-1694848

routes. All eight long-haul routes were loss-making because of the use of older generation four-engine planes. Acquiring the more-fuel efficient aircraft was the top priority in SAA's turnaround strategy to return to profitability.

Publicly, it was known that the acquisition of the new planes was delayed when then Minister of Public Enterprises, Malusi Gigaba, sent the airline back to the drawing board to redo its draft tender proposal because the initial tender did not contain crucial elements of industrialisation and localisation.[7] By that time, 'localisation' had become the buzzword for skimming – raking off a percentage of the action in the name of 'empowerment'. It was nothing short of unlawful enrichment, and Myeni was 100% behind it. 'Localisation' was intended for industrial contracts to ensure that an element of the government contract involved locally manufactured products. How do you tell Boeing, or Airbus, to include locally made components? You don't – but Myeni used it to involve local 'middlemen' in skimming from the top of the valuable aircraft supply contracts.

Kalawe told me, however, that behind the scenes, there was a disagreement between him and Myeni. He wanted to appoint an advisory firm to ensure proper process was followed in the awarding of the tender, but Myeni was opposing this.

In November 2014, Kalawe was suspended from his position as CEO. I noted from media reports that there appeared to be some power play, as the Minister, by now Lynne Brown, instructed that the suspension be lifted, but Myeni would not allow this to happen. By this stage, it was already being hinted at that Myeni was untouchable because of her alleged close connection to Zuma and that she could do anything she wanted at the national airline, with or without the Minister's approval.

7 Londiwe Buthelezi, SAA plans to lease new aircraft to cut costs, Business Report, 2 June 2014, https://www.iol.co.za/business-report/companies/saa-plans-to-lease-new-aircraft-to-cut-costs-1696986

MYENI AND HER PARIS RENDEZVOUS

In the meantime, Myeni's personal relationship with Zuma had come into the public spotlight.[8] I had also discovered a close connection to 'fixer' Fana Hlongwane. Hlongwane is best known for his role during the Arms Deal when he allegedly received R100-million into his bank account from BAE Systems. His name would pop up repeatedly in the years to come as a key player in the state capture project.

Zuma and Myeni's son, Thalente Myeni, would later be fingered in a dodgy PRASA deal.[9] He was also dragged into the mess at Eskom.

I decided to shake the tree and let Myeni know I was onto her. I wrote her an email on November 7, 2014:

> *I am writing to you now because I believe my Lifetime Platinum card is at risk. For your information, it took me seven years and a lot of money to get it. A lot of money to me, but not a lot to someone like you that's getting spoon-fed by taxpayers like me.*
>
> *I believe my Lifetime Platinum card is at risk because you are driving a once fine airline into the ground. I will not allow that to continue. As a significant taxpayer, I believe I have a duty to stop what you are doing...*
>
> *I will rise to the challenge and use all lawful means to stop you. The fight begins here, today. I am hereby formally declaring you to be on my radar screen.*

I then highlighted the accusation that she hired a private detective to spy on directors at SAA and that she was trying to get rid of Kalawe so that she could take charge of the wide-bodied aircraft tender.

> *There are rumours circulating that Fana Hlongwane, who is known to have assisted your family at various times with accommodation,*

---

8 Amabhungane, Is Myeni's next move to the Central Energy Fund? Mail & Guardian, 7 November 2014, https://mg.co.za/article/2014-11-07-is-myenis-next-move-to-the-central-energy-fund

9 Matuma Letsoala, Jacob Zuma links to 'untouchable' SAA boss, Mail & Guardian, 6 November 2014, https://mg.co.za/article/2014-11-06-jacob-zuma-links-to-untouchable-saa-boss

Porsche's etc., has been seen in Paris recently. This is the same Fana that woke up one morning and found an inordinate amount of cash in his account (I believe R200m, courtesy of the Frenchies) and could not explain it.

There is even a rumour that you were in Paris at the same time? I feel the best way to dispel these rumours would be for Fana to join you at the Polygraph Institute of South Africa for an hour or two. Indeed, it might be better if you were to book the institute for a week or so, as the questions are going to keep on coming if you keep on trying to ruin my Lifetime Platinum card...

So, it's over to you, Dudu.

Polygraph Institute with Fana, or I start ramping up the questions in public. What's it to be?

Please accept my apologies if this comes across as rude. I've never even met you, so I'm sure you're a great person. I just want you to get out of SAA and any other government institution so that I can reduce my workload on dealing with the ills caused by conflicts of interest and/or corruption.

Best wishes

Paul O'Sullivan

I knew I was being facetious and that my email would be met with anger, but sometimes, when dealing with crooks, this is the best approach. In many of the cases I had worked on, I found that being direct was akin to throwing a stone in the grass. It would get the snakes moving around quickly. This later proved to be the case with Myeni.

THE FAKE MYENI DOCUMENTS

One month later, I received a call from Kalawe, who said he would provide me with evidence of wrongdoing at SAA. Just before

Christmas, I tried to get a hold of him, but his phone was constantly off. Then he contacted me from a different number.

"Chief," he said, "if anything happens to me, I want you to investigate it."

The man was terrified and convinced his life was in danger.

Kalawe said someone had evidence of looting at SAA, but it would not be given to him as it implicated too many people in South Africa. His source told him his life was in danger. I advised him to open a case, but he said he was too scared to do so.

On the 25th of February 2015, I was in Europe on business when I got a call from Kalawe. He sounded stressed and said he had received some sensitive documents purported to have been obtained from Interpol. They allegedly showed that Myeni had overseas bank accounts with lots of money in them. He sent me four emails. Each had one photograph attached. I decided to act quickly to protect Kalawe's life by sending the photographs to the chairman of SAA and the authorities. I asked for an urgent investigation.

I called a trusted journalist at the *Sunday Times* whom I had spoken to previously about SAA. She told me they had received the documents from a different source and that they had six pages and in colour. I asked the journalist to send the emails to me. These documents were much clearer and appeared to show that Myeni had more than R250-million in two overseas bank accounts.

I sent my first email to Myeni at 10.02 a.m.

> *Dear Dudu*
>
> *You may recall I wrote to you last year in November. For some reason, I never got a reply, which in the work I do sort of gives an indication that there may be more than just smoke coming from the fire. This prompted me to unpack things a little bit more and dig a little deeper. It's important that you should now know the true meaning of being on my radar screen, and I did, in all fairness, ask you to resign from SAA or face further scrutiny.*

I am now writing to ask about your overseas bank accounts because I've been given the attached by an informer, who is normally bang on the mark with the information she provides. I've picked up two accounts which, according to the informer, are yours (unless there's someone else using your name) with extremely high balances (in excess of R250-million), which my informer says is linked to transactions in respect of the wide-bodied aircraft tender for SAA and the e-toll systems of Gauteng's roads.

Bank Austria – link to e-toll EUR 817 000

BNP Parabis – link to wide-bodied aircraft tender for SAA EUR 17.7 million

If the above are not your accounts, please let me know right away, so I am not off on a wild goose chase here.

What should you do now?

Well, if the attached accounts are yours, and they do look like they are, then I feel what we need is a come-clean approach, and you could get off lighter if you place the names of your accomplices on the table.

Since I am fairly certain that ENS will not want to be part of the unlawful attack you launched on Monwabise Kalawe for instilling counter corruption controls into the wide-bodied aircraft tender process, I am copying them in on this email. At the very least, they should bring about your dismissal from SAA and the cessation of your unlawful witch-hunt.

Needless to say, your resignation before sunset would be a good thing to do.

Oh yes, one more thing, please: #pay back the money.

I think it's now fair for me to say GAME OVER.

Myeni did not reply to the email, and I immediately sent what at face value looked like genuine documents to the authorities requesting that they investigate. The email was sent to the Deputy President (Cyril Ramaphosa), the Deputy Minister of Finance, the Minister of Public Enterprises and the Commissioner of Police.

While attending business meetings all day in Geneva, I also started a process to verify the documents. Within hours I knew they were fake. I was not happy with the spelling on the Austrian document, the signatories to the BNP document did not exist at the bank, and the so-called Surveillance Unit in Luxembourg was an institute with no legal standing in the rest of Europe. At around the same time, I got a call from journalist, Sam Sole, to whom I had also sent the documents. He asked me if I thought they were real, as he had concerns. I told him that by then, I could see they were fake. Someone was playing a high-stakes game, and I needed to find out who and why.

I contacted the authorities immediately to tell them I had verified the documents were fake and that I had started a process to investigate who the shadowy figures were who had produced the documents – and why:

> *It has been brought to my attention, whilst attempting to verify the attached document, that same may, in fact, be a fraudulent document, with its sole intention to use me to destabilise the situation at SAA.*
>
> *If that is the case, then clearly, what we have here is a monumental fraud against myself and the Chairman of SAA.*
>
> ***I must now request you to exercise extreme caution BEFORE doing anything.***

In the meantime, I will carry out further investigations and revert.

I promptly sent out another email:

> *Dear All,*
>
> *I am now very certain that a 3rd force is very hard at work, with its sole intention to cast aspersions on the Chairman of SAA, Ms DC Myeni. I have not yet got the motive for it, but I am working on this.*

By way of example, the two signatories on the 'document' from BNP do not exist, and the so-called 'Commission de Surveillance de Secteur Financier' otherwise known as CSFF, is not an EU monitoring or policing unit at all, but a monitoring entity based in Luxembourg, and only applicable in Luxembourg.

Competing interests in the aviation industry cannot be ruled out, as there seems to be a connection to another part of the world, which I do not wish to mention at this time.

I have indicated to the source of the information that I have taken the bait. I did this by blind copying the source on my earlier email. I want that situation to prevail in the hope that the originator can be unmasked.

I have done this in an attempt to flush the original source out and get them to make a mistake. I believe this will bear fruit. This process has already started, and no one copied on this email should let anyone know the course of action that has been embarked upon, or it could result in not being able to get to the origin of the fabricated documents.

I believe I will soon (in the next few days) be able to get information that will lead me to the architect of this grand plan. However, being located in Geneva, as I am at the moment, has led to certain communication difficulties.

Please do nothing with the earlier emails except sit and wait, and as soon as the architect of the deception has been identified, an appropriate criminal docket in respect of the offences of forgery, utterance and fraud, will be opened. In order to do this, I have to get to the originator, and it's a little difficult given my current communication challenges.

THE INVESTIGATION INTO SAA BEGINS

I was furious. Why had I been dragged into whatever fraud was being perpetrated here? I came down hard on Kalawe. I wanted to know why he had sent me these fraudulent documents and who had sent them to him. Was he a part of the fraud, or was he, too, an innocent victim of a group of people that had some nefarious plan up their sleeves? I later realised that it was Kalawe who had also been set up, not just me. It appeared that Myeni and her accomplices were desperate to get rid of Kalawe since he was standing in the way of them getting their hands on the piggy bank. I believe they expected him to 'bite' on the false documents, which would, in turn, act as a red herring for the looting unfolding at SAA. When he sent the documents to me, it upset the game plan as he was expected to go public with the documents himself – which would then be used as a ploy to get rid of him.

At first, Kalawe was reluctant to say where he got the documents from as he genuinely feared for his life. But then he gave me the names of a couple he had met in Rosebank and their telephone numbers, as well as the person who had given him the documents, a certain Abednego Mbulawa, the Chief Operating Officer of the Mogale City Council, west of Johannesburg, but who had an intelligence background.

In the meantime, I was contacted by a company called ENS Africa Forensics. They had been hired by Myeni to help get rid of key staff at SAA and were being paid a small fortune in public funds to do so. ENS director George van Niekerk said that Myeni would not seek legal recourse against me for sending the false documents to the police if I provided evidence of who was responsible for creating them. I was, at this stage, happy to do so. I had made a mistake by sending out the emails before verifying them and was keen to try to make up for that while leaving the coast clear to still go after Myeni.

The deal we came to was that I would do the investigation and provide my findings to them:

> *Our clients are grateful to you for your offer of assistance. More importantly, the Board of Directors at SAA is anxious to determine the source of the campaign in order to enable the law enforcement agencies to take appropriate steps against the perpetrators. To this end, the Board is comforted by your confident assurance that you can secure the unequivocal evidence to establish the involvement of such individuals.*

I quickly established that it was Mbulawa who had sent Kalawe the documents. He was also the person who created them, using office equipment at his work. I picked this up from the metadata on the PDF file sent me by the *Sunday Times* journalist. I also discovered that Kalawe had paid Mbulawa R150 000 to obtain what he, too, thought were genuine bank account statements since Kalawe wanted to 'out' Myeni himself. The question for me was, was this a money-making scheme for Mbulawa, or was he part of a sinister plot?

I provided the information to ENS, made a sworn statement and in March 2015, opened a docket with the police asking them to investigate Mbulawa for uttering a forged document and fraud. In the same docket, I asked the police to investigate the attempt by Myeni in January 2014 to unlawfully acquire cellular records and bank statements. I linked the two inextricably so that Myeni would also be subject to proper scrutiny.

MYENI'S ABOUT-TURN

Ten days after I had signed the agreement with Myeni's lawyer, George van Niekerk, he attempted to unlawfully cancel it. I was finalising Kalawe's sworn statement at the time, and, before I could get Kalawe to sign it, Myeni instigated disciplinary charges against him, based on the fake bank statements. This forced Kalawe into a position where he would not cooperate any further with me. This decision stymied my investigation, which I believe was deliberate on Myeni's part as well as that of George van Niekerk.

I had provided van Niekerk with all my evidence, but he claimed it wasn't enough and he then drafted and opened a false police case for Myeni. I entered into a dispute with Myeni and van Niekerk over this since I had followed my side of the agreement. Furthermore, the docket I had opened had already yielded results. The cops at Bramley Police Station were wide awake and had already knocked on Mbulawa's door and obtained a warning statement from him. Needless to say, Mbulawa lied in his warning statement and then chose to keep quiet about the money he had been paid by MK.

In Myeni's affidavit, she stated that "...the bank statements presented by Mr O'Sullivan to me are fictitious and fraudulent and are being used to threaten and intimidate me into making irregular and unlawful decisions as the Chairperson of the Board of SAA".

Of course, she knew that was a lie because I had invited her to tell me if they were genuine or not in my email and, a few hours later, I wrote and declared them to be fake. In fact, I was the first to publicly declare them to be fake – a fact Myeni deliberately chose to keep quiet about when opening her false docket against me. I later realised she kept quiet because I believe she already knew the documents were in circulation as part of a sinister plan to create a red herring aimed at fabricating a reason to fire SAA's CEO, Kalawe. This was all while she was looting the airline with apparent abandon and disregard for the law.

I would later realise that Moonoo's team had magically gotten hold of the false case opened by Myeni and van Niekerk. They wanted Myeni to cancel the agreement George van Niekerk had signed with me so that they could use the case to pursue me. What had happened with the fake bank statements had been an error on my part, but I had done nothing illegal. In fact, the law requires any person who may be aware of corruption to report it, and that is exactly what I had done, by sending the documents to the police, minister and deputy president. As soon as I had realised that the documents were fake, I alerted everyone I had sent them to. I then opened a criminal case and linked the case to the attempt by Myeni to get hold of Kalawe's bank statements the previous year.

But Myeni went ahead and opened a false case anyway. In her statement, she conveniently left out some important bits of information. She included the original emails I had sent (with the bank statements attached) but deliberately left out the subsequent emails I sent, alerting her and the authorities to the fact that the documents were fake and that I was investigating what had happened. She also left out the agreement I had signed with her lawyer, George van Niekerk, as well as the evidence I had amassed against Mbulawa. In her statement, she claimed that ENS had investigated and discovered that Kalawe had paid Mbulawa R150 000. Nowhere did she mention that it was, in fact, me who had uncovered this. She was lying, with lies drafted for her by George van Niekerk and both she and I knew it.

I would later open a case against her for this. Her omission of facts amounted to perjury. She was lying under oath. Nevertheless, Moonoo now thought he had the ammunition he needed against me, and he wasted no time in using it. Colonel Amod Hoosen, the man who would subsequently unlawfully arrest me at the airport in 2016, was part of the National Task Team for Narcotics formed by Moonoo in KwaZulu Natal, and he was made the lead investigator in Myeni's fake case, along with Vlok. I subsequently found out that Hoosen had a corrupt relationship with a group of well-known drug traffickers. Hoosen later stated in an affidavit that he was involved because Myeni lived in KwaZulu Natal. Vlok, they said, was assigned to the case because he was based in Johannesburg. There was no mention that they had been hand-picked by Moonoo as the special team assigned to 'deal' with me. Vlok was a part of Moonoo's NINU Unit in the police – Moonoo's privately controlled Detective Unit that did not report to any policing station or geographical area. The SAA matter was one of his handpicked cases. I opened the docket in Bramley, and it should have been investigated in Bramley. Instead, it was picked up by Vlok. So, we had Moonoo's team investigating both cases I had opened against Myeni *and* the fake case that had been opened against me by Dudu Myeni.

On March 31, 2015, my lawyers wrote to Vlok. I had received a call from a journalist asking if I had been arrested on the SAA matter as he had been tipped off that an arrest was planned in what was to be a grandiose public show. This was earmarked to take place on a Friday so that I would be detained for the upcoming long weekend. I had called Vlok to ask him about this. He claimed it was a lie. I did not believe him and asked my lawyers to write to him and provide him with the agreement that I knew was still in place between Myeni and me. I argued that arresting me on this fake case was unlawful.

Vlok used the fake case to fraudulently apply for a search warrant of my premises. In it, he stated that he needed to search files and computers that might show who had fraudulently generated the documents. He knew full well where the documents had originated since he already had the docket I had opened, which made it clear that Mbulawa had provided the documents to Kalawe, who had, in turn, supplied them to me.

There were several anomalies in Vlok's search warrant application. They were so glaringly obvious that a magistrate should never have granted him the search warrant in the first place. I launched an urgent application, which resulted in the search warrant being set aside and punitive costs being awarded in my favour.

I made this clear in a case I opened in June 2016 against Vlok, Moonoo and Myeni in Randburg for perjury, defeating the ends of justice, fraud, and corruption. In my statement, I revealed that Vlok had signed out the docket I had opened against Mbulawa from the Bramley Police station, just six days before he applied for a search warrant. He had also obtained the docket I opened against Myeni, Lindiwe Nkosi-Thomas, and private investigator Hennie Theron for attempted corruption when, in January and February 2014, Nkosi-Thomas, at the instance of Myeni, hired Theron to unlawfully procure the cellular records and bank records of three SAA directors. Theron said they were to dig up whatever dirt they could find on the three directors. Some PI's will do anything for money.

Vlok should have had no business with the dockets I had opened since he was purporting to investigate me on Myeni's false charges and could, therefore, not objectively investigate Myeni at the same time. It was a massive conflict of interest. Of course, the reality was that Myeni was a 'protected species', and it was really me they were all after. They would do whatever they could to silence me because I was exposing too many highly placed criminals. The dockets only came into Vlok's possession and control because Lieutenant General Moonoo wanted to make sure that all steps would be taken to thwart investigations against himself and commissioner Phiyega that implicated them in fraud and/or corruption. I said as much in my docket against Vlok.

Vlok falsely stated:

> *The reason is that despite the evidence, information is that the fraudulent documents were generated by Mr O'Sullivan on his personal computer or another electronic system or devices which are under his control.*

This was a bold fabrication by Vlok intending to deliberately mislead the Magistrate into granting a search warrant that would never have been granted in the first place had the true facts been placed in front of him. There was not a shred of evidence pointing towards me as the document fabricator. All the evidence pointed towards Mbulawa as the person behind it. Vlok knew this but decided not to divulge this important information so that he could raid my office and search my computer for any evidence I might have had against Moonoo, Phiyega, Myeni, and any other corrupt cops. The warrant gave sweeping and broad powers to the executor of the warrant, the purpose of which was to seize all the information on my computers. It should have only stated that they sought all information *related to SAA*.

In the middle of the search warrant debacle, Vlok strangely inserted that he was looking for any SAPS document (or documents) bearing a SAPS insignia. No case was made for why the police would be searching for such documents. The warrant was simply a trojan horse to gain illegal access to my office so that a deep fishing expedition could be embarked upon for no other purpose than digging for information of an intelligence nature that could be used against me – or for finding out what dirt I had on the hierarchy of the police, including many generals (of which Moonoo was but one).

A few days later, Vlok visited the Norwood Police Station and uplifted three cases. The first was a case I opened in 2015 against Denis Krejcir, the son of Radovan, for threatening on Twitter to kill me. The other two were fake cases opened by criminal associates of Krejcir against me as a distraction.

My lawyers again wrote to the police. The purpose was to keep an official record of their pursuit of me, as well as to let them know that I knew what they were up to. I would not be a victim of their games:

> *There can be no doubt that the ongoing fishing expedition carried out by Warrant Officer Vlok, at the instance of General Moonoo, is unlawful and is further intended to abuse our client's constitutional rights. It is the culmination of more than a year of General Moonoo unlawfully deploying police officers against our client for no other reason than to discredit our client because our client has exposed the allegations of generally corrupt relationships. Simply put, all of the above makes out a case for a gross violation of our client's*

constitutional rights for no other purpose than to cover up and/or quash corruption investigations laid by our client against senior police officials and the NPA officials.

I then stated that I would continue pursuing my investigations without fear or favour to ensure that South Africa did not become a police state.

We later learned that Vlok had taken the SAA docket to a prosecutor who declined to prosecute. Unhappy with this decision, the prosecutor was removed from the case, and a more compliant prosecutor was appointed – Advocate Mlotshwa. In my opinion, the reason Mlotshwa was so happy to go along with Vlok is that he too had a lot to hide (which I will expand on later in the book) and so would do anything to keep his secrets hidden. He was to become a major player in Moonoo's all-out campaign against me. Mlotshwa, alongside Advocate Sello Maema, was also busy prosecuting Johan Booysen, the head of the DPCI in KwaZulu Natal, who had been set up on fake charges, to stop him arresting and charging persons in business with Zuma family members. Maema was also prosecuting Sibiya and Dramat from the Hawks, as well as IPID officials Sesoko, Khuba and Robert McBride.

I had been forewarned and was expecting to be arrested on the fake SAA case. I knew the police didn't have a case against me – and I knew they knew it too – and that the case would be quickly dismissed if I were to appear in court. What I had not expected was to be arrested on some virtually non-existent immigration law that nobody had even heard of. Nor had I expected to be dragged off a plane in front of my daughters.

What I would learn is that these criminals with badges would do anything to try to stop me. I didn't know it yet, but I was about to find out that the SAA case would get me into the heart of the state capture project. The people Moonoo's unit were protecting now included Myeni.

With her proximity to the President, anything that could be done to keep me away needed to be done. There were too many fiendish plans underway in 2015 to loot the SAA money pot, and it wouldn't serve any of them to have me sniffing around, threatening to expose it all. I had already by that stage fingered Moonoo for protecting many other criminals, including the Bhana father and son team, Jen Chi (Robert) Huang, Yusuf Kajee, and the by-then infamous Radovan Krejcir.

SARAH-JANE TRENT

Between dealing with Myeni, Moonoo (and his chosen team), investigating various other state-owned agencies, and keeping an eye on underworld characters like Krejcir, I had my hands full.

Sarah-Jane Trent had come to work for me as an intern during February 2015, and by May 2015, impressed with her work ethic, I employed her full time on condition that she be registered as an attorney within two years and as a Certified Fraud Examiner within a further two years. She did both. I also made her the Executive Director of Forensics for Justice, a charity I had formed. It was this charity that would become a potent weapon against organised crime in the criminal justice system of South Africa.

SAA NOSEDIVES UNDER MYENI, THE CAPTAIN OF PLUNDER

Fighting Moonoo would occupy a lot of my time, but with the extra help from Sarah-Jane, I was able to focus on Myeni again. SAA's debt continued escalating, becoming an ever-yawning hole that would ultimately see the airline crash.

The wide-bodied aircraft interference was just the beginning of a number of irrational moves Myeni would make on tenders at SAA that would see her attempting to line her own pockets – and others associated with her – while SAA's liquidity nosedived. At the end of 2015, The amaBhungane Centre for Investigative Journalism published an article titled *How Myeni broke SAA.*[10] It described how Myeni's unlawful and "reckless pursuit of an empowerment fantasy" was bringing the airline close to bankruptcy – all due to Myeni overturning a R9-billion deal 'swap transaction' with Airbus, which Treasury had checked and approved. After Myeni had openly defied Minister Lynne Brown over SAA CEO Kalawe, political oversight of SAA was handed over to Treasury – and Finance Minister Nhlanhla Nene – to deal with.

Myeni unlawfully stopped the Airbus swap transaction deal from going through because she wanted, at the last minute, to include a hand-picked transaction advisor to manage the process of acquiring five Airbus A330 planes. The company was an Illovo-based investment group called Quartile Capital, run by Harmony Gold non-executive deputy chairperson Modise Motloba. Myeni had written to the SAA board to obtain approval to bypass normal tender procedures to secure Quartile Capital's appointment. Later, after further investigation, it would emerge that Quartile Capital had a bad debt history and had been hauled to court twice by SARS for failing to pay more than R1.8 million in VAT.[11]

Myeni's unlawful interference prompted Airbus to demand immediate payment of a R240-million default notice, which SAA could ill afford. Then, Wolf Meyer, Chief Financial Officer of SAA, warned the SAA board in an internal memo that if Airbus issued a default notice, it could trigger cross-default clauses on other loans and leases, which could have led to claims against the government of R11-billion. Meyer resigned soon afterwards, stating that he could no longer associate himself with the conduct of the board.

---

10 Sam Sole, Craig Mckune, Tabelo Timse, How Myeni broke SAA, Mail & Guardian , 27 November 2015, https://mg.co.za/article/2015-11-27-00-how-myeni-broke-saa/

11 Susan Comrie, Myeni's dodgy saviour for SAA, City Press, 26 March 2016, https://city-press.news24.com/News/myenis-dodgy-saviour-for-saa-20160326

In the article, *amaBhungane* explained that the Airbus deal had been under negotiation since 2014. The plan was to swap an onerous contract for ten shorter-range A320s, with an agreement to lease five modern long-range A330-300 wide-body aircraft. Airbus would have funded the lease initially but was open to later devolving it to another lessor, approved by SAA.

The A320 contract, first negotiated in 2002, had lumped SAA with an obligation to buy ten outdated aircraft it didn't need. The contract made provision for pre-delivery payments, some of which SAA had paid, whereas other payments, amounting to US$17-million, were overdue. The swap deal approved by Treasury would have seen Airbus repay unspent pre-delivery payments to SAA and waive new payments, making for a desperately needed cash injection. By committing to five new A330s, Airbus was all but assured of benefiting from any future expansion of the SAA long-haul fleet (rather than Boeing) because of the extra cost of maintaining a multi-vendor fleet.

The SAA board approved the swap transaction in principle, and Nene gave approval in terms of section 54(2) of the Public Finance Management Act. Nico Bezuidenhout (SAA's Acting Chief Executive) and Wolf Meyer sought SAA board ratification for the final agreement. The attempt to ratify the deal with Airbus was blocked because the board, which was largely filled with Myeni sycophants, failed to achieve a quorum. Other non-executive directors had ditched Myeni and left the airline with no proper board of control.

Instead, Myeni wrote to Airbus, stating they had engaged an African aircraft leasing company to work with them, effectively introducing an unnecessary but costly middleman – and an opportunity to skim millions off the top of the now-inflated prices.

An insider told *amaBhungane*:

> *When Airbus received this letter, they were flabbergasted. This was September. The deal had been done. Their Head of Sales, Hadi Akoum, called Meyer to say: "What the fuck is going on here?"*

A scheduled board meeting was called with Airbus to finalise the swap transaction, but the company secretary apologised, saying that Myeni could not attend. After Meyer and another board member left, Myeni, who had allegedly been hiding in the corner of the hotel, arrived with Modise Motloba from Quartile Capital. Motloba said he could give Airbus R6-billion of the purchase price and that they should do a deal. Airbus's Akoum said it was not possible – they would have to start a new process, which would take months, and Quartile would have to bid. Minister of Finance Nhlanhla Nene put his foot down and said that SAA must stick to the original Airbus deal. Six days later, President Jacob Zuma fired Nhlanhla Nene, sending the country's financial markets reeling.

In January 2016, on the back of this information, I opened a further criminal case against Myeni based on the Quartile Capital revelations. I asked that charges of reckless trading, fraud and corruption be investigated. My complaint read as follows:

> *Myeni's conduct was not only reckless in the extreme, but it was calculated and planned as part of a conspiracy to introduce a third party. When she did not get her way, she took the matter further, and the repercussions were immense and extreme... Not only did Myeni and the board engage in reckless, fraudulent and patently disgraceful ethical conduct but, when it became clear that Treasury, and in turn, the Minister of Finance refused to kowtow to Myeni's desires, she managed to procure, through Jacob Zuma to arrange for the then Minister of Finance to be (unlawfully) fired. The unlawful dismissal of Nene by President Zuma sent the world markets into turmoil and wiped billions of rands off the balance sheets of many South Africans and South African companies by causing a run on the Rand.*

In February 2019, National Treasury's financial modelling revealed that Nenegate, as it came to be known, had hiked the country's long-term debt from R3-billion to R5-billion.[12] At the State Capture Inquiry, Catherine MacLeod, the National Treasury's Chief Director of Macro Economic Policy, illustrated this long-term debt, which saw the rand tumble from R14,59 against the US$ to R15,90 in just forty-eight hours.

But Myeni wasn't done. More information kept on coming out pertaining to her allegedly reckless behaviour at SAA. In March 2016, I opened a second case against Myeni and the Board of SAA for fraud, corruption, and reckless management when a letter emerged revealing that Myeni was a repeat offender in terms of interfering in the procurement of tenders. In my opinion, the only reasonable explanation available for why she would be doing this was so that she could get a cut after appointing her friends to secure the deals. It was soon after this second docket was opened that Moonoo's crooked cops began to turn the wheel against me.

The letter emerged through Kalawe, who had been fighting the trumped-up disciplinary charges that SAA had brought against him. The case had landed up at the Labour Court. One of the court documents attached to Kalawe's application – which was ironically supplied to the court through ENS via Colonel Hoosen – was a letter titled "Leadership Challenges in Relation to the chairperson of SAA".

The letter was from 2014 when Myeni had organised, through Adv Nkosi-Thomas, to hire a private investigator to illegally acquire the phone records and bank statements of three SAA board members. Six of the then non-executive directors – Andile Khumalo, Nonhlanhla Kubeka, Raisibe Lepule, Andile Mabizela, Bongisizwe Mpondo and

12 Jessica Bezuidenhout, The impact of Nenegate: No you can't simply pick up a plunging rand, Daily Maverick, 19 February 2019, https://www.dailymaverick.co.za/article/2019-02-19-the-impact-of-nenegate-no-you-cant-simply-pick-up-a-plunging-rand/

Carol Roskruge – collaboratively wrote a letter addressed to Myeni and the then-Minister of Public Enterprises, Malusi Gigaba.

The letter showed that Myeni was repeatedly interfering in large tender processes to the detriment of the airline. It stated that at a board meeting held in January 2014, a matter was tabled and discussed relating to Myeni's conduct. The chairperson was not there, so a special board meeting was convened to discuss the matter. Myeni said she would not attend. The six decided to express their dissatisfaction with Myeni's leadership in writing. The board was trying to fulfil its mandate of having a long-term turnaround strategy to lead the airline out of its challenges – but they were being deliberately hampered by Myeni.

The letter further highlighted that Myeni was already (at that stage) interfering in the financing of the A320 narrow-body fleet. Despite repeatedly saying that the board had resolved to go ahead with the financing of all ten aircraft, Myeni repeatedly insisted that it was for just two aircraft – even writing to the Department of Public Enterprises and fraudulently stating that the board had resolved to finance only two aircraft.

There was a four-month delay in delivering the A320s, which negatively impacted the pre-delivery payments by an estimated R800-million – funds that were not being made available to SAA at a time when cash was urgently needed. In their letter, the honest members of the Board wrote:

> *This letter demonstrates repeat transgressions of corporate governance, undermining due processes approved by the Board and a lack of diligence and care on the part of the Chairperson on extremely important matters.*

In my statement to the police, I said that the letter should have led to an immediate investigation:

> *Gigaba, however, consulted President Zuma. Zuma, who is [allegedly] both romantically and financially involved with Myeni, and moved Gigaba away from Public Enterprises to Home Affairs and appointed Lynne Brown there instead.*
>
> *Brown then brought about the dismissal of the six directors who complained about Myeni.*

Poof! The magic wand had been waved, and Myeni was free to carry on looting SAA. She even had her photograph pasted on the front page of every in-flight magazine, waxing lyrical about how great she was, all while bringing the airline, and by implication the country, to its knees.

DEBT RESTRUCTURE

I had also discovered that Myeni was about to pull off the sting of the century by siphoning off R256-million from the airline's already depleted available cash reserves. In a subsequent supplementary statement made to the police, I made it clear that Myeni had no skills whatsoever to even run a two-plane airline, let alone South Africa's national carrier. Sarah-Jane Trent and I had a half-day meeting with OUTA (Organisation Undoing Tax Abuse) and handed them everything we had. OUTA subsequently launched an urgent application to stop the payment of the R256-million and Myeni, the first primary school teacher to run a national flag carrier, became the laughing stock of the global aviation industry.

The red flag to the proposed fraud was found in an email leaked to me, written by SAA employee Silas Matsaudza, which mentioned the potential appointment of the services of a transaction adviser to provide advice on the possible restructuring of SAA's alleged R15-

billion debt. I pointed out that SAA had its own staff who could have easily done the work themselves.

Seven bids for the provision for this advice were submitted. Six were delivered electronically, and one – from BNP Capital (Pty) Ltd – was hand-delivered. BNP Capital was appointed, and suddenly, the scope of the bid changed. With no second or third opinion, BNP revealed to the Board that, over and above their R1- to R2-million advisory fee, they would raise loans of R15-billion at a rate 600% higher than market norms. A fee of R256-million was then added, with BNP claiming that there was an urgent need for the loans to be secured by 30 June 2016 or the airline would collapse. The normal fee for transaction services of this nature is 0.25% and not the 1,5% BNP wanted to charge SAA. This meant their fee was R213-million more than it needed to be for the service. It was a service that SAA did not even need. Group Treasurer Cynthia Stimpel pointed out this overcharge to Interim Chief Finance Officer Phumeza Nhantsi, but Nhantsi allowed the deal to go through. When a resolution to appoint BNP Capital was made by the SAA board, no contract was drawn up with the company to include the fees payable. SAA essentially signed off a blank cheque.

Before the deal could go through, it was leaked to the media, which immediately derailed the whole process. It was only when Zuma was removed from office that Myeni finally saw the end of her time at SAA. The airline paid the cost for her tenure at its helm.

For Myeni, her high life was finally over. Or was it? I later discovered that she had been given a position as 'special advisor' to the Transport Minister, but I ensured that the position attracted media attention and the position was withdrawn. Five years earlier, she had marched into Kalawe's office and accused him of not allowing her to go on pension by appointing external transactional advisors. Finally, she had become a pariah. Nobody in the world would hire her, and many hoped that she would get to spend some of her retirement sitting around waiting for prison.

Through Bosasa whistle-blower Angelo Agrizzi, the State Capture Commission revealed that Myeni was allegedly being paid monthly by Bosasa, which received billions of rands worth of correctional services tenders. Agrizzi said Myeni was given R300 000 a month in cash for the Jacob Zuma Foundation. On one occasion, the money was handed to her in a Louis Vuitton handbag. Agrizzi said that because of her connection to Zuma, Myeni was viewed as powerful and untouchable. According to statements I obtained from Angelo Agrizzi, Bosasa had also installed state-of-the-art CCTV and security fencing at her luxury house in Richards Bay.

Because of her disastrous running of SAA, the Organisation Undoing Tax Abuse (OUTA) and the SAA Pilots' Association (SAAPA) brought a case against Myeni to have her declared a delinquent director – a slam dunk case that they won in May 2020 – ensuring that she would never be able to serve on any board, ever again. At first, Myeni pleaded guilty, but then she asked to change her plea, saying that the whole SAA board should be held responsible for what happened at SAA, and not just her. She also repeatedly failed to show up at the Pretoria High Court, claiming she could not afford to travel from KwaZulu-Natal to Pretoria.

We did not waste further time on Myeni. We knew she would not be able to escape the slippery slope she was on. We have consistently called for an opening of the books of the Jacob Zuma Foundation (run by Myeni) because we believe it was used to channel cash to both her and Zuma.

How far the mighty have fallen.

Unfortunately, she managed to take SAA down with her. By the end of 2019, the embattled airline was facing a debt spiral. SAA had lost more than R28-billion over the previous thirteen years and had no choice but to restructure. The airline went into business rescue, but so much had been looted that there was no wriggle room left. By May 2020, amidst the devastation that COVID-19 had wrought on businesses across the world, the business rescue practitioners announced that they had no options left – either SAA must retrench staff, or it must go into liquidation.[13] There were more than four thousand employees at SAA, many of whom would probably lose their jobs.

The picture looked bleak, and it was clear to me that my Lifetime Platinum Card that I sought to protect back in 2014 really *was* at risk after all. The airline eventually resurfaced in a much smaller version and has now started a long struggle to regain its market position. All thanks to corruption.

13 Clement Manyathela, D-Day for SAA as BRPs to decide on future of airline employees, EWN, 1 May 2020, https://ewn.co.za/2020/05/01/d-day-for-saa-as-brps-to-decide-on-future-of-airline-employees

CHAPTER 6

PRASA – A STATE CAPTURE TRAIN WRECK

2010 TO 2012 - THE BIRTH OF STATE CAPTURE

For many years, Lucky Montana went under the radar. He started his tenure as CEO of the Passenger Rail Agency of South Africa (PRASA) in 2010. Nothing much happened (that we know of) until 2012, a significant year for state capture. While corruption had been a problem for years and increased exponentially when Zuma took office in May 2009, it seemed that between 2011 and 2012, it really took flight. It was during this time that many of the country's state owned companies went on a buying spree, and the large-scale looting began. It was also when watchdogs, including myself, started to notice something was happening – but we weren't quite sure yet what it was.[14]

Between 2011 and 2012, I was already aware that the criminal justice system was undergoing capture but did not fully comprehend how deep the waters ran. It would take another year or two for us to fully comprehend the scope of the systemic corruption that had overtaken the state.

---

14 Lameez Omarjee, NEC has known about State Capture since 2012 – analyst, Fin24, 30 May 2017, https://www.fin24.com/Economy/nec-has-known-about-state-capture-since-2012-analyst-20170530

The capture of state owned companies followed a set pattern. The first step was the appointment of trusted cadres at the head of these organisations. Once that person was in place, the boards would be obliterated, either slowly or in one fell swoop. New people would be brought in. They would either have their private interests at heart – like in the case of Gupta mole/lackey Rajesh Naithani at SAA[15] – or they were happy to take home handsome paycheques and close their eyes to anything they saw and heard. In some cases, the new appointees saw their appointment as sincere and were oblivious due to their personal naivety (or arrogance) in their duties as non-executive directors.

In 2012, as mentioned, Dudu Myeni was appointed the chairperson of SAA following the resignation of eight of its fourteen board members. In July 2012, Anoj Singh – the Gupta man at Eskom – opened a bank account that allegedly grew from R200- to R16-million, way more than his salary earnings.[16] In 2011, Brian Molefe was appointed to Transnet, and Hlaudi Motsoeneng was placed as the Acting Chief Operating Officer of the SABC.

Assets were audited to see where improvements, often legitimate, needed to be made. Money was budgeted for and allocated by Treasury. Large projects were initiated, tenders were handed out to companies with links to a limited set of private individuals, and, slowly but surely, through the issuing of corrupt tender after tender, the looting began. This was certainly the case at PRASA. It was around this time that then-President Zuma announced the Passenger Rail Agency of South Africa would receive significant cash injections to modernise the rolling stock fleet.[17]

---

15 Sabelo Skiti, Unmasked the Guptas SAA 'mole', Times Live, 30 May 2017, https://www.timeslive.co.za/politics/2017-05-30-unmasked-the-guptas-saa-mole/

16 Ferial Haffajee, Report tracks amazing growth of Eskom finance boss Anoj Singh's bank account, Daily Maverick, 16 November 2018, https://www.dailymaverick.co.za/article/2018-11-16-report-tracks-amazing-growth-of-eskom-finance-boss-anoj-singhs-bank-account/

17 Parliamentary Monitoring Group, Passenger Rail Agency of South Africa (PRASA) on its modernisation strategy for passenger rail, 18 June 2012, https://pmg.org.za/committee-meeting/14573/

Investments at PRASA were much needed. With a stuttering public transport network, trains and private taxis were often the only way that millions of poor South Africans were able to get around. A properly operating rail network was essential for the growth of the economy. South Africa is a large country, and trains were the only viable way of transporting goods across the country. The road network was being put under strain by all the big fuel-guzzling trucks that were being forced to use the roads when the railways weren't working. The rail locomotives were old, the infrastructure was falling apart, and the train stations were notoriously dangerous.

EXPOSED

For the next three years, PRASA went on a buying spree but publicly, all was relatively quiet. That would all change in 2015 when several scandals detonated one after the other, blowing the lid open on a horde of shady dealings and a slew of crimes that would ultimately bring a previously functioning rail agency to the edge of collapse.

In June 2015, Pieter-Louis Myburgh, a journalist then at *Rapport*, revealed that PRASA had purchased twenty-five diesel and forty-five electric locomotives from an unknown shelf company called Swifambo Rail Leasing, which then subcontracted a Spanish company, Vossloh España to build the locomotives.[18] This cost R3.5-billion. When the first batch of the Afro 4000 diesel locomotives arrived, it was discovered they were too tall for our rail infrastructure. This story caught my attention.

Lucky Montana was furious at this exposé and spent the next few years vehemently denying the trains were too tall. In this instance, and numerous times afterwards, he was shown to be a stranger to the truth. In 2019, the locomotives were auctioned off – a desperate

---

18 Pieter-Louis Myburgh, SA's R600 million train blunder, Netwerk24, 7 April 2015, https://www.news24.com/SouthAfrica/News/SAs-R600-million-train-blunder-20150704

attempt by Swifambo to recoup some of the money they owed PRASA after the agency had successfully cancelled the disastrous contract through the courts. PRASA sued Swifambo for R2.6-billion.

Two months after the first stories emerged about the too-tall trains, Public Protector Thuli Madonsela released a report on widespread maladministration, tender irregularities and financial mismanagement at PRASA, titled *Derailed*. Madonsela investigated thirty-two complaints of wrongdoing against PRASA, nineteen of which were substantiated.[19]

The report also made several personal findings against Montana, including that he had acted in breach of the constitution and the promotion of administrative justice act for terminating the contracts of seven cleaning companies in 2012; that he had improperly appointed Joel Chimanda's company AR Chimanda Consulting as a special advisor at a cost of R2-million; that he had suspended seven employees without following proper disciplinary procedures, and that he terminated the services of five executives between 2008 and 2013 without following proper procedures.

Madonsela found that PRASA improperly incurred an over-expenditure amounting to more than R523.7-million. She recommended that the chairperson of the PRASA board, Popo Molefe, ask National Treasury to conduct a forensic investigation into all contracts awarded at the agency since 2012 that were above the value of R10-million, and that he address findings regarding systemic administrative deficiencies allowing ongoing maladministration and improprieties in the procurement system.

The finding I was most interested in was a tender that had been awarded to Siyangena Technologies worth R1.95-billion – that later

19 Thomas Hartleb, 10 of Thuli Madonsela's findings against Prasa, News24, 24 August 2015, https://www.fin24.com/Economy/10-of-Thuli-Madonselas-findings-against-Prasa-20150824

ballooned to more than R4-billion – to install high-speed passenger gates at the Doornfontein and Nasrec train stations.

BID-RIGGING RED FLAGS

I had first started investigating PRASA when I received a tip-off that Montana was becoming insanely rich through dodgy electronic security contracts and station security upgrades. In September 2015, a few weeks after the Public Protector's report came out, I opened a criminal docket of corruption, money laundering and fraud at PRASA. I opened the docket, comprising three lever arch files, at the Brooklyn Police Station in Pretoria. It was based on an investigation I had conducted into the contracts awarded to Siyangena for an Integrated Security Access Management System (ISAMS), a project PRASA was undertaking to secure and monitor all the rail stations. Some R4-billion had been syphoned out of the rail operator.

As the Public Protector's report *Derailed* explained, PRASA awarded a tender for the installation of high-speed passenger gates at the Nasrec and Doornfontein stations to Siyangena in 2009. This tender was later extended to include seven other stations across the country. Montana justified the increase of scope by stating that the seven stations, which had been designated as 2010 FIFA World Cup stations, had excluded the critical work of installing modern speed gates. Montana dishonestly claimed the extension was done to ensure World Cup 2010 readiness and that the closed tender complied with supply chain management policy requirements. At the time, PRASA said only two tenderers met the minimum technical requirements – Protea Coin, which tendered at R698-million, and Siyangena at R1.1-billion. It came to light, however, that the rollout only took place after the World Cup. Siyangena was appointed, and the price suddenly shot up from R1.1-billion to a total of R1.959-billion – an R859-million increase, with virtually no procurement process followed.

Madonsela did not accept Montana's submission that the rollout was to meet the 2010 FIFA World Cup needs. She indicated that Montana's changing narrative over what happened was a cause for concern. She concluded that the extension of the Siyangena contract to more stations than specified in the tender advertisement constituted maladministration and improper conduct. The tender was extended beyond the advertised scope, in violation of PRASA's supply chain policy.

I was keenly interested in the second part of the ISAMS tender. The project had been split into two phases, which, in total, was valued at over R4-billion. A letter of invitation for the second phase of the tender was issued in June 2013, valued at approximately R2.5-billion.

At the time, a company called SA Fence and Gate had a depot fencing contract with PRASA to the value of R209-million. This project was, however, allegedly unlawfully halted while SA Fence and Gate was bidding for the ISAMS tender. Later, this tender would also be surrounded by controversy, with reports indicating the scope of this project was also increased by more than R100-million.[20] The allegations were made by Lucky Montana, who filed a complaint with the Public Protector.[21] It seemed like another act of revenge by the CEO, who would soon be ousted from the organisation. He would spend the next few years throwing around accusations and denying all responsibility for what happened at PRASA. In my opinion, Montana was nothing more, or less, than a corrupt criminal.

I wrote in my statement that the unlawful halting of the fencing project flowed from the company, raising material concerns about the bidding process for the two ISAMS projects. It was, therefore, assumed to be revenge against them on the part of certain PRASA officials. There were numerous red flags that indicated tender rigging

20 Steve Kretzmann, Why are the lights off at PRASA, GroundUp, 13 December 2018, https://www.groundup.org.za/article/why-are-lights-prasa/

21 Nicky Smith, Fencing firm denies claim by former PRASA CEO, Business Day, 4 August 2015, https://www.pressreader.com/south-africa/business-day/20150804/281612419114752

had taken place in the second phase of the ISAMS project. The main red flag was that the scope of the tender was deliberately specific, requesting a certain type of equipment when others would have been perfectly suitable. At a meeting held with prospective bidders, many raised the exclusivity of the products being requested as a concern. One such product, the Dallmeier system, had a single, sole distributor in South Africa – Siyangena – immediately biasing the tender towards that specific bidding company.

In response to bidder concerns, Josephat Phungula, a PRASA employee, sent out an email in which he falsely claimed the Dallmeier system was supplied by four vendors. Our investigations revealed that this was simply not true. In all of Phungula's correspondence on the project, he called himself "Doctor". I believed his use of the title "Dr" was also fraudulent. When I opened the docket, an investigation into his CV was already underway at PRASA, and he subsequently resigned.

Despite not having the unlawfully specified equipment, SA Fence and Gate still tendered for the second phase of the ISAMS project. In response, a PRASA employee sent an email out to a list of ten people saying that the technology SA Fence and Gate offered within the fencing project was not compatible with the technology PRASA was using. It was a subjective email and made no factual basis for why the technology was incompatible. The intention, it seemed, was to scupper any chances of any other potential bidder competing against Siyangena for the ISAMS Phase 2 work. The email was distributed widely within PRASA, poisoning the well not only for SA Fence and Gate but also for any other potential bidders.

I interviewed and took a detailed statement from SA Fence and Gate. I said in my statement that the email itself amounted to an act of fraud. SA Fence and Gate submitted what should have been a potentially winning bid priced at R1.9-billion, but with the equipment requirements unlawfully specified by PRASA, there could ultimately only be one winner – a joint tender between Engineered System Solution (Pty) Ltd (ESS) and Siyangena. They had the same directors, Mario Ferreira and Pragason Reddy. Both companies fell under the umbrella company TMM Holdings. Siyangena was the only company certified in all the specified products, which meant that any other potential bidder would have been prejudiced from the very outset. The tender documents were intentionally crafted to favour one single contractor and exclude all others. This was a clear-cut case of bid-rigging, a pattern I had seen many times over the years and one I had published a paper on in 2005, explaining the different bid-rigging schemes.

BUYING UP HOUSES

I also found some links between Dallmeier and Mario Ferreira. Dallmeier sponsored the Vasco Da Gama soccer club in Cape Town, which happened to be owned by Mario Ferreira. But, more interestingly, I proved a connection between Siyangena and PRASA CEO Lucky Montana. While conducting forensic checks on everyone involved, I confirmed a highly suspicious housing transaction, one that had originally been reported by Peter Louis Myburgh in June 2015 in *City Press*. I thought this would be a good starting point. Jan Adriaan van der Walt, the attorney for Siyangena, owned a company called Precise Trade and Invest 02. This company purchased Lucky Montana's house in Parkwood for R6.8-million, bond-free. Montana had previously bought the property for R1.850-million, and I did a market comparison to see what the property should, in fact, be valued at. I found it had been sold for at least R3-million above market value. It was clear that despite 'selling' the house, Lucky Montana's mother stayed on in the house as a 'tenant', which meant that Montana still had control of it. This prompted me to expand my investigations into other properties linked to Montana.

There was another link between van der Walt and Ferreira. They were co-directors of a company called Triple Trade and Invest 04. This appeared to me to be a cut and dry case of gratification. The purchase of the house was done to conceal a corrupt payment, which may have amounted to the offences of corruption and money laundering.

Aside from this house purchase, there were several other suspicious property transactions linked to van der Walt, worth more than R37-million. I then carried out a detailed investigation, which I passed on to the police in my criminal docket.

During our months of investigations, we tracked down the previous owners of the properties in question and managed to obtain copies of the original offer to purchase contracts signed by Lucky Montana. We also obtained detailed sworn statements from the previous property owners and the estate agents involved in the transactions. They were all resolute that Lucky Montana personally chose the properties and signed the original offers, which were then mendaciously replaced with substitute contracts with an opaque company, set up and shadow-run by a crooked Pretoria lawyer, the 'owner' in Montana's place. For this reason, we added money laundering to the charge sheet.

Montana had also bought three properties worth over R15-million for cash. Where was the source of this money, I asked? It appeared evident that money laundering had taken place. On one of the properties, improvements were underway, which I estimated to be worth around R3-million. I had picked up that one of the contractors was a company called Tilespace, owned by a man called Michael Ferreira. Wondering if he was one of Mario's relatives, I asked the police to investigate the link. I even had this house under surveillance for a few days and witnessed a curious incident where a white man was taking photographs outside the house. Lucky Montana arrived and threw a brick at his car while the latter beat a hasty retreat. The next day, Pieter-Louis Myburgh wrote a story about Montana throwing a brick at the photographer's vehicle. After that, I collaborated with Myburgh and gave him everything I had uncovered, which added extra depth and width to his stories. When I opened the criminal docket against Montana and Ferreira, Myburgh was the first journalist to get a copy of it. Although Myburgh played down my role in the Montana investigations, as some journalists seem to do in my investigations, I was happy to see Montana finally getting a good dose of public attention.

I also picked up that Mario Ferreira and Lucky Montana had a previous business relationship in 2012 where a €160-million Thales-Portugal/Thales-South Africa/PRASA deal had taken place. Mario was a director of Siemens at the time, and Siemens was involved in the contract.

I argued that both Mario Ferreira and Lucky Montana be charged with corruption since the two of them were engaged in a generally corrupt relationship that prejudiced PRASA to a total of R1.86-billion. I added that along with Ferreira and Montana, Jan Adriaan van der Walt (Ferreira's lawyer and alleged money launderer) should also be charged with multiple counts of money laundering, as well as racketeering. The true value of their crimes exceeded R4-billion, but I narrowed the docket to what I considered prima facie evidence that could be acted on quickly, which came in at a little under R2-billion.

HAWKS DUCK RESPONSIBILITY

Of course, nothing was going to happen to any of these alleged crooks. The investigation, like all the others I opened, went nowhere. Instead, the scandals at PRASA deepened. Every few months, a new outrage emerged, and the crises at the rail agency, like at SAA, grew worse and worse. No investigation was carried out by the captured Hawks, and no decision to prosecute has ever been taken. Not a single rand of the estimated R4-billion I estimated to have been stolen from

PRASA was seized by the Asset Forfeiture Unit. Hawk's boss General Berning Ntlemeza and his crew at the NPA – Abrahams, Jiba and Mrwebi – appeared to have put a lid on all state-owned company corruption dockets, which, by then, were probably gathering dust in a meeting room next to the office of Zuma's appointed Head of Prosecutions, Shaun Abrahams.

When I realised that PRASA was about to make a R300-million payment to Siyangena in late September 2015, I instructed law firm Schindlers to launch an urgent application to stop the payment. I sent PRASA an email attaching a part of the docket, informing them that since this was such a blatant waste of public funds, they should suspend all payments to ESS and Siyangena or any other entity related to Mario Ferreira. I told them that unless I received an undertaking that they would freeze further payments to Siyangena, I would launch an urgent application. The board of PRASA took the docket and my threat of the court application seriously. Just prior to launching the application, Popo Molefe gave an undertaking to Schindlers that the payment would be stopped – and it was.

A couple of weeks later, I received a call asking me to attend a meeting involving PRASA. I was asked to give an irrevocable undertaking that I would not mention the initiator of the meeting, where the meeting took place, or who would attend the meeting. My word is my bond, so I was obliged to keep to it. However, without breaking my word, I can say that the meeting took place on a Sunday morning at the offices of the convenor of the meeting. I was told that 'someone special' would be at the meeting and that the purpose was to discuss the 'settlement' of the PRASA matter. I took this to mean that they would refund all the monies that had been stolen and provide inculpatory evidence against Lucky Montana. I was excited.

I duly arrived for the meeting at 9 a.m., and 'someone special' arrived in a chauffeur-driven car about ten minutes later. When I saw who I would be meeting with, I made it clear that I did not want to sit in the same room as him, so he was ushered into one office, and I was ushered into another. The convenor then acted as a messenger between the two of us.

I was then asked what it was that I wanted for me to stop the investigation against Montana and bring this thing to an end. I said I wanted the money to be paid back to PRASA and that evidence that could be used against Lucky Montana be provided. A counter offer was made, and I was offered £2-million, paid offshore if I would withdraw the criminal charges, withdraw my requirement for PRASA not to pay Siyangena the three hundred million Rand, state that I had found nothing wrong in the deal between Siyangena and PRASA, and publicly apologise for opening the docket. I played along for a while, hoping the man involved would put something in writing so I could catch him at his evil game. But the written offer never materialised, and they disappeared. I think they smelt a rat. What a pity. I would have loved to have caught the corrupters in the act. Some said I was mad to decline the £2-million, worth over R40-million at the time. But I knew differently. Once you go down that road, you are as bad as – or even worse than – those you are exposing, and you'll spend the rest of your life looking over your shoulder.

I have a simple rule in my life's ethics: I must be able to tell my children what I am doing, and if I cannot do that, I should not do it. I now wish I had not given my word about the person's identity who tried to buy me off in late 2015, but I cannot change history, and I cannot break my word.

More than a year later, a clearly frustrated Popo Molefe had written to General Ntlemeza questioning why nothing tangible had been done by the Hawks in the PRASA investigations.[22] Popo Molefe specifically

22 Gosebo Mathope, Molefe demands Hawks take corrective action in PRASA probe, then board gets sacked, The Citizen, 5 May 2017, https://citizen.co.za/news/south-africa/1504127/molefe-demands-hawks-take-corrective-action-in-prasa-probe-then-board-gets-sacked/

mentioned the Brooklyn case I had opened – the files of which I had handed to Werksmans attorneys free of charge – to set aside the contracts with Siyangena.

Molefe wrote:

> *Prasa contends that DPCI has failed reasonably to comply with its constitutional and statutory obligations to investigate these matters and to bring the investigations to finality.*

Molefe went on to say that, in terms of the correspondence supplied, the officer assigned to the case, Major General Alfred Khana (the Head of the Hawks Commercial Crimes Unit), either showed that he was not acquainted with details of the investigation, which he had been leading for a year, or he was deliberately seeking to frustrate the investigation. One week later, Popo Molefe and the entire board of PRASA was fired. Zuma appeared determined that the lid should be kept on PRASA's cash flow, which included several hundred million that had allegedly flowed back to him.

The State machinery put in place to stop corruption had themselves become corrupt. Nothing, it seemed, would happen to hold anyone accountable while the country was being looted to the tune of billions of rands.

Montana was ousted from the organisation in 2015. All he has done since is refute the claims that the rail agency was captured by corrupt forces during his tenure. The proof against him, however, was just too strong. I once heard him venting his version on a late-night radio show on Power FM, so I called in and confronted him. I told him he had a right to remain silent but that we would record the show – which we did – and would later use it as evidence against him – which we will.

In a discussion on toxic leadership threatening the country, I said that Montana ruled PRASA with an iron fist.[23] He got others to get rid of people in PRASA who stood in his way. Toxic leaders like Montana protest their innocence to the end, in much the same way as dictators like Hitler, Mussolini, Saddam Hussein, and Gaddafi had done. In 2019, Montana made grandiose statements, saying he would testify at the State Capture Commission in order to prove his innocence and name key individuals in the ANC who helped the demise of the rail agency.[24] It was all a red herring, of course. I told Montana to turn up at the Commission with his personal bank accounts so we could all see where he got his money from. Unsurprisingly, he pulled out, claiming he was being pressurised to retract some of his testimony without naming what this was.[25] As far as I was concerned, he was a crook and a coward and belonged in prison for the rest of his life. He would later give his crooked version at the Commission, but in my opinion, he simply lied through his teeth and obfuscated by tendering thousands of pages of irrelevant documents that he would use as red herrings.

Six years after I opened a docket against Lucky Montana, containing *prima facie* evidence of his corruption, the State have failed to bring him to book. His freedom is an indictment on the impotence of the criminal justice system, caused by past and present criminals and sleeper cells.

In 2016, one year after my criminal complaint was laid, the real smoking gun emerged on why PRASA was being looted – and it

23 Ciaran Ryan, Paul O'Sullivan takes on toxic leaders, Accounting Weekly, 2 August 2019, https://accountingweekly.com/toxic-leaders-threaten-the-economy/

24 Luyolo Mkentane, Former PRASA CEO Lucky Montana vows to spill the beans, Business Day, 29 July 2019, https://www.businesslive.co.za/bd/national/2019-07-29-former-prasa-ceo-lucky-montana-vows-to-spill-the-beans/

25 Luyolo Mkentane, Lucky Montana pulls out of State Capture Commission, accuses Sars of settling 'old scores', Business Day, 20 November 2019, https://www.businesslive.co.za/bd/national/2019-11-20-lucky-montana-pulls-out-of-state-capture-commission-accuses-sars-of-settling-old-scores/

was bigger than Lucky Montana. There were political masters in the background, steering the capture of the agency.

THE TRUTH EMERGES

In 2016, *News24* revealed explosive claims that the ANC benefitted from PRASA's controversial locomotive deal.[26] These were contained in court papers filed by chairperson Popo Molefe in the Johannesburg High Court. Molefe was responding to Swifambo Rail Leasing in support of PRASA's bid to have the R3.5-billion contract set aside. He alleged that the suppliers of the Afro 4000 locomotives paid R80-million to 'entities who were not creditors' of the company after an Angolan businesswoman had insisted that ten percent of the tender's value be paid to the ANC. The businesswoman was Maria Gomes, who, in an earlier report, had said she was a friend of Jacob Zuma. The R80-million claim emerged during meetings PRASA had with Auswell Mashaba, Swifambo's managing director after it turned out that the trains were too tall for the rail network. Molefe's affidavit read as follows:

> *Mr Mashaba informed us that ... he had been in contact with a Maria Gomes ... Ms Gomes told Mr Mashaba that she wanted money for the 'movement'. Ms Gomes also told him that she knew the bid to supply locomotives to PRASA was worth billions, and she could not understand why ten percent of the value of the bid could not be paid to the African National Congress. Ms Gomes was insistent that money should go to the movement.*

The court papers showed that the money was paid to Similex, a company Gomes is a director of, and lawyer George Sabelo, a business partner to one of Zuma's sons. The report said that emails dating from

26 Pieter-Louis Myburgh and Angelique Serrao, Exclusive: ANC implicated in PRASA 'bribes', News24, 26 August 2016, https://www.news24.com/SouthAfrica/News/exclusive-anc-implicated-in-prasa-bribes-20160826?isapp=true

December 2013 showed that Montana was in regular contact with Gomes. Molefe's affidavit went on to say:

> *The first alarming feature of this correspondence is the familiarity between Ms Gomes and Mr Montana. For instance, they refer to each other as 'comrades'.*

According to the court papers, Montana had allegedly also provided Gomes with information on other PRASA contracts. The ANC said they were not aware of the payments, and Swifambo denied any wrongdoing.

ZUMA'S FRIEND

Another connection to Jacob Zuma came to light. Pieter-Louis Myburgh, who by now was the only journalist who truly understood the levels of corruption at PRASA, reported on *News24* that Siyangena Technologies paid large sums of money to companies directly linked to Chockalingam (Roy) Moodley, a close friend of Zuma.[27] I had supplied copious documents to Myburgh corroborating and building on his stories. According to Myburgh, Ferreira and Moodley were also connected through the co-ownership of two racehorses – 'One Man's Dream' and 'Hi Societi'. The payments Myburgh uncovered included R500-million paid to Hail Way Trading, a company where Moodley was the director, and R50-million to a company established by Moodley called Royal Security.

Despite not commenting on the story, Moodley reacted by opening a case against Myburgh as well as Jacques Pauw, author of *The President's Keepers*, alleging criminal defamation.[28] Pauw alleged in his book that when Zuma became president, he received a salary as an employee of one of Moodley's companies, but he did not declare these earnings to

27 Pieter-Louis Myburgh, Exclusive: Zuma's friends R550m bonanza, News24, 14 August 2016, https://www.news24.com/SouthAfrica/News/exclusive-zuma-friends-r550m-bonanza-20160814

28 Kailene Pillay, Mybergh, Pauw welcome probe into cop, IOL, 15 December 2017, https://www.iol.co.za/news/south-africa/kwazulu-natal/myburgh-pauw-welcome-probe-into-cop-12426842

the taxman. Moodley used a "friendly" cop, Durban North's Colonel Reuben Govender, to pursue the two journalists. Govender was seen numerous times in Moodley's company. After Pauw and Myburgh were summoned to the Durban North Police Station and allegedly threatened with arrest, Durban magistrate Irfaan Khallil eventually ordered that Govender and Ntuzuma, a magistrate be investigated for misconduct. I did an investigation on the cop and sent it to Pauw. I also leaked it to the media and derailed the attempts to intimidate Pauw and Myburgh.

MYENI CONNECTION

What I didn't know when I opened the PRASA case in 2015 was that in investigating the agency, I was inadvertently bumping into Dudu Myeni again. This time it was through her and her son Thalente Myeni. Thalente once listed Zuma's house in Forest Town as his home address, which *News24* said Thalente shared with his brother, Nhlakanipho Vusi Zuma.[29] If this were true, it made Thalente Myeni Jacob Zuma's son. I have repeatedly and publicly stated it, with not a single denial from any of them.

It turned out that Thalente and other politically connected stakeholders involved in PRASA's R51-billion contract for new passenger carriages cashed in their shares in the tender before any of the trains were built. The article revealed that JSE-listed tech giant EOH paid R16.5-million for the shares in New Africa Rail (NAR), French manufacturing giant Alstom's BEE partner in the contract. This is the same EOH that I fingered for corruption through its subsidiary, FDA, for paying substantial bribes to the chief of police. When I said I would expose them, some of its directors sold off their shares, causing the EOH share price to dive by thirty-five percent.

29 Pieter-Louis Myburgh, Myeni and co's R16m Prasa 'freebie', News24, 11 September 2016, https://www.news24.com/SouthAfrica/News/myeni-and-cos-r16m-prasa-freebie-20160911-2

News24 wrote:

> *Thalente Myeni, 'ANC tycoon' Monde Africa and Sesinyi Seopela, the late former ANC Youth League leader Peter Mokaba's bodyguard, were NAR's local shareholders when the Alstom-led Gibela consortium won Prasa's R51bn contract for the supply of 3 600 new passenger carriages in 2012.*

New Africa Rail had no discernible experience in the rail industry, and their lawyer Christo Stockenström was the business partner of arms deal middle-man Fana Hlongwane. The whole thing smelt rotten. It seemed to be a lovely little freebie for Thalente's company as they appeared to have done nothing to earn the money – a classic red flag to corruption. Thalente is now a very wealthy man. Lucky Montana had, in the meantime, mendaciously told a parliamentary inquiry that he had resisted efforts by the Guptas to benefit from the huge train tender.[30] Montana claimed that the Gupta family and Duduzani Zuma had tried to manipulate the rolling stock tender, but he had resisted, after which they attempted to change the PRASA board. Montana also named former Transport Minister Dipuo Peters and former ANC Treasury General Zweli Mkhize as being instrumental in changing the board so they could place people there who would forward their own interests. He failed to mention the Thalente Myeni and Roy Moodley connection.

(Mkhize would subsequently become Minister of Health and fall from grace after he was found with his fingers in the cash register of a corruptly awarded tender to provide communication services for the Department of Health, which became infamously known as The Digital Vibes corruption case.)

It seemed that everyone was on the take and that PRASA was a free-for-all for multiple persons. It was so bad that even Blade Nzimande,

30 Andisiwe Makinana, Lucky Montana implicates Guptas, Zweli Mkhize in explosive testimony, City Press, 30 January 2018, https://city-press.news24.com/News/lucky-montana-implicates-guptas-zweli-mkhize-in-explosive-testimony-20180130

the then-Minister of Transport, called it an "ATM" since anyone could withdraw cash whenever they wanted it. He said:[31]

> *The fact that PRASA has not submitted its annual report is a sign of the state of the entity. PRASA has been like an ATM. The financial leakages, court challenges and loss of funding is unbelievable. I have told the board to close this ATM down. The board has promised me a submission.*

In July 2020, when the State Capture Commission set its spotlight on PRASA, the country was once again reminded just how corrupt Lucky Montana was. Much like my investigations had found five years earlier, it was revealed to the Commission that Montana had purchased a number of properties totalling over R36-million in the twelve months during which the Siyangena contracts were awarded.[32] The Commission also looked at the lack of will, both politically and from law enforcement, to investigate the corruption at PRASA. In his usual blustery tone, Montana wrote a letter to Deputy Chief Justice Raymond Zondo accusing him of allowing the Commission to become a witch-hunt.[33] He also claimed he could not come to testify because his mother had died recently, offering instead to appear before the Commission in April 2021. Promises, promises...

The damage the looting did to the rail agency was immense, and it would never fully recover. In 2019, the Auditor General, Kimi Makwetu, put a figure to it all, stating that PRASA had incurred R26-

---

31 Khulekani Magubane, Prasa has been like an ATM, says Nzimande, as he urges SOEs to plug leaks, Fin24, 18 May 2018, https://www.fin24.com/Economy/prasa-has-been-like-an-atm-says-nzimande-as-he-urges-soes-to-plug-leaks-20180518

32 Sibongile Khumalo, Ex-Prasa CEO spent over R36m on properties in one year, Fin24, 2 July 2020, https://www.news24.com/fin24/companies/industrial/state-capture-ex-prasa-ceo-spent-over-r36m-on-properties-in-one-year-20200702

33 Suné Payne, Lucky Montana questions Zondo on bias during this week's Prasa testimony before State Capture Commission, Daily Maverick, 3 July 2020, https://www.dailymaverick.co.za/article/2020-07-03-lucky-montana-questions-zondo-on-bias-during-this-weeks-prasa-testimony-before-state-capture-commission/#gsc.tab=0

billion in irregular expenditure.[34] It is an enormous figure and one that is impossible for the debt-laden agency to recover from without the taxpayer coming to its aid. In December 2019, just two days after SAA had been put into business rescue, Transport Minister Fikile Mbalula dissolved PRASA's interim board and placed the agency under administration.[35] Attempts to turn PRASA around had led to multiple suspensions of senior managers implicated in allegations of improper, irregular, or corrupt conduct and fruitless and wasteful expenditure. It was rotten to the core.

I doubt putting PRASA under administration will ultimately save it. The damage, by now, is too severe. The question should rather be asked as to how it was allowed that such an organisation, a crucial element in the backbone of our economy, could be ransacked to such a degree? The country needs accountability for what has happened. Justice needs to be done. Yet to date, not a single one of those who benefitted from the largesse has been brought to a criminal court to account for their crimes.

---

34 Bekezela Phakathi, Auditor-general slaps Prasa with disclaimer after R26bn in irregular expenditure, Business Day, 8 October 2019, https://www.businesslive.co.za/bd/national/2019-10-08-auditor-general-slaps-prasa-with-disclaimer-after-r26bn-in-irregular-expenditure/

35 Sibongile Khumalo, Mbalula dissolves Prasa interim board, places it under administration, Fin24, 9 December 2019, https://www.fin24.com/Companies/breaking-mbalula-dissolves-prasa-interim-board-places-it-under-administration-20191209

CHAPTER 7

BERNING NTLEMEZA DOES HIS WORST

APARTHEID'S CROOKED COP

It was the worst possible Christmas gift the country could receive. In 2014, just one day before the festive celebrations, the Minister of Police, Nathi Nhleko, suspended Head of the Hawks, Anwa Dramat, on fake allegations that he had been involved in the illegal rendition of five Zimbabweans in 2010 and 2011 (the false *Sunday Times* narrative). That same day, Nhleko appointed Mthandazo 'Berning' Ntlemeza in Dramat's place as the Acting Head of the Directorate of Priority Crime Investigations. Replacing Dramat with Ntlemeza was like bringing in a lame donkey to replace a winning racehorse.

However, Ntlemeza's appointment was crucial to the state capture project. It was imperative that a tarnished cadre head up the Hawks – someone who would protect politicians and their gangster friends while attacking whomever they wanted to get rid of. Ntlemeza was perfect for the job. His appointment would prove to be a complete disaster for law and order in the country.

Originally from the Eastern Cape, Ntlemeza joined the police in the Bantu homeland of Transkei at the height of apartheid in 1981, purportedly completing his degree in Police Science at the University of Transkei in 1989. While apartheid-era police were generally hated for the harsh way they treated their own people during these terrible years in South Africa's past, Ntlemeza somehow shed this mantle of distrust and rose through the ranks to become the Deputy Provincial Commissioner of first, the Eastern Cape and then Limpopo.[36]

Ntlemeza's 2015 New Year's 'gift' to the country was the suspension of Gauteng Hawks Head Shadrack Sibiya on the same fake rendition case for which Dramat had been suspended. It was a blitz of getting rid of senior police officials. KwaZulu-Natal Hawks Head Johan Booysen was at the same time the target of an orchestrated campaign to oust him, on another false *Sunday Times* narrative. Dramat, whom I had no doubt had been targeted because of the investigation I asked him to carry out against Moonoo (and Moonoo's relationships with Zuma associates), felt it was best to bow out graciously and accepted a golden handshake to leave his job quietly.

I asked him not to go and said I would help him stay at the helm. Sadly, the bowing out came *after* I had requested the Helen Suzman Foundation to bring urgent applications to stop Nhleko's unlawful conduct. I was extremely disappointed because we had fought and won the battle, only to watch Dramat leave with the door behind him wide open. I called Dramat and begged him not to go.

"Paul," he said, "I'm tired of this nonsense. I would rather just go and get on with my life."

I never spoke to him again after that.

I'm willing to bet that had he known then, that to secure their position, they (being Ntlemeza, Mokotedi, Abrahams and Jiba) would subsequently charge him with serious crimes, he would have stuck to the guns that had been primed for him by the Helen

---

36 Raessa Pather, Crib notes: Why everyone is burning Ntlemeza, Mail & Guardian, 15 September 2016, https://mg.co.za/article/2016-09-15-crib-notes-why-everyone-is-burning-ntlemeza

Suzman Foundation (HSF), possibly changing the course of history and reversing state capture back in 2015. Still, we could not change history. Dramat took what appeared to be the easy way out, leaving both Sibiya and Booysen badly exposed and leaving the door open to complete the job of capturing the criminal justice system.

Sibiya decided to fight back. He was not in Dramat's position to take a golden handshake and run, as none was on offer. He knew he was being targeted because of his investigation and arrest of Crime Intelligence boss Richard Mdluli and other cases he was working on involving certain tobacco barons, including Yusuf Kajee. It would later emerge that Ntlemeza had historically compiled a report to fraudulently exonerate Mdluli in the investigation into the death of Mdluli's ex-girlfriend's husband. Sibiya immediately launched a civil case against Ntlemeza for his unlawful suspension, which was also fought by the Helen Suzman Foundation. (HSF must have loved me – I was constantly lining up new cases for them with a constitutional imperative.)

ANTI-KICKBACK COP

It was during this upheaval that a police officer from Limpopo contacted me. He arrived at my office in full uniform, every inch neatly pressed. I could see my face in his shoes. This is the sort of cop for whom one could only have respect. He spent two full days with me, telling me his story. I helped him write a sworn statement detailing a case of defeating the ends of justice and corruption that we then opened against Ntlemeza.

His name was Lieutenant Boitumelo Ramahlaha (now Captain), and he was stationed in the provincial office in Polokwane. Ramahlaha raised many concerning allegations against Ntlemeza that seemed to indicate that Ntlemeza had been running the Limpopo police as his own personal fiefdom. Ramahlaha told me that a Brigadier HC

Morakaladi was employed as the Provincial Head of Personnel. This brigadier was also allegedly Ntlemeza's girlfriend. A senior officer, Brigadier Phillip Morkel, was investigating her for corruption after she allegedly received kickbacks from applicants for placing them in junior policing positions. But the investigation was never finalised, and the docket disappeared. Instead of being investigated, she rose through the ranks. Ramahlaha said it was commonly believed she had been protected because of her relationship with Ntlemeza.

"It makes a mockery of any reasonable attempt to improve the ethical standards of policing, as it may result in having a corrupt mindset in the police if one has to pay a kick-back to be recruited in the first place," Ramahlaha said in his statement.

Curiously, Morakaladi's own husband, also a police officer, had apparently shot himself in the back of the head in a mysterious suicide. The docket had also vanished. According to Ramahlaha, the deceased must have been double-jointed to have been able to shoot himself in the back of the head.

Ramahlala also had concerning information about a police captain, a certain Matome Thomas Rallele, who was in a relationship with one of Ntlemeza's daughters, Amanda. In 2011, Ramahlaha received evidence that Rallele was using state vehicles to carry goods stolen in house robberies and break-ins. An investigation of the allegation was carried out by a brigadier who traced the tracking units in the state vehicles utilised by Rallele. His final report found that Rallele had made fraudulent entries into the vehicle registers. Instead of being suspended while further investigations took place, Ramahlaha alleged that Ntlemeza suppressed any action against Rallele – as if Rallele was already his son-in-law.

Ramahlala said that he received information from some of his informers several years later that Ralelle was involved in the break-in at a colonel's house and that he (Captain Rallele) was still in possession of a Samsung cell phone taken during the break-in. Ramahlaha reported this to Ntlemeza and the colonel whose phone had been taken. They called Rallele into their office, and, while he was there, the colonel called his stolen phone. It rang while in Rallele's pocket. Rallele was not arrested immediately, but a case was opened, and he was eventually convicted and sentenced to a fine of R2 000 or a suspended sentence of four months. Despite the conviction, he continued to work for the police for a few months. When he was eventually discharged, following the docket we had opened, he still kept his service firearm, uniform, appointment certificate, police computer, 3G card, and two phones – giving him full access to police systems. I made sure all these details were correctly recorded in the next docket I was preparing for Ramahlaha.

In 2013, while he was still investigating Rallele, Ramahlaha and his team arrested two men who had killed a policewoman in Tembisa. The duo was also committing robberies in and around Makopane. Their arrests led them to a Nigerian man they had sold the stolen goods to. But during his arrest, the man resisted, and he died while in custody. Ramahlaha said the man had suffered no trauma at their hands, and an autopsy could find no conclusions that he had died due to their actions. Despite this, Ntlemeza ordered that a doctor come up from KwaZulu-Natal to conduct a second autopsy, which came to the same conclusion as the first one.

Despite these findings, Ntlemeza changed the docket from inquest to murder and ordered Ramahlaha and four of his subordinates to be arrested. Ramahlaha was detained without bail for twenty-four days. Ramahlaha believes that despite there being no evidence, Ntlemeza ensured that charges were pursued against him as a form of revenge. Eventually, after the trial had started, the case was withdrawn due to a complete lack of evidence. As I would later discover, setting people up on fake charges was an old apartheid trick that Ntlemeza was skilled in and which he would later have his accomplices do to me.

When he was let out of jail, Ramahlaha found that his unit had been placed under the control of Captain Rallele. Ramahlaha decided to write a report on the challenges faced by the unit, which included allegations of mismanagement, PFMA breaches, and criminality of police officers. He handed it to Ntlemeza, but again, nothing was done. Ramahlaha then decided to write a three-page letter to the police minister setting out his allegations against Ntlemeza and calling for an investigation. The letter was delivered to Nhleko's chief of staff on December 13. Instead of acting against him, Ntlemeza was promoted to Acting Head of the Hawks eleven days later.

"I cannot think of a more damning travesty of justice," Ramahlaha wrote in his statement.

This meant that Ntlemeza had been appointed to run the Hawks, despite there being an unresolved criminal allegation of defeating the ends of justice made against him by Ramahlaha, an allegation the Minister had been made aware of beforehand but swept under the carpet because it appeared to stand in the way of Ntlemeza's appointment.

MCBRIDE BECOMES A TARGET

There was only one body that could investigate top police officials without fear, and that was the Independent Police Investigation Directorate, or IPID. In early 2014, with the appointment of Robert McBride as its head, this organisation grew some teeth. It had been without a permanent head for more than a year, and McBride, a former Umkhonto we Sizwe leader who had been placed on death row for the bombing of the Why Not Restaurant and Magoo's Bar in Durban in 1986, was not afraid of anything. While he had courted much controversy in the past, I had the utmost respect for him and his straight-up approach towards getting things done.

I had opened a substantial docket against Moonoo and asked IPID to investigate. The case I had opened against NPA officials and Richard Mdluli in 2012 had since been (unlawfully) withdrawn by the State. I also handed a copy of that docket to IPID and asked McBride to deal with the criminal activities of Mdluli.

Additionally, I opened a further case against Moonoo when it was brought to my attention (by an informer in Moonoo's office) that Moonoo had held several secret meetings with the NPA's Nomgcobo Jiba about a docket that had been opened against her by her colleagues. The case was one of perjury over the false charges brought against Major General Johan Booysen, the KZN Hawks Commander. Moonoo subsequently changed the investigating officer on the case. His conduct was clearly an offence of defeating the ends of justice and corruption because the quid pro quo he was seeking was for Jiba to protect him. He, in turn, would keep the cops off her back. By now, I was entirely convinced that Moonoo was an enemy of the state who abused his position to protect criminals – and for personal gain.

With Ramahlaha's statement now in hand, I personally handed it to McBride and asked that IPID also look into Ntlemeza. In doing so, I unwittingly made McBride a target.

In March 2015, McBride was unlawfully suspended by Nhleko. The two IPID officers who were working on the cases I had opened (Mathews Sesoko, Head of Investigations, who had ordered the investigation into Moonoo and Innocent Khuba, who was investigating Ntlemeza) were also unlawfully suspended by McBride's acting replacement, Israel Kgamanyane. Kgamanyane was himself corrupt and had sold his soul to the minister, in return for dropping certain investigations. The reasons given for all the suspensions was that they had all allegedly altered a report by IPID on the rendition cases against Dramat and Sibiya, with the alterations allegedly favouring Dramat and Sibiya. As it turns out, the initial report had been crafted by one of Mdluli's people and was completely false.

I would later point out in a statement I made to police that everyone to whom I had supplied evidence regarding Moonoo's corrupt activities had either unlawfully been neutralised or corruptly paid off:

It must be now apparent to anyone looking on that a dangerous 3rd force hell-bent on protecting corrupt politicians, senior police and NPA officials is now undermining the very foundations of South Africa's democracy and has to be stopped.

THAT DAMNING JUDGEMENT

In the meantime, Sibiya's soon to be successful case against Ntlemeza for his unlawful suspension was marching ahead. The Pretoria High Court found that his suspension was unlawful and unconstitutional, but Ntlemeza ignored the court order and prevented Sibiya from returning to office pending an appeal. It was during that appeal that High Court Judge Elias Matojane said the scathing words that would ultimately lead to Ntlemeza's undoing. Justice Matojane said Ntlemeza had lied repeatedly in his bid to oppose a ruling in favour of Sibiya: :

> *In my view, the conduct of the third respondent (Ntlemeza) shows that he is biased and dishonest. To further show that the third respondent is dishonest and lacks integrity and honour, he made false statements under oath.*

The Judge made his comments after he found that Ntlemeza had swept two IPID reports that exonerated Sibiya under the rug. Ntlemeza also suggested that a key witness in the rendition case had died under suspicious circumstances, while the death certificate stated that the death was from "natural causes".

Instead of being sanctioned, Ntlemeza was unlawfully appointed as the permanent Head of the Hawks. In February 2016, Nhleko also appointed Prince Mokotedi, a self-proclaimed Zuma supporter, as the Head of the Hawks in Gauteng. He had no security clearance and had left the NPA under a cloud of dishonesty to avoid being dismissed. Instead of being viewed as liabilities, they were probably judged to be positive attributes to this new leadership of the police, where service of corrupt masters was above service to the Constitution.

There were also developments in the case McBride had launched against Nhleko for his unlawful suspension. Suspended IPID official Innocent Khuba revealed in a sworn statement that General Ntlemeza had repeatedly met with him to discuss the so-called rendition case while Ntlemeza was still based in Limpopo.

Khuba said Ntlemeza was putting pressure on him to implicate Dramat and Sibiya in the rendition. Ntlemeza had told Khuba that he wanted the report finalised so that he could take up his position as Hawk's head. This meant there was high-level interference in the top management of the police if Ntlemeza knew before the current incumbent (General Dramat) had been fired that he was to get the top job.

Khuba revealed that Ntlemeza had visited him at home to convey a message to him from disgraced and suspended General Richard Mdluli. Ntlemeza had told him he had met Mdluli at the airport and that Mdluli wanted Khuba to know that he appreciated the work he was doing and that if he saw any suspicious vehicles following him, he should let Mdluli know. Was this intended to make Khuba scared, or just intended to let him know that top cops had his back?

Khuba said he was also asked to implicate McBride in the rendition case. He said he was called by a Colonel William Mahlangu, from Mdluli's Crime Intelligence division, who promised him that "the general" would look after him. Colonel Mahlangu also wanted to provide 'evidence' that would assist the rendition case against Dramat, Sibiya and McBride. This demonstrated unlawful interference. The 'I' in IPID meant 'Independent'. How independent could IPID be if dirty cops were trying to influence the outcome of their investigations? When Khuba made his statement, he was summarily fired by McBride's acting replacement at IPID, the crooked Israel Kgamanyane.

MCBRIDE'S VICTORY

It would take McBride more than a year before he was exonerated by the Constitutional Court. In September 2016, the highest court in the land declared his suspension unlawful. The National Assembly was ordered to review the law that had given the Minister of Police the power to intervene in IPID matters.[37]

"It is declared that the decision of the Minister of Police to suspend Mr Robert McBride from his position as Executive Director of IPID is invalid and is set aside," said Justice Chris Jafta at the Constitutional Court. In the judgement, Jafta said Parliament had two years to evaluate and rectify the law that gives the Minister of Police powers to meddle in the running of IPID:

> *It is declared that the present provisions are invalid to the extent that they authorise the Minister of Police to suspend, take any disciplinary steps pursuant to suspension or remove from office the Executive Director of the Independent Police Investigative Directorate. Parliament is directed to cure the defects within 24 months from the date of this order.*

The judgement was a huge victory. It made it clear that IPID was an independent body that was free to investigate wrongdoing in the police without interference. McBride was on his way back to his desk. Kgamanyane vanished from his job and was subsequently suspended. He then applied for a senior position in the Hawks under Ntlemeza. When Ntlemeza dragged his feet appointing Kgamanyane, Nhleko

---

37 Karabo Ngoepe, McBride suspension unlawful, matter now with Parliament, News24, 6 September 2016, https://www.news24.com/SouthAfrica/News/mcbride-suspension-unlawful-matter-now-with-parliament-20160906

circumvented the process and wrote to Ntlemeza and 'instructed' him to find a job for Kgamanyane. Later, when Kgamanyane's appointment in the police was in the spotlight, he slipped out of the back door and into a management position at the Private Security Industry Regulatory Authority, or PSIRA, where the door had again been opened by Nhleko, once again proving that Nhleko is as corrupt as they come.

Johan Booysen later revealed in his book *Blood on their Hands* that two days before his suspension, Dramat had called for the Nkandla docket from detective services where Moonoo had been the investigating officer.[38] When Booysen's suspension was later overturned in the Durban High Court, Ntlemeza would be censured once again for his conduct in the Booysen's case. IPID now had another case to investigate against Ntlemeza – this time for charges of perjury.

At the State Capture Inquiry years later, Booysen described Ntlemeza's reign at the Hawks as one of terror. He said that the day Ntlemeza was appointed, "all hell broke loose" at the DPCI.

A CAST OF ROGUES: NTLEMEZA PROTECTS HIS OWN

Ntlemeza certainly wasted no time in interfering with high-profile investigations, particularly the case against Mdluli. At the State Capture Inquiry in 2019, senior Hawks investigator Colonel Kobus Roelofse revealed that Ntlemeza did not want him to investigate Mdluli for fraud and corruption.[39] Roelofse said that when he told Ntlemeza what he uncovered in the Mdluli investigation, Ntlemeza became very angry:

38 News24, Nkandla investigation ongoing – Moonoo, News24, 13 November 2014, https://www.news24.com/News24/Nkandla-investigation-ongoing-Moonoo-20141113

39 Jeanette Chabalala, 'It is our time to eat' – Ntlemeza allegedly told investigator in charge of Mdluli probe, News24, 19 September 2019, https://www.news24.com/SouthAfrica/News/it-is-our-time-to-eat-ntlemeza-allegedly-told-investigator-in-charge-of-mdluli-probe-20190919

> *That triggered the reaction where he asked me who gave us the authority and why are we investigating. He was very angry and said, "I can't trust you". He didn't really say I can't investigate. It was clear to me he didn't want me to continue with investigations.*

He said that Ntlemeza indicated it was "now our time to eat". Ntlemeza also ordered Captain De Klerk of the Hawks to hand over his docket on senior NPA officials Nomgcobo Jiba and Lawrence Mrwebi. Ntlemeza had begun what he had been hired to do – to protect his fellow criminals.

He was also deliberately ignoring major investigations that should have been a priority because of the amount of money being stolen out of state coffers. The DA's Johannesburg mayor Herman Mashaba lodged a complaint alleging that Ntlemeza had personally issued orders that cases of corruption uncovered by the City of Johannesburg, be brought directly to him.[40] One of the men that Ntlemeza had illegally suspended, Sibiya, had now found his place as the head of Mashaba's Internal Investigations Unit. Since it appeared that no investigation had taken place on any of them, Mashaba said Ntlemeza was deliberately blocking the cases:

> *I am very concerned about this. I don't run the city in my name only. I run it on behalf of the residents. I find this unacceptable.*

The then-head of the PRASA board, Popo Molefe, also complained about the lack of investigation into the PRASA case. He wrote a scathing letter to Ntlemeza about the Hawk's tardiness in investigating irregularly awarded tenders worth a total of R7-billion, which included the case I had opened against Lucky Montana for R4-billion corruption in September 2015 and a R3.5-billion tender for the acquisition of

---

40 Angelique Serrao, Exclusive: Mashaba alleges Ntlemeza is blocking Joburg corruption cases, News24, 3 March 2017, https://www.news24.com/SouthAfrica/News/exclusive-mashaba-alleges-ntlemeza-is-blocking-joburg-corruption-cases-20170403

locomotives found to be unsuitable for South Africa's rail network. Molefe wrote to Ntlemeza:

> *I am deeply concerned that South African citizens and the fiscus are prejudiced by the fact that the DPCI [Hawks] has done nothing tangible to respond effectively to these matters, despite PRASA's ongoing co-operation and assistance.*

One week later, the PRASA board was fired to be replaced by more "flexible" members.

NTLEMEZA TRIES TO TAKE ON GORDHAN

The case Ntlemeza will be probably most remembered for, however, was his unlawful pursuit of Finance Minister Pravin Gordhan. Following the disastrous decision by Zuma to oust Nhlanhla Nene as the Minister of Finance, Pravin Gordhan was viewed as a stoic hero who had managed to steer the South African economy into calmer waters. The damage that had been done to the economy was too great for the country to recover from quickly, and we have been on the brink of an all-out recession since then. Gordhan was doing his best to limit the fallout from the looting of state coffers, to reassure investors, and keep the economy chugging along.

We were close to disaster, though, and many of us knew it. The whole country was waiting with bated breath for Gordhan to deliver his 2016 budget speech. We needed to be reassured that everything was going to be okay. We needed to hear that the government had found a way to stop the wastage at state-owned enterprises like SAA, PRASA and the electricity supplier, Eskom.

It was at that exact moment of crisis that Ntlemeza decided to pursue Gordhan. In February 2016, days before the Budget speech, Ntlemeza called Gordhan to a meeting where he told him he was being investigated for his supposed role in the infamous SARS Rogue Unit case. Just like the unlawful allegations laid against Dramat,

Sibiya and Booysen, the SARS Rogue Unit case was a travesty of justice and an 'invention' of Richard Mdluli and the dishonest *Sunday Times* investigative unit. The sole intention of all these cases was to get successful public servants under a cloud so they could be pushed out of key institutions to be replaced with crooks who would loot and destroy once-proud institutions. At SARS, the High-Risk Intervention Unit, the specialised law enforcement arm of the taxman, was the target.

In pursuing the unit members, the Rogue Spy Unit's allegations had three benefits for the state capture gang. The first allowed them to turn a blind eye to their criminal accomplices, like tobacco and counterfeit goods smugglers who were allegedly lining the pockets of various politicians, including the Zuma family. The second was to allow them to bring in real rogues – in this case, Zuma's old friend and family relative, Tom Moyane, who would help them in their criminal pursuits. The third was to let them pursue their enemies who were getting in their way – in this case, Gordhan, who was obstructing plans to capture the Treasury. If the country's Treasury could be captured, then people like Dudu Myeni would be allowed full reign to do whatever they wanted. It was imperative that Treasury remain free and be well managed, or South Africa could kiss its hard-won democracy goodbye.

Ntlemeza delivered twenty-seven questions that he said Gordhan had to answer before March 2016, days before the Budget speech. These questions were then leaked to the media. Gordhan immediately called out the questions for what they were – a ploy to get him to resign as Finance Minister. Three years later, at the State Capture Commission, Gordhan recalled meeting with Zuma over the investigation and telling him that he "rejected strongly to this persecution":

I asked President Zuma whether political activists like myself must now prepare to be eliminated during the democratic era even though we have survived the oppression.

The country reacted with horror, and the rand buckled. Markets lost an estimated R50-billion, but Gordhan was left alone for a short while to deliver his budget speech. However, more was to come. In October 2016, the National Director of Public Prosecutions Shaun Abrahams indicated that Gordhan, former SARS Deputy Commissioner, Ivan Pillay, and former SARS Commissioner Oupa Magashula would be charged with fraud relating to an early retirement payout granted to Pillay in 2010 and the extension of his contract.[41] Abrahams was publicly called "Shaun The Sheep" because of his apparent capitulations to Zuma's aims. Like Ntlemeza, he appeared to only pursue the cases that suited Zuma and ignore, or worse still, conceal, those that didn't.

It looked like we were losing the fight against state capture when all of a sudden, the public came to hear of the Hawks holding a SARS legal expert called Vlok Symington hostage.[42] The Hawks unit that was investigating Gordhan, including its captured lead investigator, Brigadier Nyameka Xaba, forcibly held Symington in a board room at SARS' headquarters. They came to get a statement from Symington over a legal opinion written by Symington in 2009, addressing whether SARS was permitted to pay out former Deputy Commissioner Ivan Pillay's pension fund and then rehire Pillay on a contract basis. Symington's legal opinion was that there was no technicality that prevented SARS from reappointing Pillay. This view of Symington did not suit Ntlemeza and his accomplices. In an email chain that Moyane had sent – which erroneously found its way to Symington – was a letter

41 Jenna Etheridge, Gordhan, Ntlemeza, Moyane given representations deadline, News24, 17 October 2016, https://www.news24.com/SouthAfrica/News/gordhan-ntlemeza-moyane-given-representations-deadline-20161017

42 Staff Reporter, 'Hostage' drama explodes desperate bid by Hawks, NPA to nail Gordhan, Mail & Guardian, 27 October 2016, https://mg.co.za/article/2016-10-27-how-ethical-concerns-over-gordhan-pursuit-lead-to-a-hostage-drama-at-sars

by SARS' lawyer, David Maphakela. Maphakela was a partner in the law firm Mashiane, Moodley and Monama Inc. Maphakela indicated in an email to Moyane that he did not agree with the prosecution of Gordhan, Pillay and Magashula. This would be a damning admission in the fake case against Gordhan, Pillay and Magashula. If SARS' own lawyers did not agree that there was a case, then why were the three men being charged?

At some point during the meeting with the Hawks, the Hawks unit realised that Symington had a copy of this email exchange and held him locked in a boardroom demanding the document. Symington refused, and it was these events that ultimately collapsed the case against Gordhan. The situation revealed how desperate the Hawks were and how low they would go to pursue their own ends. Symington laid a complaint against the Hawks with IPID, but Shaun The Sheep's accomplices would later refuse to prosecute in a publicly visible continuation of the capture of the NPA.

When the revelations of Maphakela's legal opinion became public, Abrahams dropped the charges against Gordhan in an amazing volte-face. The Hawks had deliberately withheld crucial information from the state prosecutors that would have prevented the charges from going ahead in the first place. Ntlemeza was furious and wrote to Abrahams to try to force him to reinstate the charges. He accused Abrahams of acting contrary to the Constitution, stating that the Hawks had a strong case against the accused. Abrahams found himself between a rock and a hard place. His original decision to prosecute was unlawful, and he knew it would contribute to his downfall. But it was too late. Ntlemeza's aim to pursue Gordhan at all costs had been blown into the open, and there was no going back. The damage to the integrity of the Hawks and the NPA was irreparable. No one believed they would act against high-level corruption. Instead, they had become a crude, blunt tool whose only purpose appeared to be targeting those fighting state capture. I was already at the top of their list.

RAMAHLAHA CASE GETS ATTENTION

I ensured that Ramahlaha's case received media attention and that questions were asked about whether Nhleko had made Ramahlaha's defeating the ends of justice case known to Parliament when he was appointed. Ntlemeza's dishonest spokesperson, Brigadier Hangwani Mulaudzi, said the young officer's affidavit was "contentless ... cheap propaganda, blackmail".[43]

Inevitably, Ramahlaha was to become a target of Ntlemeza. He discovered he was the subject of investigation in a bizarre case of a bogus cop, Alex Maake. Maake, reportedly convicted for rape in 2010, is said to have escaped from the Pretoria Central Police Station cells and turned up at the Polokwane Police Station in 2012, where he introduced himself as Captain Alex Mailula. He said he had been seconded from the national police headquarters in Pretoria to assist in Limpopo, but it appears that no one checked his credentials. He was even lauded for his exceptional detective work. Maake was finally traced and arrested in February but again managed to escape from police custody, this time from the Polokwane cells. Ramahlaha was blamed for introducing Maake to the Limpopo police – a complete fabrication.

The *City Press* newspaper revealed in an interview with Maake in prison after he was arrested (once again) that he had allegedly interacted with Ntlemeza when he was the Deputy Police Commissioner in Limpopo.[44] Ntlemeza, he said, was his biggest fan, allowing him to handle some of the province's biggest cases. He also alleged that

---

43 Sam Sole and Sally Evans, Cloud over new Hawks boss ignored, amaBhunganem 16 October 2015, https://amabhungane.org/stories/cloud-over-new-hawks-boss-ignored/

44 Poloko Tau and Abram Mashego, Hawks boss was my biggest fan, says fake cop, City Press, 11 July 2015, https://city-press.news24.com/News/Hawks-boss-was-my-biggest-fan-says-fake-cop-20150711

he was visited in prison by senior Hawks officers who told him to implicate some senior officers. Mulaudzi told *City Press*:

> *People like Mailula and his cohorts are just trying their luck ... And to those who assisted him, they must be very afraid as their days are numbered.*

Ramahlaha was suspended after charges of fraud and defeating the ends of justice were opened against him over this case. His suspension letter was signed by Morakaladi, the same Brigadier whom Ramahlaha alleged was Ntlemeza's girlfriend, whose late husband had purportedly shot himself in the back of the head. Ramahlaha's house was searched, and a Hawks officer in charge of the case allegedly told him he would not win against the General (Ntlemeza). The officer, Lieutenant Colonel Lesiba Malapile, was then withdrawn from the investigation, allegedly after his behaviour became a liability. He had also allegedly sexually propositioned at least two female suspects linked to the investigation against Ramahlaha.

The dockets opened by Ramahlaha against Ntlemeza at IPID, with my assistance, also mysteriously disappeared during McBride's suspension.

In 2016, due to pressure kept up by Captain Ramahlaha and me, the NPA requested that the closed fraud case, opened by Ramahlaha against Ntlemeza, be reopened. This was reported by *amaBhungane*.[45] The letter from the Directorate of Public Prosecutions in North Gauteng to Polokwane's Deputy Director of Prosecution stated:

> *It appears that the decision to decline to prosecute was taken prematurely without the matter having been fully investigated. Kindly ensure that ... further investigation is completed without delay.*

This decision was made after Ramahlaha requested clarity on the status of the docket. The case, it seemed, had never moved beyond the

45 Sally Evans, Case against Hawks boss Ntlemeza resurfaces, Mail & Guardian, 29 January 2016, https://mg.co.za/article/2016-01-29-00-case-against-hawks-boss-ntlemeza-resurfaces

Polokwane Police Station where it had been closed.

Ramahlaha refused to back down, and I was supporting him all the way. In another case opened against Ramahlaha by Ntlemeza for intimidation, the trial was set to start in the Seshego Magistrate's Court when it had to be cancelled because the docket had disappeared. *The Star* reported that it had allegedly been stolen from a police vehicle parked at the Hawks' offices parking lot. This was allegedly so that Ntlemeza would not be called to testify and face a potentially incriminating cross-examination. Ramahlaha, in turn, opened another case against Ntlemeza, this time for corruption and defeating the ends of justice in Silverton, Pretoria, because of the missing docket.[46]

Ntlemeza was so angry at the media story of the missing docket that Mulaudzi issued a bizarre statement against *The Star*, saying that the paper was telling the public that Ntlemeza was hideous and corrupt.[47] Ntlemeza added:

> *I align myself with Adolf Hitler when he said if you tell a big enough lie and tell it frequently enough, it will be believed. The journalist's agenda is evident, make the lie big, keep saying it, and eventually they [sic] country will believe it.*

Ntlemeza's statement was shocking. How could any police chief openly state that he aligned himself with Adolf Hitler and then expect to win the support of the people? Ntlemeza, drunk on power, clearly felt he was beyond all reproach by this stage. He genuinely believed he was above the law, which is why I ramped things up against him and became like a terrier at his heels.

Behind the scenes, Ntlemeza must have been scared. He was facing a massive court battle to have his appointment overturned, and he

---

46 Angelique Serrao and Shain Germaner, Missing docket: cop charges Ntlemeza, IOL, 20 May 2016, https://www.iol.co.za/news/missing-docket-cop-charges-ntlemeza-2027790

47 Brigadier Hangwani Mulaudzi, The Star's malicious reports on Ntlemeza nothing new – SAPS, Politics Web, 4 May 2016, https://www.politicsweb.co.za/opinion/the-stars-malicious-reports-on-ntlemeza-nothing-ne

probably suspected that he would never succeed. He thought that abusing taxpayers funds by hiring an ethically bankrupt law firm, Hogan Lovells, would save him.

TROUBLES WITH SARS

While Ntlemeza was battling Gordhan, I discovered that he had a default judgement against him related to an income tax matter to the value of R131,055. I obtained a copy of the court file relating to the judgement. The court papers showed that Ntlemeza owed SARS money. I leaked it to the media, and mysteriously, when journalists went looking for the file, they found it was missing.[48] The Hawks' spokesman refused to answer questions about what the judgement was related to. But I had already got hold of the documents and made them public.

"You guys in the media are just trying to take him (Ntlemeza) down. Every single day there is something new in the media about the general," an irate Mulaudzi told *News24*. Mulaudzi was never short of imagination when it came to protecting his scandalised boss.

Corruption Watch Head David Lewis said it was not desirable for the Head of the Hawks to have such a tax judgment against him:

> *It is particularly disconcerting given the role the Hawks are playing in relation to the various ongoing issues around SARS, including the probe into the alleged rogue unit.*

I wondered why Ntlemeza would have such a judgement out against him. A career police officer, he would have worked through the PAYE system, which meant his employer would have automatically taken money off his salary to pay his taxes. Did Ntlemeza do work outside of his normal day job to accumulate a tax bill like this? If so, what on

48 Pieter-Louis Mybergh and Angelique Serrao, Exclusive : Hawks boss in trouble with SARS, News24, 27 September 2016, https://www.news24.com/SouthAfrica/News/exclusive-hawks-boss-in-trouble-with-sars-20160927

earth could it have been for? Assuming a 25% tax rate, then it means he had 'undisclosed income' of over R500 000. To this day, neither Ntlemeza nor his paid liar has taken the country into their confidence.

The scandals against Ntlemeza were mounting. Parliament started asking questions about his appointment. It was revealed that he was irregularly appointed by Nhleko without Parliament being properly informed, as required by the South African Police Service Act. I pointed out that his age at the time of his appointment also made his appointment unlawful as it would have taken him well over the prescribed retirement age for the police, being sixty. Everything about his appointment and the man himself was highly suspect.

THE HELEN SUZMAN FOUNDATION

It was obvious by now that Ntlemeza was a serious threat to the constitutional democracy of the country and needed to be stopped. I decided to convene meetings with the Helen Suzman Foundation (HSF). They were an organisation that had the resources and the legal know-how to have Ntlemeza's illegal appointment overturned. The meetings first started in early 2015 when I gave their lawyers copies of all my criminal complaints. Mokotedi would later falsely accuse me of planning a treasonous Arab Spring revolt, along with HSF, McBride, AfriForum, and others, because of this collaboration. Mokotedi would also falsely accuse me of espionage and working for a foreign intelligence agency, a lie that Selebi and Thabo Mbeki had peddled a decade earlier.

I certainly kept Helen Suzman Foundation busy. After Dramat, it was Sibiya. After Sibiya, it was Robert McBride. The attack on South Africa's Constitutional Democracy was fought and won in those chaotic years, not only by Forensics for Justice but with the financial muscle of the Helen Suzman Foundation and the not-for-profit organisation, Freedom Under Law, who were backed up with the best pro bono legal team in the country at Webber Wentzel, headed up by Moray Hathorn and Vlad Movshovich.

Like us, HSF considered the Ntlemeza case extremely serious. The Hawks were a key component in the administration of justice, and public confidence and integrity in the DPCI was essential. HSF and Freedom Under Law (FUL), launched proceedings against the Minister of Police and Ntlemeza in March 2016. They asked the court to review the Minister's decision to appoint Ntlemeza as the Head of the Hawks.

Just after the court case was launched, HSF's offices were robbed. The circumstances surrounding the robbery were strange, with only computers, a printer and documents being stolen. It was clearly a targeted robbery. The only reason documents would have been taken was that the motive behind the crime was to obtain crucial information.

Despite this threat, the organisations fought on and in March 2017, the Pretoria High court set aside the Minister's appointment of Ntlemeza on the grounds that Ntlemeza was unfit for the position and his appointment had, therefore, been unlawful. This was based on the judgement made by Judge Elias Matojane in the Sibiya judgement, where the Judge impugned the honesty and integrity of Ntlemeza, finding that he was "biased and dishonest" and "lacked integrity and honour" by making false statements under oath. The Minister had deliberately concealed these facts from the panel that appointed Ntlemeza despite knowing about his dishonesty.

Ntlemeza appealed the decision at the Supreme Court of Appeal, but they dismissed it. He later petitioned the Constitutional Court, but they too declined his application. All his cards had been played, and he was suddenly unemployed.

When it was finally over, HSF and FUL, while pleased with the outcome, knew that Ntlemeza had done so much damage to the Hawks, it would be hard to recover, saying: [49]

> *We realise that the General's bullying and at times near-farcical conduct was only a relatively minor phase in the broad-fronted assault on the integrity of our state institutions.*

In the meantime, a regime change had taken place in the police ministry. In one of his many cabinet reshuffles, Zuma moved Nhleko out of the police ministry, placing Fikile Mbalula there instead. This was a big mistake by the corrupt president. Fikile was a good guy, and I had known him since he was Deputy Minister a decade or so before. His Twitter tag was 'Mr Fear Fokol', meaning 'Fear Nothing'. The new Minister wasted no time getting rid of Ntlemeza, who, by this stage, was nothing but a liability. He quickly announced Ntlemeza's retirement at age sixty, making it clear he would leave the police at the level of Major General and not Lieutenant General, the rank to which he had been unlawfully appointed.

It was good to see Ntlemeza go, although retirement seemed too good a result for a man who deserved to be placed in an orange uniform. I am not ruling out coming back to sweep him into prison for what he has done to our country.

ANELE'S DEATH THREATS

I would have thought that after such public humiliation, Ntlemeza would slink off and hide, never to be heard from again. But that wasn't to be the case. One of his daughters decided to leave the public with a parting shot. Ntlemeza had made another attempt to get his job back by going to the High Court in Pretoria and attempting to interdict

49 Jeanette Chabalala, FUL and Helen Suzman Foundation 'pleased' with Ntlemeza's retirement, News24, 20 September 2017, https://www.news24.com/SouthAfrica/News/ful-and-helen-suzman-foundation-pleased-with-ntlemezas-retirement-20170920

Mbalula from removing him as Hawks' head. The application was struck from the roll.

A clearly infuriated Anele Ntlemeza, whom it turned out was also a police officer, called Ramahlaha – and then me – and threatened to kill us both. All her calls were recorded. She also insulted Mbalula during the call saying she "didn't give a fuck" about the Minister. Anele accused Ramahlaha of intimidating and harassing her sister Amanda, saying that she knew where he lived, and she would go as far as killing him.

Ramahlaha asked: "Are you willing to kill me for Ntlemeza?"

Anele responded: "You think you are clever? You psychotic motherfucker. You need a psychiatric evaluation. If I ever hear you contact or insult my sister, you are dead. I will kill you. Call her now, and it will be your last day."

In subsequent phone calls – all recorded – Anele repeated that she wanted to kill Ramahlaha that night, that she planned to attend his funeral, and that the Ntlemezas were roaming the streets of Pretoria looking for him.

I went with Ramahlaha to open a case of intimidation and conspiracy to murder against her at Pretoria Central. I then messaged her to tell her what I'd done:

> *You have alleged that you and your family are looking for him (Ramahlaha) now. We assume your family includes your father.*

I asked her to stop what she was doing.

She responded, saying, "See you in hell", adding, "you don't scare me, you terrorist. You come to South Africa to promote your criminal ways. You are messing with the wrong family. I'm not scared of you Paul."

Her messages then became increasingly crude:

> *Hahaha. Like I give a fuck. Oops maybe you need one. U look like u could use some. Let's see who goes to jail first, u or me. U think u*

> *the only one who can dish out threats u foolish kwerekwere. Now tell your client that he must harass my family again, he will never see light of day.*

She told me I would be deported from South Africa and that she hoped I was executed. Even more shockingly, she told me that I should "fuck my own daughters".

Not surprisingly, Anele was charged and convicted for *crimen injuria* and intimidation and sentenced to two year's imprisonment or a R3 000 fine suspended for five years. I felt she was just a scapegoat. The real person who should have been criminally charged was her father. I still hope that one day he will be. One day, when I have finished with other crooks, I will come back for him.

If you're reading this, Ntlemeza, I have a message for you: *Stop me if you can.*

CHAPTER 8
PHAHLANE

A NEW (CORRUPT) POLICE CHIEF ENTERS THE PICTURE

When National Police Commissioner Riah Phiyega was suspended in October 2015 following the recommendations of the Farlam Commission of Inquiry into the deaths of protesting miners in Marikana in 2012, it really didn't feel like much of a loss. She had sat on the information I sent to her on Moonoo and appeared to show no real initiative in tackling corruption within the police.

One thing I will say for Phiyega is that even though her stint in the police was an unmitigated disaster, there were others who were far worse. Specifically, the man who replaced her, Lieutenant General Johannes Khomotso Phahlane. He was worse. He was much, much worse.

Phahlane had served as the Head of the Forensic Services division of the police before being promoted to the position of Acting Commissioner. When his appointment was announced, his name rang a bell.

THE WHISTLE-BLOWER MAKES CONTACT

It was just a few months earlier when I had received an email from a senior policeman who worked in the Forensic Science Services division of the police in the Eastern Cape. His name was Colonel Sandragasen Moonsamy. He told me that he was sitting on information involving irregularities on the procurement of chemicals in the forensic science division, valued at more than R50-million. Moonsamy had become disillusioned not only with what he saw going on in the police but with the conduct of Phahlane, who appeared to be destroying morale and was acting unlawfully and wasting public funds by purchasing useless chemicals.

> *There are millions of Rands of chemicals lying all over the country that have expired due to unnecessary purchasing, and we now have to pay millions to have them removed.*

Moonsamy was an honest career policeman who decided that, rather than taking the easy way out and leaving the service, that he would do something about it. That, he said, is why he contacted me after all other routes had failed. Little did he know that this butterfly flapping its wings in the Eastern Cape would have far-reaching effects nationally, especially for Phahlane and his accomplices.

Moonsamy had reported the information he had to the Deputy National Commissioner more than a year earlier, and it appeared, just like countless other corruption allegations, that nothing was being done. He then went to the National Commissioner (Phiyega) with his complaint in August 2014, and again, nothing happened. Next, he tried the Zuma Corruption Hotline, but the complaint went to the same divisional commissioner (Phahlane) whom Moonsamy was complaining about. Months had gone by since the career policeman had laid out a complaint of corruption against Phahlane, and no investigation had taken place. He had exhausted all lines of communication in raising the complaint in terms of the Protected Disclosures Act.

In his email, he told me that he had twenty years of service in the police and had followed all routes he could take regarding his criminal complaint without success and that he was turning to me as a last resort. Moonsamy had contemplated resigning after his many years of service because of the acrimonious relationship that had now developed between him and Phahlane but decided to take one last shot at fixing things. Another dedicated police officer was being hounded out of the service because he refused to turn a blind eye to corruption.

> *I am implicating a senior officer within the SAPS at the level of Lieutenant General and I now seem to believe that I have lost my battle. If you could assist, even if it means me getting fired from the SAPS, then so be it.*
>
> *Please let me know if we can do something so that we can prevent wasteful expenditure by senior government officials who think they can get away by wasting taxpayer's money.*

I engaged further with Moonsamy, but he pulled back from giving me all the information at first because, just after contacting me, he received a response from the police to say they were investigating his complaint. He said he would try his best to follow the correct channels as a whistle-blower.

While Moonsamy never mentioned Phahlane's name, I knew that Phahlane was the Head of the Forensics' Division and that the corruption was taking place under his watch. Phahlane came to my attention again in August 2015 when I saw media reports on serious issues related to tender fraud and mismanagement in the Forensic division of the police. As Divisional Commander, Phahlane ought to have known that his division was a mess and not fit for purpose.

BAD CHEMICALS

Stories were published in the *Mail & Guardian* concerning a leaked police report that indicated that a chemical supplier, Crimetech Laboratories, had supplied chemicals of a questionable standard to the police.[50] I noted that Crimetech's directors, Jolanta Komodolowicz and John Henry Deale, strongly denied any wrongdoing in the reports, but the allegations against them were detailed and extensive. The reports stated that the local criminal record centres nationwide were overstocked with chemicals and that there was a dramatic increase in orders over the years – from R12-million in 2010-2011 to R33.8-million the following year.

In a second story, the *Mail & Guardian* reported that another company owned by Deale and Komodolowicz was being criminally charged for dumping dangerous chemicals and even feeding material meant for incineration to wild pigs.[51] The information was something I took note of, but without more information, there was nothing more I could do – yet.

When Phahlane was appointed as Acting Police Commissioner, I immediately made him aware of my evidence against Moonoo, including evidence that Moonoo was involved with Radovan Krejcir. It was around this time, as mentioned earlier, that Moonoo exposed a key state witness, Jacob Nare, in the cases against Krejcir, putting Nare in a position that he could be murdered so that all the Krejcir cases would collapse. Jacob Nare's name was an alias. He was a witness in the case where Krejcir conspired to kill me and Crime Intelligence officer Colonel Nkosana Ximba. He was also a witness in the murder case against Sam Issa, Phumlani Ncube, and a case of house robbery and attempted murder of a Hawk's Colonel in Soweto. Nare had infiltrated the syndicate surrounding Krejcir and fed the information back to his police handlers and myself.

The many incidents Nare had witnessed made me wonder if Moonoo was on Krejcir's payroll. On the day Nare was arrested, along with the

---

50 Staff Reporter, Police question forensic supplies, Mail & Guardian, 20 August 2015, http://mg.co.za/article/2015-08-20-police-question-forensic-supplies

51 Staff Reporter, Firm fed toxic waste to pigs, claims government, Mail & Guardian, 3 September 2015, http://mg.co.za/article/2015-09-03-firm-fed-toxic-waste-to-pigs-claim

rest of the syndicate (for trying to murder me), Moonoo visited Nare and took a picture of him using his cellphone. Later the leader of the sub-syndicate, Sibonisa Miya, told Nare that the 'Indian guy' at the crime scene, whom he named as Moonoo, was going to help them out as he was Krejcir's connection. Instead of being protected the way he should have been, Moonoo unlawfully cut Nare loose from witness protection in the United Kingdom. In fact, it was Phahlane who said the witness should be 'cut loose' after consultation with Moonoo.

I now knew that Phahlane was supporting Moonoo, so I decided to look deeper at Phahlane to understand his motive in protecting Moonoo. Often someone will protect a colleague's corruption because they have similar dirt in their own past that they do not want to risk being exposed. It is easier to protect so-called friends in crime than go against them. If Phahlane did go after Moonoo, he would open himself up to closer scrutiny by Moonoo.

"What I found has shocked me and will shock the nation," I wrote in a sworn statement in February 2016 when I opened a case against Phahlane for corruption, money laundering and racketeering.

DANGEROUS CHEMICALS

I then made contact with the good cop, Moonsamy and invited him to my offices. The Police had not followed through on their promise to investigate his allegations. Instead, the man Moonsamy had indicated was involved in tender fraud was promoted. Moonsamy came through and spent the day with me and my in-house legal counsel, Sarah-Jane Trent, in February 2016. Over a period of many hours, Moonsamy was interviewed, and a detailed statement was taken from him by Trent and myself. Moonsamy made it clear that Phahlane unlawfully and intentionally condoned tender rigging and fraud on the part of the same man who had been named in the *Mail & Guardian* – John Henry Deale. Moonsamy alleged Deale had grossly over-supplied chemicals to the South African Police, resulting in a loss of R50-million of public funds when the chemicals passed their use-by date.

It was clear from Moonsamy's sworn statement that lives were put at risk and crime scene investigations compromised because out-of-date chemicals were being used and the wrong equipment supplied. Moonsamy implicated Phahlane by virtue of the fact that Phahlane had allegedly victimised and intimidated anyone who raised questions around the supplier in question. Moonsamy felt he was victimised by Phahlane and those reporting to him.

Moonsamy set out, in detail, what he had discovered while he was working as the commander of the Local Criminal Records Centre (CRC) in East London. He explained that, in 2011, the same company mentioned in the media reports, Crimetech Laboratories (Pty) Ltd, was awarded the tender for the supply of chemicals, Aeroprint spray canisters, and fingerprint brushes to the CRCs countrywide. Moonsamy became aware of incidents related to the delivery, storage and use of expired chemical stock and exploding Aeroprint spray canisters due to the delivery of a sub-standard quality of product and the supply of incorrect fingerprint brushes, which destroyed crime scene evidence instead of preserving and recording it.

In March 2014, the Colonel was busy with an evaluation at the Pietermaritzburg centre when he found a large quantity of expired chemicals delivered by Crimetech to the floor of the investigation booth. He said that the chemicals had expired because a needs analysis had not been carried out, and the incorrect amount of stock had been ordered. This amounted to a criminal offence in terms of the Public Finance Management Act, bordering on corruption.

Moonsamy compiled an evaluation report with photos of the chemicals and their expiry dates. The expired chemicals, at that one police station alone, amounted to R235 000:

After further enquiry, I have reason to believe this happened throughout the country and would amount to millions of Rand wasted. King Williams Town was storing chemicals expired 20 months before.

Moonsamy also discovered that a Major General Khunou had written a letter to Crimetech in 2010 stating that the one thousand fingerprint brushes they had delivered to the Pretoria CRC did not meet specifications. Instead of supplying brushes with squirrel hair bristles, Crimetech had supplied inferior synthetic make-up brushes, which were already out in the field destroying otherwise perfect fingerprints. Khonou, in his 2010 letter, demanded that Crimetech urgently replace the brushes.

There were also complaints about the Aeroprint spray canisters. In 2011 and 2013, Moonsamy reported that there were several incidents around the country of exploding canisters. Aeroprint was a novel product developed by Crimetech but with no proper product development process. It was supposed to replace the traditional fingerprint powder and squirrel hair brush process. However, the product did not work because it would not spread the powder in the same way the brush did. In April 2012, a can exploded in Lichtenburg, and a report recommended that the use of these canisters be put on hold until their safety is guaranteed "in order to safeguard our members".

During 2012 or 2013, Phahlane visited Bishu College, and Moonsamy recalled him saying that despite the risks from the canisters, "we must use them or suffer the consequences." Phahlane then instructed his accomplices under him to go and buy special containers in which to store the useless spray cans so that when they exploded in a car, the driver or passengers would not be hurt. When union officials wanted to see the 'factory' where the product was being made – which was suspected to be a make-do-and-mend shed somewhere – Henry Deale announced that the 'factory' had burnt down and that the product was being discontinued.

A police captain approached Moonsamy in 2013, saying he believed there was a deliberate and unlawful excessive purchasing of chemicals from Crimetech. In his statement, Moonsamy said:

> *The only possible inference was that Crimetech were involved in a corrupt relationship with someone. He also said he was reprimanded by Phahlane for making statements alleging loss of stock, specifically the chemicals. It appeared to me that anyone raising issues about Crimetech supplies would be victimised by Phahlane.*

While the information Moonsamy had supplied was interesting, it was not a smoking gun. Corruption by its nature is a covert activity and is, quite often, difficult to detect – the perpetrators always attempt to cover their tracks. What I was looking for was evidence of cash payments or kickbacks in kind to Phahlane. I decided to get stuck into my own investigation.

CAUGHT OUT

I conducted further investigations and found another potential witness, Deale's ex-wife, Suzette Hartmann. She made it clear that she believed Deale was corrupt and said she had given a lengthy statement to Derek Homan at the Special Investigating Unit in 2014. She sent me the statement. It was clear that the target of their investigation was the corrupt supplier and not the corrupt divisional commissioner.

Hartmann explained in her statement that she believed Deale was not disposing of chemicals correctly, that he was dumping waste illegally, that his company had no proper tax clearance certificate, and that he had been involved in tender fraud to win contracts with the police. Hartmann also stated that she refused to meet with Phahlane because another businessman who had gone to him to complain about Deale had been sued for defamation of character. Hartmann said she witnessed Deale paying a police officer and that she had heard that he (Deale) had financed a holiday in Poland for Phahlane. Poland was the country of origin of Komodolowicz, the second owner of CrimeTech.

Hartmann also alleged that Deale was relabelling and resupplying expired products. He had also boasted that he was paid three times for the same product – their initial supply, the removal and disposal after they expired, and then the resupply of the same product. I met with Hartman and had her update and re-sign her sworn statement for inclusion in the docket I would later open. I initially thought Hartman to be a bitter, jilted ex-wife but then realised that she had once been a director of the business with Deale and could attract criminal liability in terms of the Prevention and Combatting of Corrupt Activities Act if she remained silent.

After reading Hartmann's statement, I decided to see if Phahlane's lifestyle had any red flags that could indicate corrupt activities.

THE MANSION

I have found from experience that a gratification unlawfully received is extremely difficult to hide unless it is insignificant. I decided to look at Phahlane and his wife, Beauty, who was also a senior police officer. Two career cops should lead relatively modest lives, even with Phahlane's latest promotion. However, their lifestyle was indicative of a cash-flush existence. I discovered that:

- *Neither Phahlane nor his wife had applied for credit anywhere. This is most unusual, except for high-net-worth individuals.*
- *Both Phahlane and his wife lived in the Sable Hills Waterfront Estate, an upmarket and exclusive game farm residential estate to the north of Pretoria.*

I decided to carry out an investigation into the residential property, including research into its ownership and bond registration. I looked at the property details, Google Earth history shots, and a street photo taken (by me) outside the house in February 2016.

The property was purchased by Phahlane and his wife as a vacant plot in August 2010. The purchase price was R850 000 with a bond of R595 000. With transfer costs, I estimated Phahlane and his wife would have had spare cash of R275 000 after buying the plot. A major building project commenced around April 2011 to construct a double level luxury villa of approximately 575 square metres.

The bond on the property then increased by R1 605 000. This would have provided cash of about R1 580 000 after taking bond registration fees into account. In studying my Google Earth history, I was able to ascertain that construction was completed around May 2012, but before the increased bond had been registered, the building was already up to roof height with the floor slab cast. I calculated that the value of work done by the time the increased bond was registered was in the order of R2-million – a lot of cash for a career cop and his wife, whose combined take-home pay was in the order of R45 000 a month at the time.

I am, by profession, an engineer and practised as such until about 1995. I also have property development experience and have personally managed the construction of more than 1500 houses in South Africa from 1987 through 2010. I am, therefore, fully conversant with building costs in South Africa and abroad.

Looking at Phahlane's luxury house, I made the following observations:

- The finishes were extremely high end. The property included two double hardwood door garages, air conditioning in many areas of the house, and solar heating for the swimming pool. In a nutshell, no expense had been spared on the Phahlane mansion.
- Building costs for such a mansion (back in 2011 and 2012) would be in the order of between R10 000 per square metre to

a high of R12 000 per square metre, giving a construction cost of between R5 750 000 and R6 900 000. Architects, engineers, and quantity surveyor fees would add a further approximately R550 000 to the project value.

- The total cost of the project would, therefore, have been somewhere between R6 300 000 and R7 450 000.
- Since the bond increase would have only yielded cash of R1 580 000, this meant that the Phahlane's must have had access to free cash of between R4 720 000 and R5 870 000.

Accordingly, Phahlane had to explain the source of funds of at least R4 720 000. Failure to do so would result in a corruption charge against him for a gratification of at least that amount. I asked IPID to look at the luxury cars parked in the two double garages and the luxury finishes inside the house, including fixtures and fittings that simply did not befit the paycheques of two serving police officers. I also included this request in my docket.

I subsequently discovered that the bond increased amount was only used for furnishings and the like, with no money spent on construction at all. The mansion had been built for free.

From my investigations, I suspected that Phahlane was abusing his Acting Chief of Police position to commence a process of criminalising the police. I believed that the criminalisation of the police was Phahlane's intended course of action, perhaps in the hope that, with his hand-picked people in office, he would be insulated from criminal charges himself. But South Africa simply could not afford any more corrupt heads of police or incompetent cadre appointments. I recorded that, since 1999, there has not been a single Chief of Police who has not gone out under a cloud of suspicion of criminal conduct or even (in the case of Selebi) having been convicted of corruption:

> *The criminalisation of the police would appear to me to be part of a more sinister plot by rogue elements in the State to criminalise the*

whole of the criminal justice system. By way of example, we have criminal charges being unilaterally dropped against the likes of Jiba and Mrwebi, who clearly deserved to stand trial, whilst Mrwebi and Jiba are setting others up for criminal charges as part of a purging of the system of good people.

By way of example, we had the IPID Head suspended on trumped-up charges just before he was about to have a Zuma ally arrested. We had the previous Head of the Hawks brought up on trumped-up charges. We have people like General Ntlemeza being appointed in Dramat's position, even though he was facing possible prosecution for defeating the ends of justice. Then we have a half-decade long vendetta being waged against the Head of the Hawks in KZN, apparently to silence him because he had the guts to take on Zuma's crooked friends and benefactors in Kwa-Zulu Natal.

I wrote in my statement that although I feared there would be no proper investigation into Phahlane's conduct, I was opening the docket and reserving my right to go to the International Court of Human Rights in The Hague if the State, once again, failed the people of this country:

Corruption in South Africa has almost brought this country to its knees, and I will not stand by and watch this happen any longer. I, therefore, request an urgent investigation to establish Phahlane's source of cash for his extravagant lifestyle.

I first handed the docket to IPID's then Acting Head, Israel Kgamanyane, in February 2016, but when McBride came back into his post, I redelivered it to him. I suspected that Kgamanyane had tipped Phahlane off and done nothing more with the case.

AN ATTACK ON THE WHISTLE-BLOWER

It didn't take Phahlane long to go for Moonsamy. In April 2016 he was suspended from the police.[52] He received his notice of suspension

52 Sally Evans, SAPS suspends Colonel who blew whistle on Phahlane, Mail &Guardian, 15 April 2016, https://mg.co.za/article/2016-04-15-saps-suspends-colonel-who-blew-whistle-on-phahlane

on the same day I would appear in court after my unlawful arrest, detention, and torture as part of a well-orchestrated attack on anti-corruption elements. It was clear that Phahlane and Ntlemeza were carefully coordinating their defences to my allegations.

Despite Moonsamy's case having now received media attention, Phahlane still went ahead and victimised him, refusing to clarify why. Phahlane did it by proxy. While the criminal conduct would not have his fingerprints on it, we all knew he was behind it.

Moonsamy knew it would happen. He knew the type of man he was dealing with. In his statement, he wrote: "Whilst I do expect to be victimised for opening this docket, I request that no stone be left unturned."

It was clear that Moonsamy's suspension was part of an unlawful attempt to stifle the truth from coming out about our new heads of the police. I believe it is police officers like Moonsamy, who refused to bend in the wind of corruption, that should be receiving medals for their brave work. Our country owes him a great debt.

THE EMAIL

In February of 2016, as mentioned earlier, the Hawks sent Pravin Gordhan their letter containing the twenty-seven questions they wanted him to answer regarding the SARS Rogue Unit, right before the budget speech.

The dishonest Hawks spokesman, Hangwani Mulaudzi, who had been dragged south from Limpopo by the unlawfully appointed Ntlemeza, put out a press release after Gordhan said he could not respond due to his preparations for the Budget. The Hawks responded by saying that their investigation "*would not be stalled by an individual who refuses to comply with their authorities and demand a preferential treatment*". Mulaudzi as good as insinuated that Gordhan may face arrest.

In March 2016, I sent an email to Mulaudzi. I copied Phahlane, Moonoo and several other top policemen in response, as well as then deputy president, Cyril Ramaphosa. I informed them that I intended to host a press conference in London to expose that South Africa had been taken over by a corrupt regime of Zupta-led criminals:

> *I shall be departing here on 2016-04-01. Be like the apartheid government and stop me from leaving, thereby giving a global voice to my campaign to stop the corruption that is tearing this country apart.*

In the same email, I said I had just come from a secret meeting where R20-million had been pledged to stop the Zupta crooks in their tracks. Of course, there had been no such secret meeting – it was my own cash that would be used – but I wanted them to think there was a group of us, and that taking me out would not make their problems go away. Meanwhile, I acted alone.

I did not believe they would be so audacious as to stop me from flying to London after sending them a mail like that. But I had not calculated that this mob included apartheid-era cops.

In the email, I also attached the photo I had taken of Phahlane's house and asked Mulaudzi how he thought Phahlane could afford it. I concluded my email with the following words:

> *I shall leave no stone unturned (and no cost will be spared) to put those who are criminalising the criminal justice system (to protect corrupt politicians and their lackeys) behind bars where they so rightfully belong.*
>
> *All the appointments that are criminalising the criminal justice system will be set aside.*
>
> ***Stop me if you can!***

CHAPTER 9

I BECOME THE TARGET

INCARCERATION

When I sent my email to Mulaudzi and Phahlane saying, *Stop me if you can,* I didn't think they would do just that. And not in the way they did, dragging me off that plane with my two small daughters.

After spending a hellish night inside the stinking, rat-infested cell in the Pretoria Police Station, I was let out of the cell at 11 a.m. the following morning when my attorneys arrived. I was taken into an open visiting area where we tried to take stock of the situation, which was difficult as so little information was available. I knew that I had been arrested for allegedly contravening the Citizen's Act by using my Irish passport to enter South Africa instead of my South African one. But I still had not seen my arrest warrant. I was later to find out, despite an assurance that an arrest warrant had been issued, that no such warrant existed.

During the Selebi investigations, I was forced to move my whole family out of South Africa after receiving information that people close to Selebi had been instructed to murder me. If they could not get to me, they were to murder my family. Having worked at the border police at what was then Johannesburg International Airport, I knew some senior officers there. I called one of these officers from the UK and asked if I could enter and leave the country on my Irish passport. I explained that I had reasonable grounds to believe that I might be singled out for murder if anyone knew I was in South Africa. He consented, and I distinctly recall him telling me that nobody took any notice of the relevant Section 26B and that it would be safer for me to come and go with a foreign passport whenever I felt at risk. It seemed logical that it would be absurd to enforce a rule that could put people's lives at risk, given the number of dirty police officials at the airports. If the police were *not* corrupt, I would have no need to use my Irish passport.

I used my Irish passport to enter South Africa in December 2015 because I had received credible intelligence that Radovan Krejcir knew I was overseas and that I had been in the Czech Republic, where I opened a case against his mother for aiding and abetting the murder of two Czech citizens on Krejcir's Czech hit-list.

I also knew that he had many police officials on his payroll to tell him when I was back in South Africa so that he could arrange to kill me, most likely while travelling from the airport, unarmed. Krejcir had attempted to murder me several times by that stage and was now extremely upset that I had foiled his prison escape plans by tipping off the authorities. Hence, when arriving back in South Africa on the 15th of December, 2015, I entered the country on my Irish passport. I knew that since I came in on my Irish passport, I would also have to leave on it the next time I travelled. If I left the country on my South African passport, there would be an anomaly in the Movement Control System managed by the Department of Home Affairs. Consequently, the next time I left the Republic, which was on the 13th of February 2016, I left using the same Irish passport.

At around 3 p.m. on the 2nd of April 2016, I was interviewed by a Lieutenant Ngogodlo from the Hawks, and a warning statement was taken. I answered every question put to me. Curiously, I was not asked any questions pertaining to my entering or leaving the Republic on my Irish passport, which was ostensibly the reason for my arrest. When the interview concluded, I again asked to see the warrant of arrest. My request was declined. When I asked why I could not see it, I was told there was no arrest warrant. This added to my concerns that my arrest was unlawful. I complained bitterly to my attorney about the rat-infested conditions of the prison cells with the raw sewage, the blocked toilets, and no running water. I complained to the police officers at the station and to some journalists who came to the cells to visit me.

At around 7 p.m. or so, I was taken from the Pretoria Central Police Station to Villieria Police Station in Pretoria. I only knew where I was going when we got there, after spending another twenty minutes in a high-speed, blue-light convoy.

MOKOTEDI

I saw Major General Prince Mokotedi in the basement of Pretoria Central when I was being moved on Saturday night, and it was clear that he was in charge of things. I found this somewhat poetic since I had opened the NPA docket against him in 2012 and called his appointment to the police into question only a few days earlier. He had been appointed by the then Minister of Police, Nathi Nhleko, after eighteen months of unemployment after resigning from the NPA on the back of them launching an investigation against him. Mokotedi did not go through any proper vetting process, nor did he obtain the required security clearance.

As we pulled out of the station's basement in the high-speed blue-light convoy, I also saw Lieutenant General Ntlemeza. He was standing on the street talking to an unknown person, and Ntlemeza watched as we drove past. It was clear that he was one of the puppet masters pulling the strings on what was happening to me.

When we arrived at Villieria, I was taken out of the car and inside the station. It was here that Mokotedi first approached me. He started by asking where I had studied engineering, and I told him I did not have to answer that question.

"Paul," he said, "you are not an engineer. We know that you were never an engineer, and we will charge you for lying under oath by saying you were an engineer."

I told him he could go ahead.

I had stated that I was an engineer in the docket I opened against Phahlane. Later on, I would attach annexures to a statement I made about my unlawful arrest, proving that I worked as an engineer twenty years ago and that I was also a member of the relevant institutions. Mokotedi was grasping at straws and scraping the proverbial barrel in a desperate attempt to nail me as punishment for opening dockets against him and other senior police officials. Not only was he arrogant, but also very stupid. He constantly showed me the cards he was holding. If he were a poker player, he would have been bankrupted.

"You must get used to prison," Mokotedi continued. "You will be the rest of your life in prison. We will be charging you with offences relating to treason, terrorism, fraud, forgery and many others."

I started laughing. I had never heard such rubbish. I certainly never expected to witness Police-State activities in the new order South Africa, let alone be subjected to them myself. Although I was laughing, deep down inside, I started to think that maybe these criminals in uniform could succeed in their evil plans against me.

While I was up against a wall, my hands cuffed tightly behind my back, Mokotedi poked me in the chest.

"Paul," he said, "you don't know how you've upset Dudu Myeni."

Mokotedi told me that they would also be charging me with intercepting people's phones. He said they had a sworn statement from Sam Sole, a reporter from the *AmaBhungane Centre for Investigative Journalism,* where I allegedly told Sole that I was authorised to intercept phones. I told Mokotedi the statement was rubbish. Had I not had handcuffs on, I am sure I would have broken his crooked nose.

Being in my line of business, where we investigate fraud and serious organised crime, I have made a few enemies along the way. Radovan Krejcir and Dudu Myeni are just two examples of the type of people on the receiving end of justice who came across my path. It is, therefore, not entirely impossible that corrupt police could persuade people to give false evidence against me. While the evidence would not stand the test in court, it would be enough to open further false charges against me to further punish or vilify me in public. This was in their plans.

"Listen," said Mokotedi, "if you cooperate with us, and tell us how you got the intercepts done, then we'll let you go on police bail."

The intercepts he was referring to were those I had of Moonoo speaking to a known criminal involved in drug trafficking and money laundering. This furthered my belief that Moonoo was also one of those behind my arrest. I agreed to give him the information he was looking for if he would give instructions to release me.

"Okay," he said. "We'll come here tomorrow. You have your attorney here, and we'll cut a deal." Mokotedi then left.

When my attorney Darryl Furman arrived an hour or two later, I put a call through to Sam Sole, who told me that he had never given any such statement implicating me and had never been asked to do so. I knew then that Mokotedi was bluffing. I then told my attorney to call Mokotedi and arrange to meet again the following day. I decided I would play games with him.

I spent the next two nights in the cells at Villieria Police Station. Although there were no rats, the place was extremely noisy thanks to all the drunkards who were in there with me. One of the people in my cell was mentally unstable and kept shouting to people in another cell. I spent another night without sleep. At 6 a.m. the following morning, another drunk was brought in, who promptly vomited all over the floor. The smell was putrid.

THE TORTURE CONTINUES

At about eleven on Sunday morning, Mokotedi returned with four other police officials, who began interrogating me. However, the interrogation had nothing to do with my Irish passport, which was the alleged reason for my arrest. Mokotedi began pressurising me and told me, yet again, that I would be charged with treason. He said he wanted to know who all my contacts were and who was funding me. I told him the claims were not true. I had never been involved in treasonous activities, and I had no funders.

He said I would be charged in terms of the Terrorism Act. When I queried this, he insisted I had knowledge of terrorists from al-Qaeda in South Africa and that I had committed an offence by not reporting it to the police. I assured him that I had reported it to the police and that I had, in fact, reported the matter to the Commissioner of Police (the now-disgraced Phiyega) and later to the Acting Commissioner of Police, Phahlane. I told him that when I reported it to Phahlane, I had copied in the deputy president, Cyril Ramaphosa, and still had the emails to prove it.

Mokotedi told me that I would be charged in terms of Act 70 (RICA) because I had carried out unlawful telephone interceptions. I pointed out that I had not carried out any interceptions and that the claims were deliberately false. I had received the interceptions in question from others who were concerned about the criminal influence in the police and the fact that police management appeared to be turning a blind eye to the mounting levels of corruption.

I had raised concerns with Mokotedi the previous evening that the police were wasting their time trying to establish how I came into possession of the interceptions when they should have been more concerned by the fact that a Lieutenant General in the police (Moonoo) was engaged in secret meetings with persons involved in drug trafficking and money laundering for terrorists.

All the cases Mokotedi alleged I would be charged with stemmed from my investigation into Moonoo. I had clearly hit a nerve in my pursuit of justice against him.

Mokotedi went on to bring up the SAA matter and said I would be charged with fraud and forgery. I explained that the case had no legs either since I had done nothing wrong, that they were grasping at straws, and that the person who belonged in court and on trial was Dudu Myeni herself.

Mokotedi then agreed that, on the understanding that I gave a detailed explanation pertaining to the Act 70 interceptions, I would be immediately released on police bail and allowed to leave with my attorneys. On the counter side, he made it clear that if I did not cooperate and answer the questions, I would be kept in custody ad infinitum. By now, I had been without food and sleep and unable to relieve myself for forty hours. I could not eat because I was afraid that the food given to me was poisoned. The toilets stank so much that I was reluctant to use them. I was exhausted and under tremendous emotional strain. I was told that I should talk or face further detention.

I later rationalised that this amounted to the offence of torture by Mokotedi and his accomplices. My legal team pointed out to me that while I was being questioned on things ranging from terrorism to treason to illegal interceptions, I had, in fact, been arrested on relatively minor passport offences. It clearly demonstrated the true motive behind my arrest – to extort or torture information out of me. I was arrested on a plane as the doors were closing, assaulted in front of my two young girls, and then dragged away and rushed to Pretoria at extreme reckless speed in a blue-light convoy. My phones were illegally downloaded, I was detained in conditions best described as putrid and inhumane and then snatched at short notice, with no knowledge of where I was being taken. I was certain that my murder was imminent, especially after being rushed off to another police station in another white-knuckle ride of terror and again detained without sleep.

"Cooperate and answer our questions, and we'll let you go," Mokotedi said. "Refuse to cooperate, and you'll be staying here."

The conduct of Mokotedi and his four officials met three of the four conditions for the description of torture, as set out in the Prevention and Combatting of Torture of Persons Act, which describes torture as:

> *Any act by which severe pain or suffering, whether physical or mental, is intentionally inflicted upon a person*
>
> *(a) for such purposes as to –*
>
> *(i) Obtain information or a confession from him or her or any other person;*
> *(ii) Punish him or her for an act he or she or any other person has committed, is suspected of having committed or is planning to commit; or*
> *(iii) Intimidate or coerce him or her or any other person to do, or to refrain from doing, anything;*
> *or*
>
> *(b) For any reason based on discrimination of any kind, when such pain or suffering is inflicted by or at the instigation of, or with the consent or acquiescence of a public official or other person acting in an official capacity.*

I pretended to succumb to the torture and, because of the jam I was in, provided false information that I otherwise would not have given out. Not only did I give out false information, but I even embellished it since it was clear they wanted to hear something special if they were to release me.

What else could they have expected after subjecting me to such torture? Like the fools they were, they lapped it up.

THE INTERROGATION

Present at my interrogation was Mokotedi, a Captain Mpuku from the Hawks, my attorney Darryl Furman and Sarah-Jane Trent. The Police did not know this, but my legal team recorded the entire conversation. We did not know it then, but these recordings would save me from further time in jail.

Mokotedi began the interrogation by promising me bail, reminding me that I would be able to spend some time with my daughters before they flew back to London. I was worried about Anna and Mary. I could only imagine how distraught they were after witnessing my assault and arrest.

"You have some of the stuff you must give to us," Mokotedi urged.

He kept asking me for information on how I got the telephone intercepts that revealed that Moonoo had been in contact with criminals. I told him that any information he wanted was in my office. He replied that his hands were tied and that I would have to appear in court the following day.

Furman, aware that I had been arrested on a minor misdemeanour and could easily have been given police bail, interjected:

> *This matter can be rolled over. He doesn't have to appear. You speak to the DPP (Director of Public Prosecutions), and he can remove it from the roll, or it can be set down until Friday.*

But Mokotedi insisted I had to appear in court the next day. I agreed, but on one condition:

> *I will appear tomorrow. Let me go home and see my children, take them to the airport tonight, and then I will be at court tomorrow. I will explain the intercepts to you and then hand you a memory stick with the information.*
>
> *If I have to spend another night in jail, it is going to kill me. General, I want to go home, put on my suit, and appear in court nicely.*

Mokotedi ignored my pleas and said we could go to my house to collect the information he wanted. I reminded him that yesterday he had told me that he would let me go if I gave him information.

What follows is a transcript of the conversation:

> **MOKOTEDI**: *We can take the case off the roll, but then we continue to work together. Put it in writing tomorrow, but today you give us everything.*
>
> **FURMAN**: *Are you saying you will take the case off the roll, but he is still in detention?*
>
> **O'SULLIVAN**: *Why can't I go home today? If I'm going to give you all this, I want to go home today. When you get it, you will be shocked. But I'm not going to spend another night here. Then I will rather go to court tomorrow, get bail, then sit with you and work. Because where is the benefit for me?*
>
> **FURMAN (TO MOKOTEDI):** *He could have got bail. He should have got bail on Friday night. This is not a Schedule 5 offence or a Schedule 7. This is a basic statutory misdemeanour.*

Mokotedi replied that he would be willing to give me bail on that same day. I would have to appear in court the following morning, and the Hawks would not oppose bail. After that, I would have to give them a sworn statement on how I got the Moonoo intercepts.

We agreed, and I began telling them how I began my investigation of Moonoo while investigating the corrupt Tracker contract. I explained that I implicated General Phiyega and General Moonoo in the docket I opened. I further explained that, while this investigation was underway, Krejcir had escalated his plans to murder me and that I met Crime Intelligence officers who were working with me to thwart his plans. I told Mokotedi that some of these officers, who were fed up with corruption in the police, gave me information on Moonoo, which included allowing me to listen to telephone intercepts of conversations between Moonoo and Preggy Padayachee. They wanted to see if I could identify the voices and the people they were talking about. I explained to Mokotedi that they were not intercepts done on Moonoo – they were done on Preggy Padayachee's phones. The officers then told me that Padayachee was under investigation for allegedly doing money laundering for al-Qaeda and receiving payments from Krejcir as Moonoo's middleman. I was then handed a criminal network drawing that showed the links between different people and that one of the names listed on that drawing was linked to al-Qaeda.

"So that's it," I said. "It's short and simple, but it's shocking." "It's Moonoo you want, not me."

Mokotedi said the problem was that I had distributed the tapes and that, in terms of Act 70, one is prohibited from alerting the suspect.

"You confirmed what was our theory around this thing," said Mokotedi, "and we will not retract from our deal with you."

He then asked if I had sent any of this information to the United States, as I had said I would do in my emails to the authorities. I replied as follows:

> *No, I never gave it to anybody. That was to put pressure ... What I wanted is for Phiyega to think that if she didn't act soon, there will be trouble from overseas, but I never gave it to anybody. I wanted her to take action against Moonoo.'*

I added that I said that to tease Moonoo because he kept claiming that I was a spy.

"You see, they took that very seriously, Mr O'Sullivan," said Mokotedi. "They took it very seriously."

Of course, none of this was true. I had indeed shared the information with both the UK and US secret services. I have family living in both countries and regularly visit both. Since the South African authorities were involved in assisting terrorists, it was my duty to tip them off about what was going on in South Africa.

"I've told you everything," I said.

"You've told us everything we need to know for now," Mokotedi replied.

He asked again if I had worked with Foreign Intelligence Organisations, and I reiterated that I had not. A year later, he was to put the same allegations to me in writing, this time with a threat of a charge of espionage.

LIES AND AN ABUSE OF PROCESS

After Mokotedi had the information he thought he wanted, he announced that the prosecutor, Advocate Sello Maema (coincidentally – or maybe not coincidentally – the same prosecutor who worked on the trumped-up IPID case in respect of Anwar Dramat, Shadrack Sibiya, Robert McBride, Mathews Sesoko, and Innocent Khuba) had declared that I would not be granted police bail.

I believe it was Mokotedi himself who persuaded the prosecutor to deny bail and that he and his cronies were playing games to extract more information out of me. There was also the possibility that no such discussion had ever taken place and that it was Mokotedi's way of exacting revenge on me for opening a docket against him four years earlier.

In terms of the Criminal Procedures Act, the purpose of arrest is solely to secure the attendance of the accused person in court. My arrest and detention in inhumane conditions, with sleep deprivation and hours and hours of interrogation and threats of life in prison, followed by promises to release me, was clearly nothing more than a gross abuse of power that amounted to torture. Dragging me away after assaulting me in front of my crying children was entirely unwarranted for such a simple statutory matter. My arrest was completely unnecessary because no warrant had been obtained. We would later discover that, in terms of the Citizenship act, no person had ever been arrested or even prosecuted for a similar statutory matter. In arresting and charging me, they had made history.

My detention following my arrest was, therefore, also unlawful. The downloading of information from my phones was also unlawful. My interrogation, after sixty hours of no sleep after being detained in horrific conditions that could only be described as torture. Extorting me by saying that I would be released after I had spoken – and then reneging on the undertaking and keeping me in the cells – showed a shocking disregard for the law and my rights as a human being.

After my release, I opened a docket against Mokotedi and his cohorts for this torture, which carries a life sentence. After more than five years, nothing has come of that docket, and I plan to one day mount a private prosecution against them all.

COURT

I spent another night in jail believing that on Monday morning, the 4th of April 2016, I would be released on bail and have my passports returned to me. I arrived at court at approximately 7 a.m., having been without sleep since 4 a.m. on the Friday morning preceding my arrest, having risen early to complete my work before flying to London.

Despite arriving at the Kempton Park court early so that my case might be dealt with first, I was kept in holding cells below the court until approximately 10 a.m., when Furman came to see me. He told me he was going to discuss my bail conditions with the Hawks and the prosecutor. A large media contingent had gathered outside the courtroom, waiting around in the corridors, looking for any tidbits of information they could find to get a story. The Hawks and the prosecutors knew they were being watched, and the tension in the air was palpable.

The media had already started reporting that my arrest was a form of revenge for my investigations against Moonoo, Ntlemeza and Phahlane. IOL published part of my '*Stop me if you can*' email that I blind copied to trusted journalists.[53] The DA's MPL in Gauteng, Kate Lorimer, had issued statements indicating that she believed my arrest was based on trumped-up charges. Public sentiment, it seemed, was not on the side of the Hawks.

Present in the bail meeting, which took place behind closed doors, were control prosecutor Wollie Wolmarans, prosecutor Sello Maema, General Mokotedi, Captain Mpuku, as well as my legal representatives, Darryl Furman, Mannie Witz and Sarah-Jane Trent. Again, the conversation was recorded without their knowledge.

Maema indicated that they were looking at whether I had committed more offences. Witz asked if they would make me appear in court under the one offence, release me on bail, and later add the charges Maema was talking about. The prosecutor replied with a firm, "No", and said he did not want to handle the case piecemeal. He said he had been promised he would have all the charges laid out against me by Thursday.

---

53 Angelique Serrao, Paul O'Sullivan: Stop me if you can, Zuptas, IOL, 4 April 2016, https://www.iol.co.za/news/paul-osullivan-stop-me-if-you-can-zuptas-2004579

Witz asked what that meant. What would happen to me in the meantime?

The prosecutor's answer indicated that the state had no intention of releasing me on bail that morning. He said they were legally allowed to incarcerate me for seven more days, but they would only hold me for four more days to make my arrest "as less invasive as possible". He reiterated that there were potentially other serious cases against me, and these charges would be laid against me.

Maema indicated that he wanted me to appear in court, postpone the case until Thursday, and only do the bail application then.

Witz was confused by their approach:

> *If it is just the passport stuff, I mean, you guys might as well go to the airport now and go and arrest every third or fourth passenger that is getting on every single overseas plane.*

His sentiments, I was told, were being echoed in the corridors of the court as journalists and members of the public waited for my case to appear. There were discussions about how many times they, too, had left the country on their dual passports without even realising they were committing an offence. Nobody could understand what this case was about and why I had been arrested.

Maema response to Witz was:

> *But if you do it with the knowledge that SAPS is looking for you, and you say, if they are looking for me, let them...*

Again, Witz argued on my behalf. I had no charges against me when I left the country, and I, like every South African, have the right to freedom of speech. None of this was illegal, and the State was blatantly disregarding my human rights:

> *He is not a guy who runs away from SAPS. He is always fighting with them. I mean, he is the first guy to come in the open.*

Witz went on to point out that I had been taken off a plane, and I was only leaving the country to take my daughters back to school. He had my return ticket with him. Maema was having none of it:

> *We have an email that says the corruption that is in South Africa. He has a – what does he have? He has a news briefing on Thursday...*

Maema had just given away that the email I had sent was the real reason behind my arrest. He continued:

> *In the light of those utterances, we need to see what is actually happening, whether there are any acts of preparations, whether he sold his house, whether – because he says 'I'm prepared to fight this thing from outside, from Zimbabwe, from Tanzania, from London...*

THE RENEGED DEAL

Furman asked the prosecutor if this meant I must wait until Thursday to be granted bail because my legal team intended to apply for bail that day. He mentioned that we had made a deal with General Mokotedi the day before that the state would not oppose bail:

> *The investigating team were reneging on the undertaking yesterday ... General, we had an agreement yesterday ... and I've recorded it as well, by the way.*

Mokotedi replied that he had not made a deal but rather an undertaking.

"My client exposed certain information to you based on your undertaking. That is the bottom line," Furman insisted.

Furman asked to speak to Mokotedi separately, but Maema told him that Mokotedi was his witness and that Furman was not allowed to speak to him. Furman was astonished:

> *I can't talk to your witness? He is the Head of the Hawks in Gauteng!*

Maema said he did not know what the arrangement was, but he did not see the point in releasing me, only to rearrest me. For convenience, it would be better to put all the cases together.

"This is the only charge that is before the court today," Furman pointed out.

Witz suggested they grant me bail on the day and that they keep my passports. Furman pointed out that there had been a deal with the General that I would cooperate and give them a written statement. He added that if the State did not grant me bail, he would go to the High Court:

> *You can't arrest a man off the plane on one single charge of section 26B and then come here and tell me 'no' he must wait because there's other matters.*

Maema tried again to bring up the seriousness of the 'other' charges they planned to charge me with, including terrorism and treason. But Furman wouldn't have any of it. Again, he pointed out that the charge I had been arrested on was minor and asked what law would stop them from giving me bail on charges that had not yet even been laid. Again, he asked General Mokotedi about the agreement we had the day before.

THE BROKEN AGREEMENT

"What was the use of having an agreement with you yesterday?" Furman asked.

He pointed out that aside from this case, there were four other cases the General said were being investigated, among them treason, terrorism, the SAA case, and the Act 70 interceptions and monitoring case. He pointed out that Mokotedi promised me police bail if I made a full disclosure, which is what I did.

Witz interjected and reminded everyone that the press was outside, and they didn't need everything to come out into the open. He said it was better that the case be enrolled, that I be given bail and, if any other charges were laid, that I appear in court for those separately:

> *That's the most practical way that I can see it. You don't want to land up – the General is going to go in the witness box, Darryl is going to go in the witness box ... And then you start talking about these other things. It's just going to cause an absolute nightmare for everyone, from the State and from the Defence and for the whole country.*
>
> *... I mean, I saw it on overseas news already, it's gone all over the world, it's gone viral... You don't want all this coming out in the open, all this Press and everybody sitting. It's a public document. Leave it at this for the moment, let them feed on it, let them think it's an Immigration thing which it is allegedly on paper and on the 212s, and we then deal with the other stuff if and when it develops. That would be the most practical way.*

It was after Witz pointed this out that an agreement was made to give me bail – but under the strictest of conditions.

It was clear that Mokotedi had not only reneged on the agreement to release me immediately after the interrogation that took place on Sunday the 3rd of April 2016 but also on the subsequent deal that he would release me first thing in the morning and give me back my passports. Mokotedi 'made a deal with me' with the full knowledge that he had no intention of releasing me at all. He did this to try to extract information from me, extraneous to the reason I had been arrested, which amounted to the offence of torture.

We realised that it was only because we disclosed that the conversation from the previous day had been recorded and that the press was outside (and would hear in court what had happened) that the State realised they would be exposed and embarrassed, that they agreed not to oppose bail, albeit on pathetically and unlawfully stringent conditions.

No doubt, were it not for the recording, the flagrant disregard for integrity would have continued unabated.

DOG-TIRED

Physically exhausted and psychologically drained, I realised that I either had to accept the stringent bail conditions for the time being or be detained for a further four days, which, in my current state, was not something I relished. I realised that I was, for now, at the mercy of the State and the Hawks and that their abuse of power had left me with very few options. My legal representatives protested that the conditions were ludicrous, but, desperate to be released, I indicated that they accept the conditions.

When I eventually did walk into the courtroom, it was packed. The back-benches were filled with Hawks' officers, while the press occupied the rest of the seats. My appearance was brief. It was agreed that I could be released on R20 000 bail and that I had to leave my passports with the State so that I could not leave the country. The court further stated that I could not even leave the province of Gauteng. I also had to report to the Sandton Police Station twice a day. These were the sorts of conditions applied to high-profile murder accused, not someone who entered the country with an Irish passport. They also said I should not speak to the media, to which I agreed, on condition they would not do so either. They breached the agreement later that day when Ntlemeza's crooked sidekick Mulaudzi said I was a hardened criminal, so I continued to speak to the media.

I walked out of the court and into the sun only to find journalists waiting for me, desperate for a statement. At that point, I was too drained to say anything. Later, when I looked at the pictures taken of me, I looked shrunken and grey, as if years of my life had been taken from me in just a few short days. Little did I know that this was just the beginning of a continuous campaign that would go on for a further thirty months.

Most of the stories that appeared in the media revealed that I had been arrested following my investigations into the police. The journalists quickly realised that what had happened appeared to be an abuse of police process. But the Hawks were fighting back. Public statements were made, alleging that the Hawks had far bigger cases lined up against me, insinuating that I was a hardened criminal, and they would soon reveal to the world how 'crooked' I really was. While the campaign against me had stepped up a gear, I was ready to take them on and would leave no stone unturned in doing so.

GOODBYE MULAUDZI

In an interview held on eNCA after my release with Hawks' spokesman Hangwani Mulaudzi, the interviewer asked him if it were true that my immigration case was the first of its kind ever to be prosecuted in South Africa.[54] Mulaudzi responded as follows:

> *Well, I don't have the statistics. Unfortunately, I cannot answer you on that one, but we, we view this matter in a very serious light, taking into consideration the fact that if you are a naturalised citizen of a country, you are not allowed to have more than two or three passports. You can have as many as you'd want to as such, but some citizenship – I'm sorry, I'm, I'm mixing myself here. You are not allowed to have actually three passports for that, he would use from other countries. So hence this arrest was effected on Friday.*

He was not only talking gibberish – he was talking complete nonsense. South African citizens *can* have passports from other countries. The new but little known Section 26B of the Citizen's Act prohibits an individual from using a foreign passport to leave or enter the country if they are a South African citizen.

54 eNCA, Paul O'Sullivan released on bail, Youtube, 4 April 2016, https://www.youtube.com/watch?v=h5DPDXlQi9A

The eNCA anchor asked Malaudzi if I was being treated differently to others who use multiple passports. Mulaudzi replied as follows:

> *Well, I don't know... Mr O'Sullivan is a ... is a high-profile person in this country, and as such – hence we received this information from Home Affairs. We have to come in because it falls within our mandate.*

He was lying through his teeth. He knew it, and I knew it. And he knew that I knew he was lying.

He was then asked if they were investigating a charge of treason against me:

> *I don't know where this "treason" thing is coming from, but there is an investigating team that is busy probing this matter. I don't remember anybody talking about anything about treason, so I think let's just leave it to the investigators themselves. They will be able to know exactly what kind of charges, if there are any, that needs to be added.*

Next, he was asked if I had been arrested over the email, I had sent to him, Moonoo and Phahlane:

> *They're not talking about the emails that we, we get – personally that I get that involves my family as well. So, there is a lot of things that people don't know what has been happening behind the scenes. With some of those emails ... we take them very seriously because it also talks to us in the sense that there is a 'war' that is going to be raised in this country. So such kind of things we, we take them as, as very serious in the sense that we have to protect the ... the, you know, the citizens of this county – the sovereign of this county, because we don't know what kind of 'war' was going to be ... won.*

The only 'war' I had spoken about was the war against corruption. Was the dishonest spokesman trying to imply I had threatened an actual war? While I was astonished to hear this, I knew that Mulaudzi, as Ntlemeza's paid liar, did not have an honest bone in his body. It seemed the Hawks would do and say anything to make me into a criminal.

If they could state lies like this publicly, I had no idea how far they would take this. Just what were the Hawks under Ntlemeza and Mokotedi capable of? I would later find out that they would fabricate a whole host of false charges against me to try to tie me up in knots.

Mulaudzi was now on my radar, and over the next few years, I made him aware that I would not give up and that he would pay for being a part of the state capture machine. I continuously monitored his every move and sent scathing e-mails every time I caught him lying to the media. He knew that if I go the chance, he would be tickets.

I got my chance when, in 2020, I discovered that Mulaudzi had been moonlighting in Limpopo and was the corrupt beneficiary of lottery monies, which he failed to disclose to his new boss, Lieutenant General Lebeya, who promptly fired him. Goodbye Mulaudzi!

However, back in April 2016, I wondered what would happen next after my release. I would soon find out.

I later registered a criminal case against Mulaudzi, after I discovered he was money-laundering the proceeds of his fraud and theft from the Lottery. He had stolen hundreds of thousands of rands to improve his lifestyle. To launder the money, he repeatedly bought and sold double-cab four-wheel-drive vehicles at a loss each time. I hope he will soon find his place in life. In an orange uniform of course!

CHAPTER 10
UNDER ATTACK

MORE CHARGES COME MY WAY

It took the Hawks just three days to launch a volley of further false charges against me. I had barely had a chance to catch my breath after my unlawful arrest on the trumped-up immigration case and my appearance in court when the criminals with their badges and gowns fired their next salvo.

That Thursday, I received a summons and charge sheet on the SAA case. That same day, Moonoo opened a false espionage docket against me. That Friday, the 8th of April, 2016, warning statements (where suspects or accused persons are invited to give their version of events in writing after being warned of the offence they are suspected of having committed and of their right to remain silent) were taken from me on a completely different false case related to a woman called Alice Johnston. I had investigated Johnston two years earlier after she admitted to attempting to have her boss murdered to avoid being charged with fraud which she had committed.

All these charges were overwhelming. There was no question that I was under attack. In a matter of a week, I had been hauled off a plane; I'd spent a weekend behind bars in inhumane conditions, appeared in court and charged on an immigration case, received a summons to appear in court on the SAA matter, had an espionage docket opened against me, and had warning statements taken from me on the Alice Johnston case.

A barrage of false allegations was being launched against me, all at once, and I knew this was just the beginning.

There were three false charges relating to the SAA matter. Firstly, I was charged with extortion for allegedly 'intentionally inducing or subjecting to pressure or inspiring fear in the mind of Ms Duduzile Cynthia Myeni'. The charges falsely claimed that I stated that if Myeni did not:

- resign as a Chairperson of South African Airways (SAA);
- cease the disciplinary hearing instituted by SAA against Accused 2 (Kalawe); and
- reinstate Accused 2 as Chief Executive Officer (CEO) of SAA.

– that I would subject her to further scrutiny and distribute proof to the public that she had money held in foreign bank accounts.

The second false charge was that of intimidation. It was alleged that I had tried to induce Myeni to continue with Monwabisi Kalawe's employment as chairperson of the South African Airways by threatening to damage her 'good name' by publishing false information about her reputation and finances.

The third false charge was one of fraud. They alleged I had given out and pretended to Myeni that I had obtained bank accounts from Bank Austria and BNP Parabis, which was then used to induce Myeni to resign from her employment as Chairperson of the South African Airways Board.

It was clear the Hawks' strategy was to bombard me with false cases, hoping that I would either be defeated or resign myself to having to flee the country. I knew that I could not give in to their acts of intimidation. I had to keep my spirits up and continue the fight. While it was hard not to panic, now was not the time to give in to despair.

I had to take each fake case as it came at me and deal with each one individually. Like the idiots these corrupt cops were, all they achieved was awakening the Irish fighter in me and making me very angry. I had dared them to '*Stop me if you can*', and they were trying their best. However, I knew that justice would eventually prevail – and then I would go on the attack again.

PREPARING FOR WAR

After my release that Monday, I started preparing for war. A major intelligence operation was kicked into action. I pulled out all the documents I had access to, set up a server in a foreign land (away from prying eyes), encrypted it – and its contents – and started a detailed analysis of the enemy. When I say detailed, I mean *detailed*. I wanted to know everything about every single one of them. I also started a process to build a war chest worth millions of rands. I would need to sell my assets, both in South Africa and overseas, and my pension fund would have to be used up and rebuilt later.

Major General Prince Mokotedi was clearly intent on breaking me – but he was also incapable of keeping his mouth shut. Between him and his henchmen, they had pretty much let all the cats out of the bag in terms of what they planned to do to me. That Tuesday, I sat down with my attorneys and went over everything that had happened during my arrest. We also went over all the false allegations Mokotedi said he was investigating me for. I laid all of them out and refuted them one by one in a formal criminal complaint that I would open against all of my accusers:

> *These allegations are completely false and are intended only as smokescreens for the intimidation and 'punishment' being meted out against me because I took a stand against corruption within the police. However, it is incumbent on me to take any reader into my confidence, insofar as I am able to, in explaining these absurd allegations.*

When it came to the allegation of treason, I had asked Mokotedi what it was that I was alleged to have done, and he could not answer me with any specific details. He said I was the head of a 'syndicate' that was attempting to overthrow the government. It was an allegation he would later repeat – under oath – in December that year when he alleged that this 'syndicate' also aimed to murder him, Ntlemeza and Phahlane. His intellect was clearly inversely proportional to his imagination. He also made mention of my announcement that I would be calling a press conference in London to expose corruption in South Africa.

Advocate Sello Maema repeated this in the Kempton Park court, where he said:

> *What we need to do is, in the light of those utterances, we need to see what is actually happening, whether there are any acts of preparations, whether he sold his house, whether – because he says, 'I'm "prepared" to "fight" this thing from outside, from Zimbabwe, from Tanzania, from London'.*

Advocate Maema later said:

> *No, what he is doing, we have an email from him that says he is leaving on the Thursday – this Thursday he is calling a press briefing in London where he is going to tell whatever about the "corruption" in the country. ... but I think what concerns us is the fact that he is prepared to fight the corruption in the country outside the country. He is prepared to fight it from London. He is prepared to fight it from Zimbabwe.*

During the fake immigration trial, these fools would even admit that it was my email that led to my arrest. Other than my mentioning that I was planning to hold a press conference in the *Stop me if you can* email, I had absolutely no inkling as to what the 'treason' allegation was about. I confirmed to the State that I was not engaged in any activity to 'overthrow the government':

> *It is my humble opinion that, if anyone is committing treasonable offences, then it is the organised criminals that have permeated the organs of state, in particular the police and the NPA, and then use that penetration to capture the criminal justice system and use it to torture, extort and intimidate people like me, for no other purpose than to prevent my attempts at decriminalising the criminal justice system.*

As mentioned earlier, Mokotedi had also accused me of breaching the Terrorism Act, saying it was a serious offence to know about terrorists being in South Africa and not reporting it to the authorities. I pointed out to Mokotedi that I had indeed reported the presence of al-Qaeda suspects in the country and that these suspects were linked (via drug traffickers and money launderers) to Lieutenant General Moonoo.

I also pointed out that when it came to my attention that al-Qaeda suspects were in the country, I had reported the matter to the police. I had sent emails to General Phiyega and the Deputy President of the country. The fact that no action was taken against Moonoo had nothing to do with any lack of reporting him on my part and everything to do with the fact that he was being protected by fellow criminals within the police.

SAA CHARGES

The State was clearly doing everything to try to nail me on some sort of charge, whether I had committed the offence or not. The charges showed that I was just being lumped with a list of accusations with no real evidence that I had committed any of them.

The State claimed that the information about the bank accounts was furnished to me by Kalawe (the past CEO of SAA) and Abednego Mbulawa (the Chief Operating Officer of the Mogale City Council) when, in fact, they were supplied to me by a well-known journalist. The person who *manufactured* the false bank statements was Mbulawa, whom I had nothing to do with – although I had opened a docket against him a year earlier while opening a docket against Jacob Zuma's "friend", Dudu Myeni. Yet there I was, being charged with extortion along with Mbulawa as well as Kalawe. To make matters even more laughable, I was accused number one in the case, making it clear that I was the real target and not Mbulawa or Kalawe. These dirty cops were not very smart, and I was preparing to tear them apart.

It was absurd. If I had intended to defraud Myeni, why would I have sent the emails with the bank statements to the police and then, that same day, informed them that after a preliminary investigation, I had found them to be fake? I knew that once I provided my evidence, no judge could possibly find me guilty of any of the fake charges. The corrupt cops and prosecutors also knew that, but they were only interested in setting me up on as many fake charges as possible to break my bank and spirit. The cases would cost me a significant amount of money to defend and would tie up my time. The Police probably hoped that if I was busy defending myself from all these trumped-up charges, I would not have the time to pursue my corruption investigations against them.

They were wrong. I had the resources and was ready to take them on by increasing my investigations against them to prove that I could not be taken down by corrupt cops and prosecutors.

ALICE JOHNSTON

Getting back to Alice Johnston, she was an accused person facing charges for theft and attempted murder from a case I had worked on two years earlier. Imagine my surprise when I was asked to give a warning statement on allegations of crimen injuria, fraud, and intimidation against her, knowing she was facing her own criminal charges based on the work I had done. The Hawks were trying to insinuate that when I interviewed Johnston, I had intimidated and threatened her into making a confession, saying that I would make sure she received a suspended sentence if she confessed to hiring someone to kill her ex-boss.

Johnston was the former employee of a Joburg businessman, James Murray. He was best known for claiming to have been tricked into funding mining magnate Brett Kebble's murder.[55,56] Murray had money stolen from him, and he knew it was Johnston because some of the payments for livestock sales had been made to her personal bank account. After opening a case against Johnston, Murray was ambushed and shot multiple times. It was a miracle he had survived. Bullets hit him in the arm, ruptured his colon, and passed between his spine and spleen. The hitman, assuming he would not survive the ordeal, told Murray before shooting him: "This is a message from Mac". Mac was Alice Johnston's then-boyfriend.

Police arrested Johnston for the attempted murder. She thereafter contacted me to investigate the matter, saying that she had been set up by Murray and dirty cops. Since Murray had been on my radar several years earlier when I was investigating Selebi and those around Brett Kebble, I decided to take a look on a pro bono basis.

When I interviewed Johnston at our offices, I was somewhat taken aback by her body language. I was concerned that she might have been involved in both the alleged fraud and the attempted hit on her ex-boss. I, therefore, said I would only be able to help her if she agreed to undergo a polygraph test to confirm she was not involved in hiring a hitman. She failed the polygraph terribly, and it was clear that she was involved in the attempt to kill Murray. I called Murray and met with him. He came to my office on crutches and explained, in detail,

55 Shain Germaner, O'Sullivan to appear in 3 cases in September, IOL, 9 September 2016, https://www.iol.co.za/news/osullivan-to-appear-in-3-cases-in-september-2066231

56 Amanda Watson, Kebble's ghost haunts Paul O' Sullivan court case, The Citizen, 9 August 2016, https://citizen.co.za/news/south-africa/1257416/kebbles-ghost-haunts-paul-osullivan-court-case/

how Johnston had stolen money from him and then how she had tried to have him killed.

I called Johnston again and said she should visit me to discuss the results of her polygraph. I made it clear to her that I believed she was involved in hiring people to kill her ex-boss in an attempt to wriggle out of the criminal charges she was facing for fraud and theft. I told her that she would have a better chance of doing a deal with the State if she came clean and named the shooters. She admitted that she had expressed a wish to her boyfriend, 'Mac', that Murray should be killed. She also admitted to stealing from Murray. However, she would not name the shooters, so I told her I could not help her unless she was prepared to come clean. I then contacted Murray and handed him the video recordings of her admissions and a copy of the polygraph.

Two years later, after being contacted by Warrant Officer Vlok, of Moonoo's office, Johnston falsely claimed that I had represented to her that I was working for her and that in an interview I had with her subsequent to the polygraph exam, I had belittled and threatened her and had told her that if she confessed to the shooting, she would get a suspended sentence.

Her allegations were nonsense, and I had recordings of the interview to prove it. The Hawks were on another wild goose chase. I decided to keep my recording of the interview to myself so that they could not shape their false charges accordingly. Johnston was later convicted of fraud and theft and sentenced to seven years in prison. However, in their rush to nail me, the State had completely botched the attempted murder case, and she got off on those charges scot-free. To this day, she has never gone on trial for the plot to kill Murray. Murray subsequently succumbed to his severe injuries, and the chance of her facing justice is nil.

MEETING WITH DIRTY COPS

On the 18th of April, 2016, together with my attorney, I went to meet with Mokotedi at his offices on the third floor of the Old Stock Exchange Building in Diagonal Street, Johannesburg. The meeting, which was set for 11 a.m., was preceded by a letter sent to Mokotedi by my attorney three days earlier.

Upon arrival at Mokotedi's offices, we were ushered in. Mokotedi asked us to wait outside while he spoke to 'his team' of about ten Hawks members. After being kept waiting for thirty minutes, we were ushered in again, only to see Mokotedi slipping away down the corridor. It was clear he now wanted to place distance between himself and the matter. The only conclusion I could come to was that my attorney's letter had placed him in a predicament, as it well should have done.

We were introduced to a Colonel Malima, and it quickly became apparent that Malima didn't have a clue to what had been going on. He fumbled through a meeting that lasted an hour and a half, where no agreement was possible. The meeting was a farce and came to a halt so that Malima could speak with 'the team' outside. When he returned, he said the meeting was over and that we could go, but we would be contacted again for an interview. While tapping a small docket in front of him, he added, "and a warning statement in respect of this other matter".

I asked him what this other matter was, and he replied: "Spinach". I was puzzled. What did he mean? What was my involvement with *Spinach*? Was this a code name for something? When I asked what he meant, he became tongue-tied and turned to one of his accomplices.

"How do you say this offence?"

The accomplice looked at his notes and pronounced the word slowly.

"Es-pion-age."

Not only did these clowns not know what they were doing, but they could not even read the alleged offence. I decided, there and then, that I would play with these criminals like a cat plays with a mouse. It was game on.

Before leaving, I noticed the docket on the table. On it was written *Pretoria Central CAS 380/4/2016*. I noticed that the space for the complainant had *V Moonoo* written on it. It was clear that Moonoo had not given up on his conspiracy against me despite having left the police on early retirement a couple of weeks earlier.

The following day, Colonel Malima called my attorney and said that 'the team' wanted to meet with me at Gallo Manor Police Station at 3 p.m. Darryl Furman and Sarah-Jane Trent accompanied me. The farcical meeting lasted about an hour and forty-five minutes, where Moonoo's false allegations were put to me.

These included:

- *A charge of corruption. Moonoo claimed I had bribed a police official to buy secret state information. No details were given about how much was paid, to whom, or for what purpose.*
- *A charge of defeating the ends of justice. Moonoo alleged that I alerted him that he was under investigation. No details of this alleged offence were provided either.*
- *Contravention of the Protection of Information Act. Again, no details of this alleged offence were given.*
- *Contravention of RICA through the interception of telephone calls. Again, no details were given.*
- *Finally, a charge of espionage. Espionage is generally described as an act of spying, where a government uses spies to discover the military and political secrets of other nations. It can also be used to describe the use of spies by a corporation to acquire the plans or technical knowledge of a competitor – otherwise known as industrial espionage. I should mention at this stage that the*

> *offence of 'espionage' does not exist in the statutes in South Africa and that the State, therefore, has to rely on an archaic apartheid leftover known as the Protection of Information Act.*

Again, it was clear that 'the team' was grasping (desperately) at straws, hoping that I would implicate myself in some or other offence.

They had a preprepared list of questions that were put to me in turn to give the appearance that they knew what they were doing. Many of the questions appeared to focus on my sources of information while insinuating that I was being paid and was paying others to gather State information. They asked questions like:

- *Are you employed?*
- *Is there any information tape relating to monitoring and interception of telephones of individuals?*
- *Is there any information that you might share with other countries on the prejudice of South Africa?*
- *Is there any information you share with any individual organisations or institution in the Republic of South Africa?*
- *Do you have an intelligence company?*

The whole exercise was clearly a fishing expedition, with the police hoping that, if they cast the net wide enough, I would give them something to haul me in on. The whole thing had a terrible stink of desperation surrounding it.

The cat and mouse game was now well underway, and I was having fun. To each question, I told them that I would provide a written response. In this manner, I managed to trick them into laying out their whole case – or lack of a case – in front of me. I had to fight back the laughter and keep a poker face when I realised how stupid these cops were. To compare them with the Keystone Cops would have been an insult to Mack Sennett. If this was the best that Phahlane, Ntlemeza and Mokotedi could muster against me, then this would be a walkover. It also dawned on me that if this was the best elite crime-fighters South Africa could muster, then the country was in even deeper trouble.

I drafted a detailed letter for Darryl to submit to the NPA and Mokotedi, setting out my responses to these patently false allegations.

THE LETTER

In the letter I sent via my attorneys before the meeting with Mokotedi and Malima, I set out that the maximum sentence for contravention of Section 26B of the South African Citizen's Act was a fine or imprisonment not exceeding twelve months, that no other person had ever been arrested for the offence, and that what the Hawks had put me through was a form of torture. Although I had drafted the body of the letter, I had it settled by Barry Roux SC, one of the top (and honest) legal brains in the country. What Barry Roux finalised was a masterpiece and will ultimately be one of the reasons why the State would have to settle my civil claim. He wrote:

> *The law is clear that a discretion whether or not to arrest must be rational in relation to the power of arrest and not arbitrarily, or in bad faith, or with an ulterior purpose.*
>
> *The Constitution imposes a duty on the state and all of its organs not to perform any act that infringes the entrenched rights, such as the rights to human dignity and freedom and security of a person.*
>
> *Our case law also makes it clear that an arrest, being the most drastic method to secure a person's attendance at his trial, ought to be confined to serious cases, i.e. that it should be confined to cases where such person faces a relatively serious charge. The arrest of our client was not rational but an abuse of process designed for an ulterior purpose.*

We pointed out that the large contingent of officers from the Hawks who had arrested me was inconsistent with due process and that my arrest had turned into a showpiece. The arrest took place to stop me from making public disclosures on corruption in the police and to attempt to obtain information from me after torture, relating to matters extraneous to the alleged immigration offence:

> *It is significant that the Hawks were acutely aware of an email by our client on the Thursday prior to his attempted departure to London, which was sent to them and to other authorities, informing them that our client would depart from OR Tambo to London to make certain public disclosures abroad pertaining to systemic corruption in South Africa.*

We highlighted the trickery used to obtain information from me – by promising me bail and then going back on the deal.

> *Our client has become aware that a further stratagem was contemplated to arrest our client on further purported charges.*
>
> *We therefore call on you to desist from abusing the process and authority. Should you genuinely believe that there is any merit in further charges, our client offers his full cooperation to meet with the official in charge of such matters in order to secure his attendance at Court in a civilised and non-abusive manner.*

After receiving the letter, Mokotedi must have realised that his actions during my arrest could only be perceived as an abuse of process and that he would have to answer for what he did. He subsequently tried to befriend me, and I walked him into that trap, but only to gather further useful evidence against him.

RESPONDING TO MOONOO'S FALSE ALLEGATIONS

On the 25th of April, my legal team sent another letter to the NPA referring to the meeting held with Colonel Malima, Captain Mkupa, Captain Mangqalazi and Lieutenant Ngogodlo at Gallo Manor Police Station on the 19th of April where the false allegations by Moonoo were put to me. It went as follows:

> *Our client vehemently denies these absurdly false allegations, which are clearly intended by Moonoo, as a red-herring in respect of the serious charges, which Moonoo himself should be facing.*
>
> *The false allegations, coupled with the unlawful arrest of our client, as well as his detention and torture, are the continuation of a stratagem intended to punish and exact revenge on our client for no other reason than our client has attempted to expose and bring a halt to systemic corruption with the South African Police Service, the National Prosecuting Authority and certain state-owned enterprises ... If the State believes it has a case, then it is invited to issue a J175 (Summons), and we will then proceed to court where the matter can be properly and publicly ventilated. Whilst our client has a right to remain silent, he has absolutely nothing to hide.*

It was ridiculous that Moonoo, the man I had been investigating and whom I had a stack of evidence against, was being protected by the police's top management. Instead of pursuing an investigation against him, they were using my evidence to turn the investigation around and lay charges against me.

We indicated in the letter that I had opened a plethora of serious criminal cases against Moonoo, other senior police officials, the NPA, and certain directors of state-owned enterprises:

> *It is recorded that, to date, no proper investigations have been carried out by the State, and the only visible response, is the unlawful and vicious attack against our client.*
>
> *What has transpired since 1 April 2016 clearly amounts to nothing more than a well-orchestrated campaign of unlawful arrest, detention, torture, interrogation, defamation and vilification of our client, with its only intended purpose being to punish and exact revenge on our client for exposing the aforementioned corruption.*

It was clear to me that the criminal justice system had been completely taken over by a criminal network that had penetrated and 'captured' the management of Police, DPCI, NPA, Crime Intelligence, and the State Security Agencies, as well as SARS. South Africa would soon be on its knees if we did not fight back – and hard.

THE PCLU

The Hawks and NPA were in all-out attack mode. The State was doing everything possible to 'eliminate' me, just as they were doing to Shadrack Sibiya and Johan Booysen, the members of the SARS Enforcement Unit in the false 'Rogue unit' saga. And just like them, I had been assigned to the NPA's Priority Crimes Litigation Unit (PCLU) for prosecution purposes.

The PCLU was a special unit within the prosecuting authority meant to deal with high-ranking crimes – particularly those involving the Rome Statute – such as acts of terrorism and overseas acts of aggression. One of its early achievements had been the prosecution of Mark Thatcher, Margaret Thatcher's son, who paid a whopping fine after admitting guilt in sending dogs of war to the Seychelles. The plot was foiled when they were all arrested in Harare when their plane landed to refuel.

Normally this unit would be focussed on high-profile criminals, like Krejcir, who needed extra effort and special prosecuting abilities, with top-notch prosecutors who could deal with threats and expensive defence teams. With the Hawks, it was a prosecutorial-led investigative team. Instead, as I would later prove, the unit was being used as a blunt instrument against anyone the corrupt state-capture gang wanted to get rid of.

On the 12th of April 2016, twelve days after my arrest, NPA Head Shaun Abrahams belatedly sent an internal memorandum to Advocate Nomgcobo Jiba, which was later provided to me during a discovery process. Abrahams said the PCLU should deal with all the offences and the management of all investigations and prosecutions related to me. It stated that:

> *Over and above all the matters I have referred to the PCLU in my previous memorandum dated 18 November 2015, I also refer all matters related to Paul Robert O'Sullivan to this unit, which investigations and prosecutions must be managed and directed by the Acting Special Director of Public Prosecutions and Head, Priority Crimes Litigation Unit (PCLU).*

I had become a high-priority criminal in the eyes of the State, which I found to be further evidence of unlawful conduct. The PCLU admitted in court papers that they had been involved in trying to nail me since March 2016, well before "Shaun The Sheep" had issued his 'instruction' of 12 April 2016.

CITY PRESS

Three days after Abrahams made the order that the PCLU deal with all my cases, an article appeared in *City Press* saying that the Hawks would be piling up more charges against me.[57] The article, written by Abram Mashego, stated that they had learnt from the Hawks that twelve cases were being investigated against me, over and above the (fake) ones of intimidation, forgery, extortion, and contravention of the Migration Act. It went on to say:

> *O'Sullivan is hated within the law enforcement agencies. He has been a thorn in the side of many senior police officers and has laid criminal charges against high-profile political individuals, including President Jacob Zuma, Thabo Mbeki, Riah Phiyega, Head of Detectives Vinesh Moonoo, among others.*
>
> *He has sent "intimidating" emails to several people, including Acting Police Commissioner Johannes Phahlane and SAA chair Dudu Myeni.*

57 Abram Mashego, Hawks pile up charges against Paul O'Sullivan, City Press, 14 May 2016, https://city-press.news24.com/News/hawks-pile-up-charges-against-paul-osullivan-20160514

It also stated that I was facing espionage charges along with a Crime Intelligence officer "who allegedly helped him illegally intercept telephone calls" and that I gave sensitive information about a police service general and senior government officials to foreign intelligence agencies. The story quoted an anonymous Hawks official as saying:

> *The intelligence officer concerned is already facing a departmental inquiry after it emerged that she shared sensitive information with O'Sullivan. She is also facing criminal charges and has been suspended.*

Another senior Hawks member was quoted as saying:

> *Information collected by the Crime Intelligence officer was then sold to those who would use it to blackmail, intimidate or extort money from the people involved.*

It claimed several high-profile people were blackmailed using this information, which they said was gathered illegally. When I read the story, I immediately suspected that the source of the story was Mokotedi or one of his accomplices. It smacked of the threats I had received from him.

The Hawk's attack against me, it seemed, would not just be staged in court. They were taking their fight public and doing everything possible to tarnish my reputation by making it sound as if I was the worst type of organised criminal.

CORA VAN DER MERWE

Not long after this story appeared, I, together with an ex employee of mine, Melissa Naidu, received a summons to appear in the Randburg Magistrates Court. We were being falsely charged with extortion, intimidation and kidnapping related to a case I had investigated for Road Accident Fund law firm, Ronald Bobroff & Partners Inc.

Bobroff had called me to his office in September 2014 to investigate a case of theft. We were told an employee was stealing information from the firm, and we were tasked with finding out who it was. The employee was identified as Cornelia (Cora) van der Merwe. She admitted she had leaked information to *Moneyweb* journalist Tony Beamish, which Beamish then used to write a series of articles on Bobroff that showed he was allegedly over-charging victims of vehicle accidents. Bobroff and his son Darren eventually fled to Australia and were disbarred from practising law in the country.[58]

Van der Merwe, in the scandal that later ensued, dishonestly claimed to be a whistle-blower. I knew this was not true. Even the court told her that passing private documents to a journalist to write about and share with competitors cannot be described as a 'protected disclosure'.

When Bobroff asked for my help in 2014, none of the fraud allegations against him had yet emerged. As far as we were concerned, this was a cut and dry case of theft by his employee, Cora van der Merwe.

I interviewed van der Merwe in the boardroom at Bobroff's offices. While initially denying that she had passed client files to a journalist, an hour into the interview, she admitted that she had, in fact, sent a whole load of files to Anthony Beamish. I pointed out to her that some of the files she sent were of a private and confidential nature and that this amounted to theft of proprietary information. She agreed that what she had done was wrong and agreed to make a sworn statement detailing which files she had unlawfully given to Beamish.

I had a doctor's appointment later that day that necessitated me drinking a foul-tasting aniseed liquid by 1 p.m., so I asked if she would mind coming back to our offices to finalise the statement. She agreed. On the way back to our offices, she communicated to Beamish and an attorney by the name of Anthony Millar that she had admitted to me that she had stolen files and given them to Beamish. It was clear

---

58 James de Villiers, NPA cracks down on Bobroff's million stashed in Israel, News24m 11 August 2017, https://www.news24.com/SouthAfrica/News/npa-cracks-down-on-bobroffs-millions-stashed-in-israel-20170811

to us that Beamish had passed the stolen files on to Anthony Millar, which included a brief by Bobroff to senior counsel on actions Bobroff was taking against Anthony Millar for allegedly touting clients, an unsavoury practice that could lead to him being disbarred, if found guilty.

Soon after arriving at our offices, van der Merwe's phone rang, and she stepped outside to take the call. When she came back inside, she made it clear that she no longer wanted to cooperate with the investigation. I instructed Melissa Naidu to take her back to Ronald Bobroff & Partners' offices, whereafter she was suspended and subsequently resigned, during her disciplinary enquiry.

Now, two years later (and out of the blue), I was being falsely charged for allegedly kidnapping, intimidating and extorting Van der Merwe. She was falsely alleging I had taken her against her will, threatened her with jail time and told her she wouldn't see her children again. She claimed that on the drive to my office, she was desperately messaging her lawyer to help her. She said we had induced her into confessing to having committed theft by threatening to have her criminally charged.

It was all a lot of nonsense. I had taped the meeting and still had the recordings, so I knew the case would be thrown out of court eventually. I was infuriated that they included Naidu in the charges. She had merely accompanied me to the interviews. She was merely collateral damage to the State, which would do anything to try to have me charged and convicted.

FALSE CLAIMS

My attorneys wrote another letter to the State, this time to the PCLU's fake advocate – "Advocate" Jabulani Mlotshwa – who had been appointed to all the fake cases against me. He would soon become a permanent fixture in my life – at least for the next few years, anyway.

This letter was one of the last times I would refer to him as an "Advocate". I soon found out that he was nothing of the sort and had been masquerading as one and even dressing as one by wearing an advocate's gown and signing documents as Counsel for the State. He and his wife had previously been disbarred as attorneys for dishonesty, which made him perfect material for his current job, which entailed lying to courts.

In the letter, I addressed the latest trumped-up charges against me emanating from Johnston and van der Merwe. The two women knew each other, having been introduced by Beamish and Vlok. They had collaborated to run a story about me on *Carte Blanche,* a television programme that, in my opinion, had of late started acquiring a reputation for not letting the truth stand in the way of a good story. I was shocked that they had an individual like Beamish, whose ethics I questioned, on their payroll.

Both Cora van der Merwe and Alice Johnston had brought their false claims within days of my arrest and were clearly part of the campaign by the State to stop me from exposing systemic corruption.

I had discovered that the then-Head of the Detective Services in Gauteng, Major General Norman Taioe, had already refused to waste police time on the patently false claims since he could see through the lies of the conspirators, as well as the fact that the claims were two years old. This did not meet with the approval of the unlawfully appointed Major General Mokotedi and his accomplices, so the docket was then referred to Mlotshwa after Mokotedi instructed a Captain Mokovhi from the Hawks to obtain warning statements from me, despite no investigation having been done at all. Mokovhi would later admit to this in court. In addition, I had covertly taped Mokovhi admitting that Mokotedi forced him to obtain the warning statements and that he was against what was going on. He had complained to his Colonel that he was being forced to do things the wrong way round, and his Colonel told him, "Just do what the General tells you to do."

In our letter to the State, we referred to the van der Merwe case, stating that she had clearly demonstrated that she was a liar after admitting to stealing from her employer and concocting patently false allegations against me with no evidence whatsoever. I believed that she had ulterior motives in cooperating with Major General Mokotedi.

Ironically, Beamish would later receive an award for his work in exposing the Bobroffs, who were engaged in a bitter turf war with Anthony Millar, Discovery Health, and Discovery's lawyer, George van Niekerk. The same George van Niekerk who had helped Dudu Myeni open a false case against me.

Meanwhile, Johnston was currently on trial for the theft of large sums of cash from Murray. Of Johnston I instructed my lawyer to say:

> *The false case that the complainant opened in conspiracy with van der Merwe, which is being propagated by Major General Mokotedi, is her last grasp at straws, and our client is most surprised that the Hawks and NPA would give such a window of opportunity to a patently dangerous woman, merely to put a stop to our client exposing corruption within the NPA, police and state-owned enterprises.*

The conduct of the two women amounted to defeating the ends of justice, and perjury, as far as I was concerned. I demanded that the State investigate the matter with at least the same vigour that they were using against me:

> *Our client is fast reaching a point where he will be forced to launch a massive claim for damages against the police, the NPA and against the government in respect of the malicious campaign against our client, which includes unlawful arrest, torture, extortion, unlawful detention, malicious prosecutions and general campaigns of vilification and defamation. If our client is forced to follow that route, he will include the individuals concerned and request an order that they be held personally responsible, for any award, in their private capacities, as there is an audit trail to show their liability.*

But first, I had to deal with all the trumped-up charges they had laid against me, with more still to come... They thought they had me on my knees, but I knew different.

CHAPTER 11

THE FIGHT BACK BEGINS

APPLICATION TO AMEND BAIL CONDITIONS

The ridiculous bail conditions meant that I had to go to the Sandton Police Station twice a day to sign a register, either to make sure I had not absconded or to set me up to be murdered. The police station visits were always stressful. I would first carry out counter-surveillance to ensure no hitmen were lying around waiting for me. I had received credible intelligence that I would be assassinated at one of these twice daily signings. I was a sitting target. The process normally took me between thirty and forty minutes to complete and was nothing new to me. I had been well trained for such eventualities in my youth when I was employed by the British government.

When reporting to the station, I had to walk in, state that I was reporting as per my bail conditions, and be handed a register to sign. I had to fill in the form in a loose-leaf lever arch file, indicating my name, ID number, date and time. To keep my presence inside the station to a bare minimum, I persuaded the guys behind the counter to use a pro-forma with all the details completed. I would walk in, grab the file, sign it, and leave as quickly as possible, greatly reducing the risk of an ambush. I would also vary the time each morning and evening, using a roll of the dice to choose. Each number of the dice was assigned a time slot, making my visiting times completely random. I also made sure to carry a round in the breach of my firearm as well as a spare magazine so that I could defend myself if things went that way.

A few days after being released on bail, following the illegal airport arrest, Colonel Hoosen told me, while at the police station doing one of my twice-daily signings, that since I was facing serious criminal charges, I was required to hand in my firearm. As he said this, he reached towards my shirt at the beltline, where he could see the bulge on my hip. I despised the man and told him with an angry snarl that he would have to kill me before I would hand it over – unless he had a court order. I stepped back, pushed his hand down, and placed my hand on my firearm. He was shocked. I could see that he was afraid.

With my level of training, I knew that if I had my firearm and ammunition on me, whoever took me on would come off second best. I also knew that if my weapon was taken from me, sooner or later, and with no means to defend myself, I would be assassinated.

I carried out a rapid threat assessment and determined that if these crooks were authorised to seize my firearm, I would be gone like the proverbial wind. I examined ways of leaving the country so that my life would not be in danger if Hoosen obtained that court order. I worked out possible escape routes and had a friend fly in from overseas to test the routes of escape. There were a few cross-border options – one at the border with Swaziland, one at the border with Mozambique, and the other at the Botswana border. Another method, which was my preferred choice, was simply taking my aeroplane and flying out of the country on my own steam. I practised loading the plane up with fuel and loaded containers on the seats that could then be used to replenish the tanks in the bush along the way when I made out-of-sight landings. My plane already had long-range tanks and, with the extra fuel, I could make it all the way up to Kenya, where I already had an office and contacts. From there, I could easily get on a plane using my other Irish passport. While I would be considered a fugitive from justice on the trumped-up cases against me, at least I would be alive.

As it turned out, the escape route was unnecessary. Needless to say, no court order to take my gun was ever obtained. Hoosen was just trying his luck, like the crooked gutless dirty cop he was. I was even more determined now to go head to head with these villains and beat them every step of the way.

I had agreed to the bail conditions set down in April merely to escape the abject conditions of my incarceration but, by mid-2016, it was beyond time to have them overturned – by way of a gradual nibbling process.

I applied to the Kempton Park court to have them amended, my reason for the application being that, to the best of my knowledge, no person has ever been charged in court for a contravention of Section 26B of the Citizen's Act. The fake advocate, Mlotshwa, vigorously opposed my application, costing me several hundred thousand rands in wasted lawyers' fees.

An immigration expert, Gary Eisenberg of Eisenberg & Associates, had come forward publicly to state that no one that he knew of had ever been charged for this so-called 'crime':

> *The problem at hand is not charging O'Sullivan with contravening the Citizen's Act but rather the selective enforcement of the law by the South African authorities. To prosecute a South African citizen and release him on R20 000 bail for violating this law is unheard of and ludicrous. This may be the first case in the country's history.*

Eisenberg pointed out that most South Africans entering and leaving the country on incorrect passports do so with impunity. Generally, Home Affairs gives South Africans a verbal warning – if that. Matthys Johannes Thom, the chief control immigration officer employed by the Department of Home Affairs between 1978 and 2012, agreed. He had approximately twenty-eight years' service at the airport. He stated that since the implication of the Act ten years earlier, nobody had ever been arrested or prosecuted under it.

I also had good reason for using my Irish passports, and that was to conceal some of my travel movements to avoid death threats made by Radovan Krejcir, with the crooked cops on his payroll., I requested that a subpoena be issued for Major General Mokotedi to allow me the opportunity, in court, to demonstrate that my arrest was not only an abuse of the process of court but that it was done with an ulterior motive. I still could not understand why, in terms of the law, a Colonel in Durban would be involved in an arrest for alleged contraventions in Kempton Park – unless, of course, he was pursuing an ulterior agenda.

Interestingly, during the trial on the false immigration charges, my Senior Counsel, Advocate Barry Roux, extracted an astonishing admission from Hoosen that he and Moonoo met regularly at the Sibaya Casino near Durban. Curiously, this is the same casino where Moonoo was tape-recorded meeting with a known money launderer.

ROUX EXPOSES HOOSEN'S ULTERIOR MOTIVES

In late June 2016, during the fake immigration charges trial, Roux proceeded to wipe the floor with Hoosen and expose the true reason for my unlawful arrest a few weeks earlier.

Hoosen's testimony, from the transcribed trial recordings, went as follows:

HOOSEN *I had made an application for an arrest warrant for the accused. The application was based on the information that I received as well as the emails that was sent by the accused to various individuals. The email was sent to the deputy president, various politicians, various media houses, the commissioner of police, the Acting Commissioner of police, now General*

Phahlane, various other generals, including General Moonoo in there, as well as ENS forensics [attorneys for Dudu Myeni in her personal capacity as well as SAA], Advocate Paul who alerted me about this email, that the accused was basically informing everyone that he is going into hiding and one of the words that he used, that he will be going into exile similar to the previous comrades that went into exile, or previous people that went into exile. He has also said there various other things that he is going to London, but that was not the reason. The way he was basically saying in the email that he sent the email to the police bosses and everyone else, ***CATCH ME IF YOU CAN****, I am going into exile, and I will use unorthodox methods to find you men.*

HOOSEN *That was the trigger for me to bring about an application for an arrest warrant.*

Barry Roux climbed into Hoosen:

ROUX *Yes, so it means you want him to be arrested because he is going into exile.*

HOOSEN *That is correct*

ROUX *He is upset about the corruption in South Africa and the corrupt policemen.*

HOOSEN *That is correct.*

ROUX *Yes, and he carries on with it, and he said, and he talks about Zupta and the corruption, and it must be stop, and we must fight corruption, nothing wrong with that you will agree? That is what the police stand ...[indistinct].*

HOOSEN *To fight corruption, there is nothing wrong, yes.*

ROUX *The police, you also stand for that?*

HOOSEN *That is correct.*

ROUX *So there is nothing wrong there that you really want to ...*

HOOSEN *Your Worship, I just would like to point out there further on that it is a similarities to the previous emails that he had sent to the complainant [Dudu Myeni] in the SAA matter. Very similar, he sent emails to others that I am currently investigating, that attorneys [ENS Attorneys] had sent him a response to those emails.*

ROUX: *Thank you. So this is a letter that he is really upset about corruption and corrupt policemen and he said he would fight that, that is in short, and then we come to the crucial part that you underlined.*

HOOSEN *Now he sent it to various people, he wanted this in the media, and there is a whole lot of speculation that is in there that has not been mentioned by yourself, with respect, Your Worship.*

ROUX *Yes, it is speculation, but that is the message. He is upset about corruption. We can read it. Let us take it step by step. He complains about corruption. I accept what you say, also speculates about corruption, so what? Many people do.*

HOOSEN *But that is his habit in all the matters.*

ROUX *Yes, let us take a third thing, and that is his habit to do so. Must he now be punished?*

HOOSEN *No, no, I am not punishing him for it. I looked at the point where he is going into exile. I answered that.*

ROUX *I see, now let us get there, so it is fine in your mind, and I think you are fair there and it must be that he wants to fight corruption, he wants to speculate about corruption, and he has done it before because this is not his first time that he is sending out the emails.*

HOOSEN *He has done it numerously. He is going into exile; he is going to hiding.* **CATCH ME IF YOU CAN.**

ROUX *Yes, where is "catch me if you can"?*

ROUX *Excuse me, I am looking for "catch me if you can", that is what you look for, have you forgotten?*

HOOSEN *Okay, I will show you. He has got many places of "catch me if you can."*

ROUX *Please get me the "catch me if you can" .*

HOOSEN *I will show you.*

HOOSEN *He says, "Do not even dream of sending your dirty cops to raid me like you done by the crook Moonoo last year. I will tear into you like a rabid dog."*

HOOSEN *"My methods may be unorthodox, but given I am fighting corrupt state ...[indistinct] with deep pockets I will resort to tactic design to win that does not make friends,.." but it is somewhere here*

HOOSEN *... where he says catch me. Send your people to catch me.*

HOOSEN *No, no, no, that is not in totality the words. I am going in exile. Catch me if you can.*

Having searched for the words "catch me if you can" and having failed to find them, Hoosen then tried to cover up his lies:

HOOSEN *But that is not the words. What I meant from this document, what I inferred from this document he is going into exile, and he is asking us to catch him.*

ROUX *Please make it easy to respect a senior officer and let me put this to you, and then you can take your time. Your evidence was clear, and this Court will stop me, I guarantee you.*

ROUX *And "Catch me if you can." Now I want to know where is that?*

HOOSEN *That is my inference from this document. He says he is going into exile, and he says,* ***STOP ME IF YOU CAN****. It is here.*

ROUX *You can repeat it is here many times, but you cannot show me where it is. Otherwise, show me again, but recheck your underlining, I will help you. "If I have to go into exile to beat you, then so be it."If I have to do it, is that the sentence?*

ROUX *I need the sentence where he is saying "I am going into exile. Catch me if you can." Do you want to look at it again?*

The court then played the recording of Hoosen's testimony where Hoosen listened to himself, adamant that I used the words "*Catch me if you can*" in my email.

HOOSEN *Your Worship, you can play the recording, I never said that was the words exactly used...[indistinct], I said my inference on that document and the defence put to me about the highlighted portions only.*

HOOSEN *Your Worship, I beg the Court's pardon, but you cannot read small portions and expect me to give a comment on a small portion. You must read the whole sentence, that is totally* *unacceptable that the small portion are now being read to me and you asking me to comment on a small portion. Read the whole sentence ...[indistinct] the record Your Worship ..[intervenes]*

ROUX *You know what is unacceptable is what you have just done, that is what I was trying to say to you, Colonel read the whole sentence, it is unfair to read a small portion. What have you done? I read the word "exile", I read the words "Catch me if you can" that is not there whilst and in truth, when you read the whole sentence, let us get it, "if I have to go into exile", so what you preach just apply to the sentence, read it now to the Court and tell the Court if that is the true version. Just read it.*

HOOSEN *I will read this, you must read the sentence before that for you to understand what he is trying to say. He says "I will not be here and will do what I have to do and ignore your actions and carry on until you are all beaten. If I have to go into exile so be it," then so be it, the whole sentence. "If I have to go into exile to beat you, then so be it."*

HOOSEN *Amongst others, amongst others. I said I received information also. That he is going to disappear from the country.*

ROUX *Who did you receive that from?*

HOOSEN *I am not going to say to you.*

ROUX *Oh yes, that is so convenient, so I cannot test it. When did you receive that?*

HOOSEN *I received it the time prior to be making the application for ...*

ROUX *When? Surely you have somewhere a note of that. Show me a note.*

HOOSEN *I received it prior to me making the application for the arrest warrant.*

ROUX *Prior to seeing this email?*

HOOSEN *Probably it is on or about the same time.*

ROUX *That was 23 March 2016.*

HOOSEN *That is correct, 23 March 2016.*

ROUX *Yes, that is eight days.*

HOOSEN *Eight days, that is correct.*

ROUX *So where did you note this information that is what, that he is ...*

HOOSEN *He is going to disappear from the country.*

ROUX *Where is that? In the docket, in your statement at least? Is it in your statement?*

HOOSEN *No, the statement is to deal with his arrest, I investigate, the State had clarified certain points I informed him that I received information as well as I got this information ...*

HOOSEN *I agree it is not in my statement.*

ROUX *Do you agree that this statement was made post 23 March when you received this information and you saw the email?*

HOOSEN *That is correct.*

ROUX *Do you agree that as a senior officer you know that what is important to the Court, you must put that in your statement?*

HOOSEN *That is correct, Your Worship, it is in my statement for the application for the arrest warrant. I was asked under reexamination by State and I...[indistinct] however it was about the arrest ... [indistinct] his passport.*

ROUX *And you know that when you make a statement for the police docket that you must deal with full facts?*

HOOSEN *The full facts are in my statement.*

ROUX *Can I repeat? Is that in your statement?*

HOOSEN *That statement is in respect of after you have arrested and I conducted a search on him.*

ROUX *Do you agree that this statement is after you knew about the alleged facts?*

HOOSEN *Yes, I agree with you.*

ROUX *I think you should repeat that one sentence. I beg the Court's pardon. I think he should repeat that more than once because of what he is doing. Where is the "Catch me if you can"? Do you agree it is not here?*

HOOSEN *You even said that I said it previously on those catch me, and you played the recording, and there is nothing ...[indistinct] catch me if you can.*

ROUX *Must we play it back to get that as well. I will do it.*

HOOSEN *I said "**STOP ME IF YOU CAN**".*

ROUX *Did you never say "catch me if you can"?*

HOOSEN	*Perhaps I say, but nothing here in this ...*
ROUX	*Your Worship, I am so sorry, then we have to play that part back as well, and it will be the second time. It starts at the beginning of cross-examination.*
HOOSEN	*I may have said that, but let us play it.*
ROUX	*Can you not remember it?*
HOOSEN	*Because I know that "**STOP ME IF YOU CAN**" is what I have mentioned.*
ROUX	*Did you say "catch me if you can"?*
HOOSEN	*Let us play it, Your Worship.*
ROUX	*Witness cannot or denies what he said to the Court, and if you want me to play back your denial, I will also do that for you. You want me to do that?*
ROUX	*Where is the hiding part, not there?*
HOOSEN	*No, it is not there?*
ROUX	*Let us wrap it up. He did not say it as a fact. He said "if I have to go into exile", he did not say "I was going into exile", do you agree?*
HOOSEN	*"So if I have to go into exile, then so be it."*
ROUX	*Listen to my question. He did not say "I am going into exile". He says "if I have to go into exile, then so be it".*
HOOSEN	*Why are you [indistinct] on then so be it, then so be it is clarifying that he is going into exile, that is how I understand that word that he ...*

ROUX *And the hiding part,*

HOOSEN *Well, that is ...[indistinct] where hiding from the police, they were in exile.*

ROUX *And catch me?*

HOOSEN *No, it is **"STOP ME IF YOU CAN"**, and there are parts here where you can draw inference where he is saying the matters ... "send your cops, catch me" ...[indistinct] amongst other things, but the inference one can draw from this document is that he was going into hiding, no one will be able to trace him, look for him or find him.*

ROUX *Your Worship, maybe I should just hand this document in. It is **EXHIBIT E**.*

HEALTH ISSUES

My health was being negatively affected as a result of all this nonsense, and I said as much in my court application:

> *I was turning 61 that year and did not enjoy good health. The stress caused by the unwarranted arrest, the manner in which it was executed, the stress of my children and the effect of the subsequent bullying actions by the Hawks cannot be overemphasised.*

I explained that I was supposed to have gone in for a back operation, but I could not run the risk of being murdered while in hospital after being told that Moonoo had made a pact with Krejcir to have me killed. I could not tell the court this as I did not want these thugs to see any sign of weakness that they might exploit.

I also desperately needed to reunite with my children in the United Kingdom to comfort them and try to explain what had happened. They had departed that Sunday for London under tremendous stress, not understanding or knowing my fate.

Over and above this, I explained that I was also the director of a UK-based property investment company. Without my being there, business opportunities would be lost, and I risked sustaining huge financial losses. I had arranged a meeting with the Governor of St Helena Island in the South Atlantic for the Monday afternoon in London following my arrest and was hoping I could still meet up with her to advance the property development interests I was nurturing there.

I asked that the stringent conditions now be relaxed. They were incompatible with the seriousness of the alleged passport offences. Even if the State added more offences to Section 26B, they would still not lead to imprisonment as a sentence option.

SECOND VICTORY

My application was partly successful. I no longer had to report to the Sandton Police Station twice a day – it was reduced to once a day. I was able to travel domestically but had to inform the investigating officer forty-eight hours before departure.

It was my second victory in what would be a four-year drawn-out battle against the State.

My first victory had taken place in April 2015 when I had launched an application to set aside the fraudulently obtained search warrant to raid my offices. The judge ordered that I not be arrested for any alleged offences committed before June 7, 2016, and that should the State wish to prosecute me on any matter allegedly committed by me during this time, that I would be brought to court with a J175 summons. If a trial did not proceed between the 4th and the 6th of July due to the State's inability to proceed on those dates, I could apply to travel abroad. The State, of course, was not ready to proceed with a trial, leading to the conditions being amended on July the 7th.

The court order was more than just a temporary victory. It would put a stop to any further arrests the Hawks had planned. It also formed a protection over me that would help enormously over the months to come. Or so I hoped.

General Mokotedi and his team appeared furious. They were determined to stop me and, while I was away, new plots were concocted to bring me down.

I was eventually allowed to take my annual family holiday overseas between August and September that year. Or so I thought. A week after I had booked it, the fake advocate Mlotshwa got one of Mokotedi's sidekicks to serve a summons on me to appear in court in the middle of August. I believe this was a deliberate and spiteful act of revenge by Mlotshwa and something I will make sure he pays for one day. In fact, there are many crimes against me that he will be held accountable for. I shall pursue him to the bitter end.

INVESTIGATING MY ENEMIES

In the months that followed my illegal arrest, I didn't just sit back and allow the blitz of charges to come my way. It entailed head-to-head fighting, every step of the way, with what I would later call the 'Mokotedi team'. I began investigating every single member of this clique, and my stash of information that I was storing offshore (so that they couldn't get their crooked hands on it), was growing by the day.

I focused a lot of my attention on Major General Prince Mokotedi, in the same that way he and his minion, Kobus Vlok, were focussing on me. My plan was to outsmart, outwit and outplay them. They were both classic examples of the Dunning-Kruger effect – a hypothetical cognitive bias where people with low ability to fulfil a task overestimate their ability. This pair of clowns thought they were unstoppable, but I was ready to teach them a lesson.

Obviously, Mokotedi had an axe to grind against me since I had opened the docket in 2012, naming him as one of the key suspects in the offences of perjury and defeating the end of justice, following his testimony in the witness box at the Jackie Selebi trial, where he gave false evidence in a failed attempt to get Selebi off the hook. As mentioned earlier in the book, in 2014, Mokotedi was ironically made Head of the Integrity Unit at the NPA. This was a reward for his help with Selebi and awarded to him by Nomgcobo Jiba, the now-disgraced and dismissed second in command of the NPA. Putting Mokotedi in charge of ethics was a bit like putting a thief in charge of the chequebook.

After I opened the 2012 docket, it wasn't long before Mokotedi was back to his old tricks. In 2014, he went all out to get rid of prosecutor Glynnis Breytenbach, who was being targeted for leading the prosecution against Richard Mdluli. Looking back, there is no doubt Mokotedi had formed a tight allegiance with Jiba and her accomplice, Mrwebi.

Apart from being an alleged crook, Mokotedi was also an overt racist, regularly making it clear that he hated whites. Although Mokotedi denied it, he deliberately leaked his biased report on Breytenbach to the media, and he was suspended when a disciplinary charge was brought against him for it. While on suspension, he went on the John Robbie show on Radio 702, where he made many defamatory comments about me, Gerrie Nel and senior white staff at the NPA. He claimed there was a DA camp at the NPA that all the white staff were a part of, while at the same time publicly admitting he was part of a 'Zuma camp'. The interview was staggering in its audacity. He was sowing racial divisions within the NPA – an institution that must always remain free and unbiased – while attempting to politicise it.

Mokotedi resigned from the NPA before his disciplinary enquiry commenced, avoiding a dismissal. He used his quick exit strategy to later claim as proof that he left the NPA with an unblemished record. But he wasn't fooling anyone – least of all me.

It wasn't long after commencing forensic searches into Mokotedi that I discovered something very interesting regarding him and his finances. Two months after his departure from the NPA in October 2014, Mokotedi signed for a credit card from Investec Bank, fully aware that he had no income to support the repayments. He subsequently ran up a bill more than R100 000. He also defaulted on another credit card with ABSA Bank for an amount of R9,559. When he stopped paying his mortgage bond on the house in which he was living, a summons was served on him and his wife.

Judgement was awarded in the Pretoria High Court against Mokotedi in favour of Investec Bank for R1.1-million, and in the Pretoria Magistrates Court in favour of ABSA Bank for R9,559. This all happened a few short weeks before he was given the position of Head of the Hawks in Gauteng.

While on the surface, these do not look like huge infringements, they exposed a complete lack of ethics at best and fraud at worst. It is hardly the sort of conduct that would make a person fit and proper material to be parachuted into the police at the rank of Major General as he was in February 2016. The judgements meant that he was a security risk and that he could never receive security clearance since anyone with such large self-inflicted debt has demonstrated a weakness in character. They also meant that such a person could easily be targeted by nefarious characters who could use their money problems to coerce them into corrupt practices or even extortion. The legislation made it clear that Mokotedi *must* have a security clearance certificate to be appointed. Since he was appointed Provincial Head of Hawks without security clearance, his appointment was unlawful from the get-go.

Obviously, this was ignored by the Zuma camp in the police, who unlawfully parachuted him into the position of Gauteng Head of the Hawks. It was clear he was brought in to help quell the honest tide of people, like myself and many decent high-ranking cops and prosecutors, who were exposing the systemic corruption in the police force and elsewhere. If they could appoint someone to such a high position without a security clearance check, I wondered if it was only a matter of time until extra-judicial death squads would be set up and the country went the same way as Mexico.

It seemed a fatalistic prediction to make. Surely things weren't that bad yet? But my forecast would turn out to be eerily true. I did not know it then, but a special team of crooked Hawks cops in the Northwest would soon be called upon to deal with me – and that murder was not something they shied away from.

MOKOTEDI'S FINANCES GO PUBLIC

Kate Lorimer was a Member of the Provincial Legislature (MPL) in Gauteng for the Democratic Alliance in shadow charge of Community Safety. When I was arrested, she came out and publicly defended me. I had always found her to be an ethical person who got her facts straight. After I discovered Mokotedi's personal financial mismanagement issues, I decided she needed to know about them. She would be able to ask questions in the legislature about his appointment and get to the bottom of whether he had a security clearance or not.

When Lorimer received the information, she was as shocked as I was and decided to issue a press statement on the issue.[59] She called for Mokotedi's immediate removal from his job and said she believed

59 Belinda Pheto, Remove Gauteng Hawk's head now – DA, Midrand Reporter, 11 July 2016, https://midrandreporter.co.za/161836/remove-gauteng-hawks-head-now-da/

he was at risk of being lured into corrupt practices because of his bad credit record:

> *For a high-profile job like his, a security clearance was supposed to have been issued, but that has not been the case because he is protected.*

She called on Minister Nathi Nhleko to terminate his position. Of course, that would never happen because Nhleko was an integral part of the state capture machinery. The Hawks' chief public attack dog, Hangwani Mulaudzi, said this was just an attempt to derail Mokotedi from doing his job and that it was character assassination. This was further proof that Mulaudzi and the truth were complete strangers – a key requirement if you are employed to spin-doctor a cover-up of state capture. Mulaudzi, while deliberately ignoring what the legislation said about 'fit and proper', said:

> *Why target him alone? There are thousands of people in influential positions that do not have security clearances, and nothing is being said about them.*

Another media article, this time written by Marianne Thamm at the *Daily Maverick*, got Mokotedi so hot under the collar that he laid a complaint against her with the press ombudsman.[60] Thamm wrote about my allegations against Mokotedi, accusing him of perjury at the Jackie Selebi trial. Mokotedi took exception to this and said the article was unfounded and made undue attacks on his character. He denied perjuring himself in the Jackie Selebi trial and said that the NPA had charged him for laying a charge against Glynnis Breytenbach with the police when he had not been given permission to do so. He denied his employer had charged him for leaking the report on Breytenbach to the media.

---

60 Marianne Thamm, House of cards: O'Sullivan turns up the heat on Gauteng Hawks, Daily Maverick, 9 May 2016, https://www.dailymaverick.co.za/article/2016-05-09-house-of-cards-osullivan-turns-up-the-heat-on-gauteng-hawks/

Without realising it, however, Mokotedi revealed some interesting information in his complaint. He stated, as if it were fact, that I was an 'agent' of a foreign intelligence agency and that he was 'leading an investigation' on this. He also stated that he had been working on an undercover project for the SAPS Crime Intelligence Unit since leaving the NPA. Aside from the lies about me, I wondered what exactly Mokotedi had been doing at Crime Intelligence?

MOKOTEDI MAKES A THREAT

On the 8th of June, 2016, Mokotedi phoned my attorney Daryl Furman and told him there would be serious trouble ahead for me. He said he knew that I was in possession of – and had distributed to journalists – private and confidential information pertaining to his financial affairs. This was absolute rubbish. The court judgments made against Mokotedi were public documents, and anyone with the time or the inclination could go to the courts as I did, uplift and copy the file, and read the judgements.

I considered Mokotedi's oral threats via my attorney to be extreme intimidation and a continuation of his prior criminal conduct, aimed at silencing me, for exposing his criminal conduct. I took this so seriously that I opened a further criminal case against him.

In my sworn statement, I said I believed that if Mokotedi was not stopped soon, his criminal conduct would continue to escalate unabated:

> *Indeed, I believe he is becoming so desperate that he is planning my murder at this time since it is clear that his other criminal steps, aimed at stopping me from exposing him and his accomplices, are not working for him.*
>
> *I am also aware that accomplices under his command have been intimidating other state witnesses against Ntlemeza, thereby showing a disturbing pattern of South Africa moving towards a police state. I*

can already prove that Mokotedi is overtly directing his accomplices in the NPA, who have abandoned their oath of office, to conduct themselves without fear, favour or prejudice, to raise false charges against me. Indeed, Mokotedi's criminal stranglehold over the NPA makes him a very dangerous enemy of the state.

I followed this up with another docket that I opened against Mokotedi, Ntlemeza, Phahlane, Moonoo, Lieutenant Colonel AK Hoosen, Advocate Maema, fake Advocate Mlotshwa, the Minister of Police Nathi Nhleko, and the President of the country, Jacob Zuma.

I alleged that all these suspects, in conspiracy with each other and with a common purpose, committed the following offences: unlawful arrest, unlawful detention, torture, extortion, corruption, defeating the ends of justice, and breaching Section 32 of the National Prosecuting Authority Act.

The main suspect was Mokotedi, and the main co-conspirator was Moonoo. The aim of their conspiracy was to protect Phahlane, Ntlemeza, Moonoo, Mdluli, and former Gauteng Crime Intelligence boss Joey Mabasa, who all had charges opened against them (by me) for corruption, racketeering, and defeating the ends of justice, and then Mokotedi, for perjury, extortion, torture, and defeating the ends of justice.

I painstakingly went through all my allegations against Mokotedi, including my allegations of perjury against him. I dissected his interview with John Robbie (and another interview he did with Redi Thlabi) where I said he had demonstrated his hatred for the DA and for whites in the NPA, "thereby proving he is a racist bigot". In my docket, I wrote:

One would have thought that after burning his bridges so badly at the NPA, Mokotedi would then have vanished into obscurity and never have been seen or heard of again. However, this was not to be so.

I had also downloaded his Twitter account, which was under the name Rev Prince Mokotedi. The account clearly proved he lacked objectivity, that he had a blind dedication to the ANC (which is prohibited by both the NPA Act and the Police Services Act), and that he had a deep resentment of any non-ANC political parties and openly declared he was "100% JZ". His account also showed a bitterness and hatred of his (white) ex-colleagues at the NPA and that he held profound racist views and hatred towards whites in general. He was clearly not fit for a senior position in the police.

THE MOONOO AND KREJCIR CONNECTION

I also discovered a closer link between Moonoo and Krejcir. In a meeting held in my office between a prosecutor and a police officer I have never named, we learnt from an undercover agent that Moonoo had been tipped off (in advance) that Sam Issa and Veselin Laganin would be murdered by Krejcir. These men were subsequently assassinated. They were potentially extremely dangerous witnesses against Krejcir, whose criminal empire was collapsing. Moonoo, it seemed, did nothing with the information. The informer also told us that Krejcir had paid Moonoo R5-million.

More chilling information emerged that Krejcir had called Padayachee to tell him that if he did not get his R5-million back, he would murder Moonoo. Padayachee, whose phone was being monitored, joined Moonoo on a conference call to calm Krejcir down. Moonoo then allegedly gave an undertaking to Krejcir that the cases against him would collapse. The only way Moonoo could give such a guarantee is if he intended to assist Krejcir in removing key witnesses – people like myself and Jacob Nare.

It was evident that Moonoo and Mokotedi were actively engaged in a conspiracy aimed at shutting me down. In the likelihood that this failed, they were hoping that Krejcir would hurry up and murder me in the meantime, putting an end to their problem (me) for good and leaving nobody the wiser about their ulterior motives.

FIGHTING TO ATTEND MY DAUGHTER'S 10th BIRTHDAY PARTY

When I submitted these dockets, I knew that likely, they would sit on a dusty shelf somewhere. But I had to continue attending court to oppose all the false cases being opened against me by criminals with badges and gowns. Each time I looked them in the eye and goaded them, "You're turn will come."

After my bail victory in the Kempton Park Magistrate's Court, my financial revelations against Mokotedi and the criminal charges I kept on opening (revealing that I would not take their attacks on me lying down), the Mokotedi team was furious. They were like a swarm of wasps whose nest was in the process of being destroyed. Their stings were out, and they were ready to strike anything that got in their way. It didn't matter whether I had committed a genuine criminal offence or not. However, as would later be proved, the stings in their tails were impotent.

During a delay in the trial of the Section 26B case in July 2016, I used the opportunity to apply for a further relaxation in my bail conditions. I wanted to fly out of the country to attend Anna's tenth birthday party overseas. Mlotshwa tried to sway the Magistrate's decision by falsely claiming the State was investigating ten different cases against me and that I was a flight risk. At that stage, I had not been formally charged on any other cases, except the trumped-up SAA and passport matters – although this would change in the following weeks.

Captain Bonisile Mkupa dishonestly stood in the stand and listed six cases they were investigating: A Kempton Park case of extortion, fraud, forgery, and uttering; a Pretoria Central case of corruption; a Johannesburg Central case of theft, corruption, and extortion;

an Alberton case of extortion and intimidation, a Bramley case of kidnapping; and a Midrand case of fraud.

Mkupa said a complainant in one of the cases was an African National Congress councillor in Alberton, Neil Diamond. Diamond was a well-known estate-agent-cum-property-developer in the East Rand. He was also an ANC councillor who was infamous due to a murky land-swap agreement with the State that had taken place years before in Alberton. While no charges were ever formally laid against him, the allegations against him would not go away.

Diamond was powerful, and he had a reputation for being ruthless. A few years earlier, I had investigated him for the role he played in the looting of a deceased estate. I had instructed Melissa Naidu to open a criminal docket against him, alleging that he had forged a will so that he would be the executor and that he then removed most of the cash in the estate, leaving the deceased's family virtually penniless. However, like all the allegations against Diamond, nothing stuck, and he got away with it all. His ANC membership appeared to be his get-out-of-jail-free card, and he seemed to live a charmed life.

It was at this point that I wondered where the State was getting all these cases against me. Alice Johnston, Cora van der Merwe, and now Neil Diamond were all people I had previously investigated for serious criminal offences. It seemed more than slightly suspicious that the Mokotedi team had access to all these cases. I suspected that Vlok had illegally downloaded the contents of my computer, despite the court order stopping them from doing this when they raided my offices in 2015.

Magistrate Wynand Nel asked if there were any other cases that were currently before the court. Mkupa mentioned the SAA matter.

"But he wasn't even arrested on that one," noted Nel.

Vlok, along with Mokotedi and six to ten others, made sure they were present throughout the hearing, gloating over the results of their crimes against me. Vlok said he was investigating three cases: a Johannesburg Central case of extortion, intimidation and theft; two cases of fraud, impersonating a police officer, and unlawful arrest. The Johannesburg Central case was the one I had been investigating against Edrees Hathurani in 2014, which I had also linked to Moonoo. It was another one of those fake cases against me that would go nowhere.

The other charges were the trumped-up Johnston and van der Merwe cases. It was pointed out in court that all of them were, at that point, still in the investigation phase, and no charges had yet been laid against me for any of them. So all these cases, at that stage, were nothing more than pure hearsay and hypothesis. In addition, most of the people purportedly opening the cases against me had been arrested and charged for investigations I had launched against them or had criminal charges of their own to face. The grudges they bore against me and their past criminal behaviour should have made the police wary of any allegations they made against me. But the Mokotedi team clearly felt the truth should not get in the way of their vendetta.

The Magistrate agreed that the other cases against me were nothing but hearsay and said that as far as he could see from the emails I had sent, the threats I had made to the police were about my ongoing dissatisfaction with how things were being done in the country. He swiftly issued a judgement allowing me to attend my daughter's party.

COURAGE IS THE BEST STRATEGY

While I was away in the UK, I learnt that the Hawks were planning to arrest me as soon as I landed back in Johannesburg, despite the court order forbidding them to do so.[61] They alleged again that the charges included espionage and treason and were far too serious for me not to be arrested. It was clear to me that this was the work

61 Marianne Thamm, House of cards: Hawks ready to arrest Paul O'Sullivan again, Daily Maverick, 14 July 2014, https://www.dailymaverick.co.za/article/2016-07-14-house-of-cards-hawks-ready-to-arrest-paul-osullivan-again/

of Moonoo and his accomplice, Mokotedi. I had given an interview to Alec Hogg of *Biznews* while in London, where I revealed some of the information I had on the corruption taking place at SAA.[62] This was after the national carrier unlawfully suspended its treasurer, Cynthia Stimpel, who had objected to the airline's debt restructuring deal. The story was like a firecracker – as soon as it was released, it got the country talking. Not long after that, OUTA launched a court application to have Dudu Myeni declared a delinquent director.

The Mokotedi team was even more determined to stop me after my public revelations on Myeni. Knowing this made it difficult for me to step onto that flight to come back home. For the first time in my life, I had doubts about returning to South Africa. But I knew this was the police's plan. They would have relished in making me a fugitive from justice. They would have crowed publicly that I was clearly guilty of all the ridiculously false allegations they were making about me, and I would be forever forcefully stuck out of the country I loved. Letting them win in that way was unbearable for me. My every instinct screamed that I could not – and would not – allow this injustice against me to continue. I had my hard-earned rights as a citizen of South Africa, and I was determined to prove myself innocent.

So, even though I knew that I could be thrown into a police cell within the next twenty-four hours, I flew back to South Africa. I didn't sleep a wink that night, wondering if these were my last few hours of freedom. It was highly stressful stepping out of that plane, but in the end, I remained free because they were bluffing – and I had called their bluff and won.

While I had been preparing to board my flight, in the background, my legal team was seeking an urgent interdict in the Johannesburg High Court to prevent the NPA and police from applying for a warrant

62 BizNews, Paul O'Sullivan: Exposing fresh Myeni corruption at SAA. Documentary proof, Fin24, 12 July 2016, https://www.fin24.com/BizNews/paul-osullivan-exposing-fresh-myeni-corruption-at-saa-documentary-proof-20160712

for my arrest. Although my legal team was not successful, in the end, it was all the media attention that stopped the Mokotedi team from acting out their dirty plans.

By returning to South Africa, I had not only thwarted their plans but had also proved that I was not a flight risk. Every time they served me with a summons to appear in court, I made sure I was there. I demonstrated to the different magistrates that I was a reliable person with no intention of fleeing the false charges being laid against me. It made no sense to arrest someone who was neither a danger to society nor running away from any culpability they claimed I had. From then on, every time the Mokotedi gang tried to put me in handcuffs, they were revealing their hand – that their intentions for arresting me were not out of a sense of justice, but rather a clear vendetta of revenge.

PLAYING THE RECUSAL CARD

The next time I faced the Hawks and Mlotshwa in person at the Kempton Park Magistrate's Court two weeks later in August 2016, their anger was palpable. It was as if the fury was literally dripping from their grimaced faces. They knew that by returning to South Africa, I had gained a key advantage over them.

They were clearly desperate to drag out the fake passport/immigration trial. This was the only case where they had managed to suppress me with their ridiculous bail conditions, maliciously opposing me every time I applied to leave the country.

Their intentions to stop me from revealing the corruption of people like Myeni had blatantly not worked – my interview with Alec Hogg demonstrated that – and now they could not easily arrest me and intimidate me again. But try they did.

The Section 26B case was also slowly unravelling. It had always been a fictitious case and, in granting me the relaxed bail conditions, Magistrate Nel appeared to be sympathetic to my plight. The passport case was an administrative issue and not something that should be appearing before the courts, despite the fact that it was being used to hold me down and control me.

Mlotshwa knew this and, in a move that stank of desperation, he filed a fraudulent application for the Magistrate to recuse himself. Mlotshwa dishonestly argued that in having allowed me to go to London to celebrate my daughter's birthday, the court seemed to agree that I was a corruption fighter. He was upset that the court viewed me as a corruption fighter when I had not even taken the witness stand. He argued:

> *There is absolutely no evidence before this court that the accused is fighting corruption. It can only be assumed that the court made this finding based on what was put by the defence counsel to the various state witnesses. It is therefore difficult to comprehend how the court could make this finding taking into account that the accused has not yet given evidence in this matter, and the issue in question was not even relevant to the application.*

He said that in giving this finding, it gave credence to a perception that the court was not impartial.

Adding to this appallingly dishonest argument, Mlotshwa said that the investigating officer, Captain Bonisile Mkupa, had also seen Magistrate Nel talking to my instructing attorney, Daryl Furman, in the corridor of the court without the state prosecutor being present:[63]

> *The conversation between your worship and Mr Furman may well have been innocent and had nothing to do with this matter at all but what is important is the perception created by the conversation.*

Mlotshwa said that if the conversation was innocent, the Magistrate would have to come forward and state this, making him a witness in the case, which was undesirable – and that, as such, he should recuse

63 Angelique Serrao, Magistrate in O'Sullivan trial asked to recuse himself, News24, 2 August 2016, https://www.news24.com/SouthAfrica/News/magistrate-in-osullivan-trial-asked-to-recuse-himself-20160802

himself. Barry Roux was astounded. He stood up and said that in his thirty-five years before the courts, he had never heard of such a weak recusal application. Roux said he had listened to the recording of the bail judgment that morning after learning the recusal application would take place.

Referring to the email I sent to the police on the 15th of March 2016, indicating that I would hold a press conference in London to discuss corruption in the country, Roux quoted Nel as saying, "I am not going to venture into this, but the email seems to say..." – which, as Roux stated, showed that Nel was not making a statement of fact about the case. Roux said the alleged conversation between Nel and Furman did not take place before the bail application but rather the previous day when they were waiting for an interpreter for one of the witnesses:

> *You probably won't even remember this, but Mr Furman bumped into your worship in the corridor and said, "I am sorry your worship. We are still looking for an interpreter".*

"This is all nonsense," Roux said of the application. "You did not make a finding. You did not have a discussion with the defence. There is no merit to this application." He asked why, on such a basis, the whole trial should start afresh, with all the costs and time spent so far, being for nothing.

While I was winning in court, a different fight had been launched against me outside of it – this time in the court of public opinion. The Police and Prisons Civil Rights Union (POPCRU) issued a press release saying they welcomed the call for the Magistrate to recuse himself.[64] Certain factions of POPCRU were clearly running with the foxes while hunting with the hounds. They falsely stated that:

> *We have always maintained that Mr O'Sullivan has ulterior motives in his "white knight" activities in the country. His reasons to stay*

64 POPCRU, Magistrate Nel must recuse himself from the Paul O'Sullivan hearing, 2 August 2016, https://popcru.org.za/magistrate-nel-must-recuse-himself-from-the-paul-o-sullivan-hearing/

> *in this country have always been to advance the cause of white oppression and privilege.*

Their statement struck me as having the same anti-white sentiment as the opinion often given by Mokotedi on his now-closed Twitter account. My race was clearly a card that would be used against me. There were certainly no holy cows left in this all-out war.

POPCRU added:

> *It is abundantly clear that Mr O'Sullivan's main purpose to "settle" in this country was mainly to destabilise the progressive forces of this country in the pre-1994 era. His association with opposition parties, namely, AgangSA and the DA, that advance white privilege is, therefore, not surprising.*

With a police service battered by corruption and ineptitude, I had to wonder why my matter would warrant the time they must have spent writing up the press statement. I was not a police officer. Surely, they had better things to fill their time than attack an ordinary member of the public who was fighting wrongdoing in the police? – something they should have been more vocal about, themselves.

What POPCRU also failed to mention was that I was investigating their leadership for emptying the union's coffers and had opened a docket in that regard. If the rank and file members of POPCRU could see that docket, they would all be forced to resign en-masse.

I was angry that the state capture gang was out to paint such a false and clearly defamatory picture of me. They were using my race to tarnish me, twisting everything I stood for to make the public distrust me. But I also took heart from it. It showed they were desperate. They were clearly unsure that the false cases they kept throwing at me were going to stick, so they were trying all, and any means to injure me and stop me in my tracks.

Sadly for them, Magistrate Nel refused to play their games. He quickly dismissed the application. It had been nothing more than an insult to a magistrate who was carefully following the law, and it did nothing to engender warmth towards their crooked cause. I am not sure their strategy was well thought out – a characteristic I would find increasing as the months went on. Their cases were false, and every single one was torn to shreds when revealed in court.

If this was a war, the generals on the prosecution's side were clearly inexperienced in the art of it. After my initial reaction of flabbergasted amazement at their rotten audacity wore off, I had a small chuckle. Watching the drama unfold in court, I felt that maybe, for the first time in this crazy episode in my life, there was light at the end of the tunnel, despite the fact that a real possibility existed that Zuma would take control of the courts.

CROOKED JUDGES

In 2009, Judge Leona Theron, married to controversial millionaire Charles Sarjoo, one of the most protected tenderpreneurs in South Africa, presided over Jacob Zuma's corruption trial. During this time, Theron was in business with Michael Hulley and Jerome Brauns, Zuma's legal representatives. Theron was a shareholder of Hulley's company, MLI Property Holdings. She was also a shareholder of Brauns' company, Umthombo Entertainment. Lucky for Zuma, Theron allowed for an extensive eight-month postponement of his corruption trial, while the prosecution team only wanted a month. By the time Zuma was to appear back in court in early 2010, the charges had been dropped, and he had become the President of South Africa. Of course, it was no surprise that the charges against him had been unlawfully dropped during the "grace period" that had been created by Theron. In 2010, Theron was promoted to Judge in the Supreme Court of Appeal and, in 2017, was appointed a Constitutional Court Judge. It was hardly a surprise that she later became the main dissenting Constitutional Court Judge to vociferously oppose Zuma's fifteen-month prison sentence in 2021, confirming that she was indeed a Zuma loyalist, just like the disgraced Arthur Fraser, who cancelled Zuma's prison sentence on false pretences.

Another suspicious instance of what appeared to be a capture of the judiciary was that of Zuma's 2006 rape trial, initially presided over by Judge Jeremiah Shongwe, the uncle to Zuma's son, Edward Zuma. After having refused to recuse himself from presiding over this case, Judge Shongwe was eventually forced to do so. It is important to note that Edward Zuma was born to a teenage girl in Swaziland, the precise age of whom has been kept a family secret, to avoid scandalous allegations. Yet Zuma was to be tried for the rape of "Kwhezi" by the uncle of Zuma's eldest child, who had been conceived of an affair with a schoolgirl. Ludicrous.

Despite the depth of the state-sponsored corruption around me, despite the threat of the country descending into a police state, and despite the paucity of strong leadership, the judiciary still stood firm. The state capture looters were doing their best to chip away at its structure, but the rule of law was still strong. As long as that continued to be the case, I had faith that I would win the fight. I knew I was on the side of the right, and every time I felt uncertain in this battle for my life and freedom, I tried to remember that. I would need to draw on these small moments of positivity in the months that lay ahead as the attacks against me became more frenzied, and I found myself close to losing hope all too often. I worried what would happen if these criminals took control of the courts in the same way they had taken over the police and prosecution service. I had serious grounds to question the future.

LETTER TO ABRAHAMS

By now, I had amassed enough evidence to file a formal complaint with the NPA about what I had been unlawfully subjected to. My legal team wrote a letter of complaint to Shaun Abrahams on 22 July 2016 and handed him a lever arch file detailing the conspiracy by senior members of the police to target me.

The letter stated:

> *The documents reveal evidence of an orchestrated effort by high-ranking law enforcement officials to silence Mr O'Sullivan who has implicated them in corruption. In other words, the people that Mr O'Sullivan has fingered as corrupt are now abusing their power to both punish and silence him. This has created an untenable situation. The proper functioning of our criminal justice system depends on the lawful exercising of power by those charged with upholding it. The most basic principle, and the very foundation of any constitutional democracy, is that those vested with law enforcement powers must exercise them without fear, favour or prejudice. This principle has been violated by the circumstances animating Mr O'Sullivan's complaint.*

The documents in the file detailed how Major General Mokotedi abused his power by subjecting me to continued harassment, including the arbitrary deprivation of my freedom:

> *Major General Mokotedi and other functionaries acting under his control or influence are clearly abusing their powers. Perhaps the most troubling aspect of this abuse is that it is designed only to conceal corruption.*

The paradox, of course, is that the Hawks unit was expressly established under Chapter 6A of the South African Police Act of 1995 to combat corruption. In Glenister versus the President of the Republic of South Africa, 2011 – which specifically examined the role of the Hawks – the Constitutional Court found that corruption undermined the constitutional rights and freedoms of all South Africans. It found that corruption constitutes 'a fundamental threat to the rule of law', 'imperils our democracy', and 'endangers the stability and security of our society'.

In the face of this pernicious threat, the Constitutional Court held that the State's constitutional and international law obligations require our law enforcement agencies to actively take appropriate measures to combat systemic corruption.

The documents contained in my file described the corruption that Major General Mokotedi was *concealing* instead of combatting. Corruption, I pointed out, is not restricted to that which occurs at a political level – like the corruption I exposed at South African Airways, as perpetrated by its chairperson, Duduzile Myeni – but also extends to law enforcement agencies, like the South African Police Service, the Hawks, and the National Prosecuting Authority. The letter laid out the difficult situation in which I found myself, with seemingly nowhere to turn for help.

We showed that I had been arrested just to get me into police custody where I could be interrogated, tortured and threatened:

> *This kind of intimidation and psychological abuse cannot continue. Our Constitution means nothing if ordinary citizens cannot be protected, and it means even less if they cannot be protected from those who are supposed to protect them.*

We requested a meeting with Abrahams to find someone to look at the case from all sides. I was not trying to hide from a genuine prosecution, but I needed someone to view my situation objectively and see the abuse for what it was. My pleas, of course, went unheard. Abrahams, just like his public moniker "Shaun The Sheep" suggested, did nothing. The leadership of the NPA would not be rendering me any help whatsoever. This was the proof I needed that the whole criminal justice system was now well and truly captured.

I was truly on my own. If anything was going to get me out of this mess, it was my Irish upbringing and hatred for injustice – and the criminals who perpetrated it.

CHAPTER 12
A DIRTY WAR

THE POLICE GET EVEN MORE DESPERATE

Mokotedi's threats of levelling treason, espionage and racketeering charges against me were substantial. The simple mention of such significant charges would cause fear to arise in anyone accused of such activities.

As the months of 2016 rolled by, with the only real charges thrown my way being made-up, petty cases (and whose complainants were nothing more than tainted individuals with vengeance darkening their hearts), it became obvious that Mokotedi and his sidekicks were filled with more gas than a clump of helium balloons decorating a child's birthday party.

This gave me hope that, if I stuck to my guns, the attacks on my character and freedom would eventually come to an end, but I was also aware that the bunch of villains leading the Mokotedi' team would stop at nothing to bring me down. I was in a perilous situation, with nothing but the truth to protect me from what would come next.

What I would soon come to learn – through a diverse range of people who were both ethical and brave – was that the Hawks were becoming increasingly desperate to nail me on something. Anything. However, the cases they were accusing me of would not stick. They were made-up, nonsensical crimes that only served to drain my time, my energy and my resources by tying me up in criminal and civil litigation, keeping me away from investigating them and their leaders.

Thirsting for revenge, they searched for something solid to get me behind bars. I am not sure why Vlok was the man specifically chosen for the job, other than the fact that he would listen to any instruction in what I can only assume was a futile attempt to climb up the police's structures, but he was in charge of finding – or fabricating – something substantial that could be used against me. He wasn't exactly a particularly impressive foe. Of all the mistakes Moonoo ever made, his biggest mistake was assigning an idiot to cover his back.

In the second half of 2016, I received numerous reports from ex-employees, police officers and other people I had worked with in the past that Vlok was contacting them to try to get them to make false statements about me. When they refused to participate in such blatantly unethical and criminal behaviour, he quickly turned to threats to coerce them into doing what he wanted.

It became a dirty war, and Vlok was clearly a man who would use any means at his disposal to try to conjure up non-existent muck against me. Vlok began engaging with low-life private investigators, many of whom had tarnished pasts, to dig up dirt on me. Many private investigators in South Africa have investigative skills that are inversely proportional to the number of tattoos and gold chains and bangles on show. I surmised that they joined in this game of slander to line their own pockets. Firstly, they expected to get a substantial pay-out from the Hawks as 'suppliers' of information and secondly, they believed that if I was out of the picture, some of my clients would turn to them. What they failed to realise was that I was a Forensic Consultant and Certified Fraud Examiner, and most of my clients were corporate clients who would not be seen dead with this motley crew of misfits.

Vlok and Mokotedi's campaign – or 'special project' as they called it amongst themselves – didn't quite turn out as planned. Instead of giving in to his blatant extortion, many courageous people told me that Vlok had approached them. They signed sworn statements and opened cases against Vlok instead.

TRYING TO STRONG-ARM MELISSA

Vlok then attempted to turn my ex-employee, Melissa Naidu (and my co-accused on the fake Cora van der Merwe 'kidnapping' case), against me. Perhaps Vlok thought she would be easily intimidated because she was already facing false charges of extortion, intimidation and kidnapping (alongside me). Since Melissa knew as well as me that the case was nonsensical and would not hold up in court, Vlok's attempts to gain her trust went nowhere fast. More importantly, Melissa could not get out of the corner she was in by spilling the beans on me because she had no beans to spill.

Even Vlok's fellow Hawks' officers thought the case was ridiculous. In a meeting with the Hawks held at my office in July 2016, the purpose of which was to take our warning statements in the case and our fingerprints, Captain Mokovhi expressed dismay that the van der Merwe case was going before the courts. He told Naidu and me that the docket had no evidence in it and that he believed the case was nothing more than a vendetta against me. Since Captain Mokovhi was expressing his opinion on what was clearly a weak case, it gave us confidence that any magistrate who was impartial would quickly see the same thing.

But Vlok must have believed he had a fearful suspect on his hands with Naidu because he called her a month later to tell her not to communicate with me because he wanted to offer her a section 204 if she became a state witness. Section 204 of South Africa's Criminal Procedures Act makes provision for any person who was involved in a crime to give evidence against the ringleader of the crime and, in return, receive indemnity from prosecution. Vlok dishonestly claimed to Melissa that another employee of my company, Kim Marriot, had called him and given him information against me. He was lying through his teeth, and Marriot signed a statement avowing to this. Naidu also turned Vlok down. She contacted Daryl Furman soon after the phone call and told him about everything that had transpired.

VLOK'S FISHING EXPEDITION

Detective Warrant officer Gysbert Coetzee, stationed at Hartbeespoort Dam in the Northwest, also told me that Vlok had contacted him.

During 2014, Coetzee was working with what was then known as the National Intervention Unit, a group of detectives who operated under the direct control and management of the then Divisional Commissioner for Detectives, Lieutenant General Moonoo. It was while working under Moonoo that Coetzee first came across Vlok. As Coetzee explained in his sworn statement:

> *I could see that his conduct, in late 2014, appeared to be directed towards finding any information he could find which could incriminate Paul O'Sullivan in any crimes at all. It was not as if there was a specific complaint. It was more like he was on a fishing expedition. I say this because he asked me several times if I could help him find any dirt on Paul O'Sullivan. I made it clear that I had previously worked with Paul O'Sullivan's office, and he was professional at all times.*

I had worked with Coetzee in 2012 when we were investigating a case of robbery with aggravating circumstances and conspiracy to commit murder. Kim Marriott and I assisted Coetzee with the case. In his affidavit, Coetzee explained that we helped him prepare the relevant Section 205 applications, search warrants, and J50s. There is nothing new about this. Many forensic firms assist the police in such a way, and it greatly speeds up the administration of the work that must be done. Coetzee said it was our assistance and perseverance that helped him track down and obtain good-quality evidence in the form of sworn statements from many valuable state witnesses.

In September 2016, Coetzee received a call from Vlok, which, on reflection, Coetzee found troubling. Vlok started the call by telling him he was Coetzee's friend and that he wanted to help him. Vlok went on to say that Coetzee was in big trouble because he (Vlok) had copies of search warrants and arrest warrants that were given to him by Kim Marriott. He said that Kim Marriott had visited him and given him a sworn statement, implicating Coetzee and me in producing fake search warrants and arrest warrants. Vlok alleged to Coetzee that it was me who had stamped and signed the warrants and not the court. He also said that he recovered these documents from Marriott's old work computer, which she had apparently given to him.

Coetzee said he knew that Vlok was lying for three reasons. Firstly, he knew that Marriott was an extremely ethical person and would not, under any circumstances, fabricate lies like these. Secondly, it was Marriott and not me who helped him with the administration of the cases, and there was nothing wrong or unlawful about that. Finally, Coetzee told Vlok that he himself took the documents Marriott printed to the Magistrate's court in Brits and that they were signed and stamped there:

> *In the telephone discussion with Vlok, I pointed out to him that I personally took the dockets to the Magistrate's court to get the various 205's, search warrants and arrest warrants signed. He then accused me of lying and said he had been to the courts and could not find any trace of the documents. He also again stated that the documents he had from Marriott's computer made it clear that Paul O'Sullivan was the one that signed them.*
>
> *I again told him that he was talking rubbish and that if he could not find the court files, some four years later, that is not a reason for him, or anyone else for that matter, to suspect me of wrongdoing. He then*

> *told me that if I did not cooperate by implicating Paul O'Sullivan, I would be arrested and charged with corruption and fraud.*

Coetzee promptly opened a case against Vlok for the offences of fraud and extortion, stating that he considered the allegations against him to be false and a deliberate lie intended to extort him into saying something against me that was not true. This, he felt, was being done to satisfy Vlok's personal vendetta against me, adding:

> *I therefore request a high-level investigation into Vlok's patently unlawful conduct, in particular the aspects of fraud, in that he falsely claimed Marriott had made a sworn statement implicating me and secondly his attempt to extort me into lying for him to frame Paul O'Sullivan.*

Kim Marriott also denied Vlok's lies against her. In an affidavit, she made it clear that his allegations were false:

> *I wish to make it clear that I have never contacted either Vlok or anyone else at the Hawks regarding O'Sullivan. Nor have I been contacted by Hawks members regarding O'Sullivan. I have never met nor spoken to Vlok. Nor have I made any sworn statement as alleged, nor have I handed any computer to either Vlok or anyone else for that matter. If Vlok has stated what has been attributed to him, then he is not being truthful. I do not know what his motive is, but I do not consent to him using my name like this.*
>
> *For the avoidance of doubt, in the six years that I have worked with Paul O'Sullivan, I have seen him turn away business that he considered unethical. Client's mandates have also been cancelled once our firm ascertained our clients were being unethical and/or criminal.*

THE NEIL DIAMOND SAGA CONTINUES

I met Hennie Els, a fellow forensic investigator who ran Hennie Els Forensic Legal and Audit Investigations, in 2012. He was also working on a case against ANC Ekurhuleni councillor Neil Diamond. Their case was like the fraudulent estate case I had been working on. Els was a professional Forensic Investigator and not one of the tattoo and bangle brigade.

In a sworn statement Els made in 2016 against Vlok, he described how Els was employed by the executrix in the estate of the late Deon Fourie to investigate allegations of criminal activities against Diamond. During his investigation, he found a document – allegedly used by Diamond in various High Court actions – where the testator's signature had been forged. A criminal case docket with charges including the forgery of a will and theft from the estate for R2.6-million was registered by Els at Alberton SAPS.

During this time, Els learned about the criminal case I had opened against Diamond (also related to the forgery of a will), and we met and discussed the similarities in the cases. We hadn't seen each other since, so it was a surprise for Els when he received a phone call from Vlok, four years later, in 2016. In his statement, Els said that Vlok had introduced himself as a Captain and said he was working for a special task team at the SAPS head office. He scheduled a meeting with Els to discuss what he said was the "O'Sullivan and Diamond Case".

Believing that their case was finally receiving high-level police attention after years of trying to get someone to take them seriously, Els invited Rynette Farrar, a colleague who had gathered a large amount of evidence against Rean Booysen (a developer who worked with Diamond), to the meeting. Again, Vlok introduced himself as a Captain who said he was part of a specially formed task team to investigate corruption. Els said that Vlok told him about the criminal case he had opened against Diamond that the prosecutor declined to prosecute as well as other issues in which Diamond played a part. Farrar handed Vlok a wall plan indicating who was connected in the cases against Diamond.

In his statement, Els explained what happened next:

> *He [Vlok] then told us that he had employed various private investigators to assist in the special investigation, which involved Mr O'Sullivan and matters he is involved in. He named a Mr Chad Thomas and a Mr Mike Bolhuis. He wanted to know what we know about O'Sullivan, and Rynette told him that she had never met Mr O'Sullivan, and I told him that I have never worked with Mr O'Sullivan and had only a brief meeting with him to discuss similarities in the two estate matters under investigation.*

The investigator said Vlok did not show much interest in what they had told him, but he took all the documents supplied by Farrer:

> *It became apparent to me that he was not at all interested in the cases I had opened against Diamond, of forgery, uttering and theft, or the case Rynette Farrar had opened against Booysen for fraud, but Vlok was only interested in getting information that he could use against O'Sullivan.*

When I read Els' statement, I wondered what kind of special task team Vlok was a part of, if it ignored genuine complaints of corruption against a powerful ANC politician like Diamond. It was becoming increasingly clear this so-called special team, as Vlok had described to Hennie Els, was not formed to tackle corruption. It was simply there to target me and protect the corrupt.

Sometime later, Vlok called Els again. He said he wanted to update Els on some issues and that he was sitting with an advocate who was dealing with the matters against me. I imagine this must have been the fake 'advocate' Mlotshwa. Vlok told Els that he had an affidavit from Els in which Els made allegations *in favour* of me in an Alberton case I had opened against Diamond. Of course, Vlok was lying.

In his statement, Els said:

> *I told him that I did not recall making any affidavit either in favour of Mr O'Sullivan or against any other person in that specific case docket, as I did not know enough about the case. However, I had*

> *made affidavits and a representation in the case docket I investigated against Neil Diamond in the Fourie Estate matter. Vlok then told me that he had a warrant of arrest for me, for corruption.*

Before the arrest was carried out, Els said that Vlok claimed he wanted to talk to him first. Els said that he got the impression that if he assisted Vlok with his case against me, he would not be arrested:

> *I then asked why they were not also investigating the theft and fraud against Diamond as, from what I have seen, I was of the opinion that the state had a watertight case. I also said it is Diamond's modus operandi to open fake cases against people, to divert attention from himself. He then said to me that his team's mandate was to investigate Paul O'Sullivan and not Neil Diamond.*
>
> *This attitude from a member of the SAPS and or Hawks is worrying as it is clear that he is focussing on small issues and is not prepared to investigate criminal cases that were declined under very suspicious circumstances where prominent people with political connections are mentioned, although there is more than enough evidence to prosecute them. From my conversation, it is clear that he has a mandate to find anything he can and to build a criminal case against Mr Paul O'Sullivan and nobody else.*

Els said that he felt Vlok was trying to intimidate him and that the affidavit with his name on it was a set-up.

The investigator opened a case of fraud against Vlok for saying he was a Captain when he was only a warrant officer, for defeating the ends of justice in the Diamond case, for intimidation for threatening to arrest him on fake charges, as well as extortion for using the threat of arrest to try to get him to give him information on me.

In March 2017, during one of my appearances in the Kempton Park Magistrate's Court on the passport case, I was handed a summons informing me I was being charged for extortion related to my

Diamond investigation.[65] At this point, it was the sixth case I had been charged with, with the total number of charges in all six cases close to fifty. After Els' statement, the charge came as no surprise. It was just another aimless volley being thrown my way.

DAVE SHEER GUNS' CASE

Dave Sheer, the original owner of Dave Sheer Guns, a leading distributor of firearms in the country, had sold the business and was no longer involved in it. In 2014, I investigated several allegations of criminal activity against the staff of Dave Sheer Guns. According to the statements made by key witnesses, the scale of the corruption that had been underway at the firearm trader was astonishing. One of the numerous police officers named in the case for allegedly accepting bribes to secure gun licences was the Head of the Central Firearms Registry, Brigadier Miriam Mangwani. According to an employee of the shop, Mangwani had received cash payments of between R5 000 and R10 000 twice a month for four years.

I leaked my investigation to the media, and journalist Angelique Serrao wrote numerous articles about the case, which saw the Brigadier being fired.[66,67] One of the main cases we investigated alongside the military police was the theft of more than two hundred thousand rounds of military ammunition from the Doornkop Battalion in Johannesburg and the subsequent resale of the stolen ammunition, which was valued at between R400 000 and R1-million. According to witnesses we tracked down, the ammunition was allegedly sold to Dave Sheer Guns.

---

65 News24, Hawks hits O'Sullivan with sixth charge, PoliticsWeb, 8 March 2017, https://www.politicsweb.co.za/news-and-analysis/hawks-hit-paul-osullivan-with-sixth-charge

66 Angelique Serrao, Dave Sheer Guns staff sue Ministers, The Star, 14 May 2015, https://www.security.co.za/news/27720

67 Angelique Serrao, Top cop axed over gun saga, The Star, 7 April 2014, https://www.iol.co.za/news/top-cop-axed-over-gun-saga-1672115

The investigation led to the arrest of five people in relation to the case: Gareth de Nysschen and Efthimios Demis Karamitsos, a director and manager at Dave Sheer Guns, as well as soldiers Teboho Peter Motaung and Diphang John Motloung, and Motloung's son, Thabang.

The case was complicated by the fact that the numerous crooked police officers who had been on the take repeatedly tried to interfere with the case to stop it from going ahead. The two accused from Dave Sheer Guns, de Nysschen and Karamitsos, also hired expensive legal teams that went all out to have the case collapsed. Both myself and the investigating officers from the military police received numerous threats because of our work on the case. At one point, the accused even attempted to sue the State Prosecutor overseeing the case, the ministers of defence and police, as well as the National Police Commissioner (which was Phiyega at the time) for wrongful arrest. But the team from the military police were strong, ethical police officers who would not be swayed from the case – which is still ongoing in the Krugersdorp Regional court six years later.

Stella Ngwenya, the investigating officer (and a master warrant officer at the South African National Defence Force Military Division, Western Military Police, Special Investigations Branch), was naturally outraged when, in September 2016, she received a phone call from Vlok threatening her with arrest over the case. In a sworn statement she would subsequently make against Vlok, Ngwenya stated that she had been assisted by myself and Marriott in the case, which included locating witnesses and gathering evidence in the form of sworn statements:

> *The Military Police did not pay them for their assistance which was rendered on a voluntary basis as part of their civic duty. Their assistance also included assisting with the crime administration, with the provision of sworn statements and templates for the production and application of search warrants. We subsequently became aware*

of the fact that some of the suspects had police officials on their payroll, which led to some of the searches being called off, as inside information led to the suspects being tipped off.

There was a lot of outside interference in my investigations from police officials, who clearly seemed to be more interested in derailing my investigations, notwithstanding the fact that we had gathered very strong and compelling evidence against the accused.

Ngwenya said that Vlok told her that he reported directly to General Mokotedi, the Gauteng Hawks' head. He then told her that I had made a sworn statement against her claiming that, together, we had created fake search warrants and arrest warrants for use in her case. Vlok also told her that he had a warrant for her arrest and that he would arrest her if she didn't give him a sworn statement implicating me in creating these fake search and arrest warrants. Ngwenya said:

He made it clear that O'Sullivan was the target, and I would not be arrested or prosecuted if I did what he wanted.

She told Vlok she could not say something that was not true because I had not created any fake warrants, and she had not used any fake warrants:

I am aware that this is the same accusation that some of the suspects have alleged in the hope of avoiding trial. It was Kim Marriott of O'Sullivan's offices who prepared the templates for the case. These were printed and given to me, and, to the best of my memory, the necessary completion of the documentation took place in the Magistrate's Court of Protea in Soweto. Such process was handled only by the military police with no process of either Marriott or O'Sullivan ... I would never use fake warrants for any purpose, and the allegation is absurd.

Vlok has concocted this story for his own ends. I can only assume he is part of the plot to derail the case involving the theft of military ammunition, which is a very serious case.

During the conversation, Ngwenya said that Vlok made numerous allegations against me relating to the Dave Sheer case, one being that I had *forced* one of the main witnesses in the case to make his statement. Ngwenya told Vlok this was rubbish. She said that she was present at the meeting with her colleagues when the witness was interviewed and that the whole meeting was recorded:

> *Vlok told me he had the video of the witness interview from O'Sullivan. I told him this was not possible because O'Sullivan had never been given a copy of the video. I told him the sworn statement of the witness was commissioned by Captain Mpondo. Vlok said he knew this, as he had the sworn statement from O'Sullivan's computer and that I should not deny it as he was finished with the investigation. He said that if I didn't cooperate, he would have to arrest me.*

Vlok told Ngwenya that he found the warrants of arrest on my laptop:

> *Vlok then again said that if I helped him, I would not be arrested. But if I did not give him a statement to implicate O'Sullivan, I would be arrested. He raised his voice at me. He was clearly not holding himself together. I repeatedly asked him to set up a meeting, as it was unprofessional to discuss these things over the phone, but he kept bombarding me with questions.*
>
> *I wish to repeat, for the avoidance of doubt, that I am 100% certain that Vlok mentioned several times that the source of the so-called evidence against me comprised documents he repeatedly stated he had taken from Paul O'Sullivan's computer, as well as a sworn statement from Paul O'Sullivan.*

Ngwenya said it was clear to her that Vlok's conduct could derail the entire stolen ammunition trial, which would see the accused getting away with their crimes:

> *It is for this reason that Vlok needs to be held accountable for his interference in a case that has nothing to do with him. I therefore*

request an urgent investigation into the unlawful conduct of Vlok, which amounts to:

Fraud, in that he unlawfully and intentionally misrepresented that O'Sullivan had made a sworn statement against me when he knew that not to be true.

Extortion in that he said he had an arrest warrant and would arrest me unless I gave false evidence against O'Sullivan.

Defeating the ends of justice in that his conduct is meant to interfere with the above-mentioned case, which is a serious case indeed.

In his haste to threaten Ngwenya, Vlok made a serious error – he finally, and openly, admitted to having a copy of the contents of my computer. He told Ngwenya that I had given it to him, but of course, this was a lie. He had obtained it during the illegal raid on my office, ignoring a court order that stated any mirror images of it must be destroyed. Instead, he had harvested the contents of my computer and was working through the documents – which included old cases I had worked on – and then contacting and threatening honest people to turn against me. He also turned to a bunch of criminals facing charges such as fraud, theft, forgery and child abuse, whose details he found on my computer. In this latter search, he found many willing accomplices. For these criminals, it was payback time.

CHAPTER 13

EXPOSING THE TATTOO AND BANGLE BRIGADE

MIKE BOLHUIS (Convicted Fraudster)

Illegally downloading the contents of my computer, against the clear instructions of a court order, and using my old investigation cases to try to dig up dirt on me indicated that Vlok was as unethical as they come. But he wasn't done yet. I received information that proved Vlok was bringing low-life private investigators, convicted of fraud, into the fray. He was giving these men private information about me and my clients, which was both immoral and illegal. It was nothing more than a desperate attempt to find evidence against me, and he was failing miserably.

The first report-back I received was from Frederick Daniel, a businessman from the Cradle of Life in Mpumalanga. I worked with Daniel in late 2013 to help him investigate and expose corruption in land restitution activities in former Badplaas, which had led to economic decline in the region. Land was being sold at inflated prices; most commercial farming activities in the region had been abandoned, and farms were falling fallow.

In a sworn statement, Daniel said he was called by private investigator Mike Bolhuis to help Bolhius sort out a financial matter for a businessman they both knew. Bolhuis was the investigator who had tweeted information about my arrest before I had even been handed my arrest forms, so I suspected he had somehow been involved with the Hawks, and more particularly with Vlok.

Fred Daniel met Bolhuis at his smallholding in Pretoria, and Bolhuis started asking Daniel questions about the land restitution damages case that Daniel was involved with. In his statement, Daniel said Bolhuis boasted that he was considered the country's top forensic investigator, that he had thirty years' experience, that he had the best conviction rate, and that he got things done. He also told Daniel that he was well connected and knew all the right people in authority. There was also further evidence of Vlok being in possession of – and having shared – the contents of my computer:

> *Bolhuis said he had been mandated by the Hawks to investigate O'Sullivan. He said his main thrust of the investigation is his overcharging clients and that he wants my help to nail O'Sullivan. He offered me an inducement, saying both he and the Hawks will recover all the fees I had already paid to Paul O'Sullivan and Associates.*
>
> *Bolhuis made it clear that he already knew O'Sullivan had carried out forensic work for me. He said I was wasting my time with O'Sullivan because O'Sullivan was under a cloud and under investigation by the Hawks. He warned me that all my matters will go nowhere because the authorities did not take O'Sullivan seriously, and because O'Sullivan was involved, my matters would only suffer.*

Bolhuis then suggested that Daniel should appoint him instead:

> *He wanted me to give him all O'Sullivan's invoices with a sworn statement that O'Sullivan had overcharged for the services rendered. In exchange, he would take over all O'Sullivan's work on a contingency basis, and because he had the right contacts and was the best in the country, he would guarantee immediate results, especially if*

> *O'Sullivan was out of the way. If I did what he wanted, Bolhuis said he would protect me from O'Sullivan in case there was a backlash.*

Daniel told Bolhuis that he was not prepared to run around trying to nail me. He felt that we should be fighting corruption together, not destroying those making a difference:

> *There is no doubt in my mind that O'Sullivan has made a difference in exposing corruption in South Africa, not just on the corrupt land claims in Mpumalanga, but generally in the country and in the police and other state institutions. I have ignored further attempts by Bolhuis to contact me.*

The incriminating evidence against Vlok was mounting as the months went past. Teaming up with a convicted fraudster like Bolhuis and getting Bolhuis to go after my clients, was further evidence of his criminal possession of my computer hard drive, in breach of a high Court order.

LANCE EPSTEIN

In September 2016, Sarah-Jane Trent was having a meal at the Turn n Tender in Parktown when she bumped into a man she had met a few times before, private investigator Lance Epstein. Epstein fitted the tattoo and bangle brigade stereotype perfectly. He also looked like he belonged to a biker's gang. He inquired as to whether Trent was still carrying out work for me, to which she replied that she was. In her sworn statement, Trent said:

> *He told me O'Sullivan was in big trouble, he didn't know what was coming his way, and it was very serious.*

Epstein told her he sat with the investigating officer 'Kobus' Vlok "most days" and that the General and Vlok had said that if she wanted to meet with them, he (Epstein) could set it up. Epstein told her that

I would make her my fall guy and that she must not put her name on anything related to me:

> *Epstein reiterated that I must be very careful and look for someone else to work for. He even went so far as to offer his assistance to introduce me to law firms for jobs.*

She said Epstein mentioned specific criminal cases pending against me. One was a harassment case that I was working on involving a divorced woman and businessman, Douglas Fliess. It was apparent to Trent that Fliess had employed Epstein to assist Fliess on his matters. Epstein stated that Fliess "had big stuff" on me. Epstein also named Alice Johnston, saying he knew her well, as well as Cora van der Merwe.

The next person to come forward was a complete surprise – someone completely unrelated to me and whom I barely knew – but would be dragged into what was becoming Vlok's increasingly bizarre behaviour.

PETRUS VILJOEN

Petrus 'Peet' Viljoen, a disbarred attorney, the accused in a Johannesburg Central case involving the alleged illegal sale of state property, contacted me towards the end of 2016. While what he told me was bizarre, it also confirmed what others had told me – that the Hawks had made me 'a special project', with Vlok and others solely devoted to investigating me. With all the crime rampant in South Africa, the idea that so many resources were being used to try to take down one innocent man was mind-boggling. It was also further proof that the criminal justice system in South Africa was being run by criminals. The fact they brought Viljoen into the whole debacle proved just how desperate they were getting.

In a sworn statement, Viljoen said he was contacted in September or October of 2016 by Bolhuis to meet 'a certain Colonel Kobus Vlok'.

Viljoen said he had known Bolhuis for many years after Bolhuis had threatened one of his clients. He said he later discovered that the 'Colonel' was, in fact, a warrant officer.

Bolhuis told Viljoen that Vlok wanted to meet him because some of the cases Viljoen had opened in 2013 or 2014 had either not been thoroughly investigated or had been unlawfully closed. These cases included alleged charges against senior police officials and other prominent persons related to unlawful dealings in state-owned property:

> *In the meeting, Vlok had documents with him, and Vlok made it clear he had been investigating the matters, and he declared I had been set up ... Vlok tried to convince me that Paul O'Sullivan had taken control of the Hawks, he included Shadrack Sibiya in O'Sullivan's control of the Hawks. He then said a "project" was being registered against Paul O'Sullivan.*

I had met Viljoen briefly in 2013 or 2014 when he gave me information on one of the cases he was working on. We had no further contact since then. His version of the truth was that he had been set up. The State's version was that he had been involved in serious crimes. I did not have any inkling about the cases and could not say which version was true.

Viljoen said Vlok had called him again and said he was busy with an urgent application by me. Vlok said I was causing chaos in the Hawks with all my allegations and that this would lead to further problems for them:

> *One evening, probably around mid-November 2016, Vlok called me to tell me that he had just come from the Minister of Police and that the Minister had authorised a project along the lines of what I mentioned above and that the "project" would specifically target Paul O'Sullivan and others involved with O'Sullivan.*

Vlok told Viljoen that he believed Viljoen's cases would lead to me because his cases primarily implicated a businessman linked to me.

I had started out investigating this businessman many years before when it was alleged that he was involved with shady deals. Vlok was trying to use this to bring something against me by claiming that we were involved in criminal activities together. After investigation, I realised that, although the businessman in questions occasionally sailed close to the wind, he had since cleaned up his act and was certainly not involved in anything of a criminal nature. He had since become a friend, and I did occasional work for some of his companies.

In an attempt to draw Viljoen in, Vlok told Viljoen that after looking at all his cases, his criminal case involving the Johannesburg Property Company would be withdrawn. Vlok said that a letter had been written to the prosecutor (Advocate Dries van Rensburg) by the Attorney General to halt the prosecution against Viljoen. Vlok then told Viljoen that he was about to arrest Chad Thomas, another private investigator, for impersonating a police officer. In my opinion, Thomas ticked all the boxes on both the tattoo-and-bangle-brigade and the Dunning-Kruger tests. Vlok allegedly went out in public saying that he was investigating Chad Thomas as a fake member of the Hawks. Vlok said he would arrest Thomas to get him to give evidence against me.

Viljoen said he had helped set up a meeting with Thomas and Vlok and that Thomas had told them he had been "investigating O'Sullivan for some time". With Mokotedi, Vlok, and now a questionable P.I. like Thomas, there was a prial of idiots on my back. The only way was up. In his statement, Viljoen said:

> *Thomas also said that George Darmonovich* was working for Paul O'Sullivan. Thomas also alleged that Paul O'Sullivan is a spy for the UK, and he, Thomas, would adduce evidence to that effect eventually. Whilst at this meeting, Vlok telephoned General Mokotedi, and I heard him say he needed to have an urgent meeting with all the role players working on Paul O'Sullivan... It was agreed there would be a meeting soon, and in the meantime, everyone should keep secret*

> *about it all. Vlok said the police could not go to the papers and discredit Paul O'Sullivan. After offering to do so, it was agreed at this meeting that Chad Thomas would use his connections in the media to discredit Paul O'Sullivan. I should also mention that, at this meeting, Thomas made it clear he was best friends with General Mokotedi.*

(Gorgija (George) Darmanovich left South Africa in 2015 for his native Serbia after being accused of being an information pedlar and selling fake information to both sides of the fence. While he often supplied me with information I hadn't asked for, I always treated his information with circumspect. He was a friendly guy, and I liked him, but was not convinced that he would keep our discussions confidential. In May 2018, a month before his fifty-eighth birthday, George was shot twice in the back of the head in Belgrade by a pillion passenger on a motorbike in what was clearly an assassination. Although media speculation was rife as to why he had been killed, the truth behind the hit is still unknown.)

According to Viljoen, there was a subsequent meeting with Major General Prince Mokotedi, Chad Thomas, Glenda Paul, Mike Bolhuis, Hugo Wolmorans and Lance Epstein. Everyone present, barring the police officers, were involved in private investigations.

Viljoen said:

> *Vlok reported to the whole meeting that I was to be his star witness against O'Sullivan and others (involved with O'Sullivan) and that a letter had been issued stopping the prosecution against me. I took this to mean that there was a quid pro quo in so far as I would help them with O'Sullivan matters, and the cases against me were already gone. The generals present were clearly in agreement with this.*
>
> *I should mention that by this stage, it was clear to me the only purpose of the meeting was to seek possible ways of taking down Paul O'Sullivan. I can honestly say that I have never seen such desperation as I saw that day to target and nail one person. It is for this reason that I have reflected on it and have decided to come forward.*

> *The other reason I have decided to come forward is that I was promised the charges against me had been dropped and that a letter to that effect had been issued. It was only when I demanded a copy of that letter, it became apparent to me that, because I had not offered to give tangible evidence against Paul O'Sullivan and did not offer to give false testimony against Paul O'Sullivan, that I was no longer needed in this 'special project' and it became apparent to me that the promises made to me, about the charges being withdrawn may in fact be false, and therefore amount to an offence of fraud, in that the promise was made in order to subsequently induce me to make false criminal allegations about O'Sullivan.*

Viljoen, Thomas and Bolhuis then had a disagreement about Viljoen being present at the meeting, after which Viljoen left. Viljoen went and opened a case with IPID against all the people involved – and Vlok in particular – for two offences, one being fraud (that an unlawful and intentional misrepresentation was made to him that the charges against him had been withdrawn), and the other being defeating the ends of justice (because attempts were made to induce him to become part of a "special project" aimed at adducing false evidence against me).

THE MEDIA FALLOUT

The Citizen newspaper reported on Viljoen's statement, revealing that this "special project" against me was being orchestrated by the Hawks and several private investigators.[68] Thomas told the paper that seven private investigators had arranged to meet with Mokotedi and other police officers but that the meeting never took place because of the lack of cooperation between the SAPS, the Hawks, and the private investigators. Apparently, a standing order had been issued to

68 Amanda Watson, Fresh accusations fly between O'Sullivan, Hawks and private investigators, The Citizen, 6 February 2017, https://citizen.co.za/news/south-africa/1418379/fresh-accusations-fly-osullivan-hawks-private-investigators/

all police stations stating that the SAPS did not have to cooperate with private investigators.

Thomas denied Viljoen's allegations. He said the standing order had been issued because of my *"actions against senior police officials"*, which resulted in collective punishment against all private investigators. He said he had registered a *crimen injuria* case against Viljoen. Mokotedi dishonestly confirmed Thomas' version of the meeting. Mokotedi also disputed Viljoen's claim that a promise was made to have the charges against him dropped by saying:

> *In the legal process there is no way investigators can of their own offer that kind of a deal. Actually, it shows why he is a former lawyer. It's not possible. I don't even know what charges are against him.*

The birds of a feather were clearly flocking together. I didn't buy their excuses. Viljoen may have had a chequered reputation, but everything he said about the meetings checked out. He mentioned a special project that Vlok had told other people about. He also mentioned the same private investigators who made contact with other people I had worked with. He additionally had physical proof to back up his claims. Aside from showing me WhatsApp messages that Vlok and Epstein had sent him, he also supplied me with six telephone call tape recordings that corroborated his version of events.

RACKETEERING, DEFEATING THE ENDS OF JUSTICE, AND CONTEMPT OF COURT

I now had enough evidence to open cases against everyone involved in this so-called 'special project'. I opened a case of racketeering and defeating the ends of justice with everyone mentioned in Viljoen's statement to IPID. This followed another docket I opened at Johannesburg Central Police Station for contempt of court, fraud and defeating the ends of justice. In that docket, I described how Vlok had fraudulently obtained the search warrant for my office and how he used it to go on a fishing expedition when raiding my offices. He removed two of my personal computers, two cellular phones, and about a dozen memory sticks. Despite a court order interdicting the police from having access to mirror images of these seized items, Vlok imaged my items and kept these for his own crooked use. Vlok then bragged to his colleagues that he had made two copies of everything and that I would never be able to prove this.

In my statement, I said:

> *However, it is now clear to me, when considering the multiple trumped-up charges that were emanating from Vlok and Mokotedi, that Vlok does indeed have access to my private and confidential information in breach of and in contempt of the final order granted by the High Court in Johannesburg. Initially, I thought I could only prove this on the balance of probabilities. However, I am now certain that I can prove 'beyond reasonable doubt' that Vlok is now guilty of the above serious offences.*

I also noted that in November of 2015, Vlok was seen at Langlaagte Police Station, bragging that he was busy with an investigation aimed at "bringing down Paul O'Sullivan". He was also seen printing documents from his unlawful copy of my computer.

I laid out the information supplied to me by Warrant Officer Coetzee and Warrant Officer Ngwenya that Vlok contacted them directly, threatening them with arrest if they did not incriminate me. I also mentioned that Coetzee had stated that he was in possession of Kim Marriott's downloaded computer files. Vlok knew this to be a lie, but Coetzee's statement was necessary to conceal the true origin of the documents that he dishonestly tried to use to implicate me and others in criminal conduct:

> *It is beyond reasonable doubt that Vlok has unlawfully, intentionally and in contempt of two court orders been using 'the fruit of a poisoned tree' to acquire any 'incriminating' evidence against me from people who have been inter alia, a client, police officer or employee, or even a criminal suspect in cases I have worked on. I further submit that*

> *Vlok admits he is in possession of my computer, and the information and contacts of the people he has been using can only have come from information on my computer.*

Vlok unlawfully, intentionally, and in contempt of court, accessed data on my computer. He unlawfully reviewed this data and cherry-picked what he thought might help him. Vlok contacted people he had identified from his unlawful copy of my computer, with a view to getting them to supply (false) incriminating statements against me. In my statement, I noted that he blatantly lied to two police officials. The only lie not told to Ngwenya was that Vlok found the documents he referred to on my computer.

Where the people Vlok unlawfully contacted (even using third parties to attempt to conceal his hand in the matter) were honest, he found unwilling participants in his criminal scheme. I also noted that Vlok unlawfully and intentionally threatened and intimidated these honest people with arrest if they did not assist him with incriminating evidence against me, but that he had hit a brick wall when these police officials were not prepared to lie for him. They were, however, prepared to expose him.

Where the persons contacted were criminal suspects in historical cases of mine, Vlok's criminal conduct found fertile ground. He persuaded these people to fabricate cases against me, and they became willing participants.

Vlok was also in breach of the South African Police Service Act for the unauthorised disclosure of information. He had, without the authority of the State, employed the services of private investigators. He contacted and informed various people, including clients and suspects in cases I have investigated, that he was assisting the Hawks with their investigations on me. In calling upon these low-life private investigators, Vlok scraped the proverbial bottom of the barrel.

Mike Bolhuis was himself a convicted fraudster and had even admitted providing false evidence to prove that former Springbok rugby legend, Joost van der Westhuizen had not cheated on his wife and snorted cocaine. The evidence was later discredited, and Bolhuis was forced to admit that he fabricated it. Such was the desperation of Mokotedi and Vlok to feed the demands of Ntlemeza and Phahlane that they even consorted with criminals on parole and tried to set a trap to catch me with illegally obtained bank records. However, when the career criminal phoned me to tell me he wanted to drop off the records, I smelt a rat – and a trap – and I told him I wasn't interested.

I indicated that Bolhuis had been convicted and sentenced on two criminal charges and arrested on two further criminal charges between 1997 and 2008. He was convicted of fraud in 2000 and sentenced to three years in prison, suspended for five years. He was also convicted in 2006 for running an unregistered security company and fined R2 000.

Mike Bolhuis was in possession of inside information about my unlawful arrest and detention before anyone else in the outside world, proving that Bolhuis had an inside source – Vlok. I said in my statement:

It is apparent that Vlok has a personal interest in seeing me silenced, as I have publicly exposed his criminal conduct, and what started off as a dishonest crusade on his part, for Moonoo, has become more personal for him, and he has clearly stepped over the line and become an out and out criminal, that abuses his position to frame me on fake and trumped-up charges. Vlok has been on a fishing expedition as far back as January 2015, utilising the data he unlawfully copied and retained, and that accordingly, he is guilty of fraud, contempt of court and defeating the ends of justice.

I had caught them out. Their grand plans and their dirty scheming had been exposed, and they knew it. My fight for truth was winning, and the tide was finally turning against the Mokotedi team, and they knew it. Their crooked plans were starting to fall apart, and they could smell jail time.

CHAPTER 14

VLOK SINKS LOWER

VLOK VICTIMISES THE VICTIM

I didn't think it was possible for Vlok to lower himself any further, but I would soon discover that he was so determined to nail me that he would resort to threatening an already abused woman with arrest and the removal of her young child.

I had been helping Lynn Fliess, pro bono, to obtain a protection order against her ex-husband, Douglas Fliess. Lynn claimed she had been suffering from twenty years of systematic abuse, intimidation, and assault at the hands of her ex-husband. Douglas Fliess was a wealthy businessman who appeared to use his wealth and power to intimidate his ex-wife.

Lynn was a mother to three daughters, the two eldest in their twenties and the youngest, a small child of five. She had become divorced from her ex-husband many years earlier as part of an alleged cover-and-hide-assets process and was in the process of leaving their former family home. The settlement agreement had not been finalised because, according to Lynn, the 'divorce' was a tax-divorce because her husband had concealed assets in her name to avoid SARS taking him down. They continued living together for years after the divorce.

During a particularly heated argument, Lynn had him agree to hand his firearms to her because she had a real fear that he would shoot her or the children. She placed the weapons in her safety deposit box at a bank. Under my advice, she later placed the firearms in safekeeping with a registered firearms dealer. I had drawn up a detailed criminal docket for her and her daughters, and, with my help, she successfully obtained an undertaking that Douglas Fliess would refrain from contacting or coming near her or her daughters. She also requested that Douglas be investigated for child and domestic abuse.

It had been a long and arduous journey for Lynn to separate from her husband, so one can only imagine her confusion when, in August of 2016, Douglas Fliess posted on Facebook that Lynn had no idea of the trouble coming her way, both in civil proceedings and criminal charges being laid against her:

> *It's hurting me not to see my kids but I vowed to leave no stone unturned in this quest. I will make sure Lynn faces the wrath of a competent court, even her attorney said she is psychologically damaged. Karma is a bitch ... I'm ready to go the distance on this one. Lynn will rue the day she met O'Sullivan and took me on.*

It turned out that Warrant Officer Vlok was back in the picture, this time to avenge the 'poor' father. Vlok had unlawfully become the investigating officer in a false complaint laid by Douglas Fliess over his removed firearms. Vlok was hoping that I had the firearms in my possession so that he could charge me for keeping firearms for which I did not have a licence. I would never be that stupid. Even after learning that I didn't have them, Vlok continued with his pursuit and went to remove the weapons Lynn had placed in safekeeping with the firearms dealer. Douglas Fliess also hired the private investigator, Lance Epstein, to assist him – the same private investigator who told Sarah-Jane Trent that he sat with the General and Vlok "most days".

When Lynn learned that Vlok had taken the firearms, she called her attorneys, Wandi Steyn and Beverley Clark from Clark's Attorneys, who were helping her with the legal case against her ex-husband, to ask them what was happening. They contacted Vlok to ask him what he was doing. Vlok told them that Lynn would soon be arrested.

One can only imagine the stress and confusion this caused. Not only had Lynn managed to escape years of alleged abuse, but she had now been stalked and intimidated and was in constant fear that her ex-husband might kill her and her children.

Lynn's attorneys arranged to meet with Vlok to discuss the charges Lynn was purportedly facing.

VLOK USES A CHILD TO EXTORT LYNN FLIESS

I was later given a transcript of the meeting, and I heard from Vlok's own lips how he had once again threatened an innocent person with arrest, just to get to me. He began the meeting by defaming me, telling Lynn's attorneys that I was a spy, that I was helping Lynn because I wanted money, and that I had taken her divorce settlement payout.

In the recording, Beverley Clark listened to him and then interrupted, asking how Lynn was involved in any of his investigations around me. Vlok told her that Lynn was facing a "bigger problem" and that she would be arrested for racketeering along with me, Sarah-Jane Trent and Kim Marriott. Vlok claimed Lynn was facing these charges because she had used my services, and that she would go to jail with no option of bail and that she would lose her child.

The attorneys were confused. What exactly could a woman attempting to get an interdict against her allegedly abusive ex-husband have done to suddenly face racketeering charges?

Vlok said something about me taking money from Lynn and that this would show that we were exchanging money – which was somehow "racketeering". Even for Vlok, it was a completely illogical statement.

Vlok then went on to say Lynn was facing a firearms-related charge because she removed Douglas' firearms and that she was not allowed to touch another person's firearms. Clark interrupted him at this point and said, "But she did it to be safe."

Vlok's responded by saying, "We can arrest her."

Clark said she felt that Vlok might be using the firearms charge for some other reason, reminding him that Lynn had taken the weapons to put them in safekeeping. It made no sense that she should be facing a criminal charge over the matter.

Vlok went on to say that it was not right that the child was being kept from her father.

Vlok then tried to convince the attorneys that they should negotiate an agreement between the divorced couple so that Douglas Fliess could see his daughter. Vlok promised that if that happened, he would arrange to withdraw the firearm charges and Lynn would not be arrested and detained without bail.

Clark indicated that she knew that family law was not Vlok's expertise and reminded him that Lynn believed the father to be a psychopath and that it could potentially be very dangerous for their daughter to see him. She then explained that a civil case was before the High Court, that the court was the upper guardian of the child, and it was for the court to decide what was in the best interest of the child and not them.

Vlok tried to explain his behaviour by saying he had a relationship with Douglas Fliess (Fliess subsequently admitted to taking Vlok on helicopter rides and entertaining him with meals at his house), that he found him to be honest, and that, if they could reach an agreement, everyone would be happy, and the charges would be dropped "because there was a child involved".

Vlok, who had no idea that he was being recorded, said it would be good if Lynn were kept out of the racketeering charges because "it would make Douglas smile if she was charged". Again, proof of the Dunning-Kruger effect at work.

Even after all my years of investigating criminals, Vlok's behaviour left me astonished. How was it possible for a police officer to stoop so low as to target an abused woman, threaten to arrest her and remove her minor child, and then place the child with her dangerous father, just so that he could pin a false case on me that he hoped would stick? In my mind, his behaviour was grotesque.

The attorneys subsequently wrote to Vlok:

> *Your conduct amounts to extortion and intimidation, and as such, we will have no further contact with you in this regard.*

Vlok later visited – and threatened – the firearms dealer who had Douglas Fliess's guns. The dealer arranged with well-known firearm's law expert, Martin Hood, to take up the cudgel. Within two days, Vlok received shots across his bows from two different law firms, telling him that his conduct was criminal. Vlok quickly ran from them with his tail between his legs.

Vlok's criminal crusade was running out of steam, and he was fast running out of options – and time.

JOINING AFRIFORUM

Vlok continued to bumble along. I knew it was easier for the Hawks to target me if I worked alone. If I joined forces with a larger organisation – one whose aim of fighting corruption was like my own – I knew I would have a better chance of fighting off the baseless accusations that were being catapulted my way.

Towards the end of 2016, it was widely publicised that top prosecutor Gerrie Nel was considering leaving the NPA amid the storm surrounding Nomgcobo Jiba – and the state capture gang's dominance there – to join a new private prosecutions team that was being formed at AfriForum. The plan was to run a parallel prosecuting authority to the NPA, ensuring that cases that the NPA was ignoring (or refusing to prosecute because of political interference) would see justice done.

AfriForum is a civil rights movement based in South Africa with almost 300 000 members. Predominantly interested in protecting the rights and culture of marginalised – or disempowered – minorities, the bulk of their membership is the Afrikaans community and the farming community, although they have spread further afield in terms of whom they represent.

AfriForum had, by then, taken a strong stand against civil rights abuses. To say that my civil rights had been abused was an understatement, so we were already on common ground. I was introduced to them by an old friend, Mampela Rampela, a well-known political activist who had led the charge in the civil case launched by Freedom Under Law to review and set aside the unlawful decision to drop criminal charges of murder, fraud, and corruption against Richard Mdluli.

When I first went to AfriForum's head office in Pretoria, I was pleasantly shocked at the scale, efficiency, and professionalism of their operations. Going out of their way to do things properly and correctly, I also came to learn that they had exciting ideas of taking prosecutions private and expanding their anti-corruption scope – which was exactly what the country needed. It was clear that the State's law enforcement bodies had been completely captured, were unreliable, and steered clear of prosecuting any case that questioned the authorities in power. The only political cases that the State was pursuing were against genuine crime fighters who were questioning the brazen theft and dishonesty they were witnessing around them. The only way around this was to form a private prosecutions body to tackle the cases the state was unwillingly or politically incapable of tackling.

The truth was that I also needed access to the resources AfriForum's legal team was offering. The financial cost of fighting all these court battles was crippling me. The Selebi case had cost me more than R6-million, Krejcir more than R5-million, and so far, the tally for the cases against me by the Mokotedi team was sitting at more than R4.5-million. Without AfriForum's help, I was doubtful that I could continue the fight for much longer. Running out of money would not be good for me.

My role at AfriForum would be to advance and assist an anti-corruption unit whose aim was to expose how criminals had captured the criminal justice system. Our cooperation was announced at a media conference in Centurion where the head of the unit, Monique Taute, said they were working closely with me to eradicate corruption by focussing on worthy cases and litigating against the State to force them to comply with its responsibility to put criminals behind bars. This would be done by publicly exposing corruption and running campaigns against corruption.[69] It was a privatising of the criminal justice system, which was the only way certain cases would be properly and fairly heard without the interference of the state capture criminals. It also meant that AfriForum would be at the forefront of the battle.

"The very institutions who have been entrusted to uphold our codes of law and protect us from crime have instead been infiltrated by criminals with badges who have decided to rather form partnerships with the underworld. Now corrupt politicians can satisfy their own greed with total impunity, being held above the law. Instead of protecting South Africans, they have become the enemy of South Africans and have abandoned their oaths of office and pledges to abide by the Constitution," Taute said.

---

69 Afriforum, Afriforum's anti-corruption unit and Paul O'Sullivan unveils corrupt dealings of high-ranking state officials, 19 October 2016, https://www.stopkorrupsie.co.za/en/afriforums-anti-corruption-unit-and-paul-osullivan-unveils-corrupt-dealings-of-high-ranking-state-officials/

CEO of AfriForum, Kallie Kriel, said the formation of the unit had been necessitated by the fact that corruption had spread like cancer in Jacob Zuma's government:

> *While corrupt politicians and senior officials aren't prosecuted, state resources are used to prosecute champions in the fight against corruption on trumped-up charges, such as Paul O'Sullivan and Pravin Gordhan.*

With AfriForum as my partner, I felt confident in the fight that lay ahead. I knew the strategy of the Mokotedi team, and I knew they had nothing on me. I told Alec Hogg from *Biznews* as much when I went to London to visit my children in November that year:[70]

> *I think we've got the measure of them. They're all cowards, they're all politically corrupt, and in some cases, they're not just politically corrupt; they're corrupt in as much as they've been receiving kickbacks. We've identified them, and dockets have been opened. So, the last seven months, I haven't been sitting back, twiddling my thumbs and letting them take the upper hand. I've been fighting back, and I think we've now got the measure of them.*

I told Hogg that AfriForum planned to start out with cases where there was a lot of evidence, making them easy to prosecute. I mentioned Dudu Myeni in particular. I knew she would sink South African Airways if she wasn't stopped:

> *Here we have a woman who's closely linked to Zuma. In fact, she's the founder and chairman of the Zuma Foundation, and the Zuma Foundation itself hasn't issued accounts for the last three years. One has to wonder whether or not the Zuma Foundation's been used for money laundering. There's no ability of the man in the street to see that the Zuma Foundation is clean. So, you have this woman that set that up and runs it; she's running the national airline, South African Airways. She ditches a deal with Emirates Airline because*

70 Alec Hogg, O'Sullivan, Afriforum taking criminal prosecution private – targeting Myeni, Zuptas, Biznews, 4 November 2016, https://www.biznews.com/interviews/2016/11/04/osullivan-afriforum-myeni-zuptas

they don't make a contribution to the Zuma Foundation. Now I can't understand how the two can be linked.

She then tries to swing a deal to Quartile Capital, where the directors of Quartile Capital have, in their own personal capacity, suffered judgement against them for tax. In other words, they haven't paid their taxes, and she wants to swing a deal to them for a R6-billion deal to acquire a new Airbus, and when treasury stops her from doing that, the Minister of Finance gets fired, plunging the country into political and economic turmoil. Then we have a new finance minister appointed who lasts four days, and it later transpires that before he was appointed, the job was offered to another chap by the name of Jonas. In return, he was asked to make sure that the South African Airways route to Mumbai would be cancelled, so the Gupta Airline can get the route. When you look at all this, it's quite clear that there's low-hanging fruit there.

I knew that by making these statements publicly, Myeni would be furious. It was time I put her back in the spotlight.

I told Hogg that my arrest had been a low point in my life, that there were periods where things didn't look good, and that I was contemplating leaving the country and saying to hell with it. I explained that I realised their attacks on me had confirmed that I had been right all along, that I'm tenacious, and that I didn't get put down easily. It had also given me a good claim against the State, and these criminals would have to pay back the pension fund they had taken away from me.

With AfriForum picking up the legal work, it left me free to focus on uncovering the high-level corruption. This Irish-Afrikaans partnership was truly symbiotic in nature, especially since the Zuptas had used divisive Afrikaans racism as their way of distracting attention away from their massive corruption, with help from Gupta-paid Bell Pottinger.

Joining AfriForum gave me hope for the future. It brought me renewed energy and revived the fight in me. It was time to bring this game back onto the centre court. I would no longer be beaten down.

FORMING FORENSICS FOR JUSTICE

Sarah-Jane Trent had been by my side throughout this long battle and had become a firm fighter against injustice and wrongdoing. We decided that one way to target state capture would be through our not-for-profit organisation, Forensics for Justice, which we formed in 2015 and which I funded solely from my own pocket.

We were, however, yet to do something significant to put the organisation on the map. By 2016, I decided that Forensics for Justice should become more public. The NGO gave us a formal name under which to fight state capture. It also allowed us to fundraise to continue our good work. We registered a website and started putting the cases out there for all to see. While these criminals could still try to take me down, they could not stop me from publishing their evil deeds on the internet. I intentionally had the web server located under a mountain in an obscure part of the world – and disguised through a series of bots and routers – so that the state-sponsored thugs could not get at it. I gave strict, irrevocable instructions that nothing we exposed could be taken down, even with a South African court order. If anyone wanted to stop us from publishing their evil deeds, they would have to determine which country the server was hidden in and under which mountain.

We stated on our website that Forensics for Justice's aim was to fight public corruption and state capture:

> *We acknowledge that until this scourge has been dealt with, the South African dream, given to us by the likes of Nelson Mandela and his hero comrades, will never be realised. Some of these people made the supreme sacrifice, NOT so that greedy people could bring our country*

to its knees whilst the poorest of the poor continued to suffer. We strive to rid our beautiful country of the corruption scourge.

Forensics for Justice was now a mouthpiece that could make bold statements online and publish facts relating to the criminals we were fighting.

THE LEGAL BATTLES

Now that I had AfriForum and their team of lawyers at my side and an NGO that would carry investigations into corruption forward, it was time to take on the Mokotedi team in court.

I started off slowly. I wanted to determine whether anything could be done about the monstrous abuse of my constitutional rights. I sent a formal letter of complaint to the office of retired judge Essa Moosa, who oversaw the Hawks.

In my meeting with Judge Moosa's team, they explained that all they could do was write to the Minister of Police to explain what was happening to me. It was not enough. I knew that I had to go one step further and launch an application for an interdict in the High Court.

I launched the case in two parts. Part A involved applying for a semi-urgent interdict that would temporarily stop General Phahlane, General Prince Mokotedi, Advocate Sello Maema, Advocate Jabulani Mlotshwa, and Warrant Officer Vlok – or anyone under their authority – from supervising, conducting, or participating in any criminal investigation or prosecution against me, or from arresting me. Part B of the application would make the interdict final.

In my application, I explained that I had more than forty years of experience in investigating serious crimes, including terrorism, human trafficking, drug trafficking, arms trafficking, money laundering and other transnational organised crimes.

I mentioned my investigations into Jackie Selebi and Dudu Myeni, using these as examples of the many cases that caused me to bump heads with high-ranking political figures who believed that my investigations threatened to expose the corrupt activities of people near and dear to them:

> *It is precisely for this reason that I have been targeted by high-ranking law enforcement officials that operate within South Africa's criminal justice system but who seemingly serve these corrupt politicians rather than to the public good.*
>
> *It is these high-ranking law enforcement officials that have seemingly targeted me and are now making my life a complete misery. They have instigated a number of baseless investigations, arrested and detained me in circumstances where there was no basis for doing so, and relentlessly pursued me in various prosecutions – none of which have any justifiable foundation. I have been subjected to harassment, torture and even attempted murder – all of this done by the very people who are supposed to protect our country's citizens.*

I spoke about the charges I had opened against Mokotedi after the Selebi trial and that his subsequent interview on Radio 702 – and his statement in the press ombudsman complaint to the *Daily Maverick* – showed that he was biased towards me:

> *There is a well-published history of animosity between us. He clearly cannot act impartially when it comes to me. He has an axe to grind, and he has demonstrated this repeatedly and in the most public of forums.*

I then highlighted how Mokotedi was a fan of President Zuma and that Myeni's alleged connection to Zuma fuelled Mokotedi's antagonism to me.

I explained how the Section 26B passport charge was simply a ruse to stop me from attending a media conference in London and that its sole purpose was to arrest me and interrogate me on matters extraneous to the alleged passport offence for which I had been arrested:

> *During the trial, on what can best be described as a relatively minor statutory offence, Mokotedi and as many as eight to ten senior officers of the Hawks were hanging around the courtroom during the proceedings ... I am left wondering, with the high amounts of uncontrolled crime in South Africa, how it befits such a blatant waste of police resources whilst publicly demonstrating what they can and will do to anyone that attempts to expose the criminal conduct and corrupt activities of senior state employees in the criminal justice system.*
>
> *The mandate of the Hawks is to investigate serious crime. Clearly, since a contravention of section 26B is not a serious crime, there was something else going on. The Hawks had an ulterior purpose or motive.*

My application exposed my arrest, the subsequent torture and the interrogation I endured. I described how Mokotedi had approached me in court on one of my relaxation of bail bids and said that if I pleaded guilty and agreed to leave the country, he would let me go. And that if I didn't, he would re-arrest me as soon as I left the court. I went into all the sworn statements made against Vlok, his threats, and his extortion attempts.

My application also took a closer look at the Priority Crimes Litigation Unit (PCLU) at the NPA, which seemed to be behind almost all of what the media reported as politically motivated investigations and prosecutions in South Africa. The PCLU was meant to be for serious national and international crimes covered under what is known as The Rome Statute, which includes acts of terrorism and sabotage, high treason, and foreign military crimes. In their false charges against me, the PCLU were acting completely outside their mandate. Why on earth was the PCLU investigating me, I asked?

I pointed out that if I was suspected of committing an offence, then the investigation must take place using detectives at the police station with jurisdiction over the geographical area in question, like every other case in the country. Similarly, the decision to prosecute must be taken by the control prosecutor at the relevant jurisdictional court:

> *If this occurs, as it should, then the current unlawful conduct of the Mokotedi team and other PCLU officials who are clearly coming for me will come to an end.*

MY CONSTITUTIONAL RIGHTS

I described how the arbitrary deprivation of my freedom – and my freedom of movement – infringed on my fundamental rights enshrined in Section 12 and Section 35 of the Bill of Rights in terms of the rights of those facing arrest. I told the Court that Major General Mokotedi and other functionaries were abusing their powers:

> *Perhaps the most troubling aspect of this abuse is that its purpose is to suppress the exposure of corruption committed by persons in high office within the criminal justice system and state-owned companies. Alternatively, it is revenge for such exposure. The paradox, of course, especially where the Hawks are concerned, is that the Directorate for Priority Crimes Investigation was expressly established under Chapter 6A of the SAPS Act to combat such corruption.*

The application described the corruption I had been investigating and the extraordinary lengths that were taken to silence me:

> *Our Constitution means nothing if ordinary citizens cannot be protected, and it means even less if they cannot be protected from those who are supposed to protect them.*
>
> *I approach this court out of pure desperation. I simply do not know where else to turn. I cannot deal with each and every instance of an abuse of process by law enforcement officials on an ad hoc basis in every such instance in a separate and discrete application. I simply do not have the funds to instruct lawyers to represent me in the multiplicity of trumped-up actions that would necessarily ensue.*

What made this case unusual is that I had, during the course and in the scope of my work as a corruption-buster, opened fraud and/or corruption and/or racketeering cases against many of the respondents and others at a high level in the criminal justice system. None of those cases had ever been properly investigated. I added that this particular case was not about their corrupt or unlawful doings. Instead, it was about how, because I had exposed them, they were conflicted and thus not impartial.

> *The proper functioning of any criminal justice system depends on the lawful exercising of power by those charged with promoting, protecting and enforcing justice. The most basic principle and the very foundation of any constitutional democracy is that those vested with law enforcement and prosecutorial powers must exercise them without fear, favour or prejudice. It goes hand-in-glove with the duty that any officer in the criminal justice system has: to act impartially and fairly. The corollary is that no officer in the criminal justice system should act where his or her judgment is impaired by a conflict of interests.*
>
> *This principle has been seriously violated by the circumstances animating this application because many of the respondents can act without favour or prejudice vis-à-vis me because of the obvious conflicts of interest that they hold. They have proven this with their unlawful conduct to date.*

I told the Court that I did not seek to be immunised from criminal investigation, arrest, or prosecution if I had done wrong. I accepted that the State has the right to investigate, arrest and prosecute people suspected of criminal conduct. I accepted that I did not stand aloof on this basic principle. However, where it pertains specifically to me, the four respondents should not be permitted to be a part of any investigation, arrest, or prosecution, either directly or indirectly, because a) they were conflicted and b) in consequence of their conflict, they were unable to act without fear, favour or prejudice. The contrary was apparent – they were gunning for me to silence me, seemingly to protect themselves and other people. I was being harassed, subjected to unnecessary and humiliating arrest, and detained without good reason. I had been tortured, had attempts made on my life, and was peppered with baseless prosecutions. My welfare and life were both in danger.

It was made clear to me that this ongoing harassment would only stop if I withdrew my accusations, packed my bags, and left the country, never to return.

In my application, I argued:

> *No constitutional state can conceivably allow an ordinary citizen to be subjected to the discretionary powers of law enforcement officials who are unable to act without fear, favour or prejudice. Impartiality and rationality, as a minimum constitutional standard, is required.*
>
> *Neither the State nor the interests of justice will be prejudiced if the multiple trumped-up cases are investigated by police officers at station level, where there are many competent detectives who are capable of properly investigating cases without the input, interference or assistance of the Mokotedi team, even if the outcome may not be what the Mokotedi team desire.*

A SNIFF AT VICTORY

The Court agreed with me, and I won a partial victory in Part A of the interdict, and later Part B.

I had not quite interdicted Mokotedi, Vlok, Mlotshwa and Maema from working on my cases, but, under Part A of the application, the Court made the following order:

> *The National Director of Public Prosecutions would undertake a review of the decision to prosecute the following three cases: The passport case, the Cora van der Merwe and the Alice Johnston case.*

Needless to say, this never happened.

The judgement also ordered that the Acting Special Director of Public Prosecutions would be required to approve decisions to prosecute four other cases against me, which included the trumped-up Dave Sheer Guns and Neil Diamond cases.

In a following order that the Court issued, it reiterated the Magistrate's Court's decision that in any matter, where a decision has been made to arrest me, I must be given forty-eight hours to present myself to the relevant police station, and that I would be brought to court by way of a summons and not detained.

That was an enormous victory. The Mokotedi team would no longer be allowed to harass me as they had in early 2016. The gunpowder had been removed from their barrels, and they would have to make other plans to bring me down. Or so I thought.

As it would turn out, the orders were not worth the paper they were written on. Dirty cops would continue to arrest me and my staff. My offices would be repeatedly raided, and Shaun Abrahams, the unlawfully appointed National Director of Public Prosecutions, would refuse to comply with the order and not review the decisions to prosecute me as ordered. In fact, he would issue instructions to prosecute me on even more trumped-up charges. I decided to abandon the order and told the crooks to proceed with the trials so that I could prove that the allegations were false.

CHAPTER 15

A GOOD COP FIGHTS BACK

CRIME INTELLIGENCE

It was no secret that the infiltration of the criminal justice system had left the police's Crime Intelligence division in a complete shambles. The country's intelligence services had, for a long time, been used to score political points and to prop up organised crime syndicates. Richard Mdluli had done his worst – or his best – depending on whether or not you were a criminal.

As much as there were bad cops working in the Crime Intelligence division, there were still many good police officers. The bad cops were mostly involved in management. It seemed that their sole purpose was to follow the orders of their political masters by providing illegally obtained information on their counterparts. The good cops were those who came to me when they were looking for help in cracking a crime syndicate or thought I might be able to get them relevant information on cases they were working on. We always kept our dealings secret because if they were seen speaking to me, they would be targeted by their criminally-owned bosses.

One such highly ethical Crime Intelligence officer was Captain Candice Coetzee. Coetzee, a fifty-something female cop, was a Captain stationed at Crime Intelligence's head office since 2003. She knew her way around the criminal underworld and had plenty of 'assets' working for her. An asset is a source (usually loyal to only one person) who would provide information only to that person. I probably had more assets than anyone else in the country. While I seldom paid any of them, I always got the information I was looking for. I lost count of the times I was given information on planned crimes and passed it on before they happened, thereby giving the good cops a leg-up in the war on crime.

I had run into Coetzee a few years earlier when I was working on the Radovan Krejcir cases. She was part of the team that helped thwart his plans to murder me and her colleague Colonel Nkosana Ximba. Since then, we met a few times in the course of our investigations against Krejcir. I had also given her information in 2014 on my investigations into Moonoo, hoping that some sort of investigation would be launched against the clearly protected Head of South Africa's Detectives.

In 2016, Coetzee was targeted by her bosses for her connection with me. I had mentioned her name, along with other members of the Krejcir team, during the interrogation that had taken place during my arrest and torture. I mentioned we had shared information on the corrupt Moonoo, drawing on the first name that came into my head to try to draw Mokotedi away from the real source of my information. I believed that in doing this, I was leading him down a pointless road that would end nowhere. Little did I know that it would use this information to take aim at Coetzee and attempt to damage her career.

Even though her police record was exemplary, and the police management had no proof of any wrongdoing on her part, Coetzee was promptly suspended in May of that year. Through no fault of her own, she had become another scapegoat in an increasingly desperate game of trying to stop me. It was shocking that a police officer who put her own life on the line to ensure the arrest and jail time of a criminal kingpin like Krejcir could be treated so badly. It was also further proof that a key person behind everything that was taking place was Moonoo, using Mokotedi to do his dirty work.

When her suspension was finalised in November 2016, Coetzee wrote a letter of complaint to the office of the Inspector General of Intelligence, IPID, and the office of the Judge for the DPCI, against her bosses in the Crime Intelligence division who, in conspiracy with Mokotedi, had targeted her with no formal grounds for doing so. She said their conduct amounted to racketeering, defeating the ends of justice, and violating the Interception of Communication provision of the Communication Related Information and Monitoring Act 70 of 2002 because they had handed classified intercepted data to the DPCI (Hawks).

I later received a copy of that letter, and it was dynamite. In it, Coetzee went into her investigations of Moonoo, clearly laying out how he had surrounded himself with criminal syndicates and that it was her information on him that had ultimately led to her suspension.

COETZEE'S COMPLAINT

Coetzee said her bosses had also violated the Intelligence Act by sharing classified information with the Hawks rather than reporting the matter to Counterintelligence or the Inspector General of Intelligence:

> *I will show throughout the complaint that Moonoo has been assisting criminals for a number of years, that he has been exposed in this conduct by a certain Paul O'Sullivan and that purely because of my 'association' with O'Sullivan, I have been singled out to be silenced along with O'Sullivan and others. I will also show that attempts to have O'Sullivan murdered by Radovan Krejcir, for his own account and, at the instance of Moonoo, have been disrupted or thwarted by myself and other police officers that I have worked with over the last few years.*

In further reference to Moonoo, Coetzee stated:

> *Their conduct also amounts to corruption, maladministration and abuse of power by assisting any person who is committing a crime to continue to do so or protecting them in order to avoid investigation and/or arrest.*

Coetzee said that she had come to know me for the first time in early 2014 after the police had foiled an attempt by Krejcir to have me killed. She said it became clear to her that I had dedicated a vast amount of time and resources into dealing with the criminal syndicates around Krejcir, and I was in no small way responsible for Krejcir being brought to justice and kept there.

She described how it became her job to befriend me to get information on me:

> *It was suggested that O'Sullivan be checked out as there had been rumours during 2005 and 2010 where senior police management had complained that he was a foreign agent. Infiltration processes within the intelligence community involve befriending a person in order to gain their confidence. This was my intention whilst dealing with him on the Krejcir matters that were being investigated.*
>
> *I now also wish to state that O'Sullivan is a contact person of mine, which is exactly the same as a source (informer) but one that does not expect to the remunerated by the State. He shouldn't be regarded as just any other person; he is a source. We normally task sources and give them photos of suspects, addresses, vehicle details etc., when we request their assistance in gathering information. O'Sullivan, in this regard, has been assisting me to gather information on Moonoo, Huang and many others involved in criminal activities.*

Coetzee said that she became certain that I was not involved in any unlawful activities or engaged in any foreign intelligence activities:

> *There is no doubt in my mind that his intentions were good and that he went out of his way to assist law enforcement authorities in doing their work. I do believe that the rumoured foreign intelligence connections*

related to O'Sullivan had been planted during his investigations into the formal National Commissioner and criminals that had been associated with him. I am of the opinion that it is nothing more than a malicious campaign aimed at discrediting O'Sullivan in order that his anti-corruption activities would be undermined.

In her complaint, Coetzee laid out her evidence against Moonoo by describing the strange decisions Moonoo made on the Krejcir case while still the Head of Detectives. She described an overseas trip planned by Major General Taioe, Lieutenant Colonel Gininda and Advocate Gcaba of the NPA to meet with Jacob Nare, the Section 204 witness, who was then based in London. The team also made an application to visit Prague in the Czech Republic after the London meeting to meet with a witness I believed was important to the Krejcir cases. Moonoo denied approval for the Prague leg of the trip. His actions were deliberately detrimental to the case against Krejcir, whom I believe he was trying to protect, and a prime example of the lengths he would go to in allegedly defeating the ends of justice.

Paul O'Sullivan with Colonel (now Brigadier) Gininda in Prague in 2015

I paid for Gininda and Gcaba's trip to Prague, where I met with them and introduced them to the police there. During this time, Coetzee was in contact with an informer who told her that I would be murdered in a subsequent trip to Prague. She relayed this information to Colonel Gininda, who told her to draft an official letter addressed to me to warn me of the threat. She was then to forward the email to him, and he would sign it and send it to me from his office email address. Coetzee alerted me to the threat in an SMS, and then blind carbon copied the letter to me. Assuming it to be the final signed letter, I sent it to Prague, requesting police protection while there. The authorities there contacted Interpol and got through to Moonoo. Moonoo denied the existence of the threat and told Colonel Gininda not to send the final signed letter.

In her complaint, Coetzee stated:

> *This is evidence that Moonoo would rather see O'Sullivan murdered than see him being helped. I then learned that Moonoo had insisted that an investigation be driven against me as a result of that letter.*

Between early and mid-2015, Coetzee also picked up intelligence that Moonoo had been in contact with Krejcir through third parties, imploring him to urgently bring about my death because I was keeping a close eye on the investigations and that I had opened numerous criminal cases against Moonoo. For Moonoo to help Krejcir get off the hook, I believe he expected Krejcir to kill me, thereby getting him off the hook. Naturally, as a dead man, I would be unable to push for Moonoo to be charged with corruption.

Around the same time, the Krejcir team unexpectedly uncovered more evidence against Moonoo when a decision was taken to intercept the phones of certain persons close to Krejcir to obtain intelligence. The information at hand was that Krejcir was planning another escape from prison and would have myself, Brigadier Ximba, Lieutenant Colonel Gininda, Lieutenant Colonel Ramuhala, Coetzee, and other witnesses murdered. One of the phones marked for interception was that of Preggy Padayachee after intelligence was picked up of him bragging that he'd make sure that Krejcir got off on the charges against him.

Colonel Gininda told Coetzee he was shocked to listen to intercepts concerning discussions between Padayachee, Krejcir and Moonoo. Coetzee explained that while Moonoo's phone was never intercepted, there were allegations that Krejcir had paid a substantial amount of money to Moonoo to interfere with and possibly derail the Krejcir cases. The figure mentioned was R5-million. In a call made by Krejcir to Padayachee from prison, Krejcir demanded that, since he was still sitting in prison, Moonoo pay back the R5-million. Krejcir went on to say that if Moonoo did not pay back the money – or get him out of prison – he would have him killed.

Padayachee tried to calm Krejcir down by patching them into a conference call to Moonoo. Moonoo promised Krejcir that everything would be all right and that there was a plan to deal with the cases by neutralising witnesses. Jacob Nare's name was on that list, as was my name and those of the investigating officers.

Gininda told Coetzee about another conference call where Krejcir told Padayachee he was very upset with Moonoo because Moonoo had promised him that the investigating team would not receive approval to go to the Czech Republic to interview a certain witness, but that he had found out through his sources that the team had indeed been there. Padayachee quickly patched Moonoo into the call, who made it clear that he had not approved of the team going to the Czech Republic and that he had no idea how they were able to get approval since it should have come through his office. Moonoo had no idea that I had purchased Gininda and Gcaba's tickets and paid for their accommodation.

Coetzee said she had met with another informer who said there had been further secret discussions between Moonoo and Krejcir and that Moonoo had stated he would not be able to help Krejcir while I was still alive.

Coetzee described the atmosphere in the police at the time as being in a state of turmoil because of the infiltration by criminal syndicates. Dramat, the Head of the Hawks, had been unlawfully suspended and had subsequently resigned to be replaced by an Acting Commander, Berning Ntlemeza. Ntlemeza had suspended and then fired Major General Sibiya, the Head of the Hawks in Gauteng. In March 2015, Robert McBride, the head of IPID, was unlawfully suspended. There were rumours that the Chief of Police General Phiyega was about to be suspended. There were also rumours and media articles implicating Ntlemeza in criminal activity. There were more rumours that Ntlemeza was involved with the-then suspended Head of Crime Intelligence, Lieutenant General Mdluli. There were further links tying Moonoo to Mdluli and Mdluli to Krejcir.

In her complaint, Coetzee stated:

> *It was therefore clear to me that someone needed to take action, but who could be trusted?*

Coetzee described how, not knowing who else to turn to, she made a conscious decision to alert me to the fact that my life was in danger and that she had visited me in July 2015 to warn me that Krejcir was desperate to have me killed and that Moonoo was allegedly driving this agenda:

> *To my surprise, O'Sullivan then produced a number of files and showed me that he had been investigating Moonoo for some time and had developed a lot of strong evidence with the underworld. I persuaded him to share that with me. O'Sullivan then played me some tape recordings of one of his undercover agents speaking on the phone to a criminal named "Bhana" who had been involved in racketeering.*

> *The undercover agent was trying to lure Bhana into making an admission in respect of certain criminal activities pertaining to the liquidation of the Pamodzi and Aurora mines. It was shocking to hear Bhana saying that he was not worried about O'Sullivan, that he had already spoken to General Moonoo and he would deal with the matter.*

In that meeting, I told Coetzee that I had written to the Commissioner of Police, General Phiyega, but that Phiyega did not seem to be taking me seriously. I said I had provided strong evidence of Moonoo's alleged association with the underworld but suspected that Moonoo had some sort of control over Phiyega. Coetzee mentioned to me that she had listened to some of Padayachee's intercepted telephone calls and that it appeared he might have been in communication with Moonoo. She asked that I identify persons and suspects who were in frequent communication with Moonoo via Padayachee and others:

> *I decided it would be in the best interests of justice if I would support O'Sullivan in exposing Moonoo's shocking criminal conduct. I felt that telling O'Sullivan of the threats to his life as a result of Moonoo and Krejcir was fulfilling my obligations to his right to life. I also felt that I was a whistle-blower, in that nobody in the police wanted to step up and take action against Moonoo, as he was just too powerful.*
>
> *Furthermore, since O'Sullivan had started publicly exposing Moonoo, Moonoo had become extremely dangerous and, if he could resort to having O'Sullivan murdered, he might try and have me murdered if I lodged a formal complaint about his conduct. Regardless I have now decided that I should now expose Moonoo to scrutiny by stating what I know.*

Coetzee said she was surprised that, given my weight of evidence against Moonoo, that he had been protected for so long:

> *As part of that protection, I have now been targeted by persons that have Moonoo's back, so to speak. Clearly, their conduct is unlawful*

> *and aimed at protecting from exposing senior persons engaged in systemic corruption.*

Finally, she described how the whole Krejcir team was weary of Moonoo. Moonoo, through Colonel Botha, an officer in his team, had attempted to have Lt Colonel Freddy Ramuhala, another member of his team, arrested in court, deliberately throwing the credibility of the state's case into question.

As mentioned earlier, Moonoo later cancelled Jacob Nare's protection in the UK. Nare was flown to South Africa and put in a hotel in Sandton, where Moonoo refused to sign off for the hotel payment. This was when I stepped in and paid the bill from my own pocket. Nare was then dumped in the street outside my offices, where I took it upon myself to look after him. I later flew him back to London at my own expense, put him up in a safe house, and asked the UK government to protect him. Two years later, when the wind changed direction, I brought him back to give evidence against Krejcir and his accomplices.

MEETING MOKOTEDI

On the 8th of April 2016, Coetzee received an instruction to meet with General Mokotedi and others. This was the same week I was released following three days of torture. Coetzee was informed that the Mokotedi team was looking at charging me in terms of the Protection of Constitutional Democracy Against Terrorists and Related Activities Act, as well as charges of treason and espionage:

> *I was instructed that I had a few days in which I had to submit a statement to them ... They were looking for anything to implicate O'Sullivan and wanted me to give a Section 204 statement. In other words, they did not care if I had committed any offence – they were only interested in implicating O'Sullivan.*

A further meeting was held with the Hawks where they insisted Coetzee give them information relating to Act 70 on Moonoo's phone and Gininda's unsigned letter she had emailed me about my planned murder in Prague:

> *I question how it is that a retired General in the police is still able to have so much control over the serving officials, especially when one considers his patent criminal conduct whilst in the police.*

In the notice served on her, stating she was under a departmental investigation, Coetzee was told that the investigation was related to the letter she sent to me on the Prague death threat. The claim was that she had sent it fraudulently. The other charge she was under investigation for was related to interceptions of Moonoo's phones, which had never taken place. Coetzee said the charges were both absurd and false.

In her complaint, Coetzee described some of the criminal gangs that were propping up the police. According to one of her sources, it was Mdluli who introduced Ntlemeza to the Minister of Police as the replacement for Dramat a year before Dramat was unlawfully suspended. The instruction from Mdluli to Ntlemeza (on who should be targetted) was sent to Ntlemeza through one of Mdluli's agents with the code name 'Solly' to avoid any visible link.

When Phiyega was suspended, Phahlane was introduced to Nathi Nhleko and President Zuma as *"the right man for the job"*. Mdluli made the introduction. It must be remembered that Phahlane, the Head of Personnel in the police at the time, approved two hundred and fifty new appointments within Crime Intelligence, which included family members of both Mdluli and Phahlane, and others. Between them, these dirty cops turned the police force into a corrupt family business where making money took preference over fighting crime.

THE HUANG CONNECTION

One of the key people Moonoo was close to was Jen Chi Huang. I knew this because I had been investigating this criminal (and his daughter, who was allegedly connected to members of the Chinese mafia) for a number of years. Huang owns a company called Mpisi Group (Pty) Limited, previously known as Mpisi Trading 74 (Pty) Limited. Huang, as Coetzee said, was a convicted murderer known to be engaged in the import and distribution of counterfeit goods. Curiously, despite being convicted for murder and sentenced to twelve years in prison, Huang's criminal profile had been wiped completely clean. It is not known how this could have happened.

Moonoo's daughter, Manitha Moonoo (who since married and is now known as Manitha Naran), took up employment at her father's friend's company in December 2013. When I exposed Manitha's Chinese mafia connections, it resulted in a sleight of hand and a denial, which Coetzee confirmed:

> *In late 2014, after Paul O'Sullivan apparently questioned why Manitha Naran was employed by Huang, she no longer works there. She is currently employed by a law firm known as Chen Lin, which is in the same building, on the ground floor. It is clear that Moonoo's daughter, working for the underworld, had the potential to expose Moonoo to investigation. As Manitha Naran is an attorney, the logical step was to move her down in the same building, where she would now work for Huang's law firm, Chen & Lin Attorneys.*

Chen & Lin Attorneys' website (at the time) stated that Manitha was involved in a number of customs-related matters and was "currently involved in advising clients in matters where the disputed claim is in excess of R500-million".

The dispute in question was known to have been between Huang and SARS, involving customs and excise fraud and the import and distribution of counterfeit goods. Coetzee referred to stories in the

Daily News[71] and *Mail & Guardian*[72] that described the investigation by the Hawks and Huang's connection to President Jacob Zuma nephew Khulubuse Zuma.

Coetzee explained that Huang's efforts to avoid being arrested and charged included opening fake dockets against the SARS investigation team so that they would be distracted and their credibility would be questioned:

> *It is known that the police officials under the control of Moonoo took steps to oversee the dockets in order that SARS officials may be prosecuted. This would have been of great help to Huang, as it would effectively paralyse the investigations against him, which investigations also implicated the President's nephew, Khulubuse Zuma.*

Despite being unable to pay its taxes, Huang's company had amassed an impressive portfolio of properties, mostly warehousing and storage facilities, valued at R250-million.

In January 2015, Moonoo sent a detailed sham report to Deputy Commissioner-General Sithole. Huang had lodged a formal complaint to the Deputy Commissioner, and Moonoo was instructed to look into it. Moonoo then dispatched Colonel Botha, the same officer who was sitting in the courtroom on Moonoo's instructions, waiting for Freddy Ramuhala to make a slip-up so that Ramuhala could be arrested.

Colonel Botha visited every investigating officer on every fake case opened by Huang to move the investigations against the SARS officials along. However, the outcome that Huang sought does not appear to have been achieved since none of the SARS employees was arrested and charged.

---

71 Yogas Nair,Hawk's probe Khulubuse Zuma's pal, IOL, 20 August 2012, http://www.iol.co.za/dailynews/news/hawks-probe-khulubuse-zumas-pal-1366232

72 Sam Sole, Ex-con is Khulubuse's link to Chinese deals, Mail & Guardian, 7 January 2011, https://mg.co.za/article/2011-01-07-excon-is-khulubuses-link-to-chinese-deals/

However, under incoming SARS Commissioner Tom Moyane,[73] some of these investigations were seemingly resurrected.[74] SARS investigators were once again being targeted through a new unit formed at the tax body under the management of a man called Yegan Mundie. In 2016 I opened a criminal case against Mundie because of his links to Mpisi through his wife, Diane.[75] I discovered that Diane worked at Mpisi while Mundie was part of a team at SARS that was supposed to be investigating the company. Interestingly, Chetty Vengas, a director at Mpisi, had requested panel beating quotes to have Mundie's BMW fixed.

After opening the case at the Bedfordview Police Station, I received a call from a colonel based there who told me that, as a civilian, I was not allowed to open a corruption case against state employees and that there was insufficient evidence in the docket to open a case. It was nonsense. I immediately knew that there would be no investigation into Mundie. I sent the docket to IPID, which, by then, had McBride back in the driving seat and was operating efficiently again.

Coetzee, in her complaint, said that other steps were being taken to neutralise the cases against Huang, which were being investigated by the Hawks from 2012 to 2014 under the command of General Dramat.

As described earlier in the book, Dramat had been unlawfully suspended by Police Minister Nathi Nhleko on Christmas Eve 2014, the same day that General Ntlemeza was appointed as Acting Head in Dramat's place. All the sensitive cases being investigated by Dramat's

73 Pauli van Wyk, Scorpio: The curious case of ANC benefactor Robert Huang, a never-ending investigation and billions owed to SARS, Daily Maverick, 23 January 2018, https://www.dailymaverick.co.za/article/2018-01-23-scorpio-the-curious-case-of-anc-benefactor-robert-huang-a-never-ending-investigation-and-billions-owed-to-sars/

74 Angelique Serrao, SARS suspends last Jedi, News24, 26 February 2017, https://www.news24.com/SouthAfrica/News/sars-suspends-last-jedi-20170226

75 Angelique Serrao, Senior SARS employee involved with Zuma family linked company, News24m 16 November 2016, https://www.news24.com/SouthAfrica/News/senior-sars-employee-involved-with-zuma-family-linked-company-20161116

team were taken away from Dramat's offices and handed to Moonoo, including the cases against Huang and Khulubuse Zuma.[76]

Coetzee said, in her complaint, that there was no record of Moonoo making any declarations in respect of his association with Huang. However, in December 2014, some fifteen months prior to going on early pension, Moonoo was in China with Huang. In a Chinese media article, Moonoo was introduced as Vice President of the Mpisi Group. The article stated that "Vice-President Mr Moonoo of Mpisi and Chairman Mr Huang came to DieShiqiao International Textile City for the business investigation."[77]

Coetzee said that DieShiqiao International Textile City, located near Shanghai in China, was believed to be one of the major producers of counterfeit clothing that has been flooding the markets of the Western world:

> *Moonoo has since been closely involved and, being appointed as Vice President of Mpisi, became a regular traveller to China via Hong Kong. He is known to have made multiple trips to China via Hong Kong. Although on one occasion, it is believed he flew to China via New York.*

Coetzee said an investigation needed to take place to establish who paid for the five trips to China. Needless to say, nothing has been done to investigate these allegations of corruption.

COETZEE ON YUSUF KAJEE

Confirming what I had already discovered, Coetzee said her investigations also uncovered a relationship between Moonoo and renowned and infamous tobacco baron/smuggler Yusuf Kajee. Curiously, Kajee is also in business with the outspoken Edward Zuma,

---

76 Marianne Thamm, State Capture: keeping up with No1, hawk's boss asks for jet and more money, Daily Maverick, 10 April 2016, https://www.dailymaverick.co.za/article/2016-04-10-state-capture-keeping-up-with-no-1-hawks-boss-asks-for-a-jet-and-more-money/

77 S & C International Group, 11 December 2014, http://www.jssc.cc/html/scdt/cyxw/3777.html

one of Jacob Zuma's sons. I had been down the same path before when I emailed Phiyega in early 2015 and said:

> *Information from a reliable source indicates that Moonoo and his wife travelled Business Class to India with a stop-over in Dubai. The source implicated Kajee in paying for an upgrade from Economy to Business Class and providing a free hotel stop-over in Dubai.*

As mentioned earlier, I had exposed Moonoo's links to Kajee in my email sent to General Phiyega before she was suspended.[78] I had also attached the picture of Moonoo and Kajee at an event in Pietermaritzburg where Edward Zuma was also in attendance. Interestingly, Moonoo was also the lead investigator in the criminal investigation into the R250-million Nkandla upgrade, following Dramat's unlawful suspension.

Just like Huang, Kajee's company was also at the centre of a SARS investigation. As a result of tobacco smuggling and customs and excise duties fraud that resulted in billions of rands being lost to the fiscus, SARS set up a dedicated investigation team to establish who the main players were. It wasn't long before the spotlight was thrown onto Kajee's company, Amalgamated Tobacco Manufacturing (ATM). SARS was able to establish that ATM was involved in major tax fraud and was producing cigarettes at night after removing the counting seals from their machines so that the excise duty would not have to be paid. SARS regulations make it an offence for a cigarette manufacturer to remove the counting seals, Coetzee said.

In a raid conducted by SARS investigators in August 2014, metal shavings were found on the floor next to the machines used during the night to produce cigarettes. Criminal cases were subsequently opened against Kajee and his company. SARS also discovered that the previous company operating at the factory in Pietermaritzburg had

78 Sam Sole, Sally Evans, Selebi's nemesis target's Phiyega, Mail & Guardian, 22 January 2015, Http://mg.co.za/article/2015-01-22-Selebis-nemesis-targets-Phiyega

directors who could not be found. It was later established that the directors were fictitious and did not even exist. However, as Coetzee explained, telephone numbers for the directors could be traced back to Kajee.

In a similar modus operandi to the attack Huang made on SARS investigators – by opening up false dockets against them – Kajee's people did the same, with criminal complaints being opened against the SARS employees. The complaints were being investigated by the Hawks, and the investigation was being driven by a special team from the Pretoria Commercial Crime Unit led by Brigadier Jonker.

As the investigations against Kajee progressed, Kajee started applying pressure to have the SARS people placed under criminal investigation through the offices of his attorney Yusuf Jasat. Brigadier Jonker subsequently gave instructions to a SAPS official in Pietermaritzburg to obtain a warning statement from Kajee in respect of a matter of intimidation that had been opened against Kajee.

In an effort to avoid giving the warning statement, Kajee had his attorney allegedly intimidate the police officials. During the telephone call with the police sergeant, Kajee's attorney (Jasat) alleged that the sergeant could not investigate his client since all cases pertaining to his client could only be investigated by General Moonoo. Jasat confirmed this in writing. I understand that this required the docket to be transferred to Moonoo's office.

In her complaint, Coetzee stated that Jonker's conduct resulted in Brigadier Jonker sending him a fax querying Moonoo's involvement. This, in turn, resulted in further communication from Jasat, who launched into a vitriolic attack on Brigadier Jonker's character while also explaining why all cases related to Yusuf Kajee should only be investigated by Moonoo

Dramat had instructed Shadrack Sibiya to investigate the matter and issue his recommendations. The matter of Moonoo's alleged taking over of the Kajee cases did not materialise until after Dramat was suspended about six weeks later. It is not known what became of the dockets after Moonoo's office took them over in January 2015. Coetzee said that after linking the media stories, the sourced information concerning the trip to India, and the exchange of letters from Jasat, a proper investigation would have been warranted. It is believed that all the cases against Kajee have since fallen away.

SOLLY AND FAZEL BHANA

There have been allegations that the Bhana family have been involved in various scams, including but not limited to the liquidation of the Pamodzi mine, which ultimately resulted in the sequestration of the father-and-son team Solly & Fazel Bhana. I was involved in various aspects of the investigations into the collapse of Pamodzi and, along the way, was startled to find evidence of the Bhanas claiming protection from Moonoo against possible criminal charges.

Until the suspension of Anwa Dramat, the Hawks (from Dramat's office) were investigating alleged crimes pertaining to fraud, corruption, and money laundering in an investigation that included the Bhanas and Khulubuse Zuma:

> *During O'Sullivan's investigation, an undercover agent made a recording he had with one of the Bhana's that implicated Moonoo in providing protection from any criminal investigation.*[79]

IN SUMMARY

Coetzee's complaint showed strong evidence that Moonoo was allegedly behind her suspension in an effort to stop evidence of his criminal activity from emerging.

79 Sam Sole, Sally Evans, Selebi's nemesis target's Phiyega, Mail & Guardian, 22 January 2015, Http://mg.co.za/article/2015-01-22-Selebis-nemesis-targets-Phiyega

Coetzee's allegations implied that Moonoo:

- Was supporting Radovan Krejcir by trying to neutralise witnesses and interfering with the investigation.
- Had links with Padayachee, and payments were being channelled to Moonoo via him.
- Had an article published stating that he was the Vice President of Huang's company, Mpisi Group.
- Had made multiple trips to China on behalf of Huang while serving as a police general.
- Had arranged employment, through Huang, for his daughter Manitha Naran.
- Had arranged for diversionary cases, opened by Huang, for SARS officials to be expedited, to Huang's benefit.
- Arranged for the cases against Huang to be transferred to his office after Dramat's unlawful suspension.
- Had accepted a flight upgrade and free hotel in Dubai from Yusuf Kajee while en route to a holiday in India for himself and his wife.
- Had arranged for cases being investigated by the Hawks against Yusuf Kajee to be transferred to his own office after Dramat's unlawful suspension.
- Had assured the Bhanas that he would take care of them and then arranged for the Bhana cases to be transferred to his office after Dramat's unlawful suspension.
- Had attempted to procure the murder of O'Sullivan, using Krejcir as the tool for the job.

She went on to state:

> *It is clear that Moonoo is very dangerous. Given his obvious connections via the criminal associates with the Zuma family, it cannot be ruled out that he did not have a hand in the suspension of Dramat, Sibiya, McBride and Phiyega, for the benefit of those Zuma connections.*

> *Accordingly, it is not I who should be facing an inquiry; it is those that have brought the police into disrepute by protecting criminals like Moonoo and attacking anyone that has taken steps to stop his criminal activities. An investigation should also be undertaken into why Moonoo is being protected and I am being targeted.*

Coetzee's calls for an investigation into Moonoo again fell on deaf ears. Coetzee – a talented and honest police officer whose skill was not used during a painful period in our country, where crime continued to escalate – remained on suspension for a full year after this complaint was laid.[80,81]

In 2021, at the time of writing this book, Moonoo is still free, along with all the criminals he allegedly supported. South Africa's 2016 crime statistics revealed a steep escalation in murder and armed robbery from the year before. Armed robbery had increased 31% in the five years preceding this, and vehicle hijacking had increased by 14.7%. Had Crime Intelligence officers been allowed to focus on the jobs they were meant to do, these sharp rises in crime could have been curtailed. The situation brings home the cold reality of political interference in key institutions like the police, demonstrating the real-life consequences for everyday South Africans. The high crime rate is just one of the symptoms.

It was clear, however, that the patently fake charges that had been brought against Coetzee couldn't be sustained for long. She was reinstated a year later, one week after Ntlemeza was fired. In fact, Coetzee was even promoted and today is a Colonel in the SAPS – a well-deserved promotion for a woman who fearlessly defends our country every day.

---

80 Gareth Newham, Why SAPS needs better crime intelligence, Institute for Security Studies, 7 September 2016, https://issafrica.org/iss-today/why-saps-needs-better-crime-intelligence

81 Robyn Dixon, Year of terrible headlines sees South Africa's rate leap once again, Los Angeles Times, 29 September 2015, https://www.latimes.com/world/africa/la-fg-south-africa-murders-crime-statistics-20150929-story.html

As for Coetzee's complaint, on the 16th of March 2021, the DPCI Judge issued a 44-page report that slammed the criminal actions of the Mokotedi team and recommended they be charged for their conduct. Mokotedi was subsequently suspended and is sitting at home on full pay like many of his criminal associates before him.

CHAPTER 16

IPID BECOMES A FORCE TO BE RECKONED WITH

MCBRIDE WINS HIS BATTLE

A massive victory in the fight against the capture of the criminal justice system took place on the 6th of September 2016 – the same day the Constitutional Court ruled that the Minister of Police's decision to suspend Robert McBride was unlawful and, therefore, invalid.[82]

At the time, McBride had been suspended for a year and a half after being falsely accused of fraudulently altering a report on Anwa Dramat and Shadrack Sibiya. McBride had (rightly) found that the pair had not illegally deported a group of Zimbabweans wanted for murder in their home country. Police Minister Nathi Nhleko claimed McBride had illegally changed the report to declare the two former Hawk's heads innocent. Refusing to be put down for something he did not do, McBride – always a fighter – stood his ground and took the Minister to court to challenge the decision to suspend him. After a long battle, the highest court in the land finally ruled that McBride's suspension

82 Staff Reporter, Concourt rules in favour of Robert McBride, Mail & Guardian, 6 September 2016, https://mg.co.za/article/2016-09-06-breaking-concourt-rules-in-favour-of-robert-mcbride/

was both unlawful and unconstitutional and ruled in favour of the independence of the Police Directorate. Justice Chris Jafta said that Nathi Nhleko did not have the power to suspend McBride or take disciplinary steps against him:

> *The court emphasises the need to protect the Directorate from undue influence or political pressure by ensuring that appropriate mechanisms for accountability and oversight are in place.*

It was an enormous victory for McBride – and the country. With McBride back at the helm of IPID, the crooks who had taken over the police feared they would be held to account for their criminal actions. This was the news I'd been waiting for. By then, all the criminal justice institutions were fully captured, so this decision would start to turn the tide against the criminals at the helm of SAPS, the Directorate for Priority Crime Investigation, and the National Prosecuting Authority. The criminals had such a tight hold on the justice sector that South Africa was well on its way to becoming a police state if the rot wasn't stopped. Were it not for McBride's return, we expected the extra-judicial kidnappings and torture that were already taking place to be followed by extra-judicial killings. I was elated and knew that the wind would soon change direction. McBride was his own man and not subject to the vagaries of corrupt politicians.

PHAHLANE'S DAY OF RECKONING

When McBride arrived back at IPID's offices, he had a lot of fixing to do. In the time he had been away, the Acting Head, Israel Kgamanyane, had appeared to have lost control of the entire organisation. Case dockets were missing and staff morale was low. McBride had to get the directorate back up and running again, knowing the Police Minister was against him. State capture had already crippled the justice system, and the more time corrupt leaders and their sycophantic followers were allowed to rule unhindered, the worse the damage to the country would be.

The clock was ticking, and McBride knew it. He had to get IPID functioning – and fast. One of the first cases he decided to look into was the case I opened against Acting Police Commissioner Khomotso Phahlane. Under Kgamanyane, the case file had gathered dust. There was no doubt in my mind that the email I had sent to Phahlane with the photo of his house, asking how he had paid for it, had set up all the events that followed. The house was a sensitive subject. It was clear something untoward had taken place there, and I strongly suspected that the mansion in the luxurious Sable Hills Waterfront Estate had been built on the proceeds of a corrupt relationship with a forensics chemical supplier to SAPS.

Building a house is a popular way to launder money gained from corruption – it costs a lot of money, so you can pour millions into it. Buying a house outright leaves an easy electronic trace of the amounts paid, but when you build a house, you can pay different contractors in cash, and it isn't as easy to see how much the house cost to build or to trace where the money has come from – or gone. As a career policeman who watched criminal behaviour, it appeared that Phahlane had learnt a few tricks. He had even taken out a bond on the property to prove the construction was above board. Unfortunately for him, I had spent an even longer time working as a forensic investigator than he had as a policeman. Under close examination, his ploys to hide the money did not hold up to scrutiny – even though he tried to convince the country otherwise in the following months.

For one, the mortgage bond was far too low for a house of that size. He also paid it off far too quickly for a man who earned a salary as a state employee. Additionally, he only started drawing on the bond when the house was at roof height. I knew I was on the right track and kept the heat up.

Since opening the original docket against Phahlane in early 2016, no investigation had taken place. The appointed investigator, Dan Morema, had done nothing further with it, and that's how it would have stayed were it not for the Constitutional Court ruling in favour of McBride.

THE INVESTIGATION BEGINS

On or about the 4th of November 2016, I was contacted by Mandla Mahlangu of IPID, who wanted to meet with me to discuss the Phahlane case. I had never met him before. We met at my offices on the 7th of November 2016. I went through the case with him and explained the relevance of various components. I advised him that I felt the best way to advance the investigation would be to focus on the house and that I felt there would be evidence at the Sable Hills Homeowner's Association. We met a few days later near the Zambezi offramp on the N1 and travelled to Sable Hills. Sarah-Jane Trent and one of Mahlangu's colleagues, Temane Binang, accompanied us. I knew exactly what I was looking for, based on my January 2016 investigation, and Mahlangu knew I'd have no problem pointing out the relevant evidence.

Initially, the security at Sable Hills refused to allow us in. After Mahlangu insisted we go to the Homeowner's Association offices, we were eventually escorted to the offices. We were introduced to Chris Jooste, the Estate Manager of Sable Hills HOA. Mahlangu showed Jooste his IPID appointment card, and we explained why we were there. We were able to convince Jooste to show us the HOA house file. The file contained approved and signed architect's drawings (purportedly bearing the signatures of Phahlane and his architect), the approval notice itself, and the occupation certificate. I established that the built size of the house was 803 square metres – not far off my original estimate of 750 square metres – and that the approximate value of the house was R8.5-million. According to my docket, there was a discrepancy between the cost of building the house and the cash flowing in from the registered bond to the order of several million rands.

We asked Jooste who the contractor was, but he could not tell us. He had only started working there in 2013. I had a few ideas as to how we might establish the contractor's identity, including looking for other documentation and discussing the matter with staff who had been there from the time the house was built in 2011 and 2012. My ideas paid off, and we were able to establish the contractor's identity – a person by the name of Frederik Gerhardus Terblanche. We obtained his telephone number and called him immediately. Terblanche agreed to a meeting, so we went directly to his offices from Sable Hills.

Before leaving Sable Hills, we pointed out to Jooste that the investigation must be kept confidential and that any person breaching such confidentiality may make him or herself guilty of the serious offence of defeating the ends of justice.

Jooste later tipped Phahlane off in a phone call.

MEETING THE CONTRACTOR

We introduced ourselves to Terblanche and were shown into a room, where a table and chairs were set up. Mahlangu showed him his IPID appointment card and explained that this was an official investigation. Terblanche took one look at me and said, "I know who you are".

Trent recorded the meeting, as she did with all the meetings we have with witnesses. It was pointed out to Terblanche, as with Jooste, that he had to keep the investigation quiet. Again, this was lost upon him. We later found he had also tipped Phahlane off.

The discussion that followed revealed, unsurprisingly, that Phahlane paid for the construction of his home in cash. This was the smoking gun any investigation into money laundering was looking for. Not many people will pay large amounts of money in cash unless they are trying to hide the source of that cash. Clearly, Phahlane had a lot to hide.

The first two payments to Terblanche were for the largest amounts. Each payment was in the region of R350 000. The payments were made in banknotes, which Phahlane handed to Terblanche in plastic bags from either Checkers or Spar. Throughout the project, all the payments were made in cash. According to Terblanche, Phahlane's 'driver', Alwyn (also a dirty cop), would arrive at Phahlane's house in a black BMW and pay Terblanche from the boot of his vehicle.

The level of detail provided by Terblanche was the sort of detail one would expect from a man telling the truth. However, Terblanche had his own problems. The construction company he used to own had since gone bust, and it seemed he did not pay tax on the cash payments he received. We made it clear that we were not interested in the non-payment of his debts, just the cash receipts.

While Terblanche seemed to think the cost of the construction was only R3-million, his estimate excluded many of the finishes such as kitchen, cupboards, sanitary-ware and tiling. Terblanche said that Phahlane paid those amounts himself without going through him. This appeared to be a classic case of money laundering. These were shocking revelations but precisely what I expected to discover. I had known about it for a long time, and now we could prove it.

Terblanche initially agreed to go to his bank to obtain bank statements for his company, Terblanche Du Toit CC, saying he wanted to obtain the statements himself. He later admitted that he did not have the cash to pay the bank, so I offered to cover the costs.

I suspected that Terblanche was not being completely honest with us. I picked up negative body language from him whenever we asked certain questions pertaining to the payments. It was agreed that we should wait until the next meeting to review the bank statements to see if all the payments were indeed cash payments. I suspected there might be EFT payments from the suspect company.

On the 17th of November, in a meeting at IPID's offices, Trent called Chris Jooste. Trent had Jooste on speakerphone, and we all heard him say that Phahlane had challenged him after Terblanche had called Phahlane and made it known that IPID investigators had met with him and that they had obtained his details from Jooste. Jooste also mentioned that Phahlane had instructed him not to cooperate with the IPID investigation or hand out any information pertaining to Phahlane or his house.

As a result of this startling revelation, Mhlangu immediately telephoned Terblanche. He started by asking Terblanche when he had last called Phahlane. Terblanche admitted that he regularly called Phahlane. He also stated categorically that, despite an appointment for him to attend the IPID offices on the 18th of November at 11 a.m., he had no intention of attending the interview. Obviously, Terblanche had also been got at by Phahlane – clear evidence of the criminal offence of obstructing justice on Phahlane's part.

On the 18th of November, Mahlangu obtained a sworn statement from Jooste to the above effect. I helped Jooste to prepare the statement since I had a template on my computer. After agreeing to the wording, I emailed it to Jooste. He printed it out and signed it in front of Mhlangu.

I had no idea at the time that Phahlane would try to use this against me in an attempt to scupper the investigation in the weeks that followed. The more we closed in on him, the more he started to act like a fish out of water. He thrashed around desperately, trying to wriggle himself out of the net, closing in on him. But he was a powerful fish with the backing of the entire police force and his political masters, making him a significant foe. He also had corrupted employees of the

National Prosecuting Authority on his side. Fortunately, all Phahlane's accomplices were not too bright, and I literally ran rings around them.

Phahlane would later dishonestly claim in Parliament that he had no idea a case had been opened against him.[83] But he was caught lying in what would become a pattern when a letter came to light revealing that Kgamanyane had sent a letter to Phahlane in March of 2016 revealing the complaint I had made against him – and that IPID would be 'investigating'. Something they did not do, of course, until McBride came back to work. In any event, I had written to Phahlane on the 15th of March

2016 and told him that I had opened a corruption case against him.

KGAMANYANE SPILLS THE BEANS

While McBride was suspended, I realised that Israel Kgamanyane, the specially chosen Acting Head, had stalled the case and notified Phahlane of the investigation. I knew this because, in my original docket, I referred to my previous work as an engineer, which I had ceased doing twenty years earlier. The purpose of this reference was to show that I knew what I was talking about when it came to estimating construction costs on Phahlane's mansion. I never made any other sworn statement concerning my work as an engineer, except in this docket. Yet, when I was illegally arrested a few weeks after opening that docket, Mokotedi mentioned my work as an engineer, claiming I had lied in an affidavit and had thereby committed perjury. I later sent Mokotedi proof that my previous profession was, in fact, that of an engineer.

On the 19th of November 2016, I emailed Kgamanyane implicating him in tipping off Phahlane, which I believe was a contributing factor

83 Angelique Serrao, Did IPID inform Phahlane of probe into him in March last year? News24, 22 February 2017, http://www.news24.com/SouthAfrica/News/did-ipid-inform-phahlane-of-probe-into-him-in-march-last-year-20170222

to my next unlawful arrest a few months later:

> *I am, therefore, now under the impression, in fact, the only logical conclusion (by implication) that can be drawn is that you unlawfully and intentionally shared the Phahlane docket with Phahlane, who in turn must have discussed it with Mokotedi. Where else could Mokotedi have gotten such information from?*
>
> *I am, therefore, formally requesting an investigation against you for the offence of defeating the ends of justice by sharing the corruption docket with the suspect. When put together with my revelations with my 15 March 2016 email addressed to Phahlane and others, it is clear that your conduct led to my arrest and subsequent torture.*

I have no doubt that Kgamanyane shared my email with Phahlane because, a day later, I received a threatening SMS, which had clearly been sent to someone else but had also been copied to me. It was obvious from the SMS that whoever was behind it was threatening to kill me – and an IPID investigator.

Its atrocious grammar read as follows:

> *HALLO CHIEF. This is a warning to u. we r aware that u r workin fo a big foreign spy paul saliva who is funded by his masters. this man is in cahoot with robert. lot of junior policeman, the police comm and lot of senior policemen who r paid by him with money frm uk kindom. unfotunately u became part of them. u must stop now. we know where u stay and ur family. paul is a stupid old man. his days r numbered. we r on his heels. u must either choose to die with him. we r watchin u boy. we r about to fnish paul. we have everythin on him frm his family in uk. he is a foreiner. Robert is nt clever. tel him to leave this spy. i wil c if u r listenin. im nt goin to warn u again.*

I subsequently discovered that the SMS had also been sent to Mandla Mahlangu, who was the lead investigator into Phahlane and was intended to intimidate both Mahlangu and me. The only person who had knowledge of my involvement with Mahlangu and IPID was Terblanche. He also had Mahlangu's number from the business card

Mahlangu had given him. He had obviously shared that information with Phahlane, so the only possible and logical conclusion was that Phahlane either sent the SMS himself or procured its sending. I sent Phahlane an email on the 21st of November where I, in no uncertain terms, accused him of being behind the threats.[1]

> *I note that the SMS expresses an intention to kill me and the investigator (it says he can die with me) if he does not stop with his investigations. I understand why you want me dead, but you should not threaten senior investigators of IPID with such things. That's more likely to cause more trouble for you.*
>
> *In fact, I know you are behind it, and I will state now why I know.*
>
> *Firstly, in order to create a red-herring, you suggest that I am in cahoots with various people and include yourself in that list. You know full well I am not in cahoots with you. You know I want you in prison for the good of SA. However, you include yourself so that we will think it could not have come from you. A really unintelligent double-bluff that had failed.*
>
> *Next, you have this person, Tsholofelo Mogale, whom I have traced the cellular number to, let you use her phone to send the message, and then the phone is switched off. It's still off.*
>
> *The same message that is sent to Mandla Mahlangu is copied to me but is meant to intimidate Mandla Mahlangu of IPID.*
>
> *Your motive for the threats:*
>
> *My only association with Mandla Mahlangu is that I am helping him with an IPID docket I opened against you following intensive investigations which began last year. The docket pertains to your corrupt relationship with the owners of a supplier to SAPS Forensics Division, which you used to head, and still control. To launder the money that was paid to you in carrier bags, you used the same cash to build an 803 square metre mansion at Sable Hills Waterfront*

Estate. I know this, and now we (the "we" being myself and IPID investigators) can prove this.

I traced the builder of the house by using old-fashioned detective work and shoe leather on the floor. Mandla and a colleague were with me when I did it, as we were chasing a paper trail, and I was assisting them since I knew what you'd been up to. We then went and had a short meeting with this guy. His name is Frikkie Terblanche. Frikkie very quickly made startling admissions. He admitted he was paid in cash for the whole construction project. His discussions with us were recorded and transcribed, and this is precisely what he said.

There are a lot more admissions concerning how the house was paid for. But the above should serve to show you, you have a big problem, and you know it. Hence the threats.

Frikkie was warned not to communicate with you. I guess he was worried, and his (betrayal of you) feelings got the better of him, as last Wednesday he called you and told you what he had done, with all the detail. But he did not tell you his discussions with us were recorded, as he did not know, until last Friday afternoon when Mandla called him and told him. There is no doubt that he then called you again and told you what Mandla had said to him concerning the recording of his initial discussions, where he admitted you paid him in cash. Since Mandla had left his business card with Frikkie, with his telephone number on it and since he had my telephone number as well, he clearly supplied that information to you. In doing what he did, he broke the law, and the offence is known as defeating the ends of justice.

And what did you do? You picked up the phone last Wednesday and called the estate manager at Sable Hills Waterfront Estate. You told him, in no uncertain terms, that he was not to cooperate with the guys from IPID, and he was NOT to give anything pertaining to you or your house to IPID. That conduct makes you guilty of the same offence as Frikkie, i.e. Defeating the Ends of Justice.

> *And what did you do after Frikkie called you on Friday afternoon and told you that Mandla had called him and told him that the call with him had been recorded? You had a sleepless night Friday and Saturday. On Sunday, you asked Tsholofelo Mogale to let you use her phone, and you sent a crude message to Mandla and copied me.*
>
> *In that SMS, you tell Mandla that he can die with me or stop working with me. It can only have been you, as no one else had the knowledge that I was assisting the IPID, Mandla in particular, to obtain crucial evidence against you.*
>
> *That was a big mistake and will not only speed up your entry to prison. It will see that you get a longer time in prison.*
>
> *Of course, your criminal conduct does not just extend to the house built with cash kickbacks from a supplier to the police. There are a lot of other areas where you have been found wanting, and I have no doubt that in the fullness of time, you will face the music for all of it.*
>
> *One of these things is my unlawful arrest and torture at the hands of your accomplice, Mokotedi. I've only now joined the dots on that one ...*
>
> *I told this to Selebi 15 years ago, and I'm telling this to you now*
>
> *PREPARE YOURSELF FOR PRISON. I am sending you there.*
>
> *By copy to the Deputy President, I am requesting you to be relieved of your duties NOW.*
>
> *Don't even dream of threatening me again, or you will wake up and suffer the consequences.*

Of course, Phahlane ignored the mail. What else could he do?

THE PHAHLANE INVESTIGATION CONTINUES

IPID forged ahead with the investigation despite the threat and began to meet with potential witnesses. The first was with Phahlane's driver, Alwyn, whom Terblanche had stated delivered the cash to him from the boot of a black BMW. Sarah-Jane and I tracked him down and managed to obtain his contact details and home address.

It was clear the man was either scared or warned not to speak to us and had been coached in what to say. His answers were guarded and, while he did not give much away, he said enough for us to know that we were on the right track. Alwyn asked if it was normal for private citizens like Trent and me to accompany IPID to interviews. Mahlangu explained that I was the complainant in the case and was simply helping with the investigation. There was nothing untoward, and we had no influence over the case. We were simply helping to track down witnesses.

Alwyn confirmed that contractors were paid in cash, although he said it was in a bank bag because he would go first to the bank and withdraw the cash. He said it was between R10 000 and R20 000 each time. "It wasn't much," he said. Of course, he was lying – and those lies would see Phahlane promoting him from Warrant Officer to Captain.

Alwyn revealed that Phahlane had many meetings with Yola (Jolanta) Komodolowicz from Crimetech Laboratories since she was the interior designer for Phahlane's house. Alwyn named several restaurants around Brooklyn where they used to meet.

The conversation continued as follows:

O' SULLIVAN	*The interior design of that house itself ran into a lot of money, okay? And what you are saying is Yola arranged for all of that?*
ALWYN	*Ja.*
O'SULLIVAN	*And here's a major supplier of the police doing the interior design and the interior decorating for a house for a General in the police. It doesn't look good, does it?'*
ALWYN	*What you want to say is "conflict of interest".*

We soon discovered that Yola had acquired a fancy sound system for Phahlane, which was subsequently installed in Phahlane's home. We tracked down the shop where it was purchased – Sounds Great Audio and Electronic Equipment Sales (Pty) Ltd. An employee there explained that he assisted Yola in buying "a lot of equipment". After this, the employee was offered a sales job at Yola's company, Waste Express, which removed hazardous waste. After the Department of Environmental Affairs investigated the company and fined them for illegal dumping, Yola and her partner, Henry Deale, started Crimetech Laboratories, which did the same work as Waste Express.

The shop employee described a meeting held with Phahlane, after which he was asked to go to Sounds Great and order the same equipment Yola had purchased and have it delivered to Phahlane's house. Among the goods were a 55-inch Toshiba flat-screen TV, two or three 32 inch Samsung flat-screen TVs, and a Jamo home theatre system. The goods came to around R80 000. The money was paid to Sounds Great by way of an EFT. Although Phahlane was later able to prove he had paid the EFT, he did not pay for the installation at his mansion.

The witness (the ex Sounds Great employee) delivered the equipment to Phahlane's house and checked that it was correctly installed – all while on the payroll of a police supplier. While there, he noticed that Phahlane's carpets were the same carpets he had seen at Yola's house and was under the impression that Yola had been the interior designer at Phahlane's house.

Sounds Great confirmed that Yola had bought two sets of equipment from their Woodlands Boulevard Mall. Their system recorded an invoice for R126 900 for the first system (which was paid in cash) and R80 075 for the second set of equipment (which was paid by EFT). The employee explained that the reference on the invoice was 'Yola' since she had sourced the equipment and obtained a special discount for Phahlane.

Could this be the smoking gun we were looking for, an electronic trace of equipment bought for Phahlane from a chemical supplier to the police? It wasn't to be. In a stroke of luck (for Phahlane), it emerged that the EFT payment for the sound system was made from Phahlane's bank account. However, the employee of a police supplier had done the delivery and installation, and no payment was recorded for that. A minuscule gratification, but an act of corruption nonetheless. I knew more evidence would be found if we carried on searching and carry on searching we did.

AN INDEPENDENT OPINION

Getting back to Crimetech Laboratories' 2011 tender to supply chemicals, Aeroprint spray canisters, and fingerprint brushes to the SAPS, and the substandard products that were subsequently delivered, I sent an LCRC Operational Management Report and Moonsamy's photographic proof of the expired chemicals to South Africa's foremost forensic scientist, Dr David Klatzow. I wanted an independent analysis of the effect on the justice system if the police were given expired chemicals for use in crime investigation.

In his report, Klatzow stated that it was essential for the forensic laboratories to operate according to a standard operating procedure, which meant the chemicals needed to be within their period of use, and must not exceed the expiry date listed on each bottle:

> *If the allegation is correct that the expiry times were exceeded and that these were relabelled with a new expiry time, this constitutes a fraud on the system.*

It was also absolutely essential that the chemicals were stored under conditions that could be monitored and could form a proper chain of custody, Klatzow said:

> *Unless this is the case, it places into jeopardy any prosecution using those chemicals. If the chemicals are used, and there is no chain of their use and chain to show that these chemicals are in fact purporting to be what is stated on the label, then it becomes a serious issue in maintaining the integrity of any analysis subsequently should that come under cross-examination in a court case.*

He added that had these chemicals had been purchased in excess, it constituted, in his view, a grave breach of process and threw into jeopardy the otherwise good results that were being obtained by some sectors of the police's forensic laboratories.

With regards to fingerprint brushes, Klatzow said it was important to understand that a fingerprint, a latent print on any surface, is exceptionally fragile and needed to be treated with the utmost care:

> *Over more than 100 years of experience, it has been found that squirrel hairbrushes of the right type, specifically designed for the purpose, are the correct instrument for use for transferring fingerprint powder onto the latent print. The use of a synthetic brush with a harder nylon or another type of bristle is totally inadequate for the purpose, for the simple reason that it is likely to destroy the finer features and the detail of the fingerprint.*

In his report, Klatzow explained that a fingerprint might become completely useless when synthetic brushes are used, as there would be unexplained differences between the ten-times-inked fingerprints that are taken and kept in the docket. This could have a negative effect on the prosecution and would, in itself, be an unacceptable degradation of the crime scene to the great disadvantage of everyone concerned.

What Phahlane had done in allowing the expired chemicals and incorrect materials to be delivered to the police stores was criminal. Aside from the obvious alleged corruption and mismanagement involved in the process, he had also put countless crime investigation scenes in jeopardy.

MIXED MEDIA

By now, the media had caught a sniff of the story. They had discovered that IPID had begun to actively investigate Phahlane, which added a whole new element to the case.

News24 broke the original story on the 23rd of November, revealing that Phahlane was expected to make a statement at IPID's offices regarding the defeating the ends of justice charge by getting Terblanche and Jooste to refuse to cooperate with the IPID investigation.[84] The story also revealed that IPID was investigating how Phahlane was able to afford the house.

Whenever an independent journalist asked a probing question, Phahlane's dishonest media spokeswoman immediately went into attack mode. Phahlane's spokespeople were ruthless in their attempts to freeze out any independent, strong-minded, investigative journalists who were not afraid to report on Phahlane's misdeeds. They were not invited to Phahlane's press conferences; they were named by Phahlane every so often as being 'on IPID's side', and his spokespeople ignored their media queries while speaking 'openly' to other more 'flexible' journalists. In this way, it would be easy to accuse these journalists of being biased against him.

Phahlane's public relations team then sought – and quickly found – journalists sympathetic to their cause to write stories that suited Phahlane's version of events. Often, they were more junior members of the press who were happy to be getting in on the big story of the day. Others belonged to organisations that were sympathetic to the Zuma government. His most receptive (read: *willing to lie*) journalists

84 Angelique Serrao and Pieter-Louis Myburgh, Exclusive: IPID to charge acting police commissioner, News24, 23 November 2016, https://www.news24.com/SouthAfrica/News/exclusive-ipid-to-charge-acting-police-commissioner-20161123

were found at the Gupta-owned *New Age* newspaper and *ANN7* news channel.

As time went on, Phahlane tried to use the age-old trick of divide and conquer to cast doubt in the public's minds about whether he was guilty or not. It was an old tactic in the public relation's game – confuse the public's view of what was really happening, i.e. a corrupt policeman using his might to hide his criminal deeds. He went as far as paying liars with police badges to give his version of the truth an air of belief about it. He would use the same tactics in Parliament in the months that followed.

To *News24, Radio 702,* the *Daily Maverick,* and other news organisations whose investigative journalists weren't simply gulping down Phahlane's sugar-coated (but thinly-veiled) public relations sippy cup, the opposite attitude by Phahlane's spokespeople was on display.

Brigadier Mashadi Selepe told *News24*:

> *The Acting National Commissioner welcomes any investigation on any allegations and matters against him conducted within the confines of the law to enable the testing of any such allegations. It is unfortunate that such investigations and/or allegations, if any, are conducted through the media with the sole aim of causing harm and damage to the reputation and integrity of the Acting National Commissioner.*

What a joke. Phahlane had no integrity, so how could his reputation possibly be harmed?

Phahlane used the story to duck out of his meeting at IPID's offices. It was one place where he could not afford to be caught out.[85] He would use any excuse to avoid blowing his cover. To this day, he has not given any explanation as to how he built his mansion, which, as

85 Angelique Serrao and Pieter-Louis Myburgh, Phahlane a no-show at IPID offices, News24, 23 November 2016, https://www.news24.com/SouthAfrica/News/phahlane-a-no-show-at-ipid-offices-20161123

I have repeatedly alleged, was bought with the proceeds of crime. I stand by that.

Amid all the drama, a moment of humour entered the fray in June 2016 when a video emerged of Phahlane fighting and then hiding behind a couch during an attempted armed robbery at a spa.[86] At the time, Phahlane was dishonestly described as a hero who had fought off the robbers, chasing them away. I was reliably informed that he was subsequently given an award for his bravery. In an interview with Independent Media after the robbery, Phahlane said he used his experience as a policeman to fight the two armed men:[87]

Using his experience as a policeman, he leapt into action, grabbing the arm of one of the would-be robbers:

> *In order to change the direction of the gun that was pointed at me, I went for his (attacker's) arm.*

Suddenly, the gun was pointed at his colleague (accomplice):

> *I knew if he decides to fire a shot, his colleague could also be shot. As (a) police (officer), you have to act in a split second.*

The story stated that throughout the scuffle, the firearm was pointed at the man's accomplice. Phahlane, in his statement, said:

> *I was employed to protect the community and save lives. As an officer, you place yourself on duty if the situation demands that. I'm grateful no one was hurt.*

But the video showed that he was in the spa with his wife, wearing no shoes, when the robbers entered. At first, he fought with the robbers, punching one in the face and then falling to the floor as they ran outside. But instead of running off, the robbers stormed back

86 Angelique Serrao and Pieter-Louis Myburgh, Watch: Acting top cop fights, hides behind couch during robbery, News24, 14 December 2016, https://www.news24.com/SouthAfrica/News/watch-acting-top-cop-fights-hides-behind-couch-during-robbery-20161214

87 Solly Maphumulo, Top cop on tackling thugs: It's what I do, The Star, 7 June 2016, https://www.iol.co.za/news/top-cop-on-tackling-thugs-its-what-i-do-2031267

into the spa. Phahlane grabbed a pillow from the couch before diving behind it while his wife and a spa employee pushed the couch towards the robbers, upon which the robbers fled.

Selepe again attacked journalists in her response to questions about the true events that took place during the robbery:

> *There is no dispute on the sequence of events that unfolded on the day of the attack at the spa ... It is unfortunate that you are suggesting a misrepresentation of facts which will be found nowhere in the department's reporting on the matter. It is found suspicious or why you are in possession of such recordings, which is a subject of investigation. Such recordings can, under no circumstances, be made public.*

Selepe was obviously a stranger to the truth. By this stage, I was completely fed up with the fact that it was the taxpayer who was funding Phahlane's spin doctors. I decided to add them to my list of heads that should roll and let them all know about it. (Sally de Beer, another regular fabricator for Jackie Selebi, is now on pension while Hungwani Mulaudzi was forced to resign after I exposed his dishonesty to the new Hawks head, Godfrey Lebeya).

While I, like many members of the public, laughed when I saw the video, I realised it pointed to two key aspects of Phahlane's personality. First, it showed that the man lied easily. In giving an interview with the media after the robbery and lying about what took place, he showed he was comfortable telling lies to paint himself in a positive light. Secondly, in winning awards, he received state money based on something that did not take place. This showed a further lack of ethics on his part. I posted the video of his cowardice on YouTube for all to see. The Police Minister quickly came forward to defend his unlawfully chosen Acting Police Commissioner. In a briefing before Parliament, Nathi Nhleko claimed that anyone saying Phahlane could not afford his house just by looking at it was ludicrous:[88]

> *That's a very subjective way of dealing with issues. There has got to be a scientific way to deal with whether the house that you own, you built it through proceeds of crime. They can't just look at your place and decide you must have stolen money to buy your property.*

Of course, anyone who bothered to read up on the issue would have seen that IPID had taken more than just one look at the house. Forensic searches looking at the bonds on the property, the building costs, and interviews with witnesses revealed there was real substance to the investigation. But Nhleko, a minister with questionable ethics himself – and more than just a few skeletons in his closet – would say anything to protect Phahlane. He had no choice but to protect Phahlane because Phahlane was part of the state capture mechanism that shored up Zuma's criminal enterprise, of which Nhleko was a part.

THE RAID

In January 2017, IPID obtained search warrants to enter Phahlane's house. They wanted to confirm that the electronic equipment installed by 'Yola' as part of the R80 000 sound system purchase was in Phahlane's home, and they were also looking to see if he had any proof that he paid for the installation.

I knew that a search of Phahlane's home was the inevitable next step, but I, like the rest of the country, only learnt of it happening through the media. Phahlane begged to differ and insisted that I had master-minded the raid and tipped off the media.

Because of the threats already sent to IPID's investigators, IPID decided that the safest way to conduct the raid would be after meeting with Phahlane to obtain his warning statement.

---

88 Thulani Gqirana, Police Minister defends Phahlan'e R10m house, News24, 7 December 2016, https://www.news24.com/SouthAfrica/News/police-minister-defends-phahlanes-r10m-house-20161207

The search was (obviously) leaked to members of the media, who were waiting outside Phahlane's estate when IPID investigators entered. Phahlane, infuriated at what was going on, called police officers to the scene to take down the number plates of those present. According to a *BusinessLIVE* article, the officers arrived in marked and unmarked vehicles and took photos of the IPID officers as they arrived. They also attempted to block the IPID officers from entering the property.[89]

After the search was carried out, Phahlane's public relations campaign went into overdrive. He immediately made himself available to his carefully chosen and 'flexible' media houses to try to debunk IPID's actions. In a SABC interview, it was clear that he had either been coached on how to answer questions or had perhaps written the questions himself.[90]

The public might not be aware of this, but Certified Fraud Examiners are highly experienced interviewers trained to read body language. They can quickly see when a person is lying. In Phahlane's case, he had also been trained to gain sympathy from the public. He was always softly spoken, and he hardly ever raised his voice or spoke forcefully, even when asked direct questions about his corruption. His eyes faced downwards as if he were a victim facing unfair accusations, but he made sure he looked directly into the camera when answering direct accusations to give the impression that he was speaking the truth. This was deliberately done to make the public believe that he was an innocent man being targeted by a group of people who were out to get him.

---

89 Graeme Hosken, Cops face off in dramatic raid of acting commissioner Kgomotso Phahlane's home, Business Day, 19 January 2017, https://www.businesslive.co.za/bd/national/2017-01-19-cops-face-off-in-dramatic-raid-of-acting-commissioner-kgomotso-phahlanes-home/

90 SABC News, Kgomotso Phahlane on IPID's raid of his home, Youtube, 10 January 2017, https://www.youtube.com/watch?v=_WYHnIKHLek

He made sure to paint himself as a victim from the start when he said:

> *Where I am, I am of the view that I am treated unfairly and unethically, and there is a concerted effort, a programme, that is aimed at attacking my integrity and ensuring that I am losing the focus on the work that I am supposed to be doing as an ordinary South African.*

But when questions were being framed, he gave himself away by repeatedly opening and closing his eyes as he attempted to recollect his lies. An honest person does not have to think about their answer at all – all they have to do is recollect it from their memory. A dishonest person, on the other hand, has to think carefully about their lies if they don't want to be found out.

The SABC (naturally) asked him easy, open-ended questions that were not direct or accusatory in the slightest – a nice, warm, comfortable space for him to wriggle out of telling the country the truth, or at least his version of the truth. The Union Buildings in the background added a nice touch to the interview, giving Phahlane false gravitas – as if he were on the side of the country, a man of authority and integrity. Nothing could be further from the truth. I believe that he was a dishonest coward who abused his office for his own gain.

Phahlane's veiled threat came in at around twelve minutes into the interview when he smiled for the first (and only) time on-air and said:

> *What they should know is that this continuation and attack [sic] and assault on my integrity is never going to be taken lightly and I will warn them, together with Mr Paul O'Sullivan, also equally to cooperate with the authorities when they get closer to them for all these things, including the violation of my privacy.*

Less than three weeks later, Phahlane deployed his goons to come after me. I now knew I was not only dealing with a crook but also a dangerous criminal who would go to any lengths to cover his tracks. Phahlane also revealed that he planned to sue IPID after being humiliated by the media reporting on the raid at his house. The interviewer asked if he had been presented with any evidence of wrongdoing on his part, and he replied:

> *It is [an] allegation. Vague as they are, they remain allegations. Yesterday I have hosted officials from IPID in my office who presented two charges. One defeating the ends of justice and secondly corruption. The so-called corruption from the purchase of what has now become commonly known as the sound system in my house. The allegation there is that there is a service provider to the police that purchased it for me. There is nothing at all to support that allegation. I am clear that I contracted this particular person; yes, they happened to be a service provider to the South African police service. But I have contracted her as an interior designer, which work she is doing. It is a business relationship. She is to offer services. I am to pay for those services. She obtained the quotation from Sounds Great in Woodlands, provided me with that quotation, followed by which I approached my bank to process and EFT directly to Sounds Great in Woodlands. If that is corruption, I don't know when did we introduce a new definition of corruption.*

Phahlane focussed solely on the sound system, but that was not his Achille's heel. The entire house was his problem. It had been built for nothing yet was worth R8-million. While the public theatrics continued, the IPID investigators continued with their investigation. By now, the IPID officials had realised that something was interesting about all the expensive cars in Phahlane's family's garage. How exactly had he come to afford them all? We would soon find out.

The role we played, Sarah-Jane in particular, in exposing the hidden iceberg of Phahlane's corruption was substantial, and Phahlane knew it. He was very scared of what we were doing and was desperate to stop us. We built up a meticulous profile of him, his wife and his whole family and their ill-gotten assets.

CHAPTER 17

A NEW LINE OF ATTACK

A HARMLESS BRAAI GETS DRESSED UP AS A TREASON PLOT

Christmas 2016 was just around the corner. It was the end of a long, hard year, and I was feeling the toll of all the battles I had been fighting. November had been incredibly busy. The Phahlane investigation was in full swing, and IPID was now tackling Ntlemeza for charges of fraud, perjury, and crimen injuria.

I had just published, jointly with AfriForum, a report titled *Joining the Dots – Capture of the Criminal Justice System*, which explained how a cabal of crooks had come into power in the key institutions of the police, the Hawks and the NPA, and how they were protecting corrupt politicians who were pillaging state coffers at an eye-watering rate. The report was published by AfriForum's anti-corruption division, headed up by a bright, vigilant and dedicated activist named Monique Taute. For the first time, the public was able to get a sense of the bigger picture and a look into the patronage system of those who had come to power. A book on Krejcir had also just been released by Angelique Serrao, which contained details of how I had spent years of my life ensuring Krejcir was put behind bars.

As we entered the beginning of December, I knew I had to take a bit of a break to spend some time with my family. I also felt that it was an opportunity to take a step back and absorb some of the successes of my fight-back campaign. While I still had a long way to go, I felt like I had achieved much in the past year. Although I was still fighting the numerous criminal cases launched against me, the previous few months had given me hope that the tide was finally turning. Little did I know that Shaun (The Sheep) Abrahams and his accomplices had many more surprises in store for me in 2017.

I had a ticket booked for the 3rd of December to visit my children overseas. Before I left that evening, I planned to hold a small afternoon get-together to thank some of the key people who joined me in the hard fight against corruption – Robert McBride, the two IPID investigators, Crime Intelligence officer Candice Coetzee, and Shadrack Sibiya, who had recently joined the City of Johannesburg to form a new investigations unit under Mayor Herman Mashaba.

Buying properties on auction, fixing them up and then selling them for a profit was a large part of my daytime business dealings. Not many knew about it, but when Krejcir's house went on auction, a friend and I had successfully bid on it. We were just about halfway through a multi-million rand makeover of the property. It was a beautiful home with amazing views, but it had been neglected. I wanted to fix it up, wait for the reputation of its previous owner to dim, and then sell it. I was mindful of the evil man who had once lived there and that he had hatched more than a few murder plots from within its walls, including several attempts on my own life. Before starting the works, I brought in a priest from the Orthodox Church in Midrand to have the house exorcised of potential demons and blessed with good spirits. I video-recorded the whole process in case a future buyer was worried about bad omens.

I decided to have the get-together at the Krejcir house. It was conveniently located in Bedfordview, close to the airport, so I would not have a long drive to catch my flight. The home also had a lovely large terrace with a braai overlooking the pool – the perfect place to sit and relax on a sunny December afternoon.

At our get-together, I handed out copies of my *Joining the Dots* report and we discussed its contents. I showed them a small hidden room where I believed Radovan Krejcir had concealed himself when the Hawks had raided the property. They never found him. I reminisced about the times I had been shot on duty and where the injuries still bothered me, and we discussed recent news stories. An interesting one that had just come out was an analysis of the rise of Twitter bots using the hashtag #WhiteMonopolyCapital, creating fake images, and attacking decent people like Ferial Haffajee (and other good journalists) and businessmen like Johan Rupert. The online abuse seemed to be part of a planned campaign, and we wondered what (and who) was behind it. At the time, the Gupta Leaks were yet to emerge to reveal the part UK public relations firm Bell Pottinger had played in creating fake news through their manipulated racism campaigns in the country.

While we chatted about current events – the same sort of conversations that formed part of get-togethers with friends all over the country – the person doing the braai work was introduced to the visitors, but under a pseudonym. He was actually Jacob Nare. As one of the key state witnesses against Radovan Krejcir, he was still under my protection while Krejcir's trials were underway and which are still ongoing today.

By the time I boarded my flight, I was relaxed and content. I was looking forward to my holiday. Little did I know at the time that one of the IPID investigators at the get-together was a double agent working for the enemy.

MOKOTEDI'S ALLEGATIONS

A week and a half later, I woke up to the news that Major General Prince Mokotedi had opened a fake criminal docket against myself, McBride, Sibiya, and Coetzee, claiming our get-together had been a secret meeting, with the DA and AfriForum in attendance, where we planned an Arab Spring-type uprising against the leaders in the country. I was being accused of high treason, with wild allegations of murder plots being thrown into the mix. According to Mokotedi, I was planning to murder him and Ntlemeza and launch fake smear campaigns against the leadership of the police and the Zuma family.

I knew the police were desperate to pin something on me, but this was taking things a bit far. Mokotedi had clearly been reading too many fiction spy novels in his spare time and was either delusional or hoping the more accusations he threw my way, the more likely something would stick. The details became even more outlandish every time he was interviewed in the media about this supposed treasonous meeting. In an interview with John Robbie on Radio 702, he claimed he had been monitoring us, that we had a grabber, that we were planning a regime change through a popular revolt, and that we were called the Black Hawks.

He was correct in so far as who was at the 'meeting' (and its date and time), save for the imagined DA and AfriForum attendees. Who in our midst was a double agent, we wondered? McBride was the only person who knew the identity of the braai chef and had done some checks on him. McBride subsequently named Jacob Nare as the 'traitor' and said that he was an agent of both Phahlane and Richard Mdluli. Of course, I knew he was wrong, but, for good measure, I moved Nare to London for the next eighteen months on a three-month visa to keep him safe. I subsequently met with the UK authorities to have him stay there until the start of the future trials against Radovan Krejcir.

I always knew Mokotedi was averse to the truth – I just didn't realise (until that point) that he had aspirations of becoming a fairy-tale author. If the false charges he was trying to pin on us weren't so serious, I would have paid him for a good comedy script.

Mokotedi's allegations were contained in an affidavit he submitted to the Bedfordview Police Station when opening a docket. I couldn't understand why the head of the Hawks in Gauteng would need to open a docket at a local police station, especially on charges as serious as treason. Why did he not get the Hawks who reported to him to investigate the case?

I believed that the real purpose of Mokotedi's allegations had nothing to do with them being genuinely investigated, but rather that they be aired in the media to tarnish mine, McBride's, Sibiya's and Coetzee's reputations. Mokotedi and his people knew that, through our various investigations, we were closing in on their criminal networks.

Mokotedi's affidavit was freely handed out to the media, having been leaked by Chad Thomas, one of the bangle-and-tattoo-brigade of PIs who frequented Mokotedi's office. Thomas was a bit of an oddball. With no recognised professional skills, he had set himself up a few years earlier as a PI and had become adept at running with the foxes and hunting with the hounds. He regularly spoke on a Jewish community radio station operating out of a backroom near Orange Grove, promoting his PI business, IRS Forensics. A couple of years earlier, Thomas had told me he wanted to form an organisation of forensic consultants and wanted me to be its first 'President'. He meant well, but at my professional level – and being a highly qualified and respected Certified Fraud Examiner – I had no desire to be seen rubbing shoulders with a group of PIs who moved in the same circles as Chad Thomas. I politely declined and wished him well.

Along with Lance Epstein and Mike Bolhuis, I believe Thomas had become part of the team assembled by Vlok and Mokotedi to nail me.

At the time, I was unaware of this but later got the full story from disbarred Pretoria attorney, Peet Viljoen. According to Viljoen, Chad Thomas was allegedly at the forefront of Vlok and Mokotedi's plans to take me down. It was, therefore, no surprise that he leaked Mokotedi's fairy-tale statement to the media.

In Mokotedi's affidavit, he said he had a source who was at the braai who was party to our discussions about people we had identified for vexatious criminal investigations and shaming in the media:

> *The motive for targeting these individuals is that they are close to or are supporters of the President of South Africa, President Jacob Zuma.*

He named Phahlane, Ntlemeza, himself, Advocate Shaun Abrahams, and the Head of the State Security Agency Arthur Fraser as the main targets on our list. Conveniently, it was already public knowledge that we were conducting investigations into these people, and others.

Apparently, I had agreed to collect information and dig up dirt on these men by looking for evidence of corruption and acts of criminality. Why would I need to discuss this matter at my get-together when I had already publicly stated over the last few years that I was doing just that? I was also not sure why doing this was considered "treason". Surely stopping corruption and criminality within the security cluster was a civic duty and not an evil intent? All it did was show how deluded Mokotedi and his bosses had become, believing that crime-fighting was the true transgression rather than the open looting that was taking place.

I had also supposedly discussed how I planned to raise money for all of this to take place. I was still trying to raise money for all the court cases Mokotedi's team were illegally making me part of, but suddenly I was so flush with cash that I could hand out money for this, too, apparently. I don't think Mokotedi thought through any of these claims with any sense of logic. It seemed he and his source were just randomly throwing out accusations to paint me as some sort of evil overlord determined to take down what they seemed to think was a utopian leadership structure within the police.

Mokotedi went on to claim that we held discussions on various cases IPID was dealing with against Phahlane and Ntlemeza and that we had agreed that these cases needed to be finalised before the end of the month and submitted to the NPA for a decision. According to Mokotedi, if the NPA declined to prosecute, AfriForum and the DA would pursue a private prosecution. I assumed this was decided by the unnamed AfriForum and DA members who were supposedly at the meeting. I would still love to find out who these phantom people were.

Mokotedi also claimed that I was getting information from Candice Coetzee, whom he said was on suspension for providing me with classified information without authorisation – a claim he was happy to bandy about without having a shred of evidence with which to back it up.

SUPER-SPY O'SULLIVAN

In Mokotedi's affidavit, the claims against me were turned up a notch when I was painted as some sort of super-spy who was about to unleash an Arab Spring-type revolt in the country:

> *It was disclosed by the group that Paul O'Sullivan has collected damaging evidence against Mr Duduzani Zuma, the President's son, and that information can be used to mobilise the community revolt and pressure the President to quit office.*
>
> *The group also agreed that the activities that they have planned against the targeted group should be used to mobilise for an Arab Spring type revolt in the country. It is common cause that Mr Paul O'Sullivan has been in and out of the country and has been mobilising for support and funding from abroad and hide the source of the funds. O'Sullivan was further mandated to continue to make spurious and vexatious allegations against senior members in the security services in the country whilst he is outside the country to*

> *mobilise for international solidarity. It is also common cause that Mr Paul O'Sullivan, by his own admission, worked for a number of foreign intelligence agencies.*

Mokotedi once again claimed I was working for foreign intelligence – the same claim he had been against me since the time of my investigations against Jackie Selebi. Not once had he produced a shred of evidence to back this false claim up. Perhaps he believed that the more he told that lie, the more likely it was to be believed. It was also a convenient way to dismiss all my legitimate accusations of corruption and other acts of criminality against Phahlane, Ntlemeza, Moonoo, and himself.

Unlike Mokotedi's random hearsay and vague accusations, in his sad attempt to 'prove' my super-spy overlord role, my affidavits implicating him and his fellow criminals with badges were detailed and filled with provable corroborating evidence. They were hard facts to argue against. The only way Mokotedi could try to get the public on his side was to claim I was making up the accusations to overthrow the leadership structure in the police. To make his claims sound more legitimate and formulate the leap into accusing us of treason, he threw the President into the mix:

> *Hence the meeting of the 3rd of December 2016 was meant to concretise and put in motion a plan to destabilise the security forces of the country and to oust the President of the country through popular revolt, it is my submission that the group knowingly and actively participated in the plan to commit high treason, intimidate and harass senior officials, and to ignite a revolution.*

Proving that the real motive for the 'affidavit' was to cast doubts in the public's minds about IPID's credibility in conducting the Phahlane and Ntlemeza investigations. Mokotedi said that I was an accused person in several cases before the court and that:

> *... it is therefore O'Sullivan's interest to tarnish the images of the current leadership of the SAPS, the DPCI, and the NPA and place himself as a white knight and victim of corrupt officials.*

The only people Mokotedi fooled with his lies were the Zuptas and the Zuptoid supporters who were desperate to find evidence that their leader, Zuma, was a man of high morals. Exposing a 'foreign agent' who was paying to destabilise the country was the same tactic used a decade earlier by Jackie Selebi and his sidekick Andre Pruis when Thabo Mbeki was in power. Although it had not worked then, ten years had gone by, and people had short memories, so why not give it another shot?

ASSASSINATION FAIRY-TALES

As if he was aware that the leap he took from investigating members of the police and NPA to starting a popular revolt was too wide to be believed, Mokotedi added a supposed intelligence report from another meeting which apparently took place either in March or April of 2016. The affidavit mentions both dates without making it clear which one was correct.

This meeting allegedly took place at the Michelangelo Hotel in Sandton between former DPCI employees, members of the Zimbabwean Intelligence Agency, and Serbian nationals. Of course, just like all the other fake intelligence reports that were being bandied about at the time, the names of those who took part were non-existent, as were any concrete details – nothing more than fabricated lies.

Mokotedi claimed the purpose of this secret meeting was to discuss:

> *... the strategy of dealing with Lt General Ntlemeza, Major General Mokotedi and the witnesses on the rendition matter which they perceived General Ntlemeza as a dangerous man who may not be leaved [sic] to run the police and whom later brought Major General Mokotedi to do the groundwork as the Major Mokotedi is familiar with the law.*

In Ireland, we have a saying that goes, "self-praise is no praise". Amidst all Mokotedi's wild accusations was a compliment aimed directly at himself, a sweet little present wrapped up in a pretty bow. I was taken aback that he was vain enough to expect the media to swallow it and believe it to be true. Whoever wrote this piece of fiction must have had a good chuckle when they inserted that line. They were no doubt paid a handsome informer's fee for giving the report to him. I highly suspected that Mokotedi had fabricated the whole thing.

Mokotedi added:

> *The intelligence further indicated that General Ntlemeza and myself must be dealt with immediately and that we should be assassinated because we are seen as the ones who are pursuing the rendition matter. The strategy would include, according to the intelligence report, to implicate them to corruption to Mafia subsequently leak it to the media including the foreign media. They considered that an assassination should be conducted by the foreign people who shall after that sneak out of the country.*

Not only could Mokotedi not string a proper fairy-tale together, but his grammar would have shamed a primary school pupil.

In a leap of faith that made no logical sense, Mokotedi claimed that our 'meeting' had the same intention as the apparitions present at the Sandton meeting and that people present at the Michelangelo meeting were also present at my get-together on the 3rd of December. Surprise, surprise, he named no one. By mentioning that previous members of the Hawks were at the Michelangelo, one can only surmise he was suggesting this was Sibiya, but who knows? His affidavit was so open-ended, it may very well have been Darth Vader descending from some unknown solar system to bring the Galactic Empire to South Africa. Perhaps he was the unnamed member of AfriForum who was at the braai?

Mokotedi concluded:

> *It is my request that the matter must be investigated against the groups for high treason, espionage, conspiracy to commit murder,*

> *corruption, intimidation and harassment, defeating the ends of justice, tax evasion and immigration laws.*

Citing tax evasion and immigration laws was a nice finishing touch, I thought. Two random charges added to the other false random accusations Mokotedi was throwing my way.

I later found that Mokotedi and his accomplices used the treason allegations to unlawfully obtain wiretaps on all my phones. Knowing that he was tapping my phones, I repeatedly made statements to lead him down the garden path, referring to agents like Red Fox and Grey Squirrel and making statements like "The fox will get into the hen-house". The clowns listening in must have thought they'd hit pay dirt.

THE MEDIA STORM

On the 13th of December, one day after the as-yet-unnamed double agent leaked 'information' on our allegedly treasonous braai meet-up, Mokotedi's fairy-tale affidavit found its way into the public domain, thanks to PI Chad Thomas.[91] Mokotedi clearly spent an enormous amount of time investigating the veracity of the claims – at least twenty-four hours. Never mind my being a super-spy, Mokotedi must have fancied himself as some kind of super cop who was so brilliant that he didn't need to put old-fashioned leg work – or time – into his investigations. His pathetic sworn statement was one hundred percent hearsay of hearsay from persons who did not have names. No self-respecting police official would allow any member of the public to open a criminal docket based on such hearsay. If anything, they would send the attempted complainant packing. At the Bedfordview Police Station (Radovan Krejcir's 'owned' police station), a person could open a docket with a newspaper cutting, claiming it as fact. The captured

91 Citizen Reporter, Hawks confirm treason, assassination case against McBride, Sibiya, O'Sullivan, The Citizen, 13 December 2016, https://citizen.co.za/news/south-africa/1374367/hawks-confirm-treason-assassination-case-against-mcbride-sibiya-osullivan/

elements of South African Police of 2016 operated no differently. They would allow a criminal to open a docket with flimsy hearsay, yet a genuine victim of a crime was regularly given the run-around.

While the media clearly had the affidavit in their hands, which could have only been sourced from Mokotedi (via his accomplice Chad Thomas), their dishonest spokesman Brigadier Hangwani Mulaudzi claimed they were unable to divulge the contents of the affidavit to the public. All he could say was that the information was received from "a very reliable source". Yeah, right!

Who was this source, I wondered? Someone had known there had been a braai which we had attended. Had someone spoken about it on the phone and intercepted our calls? Had the former Krejcir house been bugged and our get-together used to create fictional conversations? Or, had someone who had been there – someone with an ulterior motive – gone to Mokotedi and spun tales about what had happened? I had no idea, and I was left scratching my head as to what happened to cause this crazy story.

IPID was quick to dismiss the whole thing as rubbish. Their spokesman Moses Dlamini said:

> *The concern is that people in high office are going to this extent to falsely implicate people in wrongdoing ... It is the same pattern that we have seen since the rendition saga began. It is being repeated by the very same characters.*

From London, I called up Alec Hogg of *Biznews* to tell him what I thought of Mokotedi's claims, calling the situation out for what it was – Mokotedi and his criminal accomplices getting desperate. In his 13 December article, Hogg stated: "Developments in Zumaland have now gone beyond bizarre", which I believed to be an accurate description of what was going on.[92] I decided there and then to put a stop to this

92 Alec Hogg, O'Sullivan on police chief accusing him of treason: 'A criminal with badge'. BizNews, 12 December 2016, https://www.biznews.com/undictated/2016/12/13/osullivan-police-chief-treason

public game of chess Mokotedi was attempting to play. In the article, I challenged him:

> *Is that why you've resorted to fabricating stories, void of all truth whatsoever and then deliberately leaking it to the media? I hereby challenge you to take a lie-detector test to confirm that a source really did tell you these things, against your own resignation if you fail.*
>
> *The questions should be:*
>
> - *Did you lie about the allegations in this affidavit?*
> - *Do you know that allegations in this affidavit are false?*
> - *Do you know who leaked the affidavit to the media?*
>
> *If you think the whole country is so stupid as to allow a self-proclaimed Zuma supporter to hoodwink them into believing this garbage, then you have proven yourself to be wholly unfit for office.*

In a statement to the media, quoted in Hogg's article, I said:

> *Mokotedi is nothing more than a dishonest criminal with a badge. He was unlawfully appointed by a corrupt Minister of Police who decided to turn a blind eye to the fact that Mokotedi resigned ahead of a disciplinary enquiry from the NPA after it had been shown he had deliberately leaked false information to the media. Nhleko also turned a blind eye to the fact that Mokotedi had taken out a credit card, then run up a bill of R100,000 and not paid it, and also had judgments against him in excess of R1.1m.*

I pointed out the fact that Mokotedi's fake claims were based on one anonymous source, reducing the affidavit to nothing more than hearsay. The fact that Mokotedi described himself and his cabal as close supporters of President Zuma was evidence that they had breached their oath of office. Where was their independence?

I used Hogg's article to hit back hard. I was growing tired of these crooked cops and prosecutors. I was as vicious as I was rabid in my response:

> *Now, when it is clear that Zuma's criminal empire is falling, which includes the likes of Mokotedi, Ntlemeza, Phahlane, Nhleko and many others, this is their last-ditch attempt at avoiding the inevitable long road to prison.*
>
> *On 15 April, 1912, when the RMS Titanic hit an iceberg, the Captain of the ship, Edward Smith, sent the crew out to rearrange the deck-chairs. It did not help, and less than two hours later, Smith went down with the ship. Right now, Mokotedi is carrying out Captain Zuma's orders and re-arranging the deckchairs in a desperate attempt at diverting attention away from the criminal conspiracy he has been involved in since his unlawful appointment in February 2016. In this case, Mokotedi, Ntlemeza and the rest of the crew will eventually go to prison with their captain. The sad part is that Mokotedi and his accomplices are using Public Funds for rearranging the deck chairs on a sinking ship.'*

In closing, I said that these criminals with badges were fools if they believed the country could not see through Mokotedi's lies that amounted to the offences of defeating the ends of justice, fraud, and perjury, adding:

> *I will not dignify Mokotedi's work of fiction with a response until he has passed a lie-detector test at a reputable independent institute. I will, however, continue with my efforts to send him and his accomplices to prison, where they all belong.*

AfriForum and the DA also denied being at the 'meeting'. They would, because none of their members were at my end-of-year braai. Chairman of the DA's federal council James Selfe said the allegations sounded like they came out of a chapter of *Alice in Wonderland*:[93]

93 Graeme Hosken, Hawks treason plot probe 'is typical of the paranoia of our times', TimesLive, 12 December 2016, https://www.timeslive.co.za/politics/2016-12-13-hawks-treason-plot-probe-is-typical-of-the-paranoia-of-our-times/

This is completely and utterly bizarre and typical of the paranoia of our times. It's Spy vs Spy come real.

AfriForum CEO Kallie Kriel called out Mokotedi for the criminal he was:[94]

It is clear that Mokotedi is telling lies because he is nervous after AfriForum and Paul O'Sullivan published a report named "Joining the dots: Capture of the criminal justice system".

Mokotedi is exposed in the report as one of the role-players in the illegal capture of the criminal justice system by Zuma supporters. Apparently, it seems that desperate cats indeed make desperate leaps.

MCBRIDE RESPONDS

McBride quickly rubbished Mokotedi's claims. Former Gauteng Hawks boss Shadrack Sibiya also denied the allegations, threatening legal action to clear his name:[95]

In a *Sunday Times* article published on the 13th of December 2016, McBride had a warning for Mokotedi:[96]

Be careful that if you play with a cat, that the cat is not playing with you.

McBride made it clear that he was being targeted for his investigations into the systemic corruption in the top echelons of the police "because people did not want to be separated from their ill-gotten gains". He pointed out that the timing of the case being opened was important. It happened only hours after a docket against Phahlane was submitted

94 TimesLive, Treason plot: Afriforum says it didn't braai with McBride, DispatchLive, 12 December 2016, https://www.dispatchlive.co.za/news/2016-12-14-treason-plot-afriforum-says-it-didnt-braai-with-mcbride/

95 Sihle Manda, McBride: No plot to oust Zuma and co, IOL, 14 December 2016, https://www.iol.co.za/news/politics/mcbride-no-plot-to-oust-zuma-and-co-7177763

96 Sipho Mabena, IPID head McBride's chilling warning to Gauteng Hawk's boss, TimesLive, 12 December 2016, https://www.timeslive.co.za/politics/2016-12-13-ipid-head-mcbrides-chilling-warning-to-gauteng-hawks-boss/

to the Director of Public Prosecutions, and a warning statement was obtained from Ntlemeza, adding:

> *This will collapse like the rendition matter collapsed... we are unafraid, we are not intimidated.*

He said there was nothing untoward about our meeting:

> *In terms of our experience with Paul O Sullivan, his information has always been accurate, and even in instances where we thought he was not correct, it was later found that his information was correct. Now, as a complainant, we would regularly meet with him.*

McBride said there had been many attempts to get rid of him, both through parliament and unlawful and unconstitutional means. He said these sinister processes were continuing and that it had come as no surprise that the recent allegations had been made:

> *The allegation made is based on a supposed set of information, hearsay of hearsay, from a single source, and the statement that has been made must be rejected completely that there is any illegal activity that IPID and IPID investigators are involved in and I am not aware of any situation where any illegal activity was discussed with me or my investigators or anybody else.*

Like me, McBride called on Mokotedi to take a polygraph test, challenging him to do the test with him on live television to prove his innocence:[97] Referring to the swimming pool built at Jacob Zuma's Nkandla homestead as part of supposed security upgrades, McBride said:

> *No matter what you do, the truth cannot be changed by smoke and mirrors. This is a hair-brained scheme, similar to the fire pool story.*

97 ANA Reporter, McBride challenges Hawk's boss to live polygraph test, IOL, 13 December 2016, https://www.iol.co.za/capetimes/news/mcbride-challenges-hawks-boss-to-live-polygraph-test-7172925

MOKOTEDI BACKS OUT

At first, Mokotedi responded to the polygraph challenge with bravado, saying he would do the test with McBride. Unsurprisingly, just a few days later, he backed out. He sent a cancellation message to the polygraph examiner I had hired, who had been trying to establish a date and time to conduct the test.

Mokotedi claimed he wanted to do the test, but he had been advised not to because it had no legal purpose, which was ripe coming from a crooked cop who had given his statement to one of his PIs to leak to the media:[98]

> *I am not a suspect here; McBride is a suspect. We will do everything following proper legal process; we are avoiding playing into a narrative that suggests we are investigating people through the media. I don't want to be seen to be investigating him [McBride] through the media.*

But Mokotedi wasn't finished. In reference to me opening the case against him, he said:

> *When I opened the case against him, I just wanted to show the integrity of my heart and the innocence of my hand, and I respect the public interest in the matter, but I believe the law must take its course. All the issues that he wants me to address in a polygraph test, we can do so in an open court of law.*

His entire statement stank of poorly constructed irony. If he didn't want to investigate us through the media, then why did he have the affidavit widely leaked in the first place? And what did the integrity of his heart have to do with anything? If his heart had any integrity whatsoever, he would have resigned there and then. What kind of a police officer opens a case of high treason against someone based on hearsay evidence without even conducting a shred of proper

98 Jeff Wicks and Jeanette Chabalalam Mokotedi backtracks on lie detector test in McBride and O'Sullivan matter, News24, 20 December 2016, https://www.news24.com/SouthAfrica/News/mokotedi-backtrackcs-on-lie-detector-test-in-mcbride-and-osullivan-matter-20161220

investigation? He appeared to be nothing more than a puppet being pulled on a string by his corrupt bosses. In calling for a polygraph test, which he readily agreed to and then reneged on, McBride and I had caught him out with his fairy-tale.

The Hawks defended Mokotedi, saying that after seeking legal opinion, they were advised that Mokotedi's participation in a polygraph test would not serve any legal purpose but would instead unsettle the network of sources and informers they had cultivated. More lies cooked up by Ntlemeza's accomplice, Mulaudzi.

Unfailing in his innocence, McBride was no coward. He went ahead with the test. A report issued by the *National Voice Stress and Polygraph Network* and published in *The Citizen* newspaper on the 24th of December, 2016 showed that no deception was detected and that McBride was, therefore, not involved in any of Mokotedi's allegations:[99]

> *It is the opinion of the examiner that the examinee was being truthful when answering the relevant questions.*

Mulaudzi had no statement to give *The Citizen* when they called him for comment other than [referring to McBride] "Congratulations to him". I felt I had no need to do a polygraph because I was not being paid by the taxpayer.

In the same article, *The Citizen* spoke to a police source who said Mokotedi's affidavit was long on allegations of treason but short on details:

> *These details are generally required in an A1 statement, which forms the basis of the charge sheet presented in court, something junior constables learn in police college.*

Mokotedi had turned himself into a joke. Even his fellow police members were mocking him. I capitalised on it and ensured he was bombarded from all directions.

---

99 Amanda Watson, Truthful Robert McBride cleared by polygraph test, The Citizen, 24 December 2016, https://citizen.co.za/news/south-africa/1382825/truthful-robert-mcbride-cleared-by-polygraph-test/

IGNORING THE GUPTAS

What made the entire situation even more ridiculous was when Mokotedi formally requested that I make a statement to him with regards to the information I had about al-Qaeda operating in the country – information I had already sent to Phiyega more than a year earlier. The request supposedly came from my allegations that Moonoo was in contact with people connected to the organisation.

I informed Mokotedi that I had already made the information known to the police and questioned why he was suddenly so interested in fighting terrorism in the country when he had shown no interest in my allegations before – other than trying to use the information against me.

On the 20th of November, 2016, only weeks before his treason allegation against me, I had emailed Mokotedi about far more important treason suspects who should have been first on the Hawk's radar – the Guptas.

The *Sunday Times* had recently revealed that while he was Minister of Finance for a few short days in 2015, Des van Rooyen had his associates supply the Guptas with classified Treasury documents.[100] It was the start of the media blitz on the Gupta family that would come to be known as the Gupta Leaks. While Mokotedi was making bizarre claims against me, the Hawks were doing nothing about what was clearly the country's largest organised crime network. I could not understand how they could so blatantly ignore the flurry of information that media organisations like *amaBhungane*, the *Daily Maverick*, *News24*, and the *Sunday Times* were revealing.

I reminded Mokotedi that although the media was doing a great job of uncovering corruption, their role was limited in that they could

100 Thanduxolo Jika and Sabeko Skiti, How Des van Rooyen's Gupta cronies leaked classified Treasury documents, TimeLive, 20 November 2016, http://www.timeslive.co.za/sundaytimes/stnews/2016/11/20/How-Des-van-Rooyens-Gupta-cronies-leaked-classified-Treasury-documents

not investigate people criminally. It was the Hawks who were the last line of defence against the Guptas, their enablers in government, and in the Zuma family:

> *But no one in the Hawks seems to want to deal with the Zupta criminals and instead pledge to charge me with espionage and treason, just for exposing the Zuptas and their crooked friends in the police, government, NPA, and SAA.*

I asked him to please let me know when an arrest warrant would be issued for them since I (and the whole country) knew where they lived and what they looked like. I said I would gladly point them out to him.

As the stories on the Gupta emails continued to flow, revealing the true extent of the government's capture by the family, the Hawks reluctance to do anything about it became a public sticking point. It emerged that the Gupta brothers had fled the country without anyone stopping them. Bizarre stories emerged, seemingly revealing that the Hawks had just missed them.[101] It was complete nonsense. They had more than enough time to make arrests. How could they have missed them when the truth of their crimes had been brazenly out there for months – even years – already? Perhaps if they hadn't been focussing on catching real corruption fighters, like myself and McBride, they wouldn't have 'just missed' the Gupta brothers' escape. The whole situation was ridiculous.

And it wasn't just the Guptas. In earlier emails to Mokotedi, I asked him to investigate revelations that Lionel Moyo, the Chief of Staff in the Police Minister's office, was a convicted fraudster.[102] Moyo, a Zimbabwean, had somehow acquired a South African ID

101 Graeme Hosken, Inside the Gupta home – officers describe the Hawks raidm Timeslive, 12 February 2018, https://www.timeslive.co.za/news/south-africa/2018-02-14-inside-the-gupta-home--officers-describe-the-hawks-raid/

102 Tshidi Madia, Police Ministry's chief of staff a convicted fraudster, News24, 30 August 2016,http://www.news24.com/SouthAfrica/News/police-ministrys-chief-of-staff-a-convicted-fraudster-20160830

under a false name by lying that he was born in South Africa. Leon Abednigo Mbangwa, as he now called himself, was arrested and charged with fraud in 2002 for supplying the Department of Home Affairs with false data. He was found guilty and sentenced to four years in prison. He served eight months before being released and repatriated to Zimbabwe, where he changed his name to the fake Mbangwa. Somehow, after all of this, the man was given a job as Chief of Staff in Nhleko's office in 2015 with no background checks. Not only that but he was placed with Top Secret clearance. When the details surrounding his identity emerged in the media, his Home Affairs file mysteriously 'emptied' as Nhleko and Phahlane scrambled to clean his criminal record and issue him with a real South African ID. Real, but fraudulent.

I pointed this information out to Mokotedi and gave him Mbangwa's address, where a default had been listed against him for not paying his rent, making him unfit for Top Secret security clearance. I told Mokotedi that having a criminal fraudster and imposter as Chief of Staff in the Police Minister's office was an absolute joke:

> *Do you think there is a chance of a treason charge here anywhere? Possibly a crime against the state by those that knowingly employed him and gave him access to TOP SECRET files. What's your view?*

I subsequently received further information that Mbangwa was, in fact, a Zimbabwean agent who was using his clearance to garner intelligence information on Zanu-PF detractors in South Africa to 'neutralise' them. I conveyed this to Mokotedi, but, as expected, I heard nothing more from him. Apparently, I was a far more interesting target for him to pursue than a real spy like Mbangwa.

"INVESTIGATIONS" FALL APART

In October 2017, nearly one year later, police revealed that their investigations could find no substance to Mokotedi's allegations.[103] By then, Ntlemeza had been ousted and replaced with Yoliswa Matakata, a policewoman who was acting as the National Hawks Head. In a status update, she told McBride that the case had been brought before the National Director of Public Prosecutions Priority Crime Litigation Unit but had been returned to the investigator 'with further instructions'. "Thus far, the investigation revealed that no one can be linked to the allegations," she said.

IPID's spokesman Moses Dlamini said the feedback confirmed their numerous experiences of the abuse of power by certain police officers serving under Ntlemeza. I subsequently uncovered that it was Mokotedi's docket that had been the cornerstone of his dirty tricks in getting my phone (and those of my staff) tapped. That would continue until late 2017 when I threw away my old Nokia E90 Communicator and got myself a fully encrypted phone.

THE DISHONEST SNITCH - CEDRICK NKABINDE

It would later emerge that Mokotedi did, in fact, have a source. The individual in question turned out to be Cedrick Nkabinde, a disgruntled IPID investigator of low intelligence who had attended my 2016 December 3 braai. It would also emerge that Phahlane and his fellow crooks had been approaching IPID officers and offering them cushy top jobs – at the rank of Brigadier – with the police if they agreed to lie about McBride. It was all part of Phahlane's desperate bid to have the investigation against him squashed.

103 Angelique Serrao, 'No-one can be linked' to treason allegations against McBride, News24, 26 October 2017, https://www.news24.com/SouthAfrica/News/no-one-can-be-linked-to-treason-allegations-against-mcbride-20171026

Cedrick Nkabinde seemed to have taken the bait. In 2018, when Bheki Cele took up the helm as Police Minister, Nkabinde wrote him a letter of complaint about McBride, which he made public. Nkabinde made several false allegations about McBride – to which I cannot respond, as I was not a part of any of it – but he did make a few allegations against me, which I completely denied. He also repeated the allegations Mokotedi had let loose in December 2016, thereby confirming that he was the traitor that had corruptly sold his soul for a higher rank in the police.

In his letter, Nkabinde said that he had been part of the specialised task team established to investigate Phahlane, where he claimed to have seen unprofessional conduct taking place during the investigation.

Nkabinde alleged that I, Sarah Jane Trent, and AfriForum had been spearheading IPID's investigations, that information had been leaked to the media to deliberately tarnish the image of specific individuals, and that we had obtained evidence illegally. Much like in his allegations about what happened at the braai, he did not name this illusive AfriForum member. The reason why is because they never existed.

Nkabinde claimed McBride had given instructions for all official information obtained during the Phahlane investigation to be given to me first for analysis, including cell phone and bank account obtained through section 205 court orders:

> *This investigation cannot be seen to be objective nor independent because the instruction given by the executive director was to damage the image of Lt General Phahlane in order for him not to be confirmed as a permanent National Commissioner.*

He spun the story to imply that Phahlane was being investigated because McBride wanted to become National Police Commissioner. He then revealed that he was the source of the treason allegations, but his story changed from the one in Mokotedi's affidavit.

In his letter, Nkabinde claimed the main purpose of the meeting was to plot how to bring down Lieutenant General Phahlane, that AfriForum guaranteed that the funds were available to carry out this mission and that I was responsible for spying on Phahlane to find out anything that could bring him down:

> *This meeting sought to plot how to usurp power of the entire security cluster such as NPA, Crime Intelligence, SSA and DPCI.*

Where were the details of the Arab Spring-type uprising, I wondered? Amazingly, his letter omitted that piece of fiction. It was all the confirmation I needed that Mokotedi had inserted that line to get the illegal wiretaps on my phones.

Nkabinde claimed that both myself and Trent would do presentations to the task team on Phahlane's bank records and cellular phone data, that we obtained information unlawfully, and that we only formalised it later.

I responded to Nkabinde's allegations in an affidavit, pointing out that they contained patently false allegations against me that amounted to a serious case of fraud and defeating the ends of justice:

> *I have never spearheaded any investigation at IPID. No official information has ever been divulged to me by anyone at IPID. I have no doubt that Nkabinde has either been inspired to write these lies, or they have been written for him, and he put his signature thereto at the instance of Phahlane or one of his accomplices.*

I further explained that I met with McBride after he had his unlawful suspension set aside by the Constitutional Court in October 2016 and advised that due to his absence of eighteen months, the police was now being run by criminals and that urgent action would be needed to restore some semblance of ethics within the police. I stated that I volunteered my time, my staff's time, and the time and resources of Forensics for Justice to assist IPID in getting back on top of things. I explained that we (my staff and I) had put in many hours during those first few weeks when IPID began working on all the cases I had opened (but had never been investigated), tracing possible witnesses and evidence to advance the investigation.

I then explained how Phahlane and Ntlemeza got wind of what we were doing and commenced a counter investigation. It is no coincidence that the false allegations made against me by Phahlane and his accomplices were echoed in Nkabinde's lies. Nkabinde was clearly in cahoots with Phahlane and his criminal associates and should be charged with corruption, fraud, and defeating the ends of justice, I said.

Trent also denied Nkabinde's allegations pointing out that they were spurious, vague, and embarrassing:

> *I never "spearheaded" any IPID investigations, and "the AfriForum representative" is but a figment of Nkabinde's imagination. I was requested by the IPID to assist in certain aspects of an investigation. There was nothing illegal or sinister about this.*

IPID spokesman Moses Dlamini said that Nkabinde's allegations were made out of spite and malice against McBride and that Nkabinde was going back on the recommendations he made during Phahlane's investigation.[104]

> *We have received information that our investigators were allegedly paid money to make false allegations against IPID investigators who are investigating Phahlane. IPID will not be deterred from pursuing its investigations.*

Nkabinde was also the chief investigator in a case against former Crime Intelligence officer Morris 'Captain KGB' Tshabalala. Tshabalala was facing charges of fraud, theft, and corruption relating to the submission of alleged fraudulent invoices to the value of R563 005 for blinds and curtains for safe houses in Pretoria.

---

104 Alex Mitchely, IPID investigator Nkabinde resigns, News24, 21 September 2018, https://www.news24.com/SouthAfrica/News/ipid-investigator-nkabinde-resigns-20180921

It was revealed in July 2018, at the Specialised Commercial Crimes Court, in the trial of Morris "KGB" Tshabalala that Nkabinde purposely misled the court while on suspension during Tshabalala's bail application.[105] This finding against Nkabinde and what he deposed in court led to Tshabalala being granted bail. In her judgement, Magistrate Nicola Setshogoe said Nkabinde's actions were tantamount to ill-conduct, stating that "*it creates doubts in the mind of the court that whatever was deposed by Nkabinde is the truth*".

Nkabinde subsequently called Tshabalala's attorney, Mpesi Makhanya, and offered to help him in court.

Nkabinde resigned from IPID shortly after making his claims, dropping all his complaints against McBride. He told the media he had come to a mutual understanding with IPID and that the charges against him for defeating the ends of justice would be dropped if he resigned and withdrew his complaints.[106] No money was exchanged. Nkabinde had no doubt realised that he would likely face jail time if he continued to lie, so he quickly abandoned all his falsehoods and left with his tail between his legs.

I also let Nkabinde have it over email. I told him that as a result of his dishonesty, I would see to it that he goes to prison when I get down to it, but that I had bigger fish to fry before I started on the sprats.

If you're reading this book, Nkabinde, just know that when I get around to scraping the bottom of the barrel of corruption, I will seek you out and deal with you. I will leave no stone unturned to send you to prison for a very long time.

Stop me if you can!

---

105 Se-Anne Koopman, Suspended Ipid investigator 'misled' court in recent KGB bail application, IOL, 2 August 2018, https://www.iol.co.za/dailynews/news/suspended-ipid-investigator-misled-court-in-recent-kgb-bail-application-16380852

106 Bonga Dlulane, Cedrick Nkabinde resigns from IPID after dropping complaints against McBride, EWN, 21 September 2018, https://ewn.co.za/2018/09/21/cedrick-nkabinde-resigns-from-ipid-after-dropping-complaints-against-mcbride

CHAPTER 18
PHAHLANE'S NEXT MOVE

SECOND UNLAWFUL ARREST

It was a Friday afternoon in early February 2017 when the doorbell rang. I was in my boardroom finishing up work for the week. Sarah-Jane Trent was working beside me. I went out to see who it was. There was a female Metro police officer at the gate. With all the threats I have had on my life, I never open my door to anyone unless I know them.

I asked the metro officer what she wanted, and she said, "Let me in".

She told me that a car involved in a hit-and-run accident a couple of weeks ago had been traced to my address. I asked her for the registration number, and she gave me one for a car I had used to visit the Sable Hills Waterfront Estate with the IPID officials in November 2016. I'd sold the vehicle shortly afterwards.

I told the metro officer that the car had been sold and that she had the wrong address. She asked me for my name. I did not give out information like that. I asked her for details of the accident – where and when had it taken place. I quickly called the dealer I had sold the car to and asked who had purchased it. While I was still on the phone, the officer said she would get more details. She walked back to her branded Metro Police double-cab and drove off at high speed.

Her actions were highly suspicious. Having now established I was home, were they about to murder me? Almost without thinking, I jumped into my car, pressed the remote, opened my garage door, and drove up the street. As I drove away, I saw several unmarked cars coming down the street. There were far too many vehicles for this to be a hit. The only assumption I could make was that it was yet another unlawful police raid on my offices. I noted that they all had Northwest number plates and that the occupants were armed. I drove past them at high speed, weaving between them as they attempted to block my route. As soon as I had driven far enough to be out of danger, I called several people for help. First, I called my lawyers. Then I called a few journalists. Calling the media was one of the best things I could have done, as the public was being kept up to date every step of the way. Then I went into 'invisible' mode while my legal teams worked to find out what was happening. I was later shocked and horrified to discover that the police had abducted Sarah-Jane Trent and driven off with her. She was subjected to what can be classed as massive abuse of her human rights in breach of the Constitution.

THE ABDUCTION OF SARAH-JANE

This is what happened to Trent in her own words, as set out in her criminal complaint:

> *It was just after 4 p.m., and I was in the boardroom of Paul O'Sullivan and Associates when the doorbell rang. I heard O'Sullivan discussing a car accident involving an alleged car he had sold last year. Whilst O'Sullivan was on the phone to the car dealership, the metro police official got into her vehicle and drove off. O'Sullivan and I became suspicious of this, and O'Sullivan said: "I think someone is trying to get me to go outside". I heard the garage open, and a few seconds later, O'Sullivan got into his car and drove out of the garage.*

I heard the screeching of car tyres, hooting and a police siren outside. I ran to the door and saw a black man about 45 years of age running towards the entrance to the office. I then pressed the garage button to close it as I thought this was a possible robbery and I was terrified. The man ducked under the closing garage door and came to the door shouting, "Open, open, open!" I told him that I needed to see his identification and that I would not allow him entry unless I was shown identification. The man struggled to find the identification card in his wallet, and when he found it, he came into the office and showed it to me.

I was then frantic because I do not trust the people who are investigating O'Sullivan because I have seen first-hand how they continue to infringe several of his Constitutional Rights. O'Sullivan is in possession of a High Court order which he had to obtain for the purpose of stopping them from doing exactly what they were doing right then and there. When police officers blatantly ignore High Court orders and do what they please, you are no longer protected from safety, and the fear for your life is instilled.

He announced his name and told me I was being arrested for pretending to be an IPID officer in terms of a section in the IPID Act. I asked him if I could see the warrant, and he merely allowed me to glance at the warrant. I was not given a copy of my arrest warrant but flashed it, and he pulled it away so I could not properly read it. I believe I was not given a copy of my arrest warrant because they did not want anyone to know where they were taking me to.

I asked if I could phone my attorney so that I could tell him which police station to go to. The officer told me that they were taking me to Cullinan Police Station. I spoke to attorney Darryl Furman and asked him to arrange for an attorney to meet me at the Cullinan Police Station as I was under arrest.

I was now frightened for my life to a degree that no one should ever have to feel. I thought maybe these people were there to murder O'Sullivan. Since O'Sullivan had driven off, maybe they would murder me instead. There have been multiple attempts to murder O'Sullivan. During 2016 alone, there were two attempts on his life, and he and the Principal IPID investigator on the Phahlane docket received a death threat per SMS.

When they took me outside, there were four vehicles with at least nine armed police officers, many with R5 rifles. When I was outside the property, I asked the woman if I could put my phone in my car that was parked in the garage, and she allowed me to do so.

I was put in an old white double cab bakkie and driven to a Shell petrol station on Marlboro Drive, Sandton. As we pulled up, I saw other cars and plain-clothed men standing around waiting. At this point, I knew that I was being abducted and wanted to faint and vomit at the same time.

When we got to the petrol station, I had not been handcuffed yet. An Indian man who told me he was Dawood told a police officer to cuff me. The police officer then tightened a cable tie around my wrists which was uncomfortably tight, so much so that it was painful. Dawood asked me if I had been searched and asked where my cellphone was. I told him I did not have any cellphone.

The police officers that were in the car with me when they drove me to the Shell Garage got out of the car. I was left alone in the car and exposed to the road where we were parked. What was going through my mind was, "Is someone going to shoot at me?". Every time a car drove past, I put my head down out of fear of being shot. This fear is also backed up by the fact I was under the impression that once a person is arrested, they are to be taken directly to the closest police station. I was not. I was made to sit in a car for an hour and a half.

These people inspired in me the belief that physical harm was imminent, and they did this on a number of occasions by addressing me in very demanding and aggressive tones.

After about 45 minutes (which felt like an eternity), the arresting officer, now known to me as Brigadier Kgorane, came to the vehicle, opened the door next to me, put his foot on the doorstep and tied his laces. He then looked at me and asked me for my cellphone. I told him I did not have it. He walked off and spoke to Dawood, who was standing next to a white VW Polo car with Northwest number plates.

After about 15 minutes, the arresting officer came back to the car with Dawood and the lady. I asked the lady what her name was, and she said, "Lucia". The arresting officer again asked me where my phone was, and I told him that Lucia had allowed me to put it in my car, back at the office. I was accused of lying for telling him Lucia had let me put my phone in my car earlier. The driver even pointed his finger at me and told me to stop blaming Lucia; I was going to give them my phone.

The officers told me they were going back to the office to collect the phone. They did not know the way back there, and I had to give them directions. I was so incredibly scared that if I did not do what they told me, they would hurt me. I have read news articles of police officers torturing and harming people in their custody, and I believe my fear was real.

I again asked the arresting officer to show me the arrest warrant so that I could see whether there was a search and seizure in there and that they were entitled to take possession of my cellphone. The arresting officer glared at me and shouted, "Ma'am, ma'am, ma'am! Your phone is part of an investigation". Everyone then got back into their vehicles, and I was driven back to the POAA office. I thought at this stage I would be assaulted or even worse.

At 17:58, we arrived back at the offices, and they took possession of the phone. I was then taken back to the same petrol station where Dawood was waiting with the VW Polo boot open. The arresting officer then took my phone to Dawood, where they were busy with it in the boot of the VW Polo. At this time, my family and friends had absolutely no idea where I was, and people were calling me and sending me messages. I believe that Dawood downloaded my cellphone in the boot of the car. Alternatively, they were doing something with my cellphone.

Eventually, I heard the officers outside of the vehicle that I was kept in discussing that the police station they were taking me to was Kameeldrift Police Station. I then started to cry and begged them to contact my attorney and tell them that they were taking me to Kameeldrift Police Station because they would go to Cullinan Police Station in line with what I was told at the time of my arrest, i.e. 16:20, and it was now 18:30. They refused. I was driven to the police station at Kameeldrift at 160kms an hour, and I made sure that I kept my eye on the speedometer most of the way. The driver had an R5 rifle across his chest and ate popcorn while driving. He finished the bag of popcorn before we got there. I thought at any moment he would have an accident as his driving was reckless to the extreme.

AT THE KAMEELDRIFT POLICE STATION

When we got to the police station at Kameeldrift, one of the officers on duty at the station asked the arresting officer, "Is this Trent because her lawyer is looking for her". The arresting officer did not answer her. I jumped and told her it was me and begged her to call my attorney. I then said I wanted my attorney there immediately, and he just ignored me.

I was then told to sign a form advising me of my rights. One of the officers that had accompanied the arresting entourage wrote the time on the form as 18:00 when, in fact, it was by then 19:15. I then crossed out 18:00 and wrote down the correct time on the form. I believe this was done deliberately to cover up having abducted me. I was then not handed the form I had just filled in. They refused to give it to me as it showed their attempt at fraud.

The arresting officer placed my phone into an evidence bag and then asked me for my pin code. I told him I would not give my pin code to him.

Two gentlemen came into the station. The arresting officer spoke to the men about downloading my cellphone. They asked for my pin code, and I refused to give it to them. One of the men came to me where I was sitting behind bars and asked me for my pin code. I asked him who he was, and he said Colonel Mike Sales. I asked him if I would be committing an offence if I refused to give them my password. Sales shrugged and kind of nodded his head. I asked him if he was lying and told him I would not give anything to him until I saw my attorney.

Sales then told me that if I did not give him my cellphone pin code that they would send it to the United States and Dubai to get the data off my phone and that I would never get my phone back... I told him I was not telling him anything, and I wanted my lawyer. I heard Sales speaking on his phone, telling someone that my phone had a six-digit pin code and that I would not give it to them. To this day, my phone has not been returned, and I had to buy another one.

Later, attorney Louis Taljaard came to the police station at Kameeldrift, and I was taken to the holding cells. I had ten minutes to consult with Taljaard. Taljaard then went to buy me some food, a toothbrush, toothpaste, and toilet paper.

When I got into the holding cell, there were no beds, just mats and old dirty blankets. I then saw two big sticky puddles of urine on the floor. The cell smelled like a dirty toilet. The toilet was full of waste, and a blanket had been draped over the toilet. The sink had old food in it that had moulded, and it was black and infested with maggots. When I lay on the floor on the mat, I could see hundreds of small white maggots crawling around on the floor. When I needed to use the toilet, I called for someone to take me to the staff toilets as I would not use the toilet in the cell. I was taken to the staff toilet. The cell that I was kept in for the weekend was a breeding ground for disease.

The unsanitary conditions of the cell are not fit for any human being to be detained whether they are rich or poor, young or old and especially when a person has not even been found guilty of any crime in a court of law. The filth and stench were overbearing, with old food on plastic plates at the entrance of the cell that no one intended on removing. At one stage, a black cat came into the cell and started eating from the old rotten food.

SARAH-JANE'S HUMAN RIGHT'S ABUSE CONTINUES

Trent spent the rest of Saturday and Sunday at the police station. She was allowed to see a friend and her uncle for ten minutes each, where she learnt that her family and friends had been beside themselves with worry. For hours, nobody had any idea where she was. She was told that AfriForum's lawyers were initiating an urgent High Court application to have her released. While still in custody, and in another illegal attempt to gain access to her belongings, the arresting officer and Lucia made her accompany them to her apartment:

They told me they were going to charge me, but they needed to prove my proof of residence first. Taljaard had furnished them with a copy of my lease agreement, but they still insisted that we travel to Sandton to confirm my residential address.

One of the police officers at the station then whispered to me that they had no right to enter my apartment and not to let them in. This police officer risked his job to inform me of this right because he knew that what the arresting officer was doing and had done to me that weekend was unconstitutional and disgraceful.

They put metal handcuffs behind my back and put me in the VW Polo with Northwest number plates. We then drove to my residential address at an average of 140km an hour. A security guard was there and confirmed I lived there. They insisted on seeing my front door. The whole drive there and back, the arresting officer was speaking to different people on the phone in respect of my High Court application. He spoke to a General several times about the application.

Late that Sunday night, after delaying the process as much as possible, the police officers brought Trent to the Pretoria High court.

She was released on bail after being falsely charged with impersonating an IPID officer. I could not be there as I was still 'invisible' and unsure of what was going on.

I believe Trent's illegal arrest was part of a fight-back by Phahlane, and his actions made him look as guilty as a puppy sitting next to a steaming pile of poo.

MY ARREST

Now that I knew what it was all about, I dropped my caution. I knew that I could not be arrested unless the police gave me forty-eight hours notice, thanks to the High Court Order I obtained in November 2016.

That Monday, I attended a meeting with Trent at the AfriForum building in Centurion. The meeting was to discuss the processes at court the following day. It was agreed that I would attend court since the police had not, at that stage, provided me with any notice of an intention to arrest me.

The meeting with the attorneys finished around 6:30 p.m. Trent and I chatted outside for a few minutes before driving back to Johannesburg. We drove out of the AfriForum building at about 6:40 p.m.

After about one hundred and fifty metres, we were ambushed by about eight unmarked vehicles, blue lights flashing and sirens blaring, blocking us from going any further. I later established that the ambush was led by a certain Brigadier Ncube (from the Northwest SAPS) and that he had deployed members from the Gauteng Operational Command of SAPS with the sole purpose of ambushing us. At least seventeen police officers surrounded us.

I stopped the car, switched off the engine, climbed out, and put my hands out in front of me, just in case they were bloodthirsty, trigger-happy cops who wanted to gun me down. Trent waited in the car and switched on her cell phone to record what was happening outside. I was approached by Ncube, a fifty to fifty-five-year-old black male, who proceeded to show me his ID.

Ncube said he intended arresting me for various offences, obviously related to the cases I had opened against Phahlane. I immediately told him that he could not arrest me, as there was a High Court order that required them to give me forty-eight hours notice. He refused to listen to me, seized my firearm and UK cellular phone, and said he did not care about any High Court order. Fortunately, he did not take my South African cellular phone, which was lying in the car.

Sarah-Jane called AfriForum's Willie Spies, who arrived within a couple of minutes. Ncube told Spies that he'd have to wait before speaking to me and then proceeded to formally arrest me and read me my rights. Spies told Ncube, in no uncertain terms, that his conduct was unlawful.

Trent managed to video small sections of the discussion, which were promptly put out in the media. In the videos, Willie Spies could be heard telling Ncube about the conditions of the High Court order and that the police were required to give me forty-eight hours to present myself at a police station. Spies held the order out to Ncube to inspect. Uninterested, Ncube said this was a new matter and that, as far as he was concerned, the order was not relevant to the matter for which he was arresting me.

Even though Spies pointed out that the order stated 'any matter', he was wasting his breath. Ncube clearly lacked the intelligence to know how to properly interpret a High Court order. As an Apartheid cop, he was nothing more (or less) than the remnants of a policing system founded on patriarchal discipline where black cops did what their white masters told them to do. With the fall of Apartheid, buffoons like Ncube were given rank and privilege far above their station.

Ncube was punching well above his weight – which would lead to his eventual undoing.

Despite it being carefully pointed out to Ncube that his conduct was unlawful, Ncube stubbornly persisted. Spies told Ncube that an urgent application would be made to the High Court, which it was. I was then placed in the back of a black Mercedes and driven at high speed (150-160km/hr) to the Kameeldrift Police Station, where I was detained, my fingerprints, photograph, and profile taken, after which I was locked in a cell. At one point, I was required to sign a warning statement. I refused to make or sign any statement other than to write on the form that I considered my arrest unlawful. I told Ncube to his face that he was a crook and that he would eventually go to prison for what he was doing. I intend to keep my word on that.

Unbeknown to Ncube, Sarah-Jane had been using her new iPhone to video record his conduct, which she sent to various journalists – and it went viral.

At about 11:45 p.m., Ncube let me out of the cell and told me that the court had ordered him to release me. The formal release procedure was then processed, after which Ncube wrote out a notice which stipulated that I must present myself at the Kameeldrift Police Station in forty-eight hours, where I would be served a summons to attend court for the alleged offence of impersonating a police official. He signed it, and then I signed it. I stepped outside with Kallie Kriel of AfriForum to wait for a SAP 13 official to return my firearm to me.

After I had been outside a few minutes, Ncube approached Kallie and me and asked that I show him the notice he'd handed me earlier. I handed it to him. With it safely in his possession, he told me that the prosecutor had instructed him to rewrite it because he had made a mistake on it. He then rewrote it and told me I could only go once I had signed it. I noted that the wording was identical, except the word *summonsed* had been replaced with *arrest*. I said this was not what was agreed and asked for the original notice back. He refused, crumpled the other notice up, and put it in his pocket. He reminded me that unless I signed the notice, I could not leave. I later found out he lied to me and that the prosecutor had said no such thing.

COMPROMISED COP MABULA

I subsequently discovered that the officers who had arrested Trent that Friday and me that Monday were part of a team from the Northwest under the direct command of Major General Ntebo 'Jan' Mabula. Mabula had a history of being involved in politically motivated arrests to protect criminals. He was a close ally of former Police Commissioner Jackie Selebi and former Crime Intelligence head Richard Mdluli. In 2008, Mabula tried to scupper the Selebi investigation by falsely arresting Advocate Gerrie Nel, who was then with the Scorpions. The day after Nel's arrest, Selebi launched an urgent application to halt the Scorpions' investigation against him.

As the previous Head of the Hawks in the Northwest, Mabula had a reputation for being a long-term associate of Mdluli, under whom he served as a detective in Potchefstroom when Mdluli headed organised crime there.[107] Mabula also led the Hawks investigation into the so-called Cato Manor Death Squad. As mentioned earlier, on Deputy National Director of Public Prosecutions Nomgcobo Jiba's instruction, he arrested KwaZulu-Natal SAPS Head Major General Johan Booysen for racketeering charges, which the court later declared unlawful. It was clear that, like Ncube, Mabula was an integral part of the team intent on stopping those near and dear to Zuma from being exposed for corruption. For that reason alone, I intend to send Mabula to prison when I get around to him.

---

107 Angelique Serrao, Inside top cop's fight-back campaign against IPID, News24, 13 February 2017, https://www.huffingtonpost.co.uk/2017/02/13/inside-top-cop-s-fight-back-campaign-against-ipid_a_21713020/

It turned out that Trent had good reason to be fearful when she was arrested. These police officers were dangerous. At the time, Mabula's mob was under investigation by IPID for the death – by suffocation – of police informer Solomon Nengwane. His death was allegedly at the hands of a task team of detectives under the command of Mabula, who was then a colonel. I was shocked at how many of these thugs were promoted for their crimes. That alone reinforced my determination to see that they all go to prison. They were subsequently criminally charged on the murder case and at the time of writing are awaiting trial.

Before his untimely death, Nengwane was allegedly involved in stealing R14-million worth of recovered heist money from a police station in Benoni in 2006 and Mabula would later be charged with kidnapping, torture and murder, along with his team members. The 2006 heist involved about R100-million in cash stolen from the OR Tambo International Airport cargo terminal. Four of the suspects were killed shortly after the heist. Prosecutor Peter Smith told the court it seemed as if the police were "knocking off" witnesses to "cover their own tracks". A post-mortem report revealed that Nengwane was tortured with "electricity shock", and a "tube was used to choke him".[108] It sounded like he died in a horrific way.

I was convinced that Mabula was now operating under the instructions of Phahlane and was, therefore, merely a proxy for an Acting Police Chief who was desperate to derail an investigation that was getting too close to the truth of his corrupt relationships. I was his number one enemy.

Both Trent and I opened cases with IPID against Mabula and his team for the offence of contempt of court, kidnapping, unlawful detention, torture and defeating the ends of justice.

---

108 City Press, Hawks boss in heist murder probe, News24, 28 July 2013, https://www.news24.com/news24/Archives/City-Press/Hawks-boss-in-heist-murder-probe-20150429

FALSELY CHARGED AGAIN

Both Trent and I were falsely charged for impersonating an IPID official, fraud, extortion, and contravention of the IPID Act. The impersonating an IPID official charge stemmed from our visit to Sable Hills Estate in November 2016. Phahlane, it seemed, had not only interfered with Jooste and Terblanche (the two witnesses we had interviewed in the corruption case against him), he also got them to claim that Trent and I were pretending to be IPID officials. It was all nonsense and, like the other cases I had to face, would easily be overcome in court. It was nothing more than an intimidation tactic by Phahlane to stop IPID from investigating him.

Furious after my first appearance in court, I emerged with a message for the corrupt police, telling them, in no uncertain terms, that I would hold them accountable, no matter what it took. A video on *News24* has me telling them that I was prepared to go to jail to protect the rights of all South Africans:[109]

> *If I have to spend time in prison, I will do it. But I will know that I am going to prison for nothing. These people – the corrupt people in the police – will be held accountable, and all South Africans will one day stand up and tell them that they are being held accountable.*

A journalist asked me about my role in the Phahlane investigation:

> *I am a complainant, going back a number of years against a number of people, including Lt General Moonoo, for corruption, defeating the end of justice, racketeering. Against Ntlemeza for corruption, defeating the end of justice, racketeering. Against Phahlane for corruption, defeating the end of justice, racketeering. Against Mokotedi for corruption, defeating the end of justice, racketeering, unlawful arrest and torture. I am the complainant in those cases.*

---

109 Angelique Serrao, O'Sullivan appears in court, out on R10000 bail, News24, 16 February 2017, https://m.news24.com/SouthAfrica/News/osullivan-appears-in-court-out-on-r10-000-bail-20170216

> *I have adduced enormous evidence of their wrongdoing, and I will pursue each and every one of those cases. My relationship with IPID is the same as any complainant in any case. I will assist with the investigation, and when they cannot understand something, they come and ask me questions, and I show them exactly how this happened and that happened and whatever. I've been subject to this criminal activity by these criminals with badges since the arrest of Jackie Selebi.*

When asked about the bail condition that I not go near Phahlane's house, I said – knowing it would infuriate him – "When it is sold on auction, I will buy that house."

The problem Phahlane had – apart from the fact that he was facing life in prison – was that we recorded, and then transcribed, everything that was said in all our meetings with potential witnesses. The transcripts clearly showed that the 'witnesses' put up by the Mabula team were lying through their teeth.

I subsequently found out that Jooste was under threat of losing his job when his employer found out that he had committed fraud by claiming to possess qualifications he did not have. Phahlane used his clout at the Homeowner's Association to let Jooste off the hook, I suspect in return for false testimony, itself an act of corruption and obstructing justice.

On the same day as my illegal arrest outside AfriForum's offices, Phahlane filed an interdict application against McBride, myself, Trent, and Magistrate JR Tsetsi. Tsetsi was the magistrate who issued the search warrant allowing IPID to search the Sable Hills house and remove the R80 000 sound system. Phahlane claimed Tsetsi launched the application to stop Trent and me from participating in the investigation and ensure the investigation against him was conducted lawfully. He also wanted the search warrant that had been used to enter his home set aside. The interdict was to stop me from "harassing, intimidating, or abusing him, verbally or by email", an almost carbon copy of what Selebi had done. And the same names were involved. In January 2008, when Mabula arrested Gerrie Nel (of the Scorpions) on trumped-up charges, Selebi launched a High Court application to obtain an order that the Scorpions could not investigate him (Selebi). These criminals were so arrogant that not only did they fail to learn from their mistakes, but they kept making the same ones.

Clearly, Phahlane was feeling the heat and would do anything possible to stop us from getting any closer to the truth. IPID, unintimidated, soon found out why Phahlane was so desperate to stop the investigation. Phahlane's corruption was much deeper than any of us could have ever imagined when we started the investigation. We would soon discover that the contracts he was issuing to chosen suppliers were worth billions of rands. Under Phahlane, the looting of the police was on the same level as the looting going on at state-owned companies like Eskom, SAA and PRASA.

CHAPTER 19
THE TABLES TURN

IPID FIGHTS BACK

IPID had been busy since McBride returned from his unlawful suspension. Sarah-Jane Trent and I had been equally busy, supporting their investigations by providing useful intelligence and data analysis. Despite Phahlane's attempts to have the investigation against him squashed, we went all out to uncover exactly what he had been up to. It didn't take long for IPID to discover one questionable relationship with police suppliers after another. Phahlane, it seemed, was as rotten as they come – and he had been living off the proceeds of corrupt relationships for years.

McBride turned the court cases Phahlane had launched against him. Now it was Phahlane who had to answer to allegations of wrongdoing, and not the other way around. IPID did this by filing responding papers in which Mandla Mahlangu, their lead investigator, revealed all sorts of dubious relationships Phahlane had when it came to purchasing his vehicles and building his house.[110]

110 Angelique Serrao, IPID responds to top cop Phahlane with more financial revelations, News24, 21 April 2017, https://www.news24.com/SouthAfrica/News/ipid-responds-to-top-cop-phahlane-with-more-financial-revelations-20170421

Mahlangu said the relief Phahlane sought in trying to have the search warrant overturned was academic because he was not seeking the return of the goods seized, i.e. the sound system. He also said that under the IPID Act, the directorate may appoint any fit and proper person as an investigator and that Phahlane was not entitled to a blanket embargo – like the one he was seeking to have imposed against me.

Mahlangu explained that the allegations of wrongdoing in the chemical contracts (that I had alleged in my original complaint against Phahlane) put lives at risk and that crime scene investigations were being compromised by using the out of date chemicals and wrong equipment supplied.

Mahlangu went into detail on the cash payments made from the boot of Phahlane's car, over and above the two cash payments of R350 000:

- The bricklayer received approximately seven cash payments of R14 000 each, an extra R20 000 (also in cash) to build a wall, and R11 000 in cash for the stairs, swimming pool, and bathroom wall. The total cash payments to the bricklayer amounted to R129 000.
- The plasterer was paid R170 000 in cash payments on a fortnightly basis.
- The electrician was also paid R10 000 on four or five occasions, amounting to approximately R50 000 in cash.
- The plumber was also paid in cash in amounts totalling R30 000.
- The tiler was paid between R5 000 and R10 000 in cash seven or eight times.

Mahlangu then revealed questionable findings they had made on several vehicles Phahlane and his family members drove. While everyone was focused on the building of his house, the IPID team had been looking at all aspects of his lifestyle. Interestingly, we found that Phahlane did not seem to have any debt, which meant he had money at his disposal. In fact, his propensity to spend and live like a king was the single largest red flag that prompted in-depth investigations.

This is what was discovered about his cars:

- Phahlane bought a Land Rover Discovery V6 in 2011 for R765 995, which he sold in 2014 to a car dealership in Pretoria for R650 000. The trade-in value for the vehicle at that time was only R557 500, which meant the dealership paid R92 500 more than the trade-in value. The car was then sold for R547 500, meaning the dealership made a loss of R106 632.
- Phahlane's wife purchased a Mercedes Benz C250 Elegance Automatic in 2012 for R482 500. The car was sold to the same dealership in January 2015. The vehicle was valued at R318 900, according to the dealership's stock card. However, their bank statement for the period (with Phahlane's name as a reference) said a total amount of R549 999 was paid, making the purchase price R241 099 above the trade-in value and R67 499 more than the vehicle cost new three years earlier.
- The proceeds of the sale for the Mercedes Benz were used to purchase a second Mercedes Benz, a new E250 CDI, for R765 000 – R250 000 of which Phahlane transferred into his wife's account.
- In 2013, Phahlane purchased a 2013 Nissan Navara for R322 927, which was financed by Nedbank. This was sold to the same dealership for R495 000 in April 2015. The book value at the time was R308 000 – a R187 000 difference.
- In April 2015, Phahlane bought a VW Amarok that the same dealership credited to another dealership for R362 963 and later valued at R132 000.

- In December 2015, a Toyota Hilux 4x4 single cab bakkie was purchased for R377 360.
- In February 2016, a VW Polo was registered in Phahlane's wife's name for R230 681. The vehicle was collected by an employee of the same dealership. This employee said that the Toyota Hilux and the Polo were given to Phahlane as a 'sponsorship', but Mahlangu said that Phahlane didn't point out the sponsorship in his founding affidavit or in his official disclosures.

The investigation into the Sable Hills house revealed that Phahlane paid up the bond on his house very quickly. He appeared to be living an extremely cash-flush lifestyle. The court papers revealed:

- Phahlane acquired the land in April 2010 for R850 000, with a cash deposit of R250 000 and a bond of R595 000.
- His bank statements showed that the proceeds from the sale of his last home totalled R513 994. This amount was paid into his account in September 2010. It is unknown where the R255 000 deposit came from, Mahlangu said.
- In 2010/11, Phahlane paid R157 000 into his bond account when he was only required to pay R47 000.
- In 2011/2012, Phahlane paid R143 000 into his bond account when he was only required to pay R36 000.
- During this period, he built the house and the only visible payment out of the bond account for construction work was for R200 000.
- In 2013/2014, Phahlane's bond repayments, pursuant to an increase in the bond amount, was R128 000. He paid R369 000.
- In 2014/2015, Phahlane was required to pay R111 000, but he paid R402 000.
- In 2015/2016, Phahlane was required to pay R73 000, but he paid R330 000.

- Between March and December 2016, Phahlane was required to make payments amounting to R51 000, but he paid R244 000.

These payments, Mahlangu said, needed to be considered along with all the other cash payments he made to the various contractors. With the dodgy house and the equally dodgy car transactions, Phahlane would be facing charges of money laundering, and he knew it:

> *The aforementioned information reveals dubious transactions in Phahlane's financial affairs. The investigation reveals that Phahlane and his wife were able to make additional payments of approximately R2m into their bond account in the last five years.*

Mahlangu said that Phahlane acquired a bond of R2.2-million, but he allegedly never used this money towards the cost of building the house:

> *He only accessed R1.1m between March and July 2012 after the house was almost finished, and this was used for finishes and trimmings.*

I knew this already and had included it in my complaint. Mahlangu then touched on how Phahlane was using his authority to undermine IPID's investigation. Aside from being in contact with three witnesses, Phahlane had also accessed a court file containing an application for the subpoena of certain witnesses and information pertaining to a list of intended witnesses. Mahlangu noted that Phahlane established his own task team, led by General Mabula and that these police officers had questioned IPID witnesses, arrested Trent and me, and sought to obtain Trent's cell phone without a warrant.

PUBLIC SPAT DISTRACTION

Phahlane took his fight-back campaign to Parliament. He made sure that whenever he spoke about the case, he accused IPID of being 'captured' by me. He started mockingly calling IPID 'OPID' – the

O'Sullivan Police Investigative Directorate.[111] It was a clever spin on his part to divert attention away from himself and his corrupt dealings and aim the public's scrutiny at me. For some strange reason, and despite the clear evidence of his wrongdoing, his public relations official's distraction campaign seemed to work to some extent, and the media kept speaking about the 'spat' between McBride and the Acting Police Chief, with calls for the Minister of Police to intervene – as if this was some sort of schoolyard fight. Certain gullible – or friendly – journalists either did not have the intelligence to unravel what had been put in front of them or were backing Phahlane.

This 'spat' was nothing of the sort. It was an independent investigation into a corrupt Acting Police Chief who was interfering in the investigations against him in every way he could think of and who was utilising a carefully crafted publicly funded communication campaign to make it seem as if he was a victim of an allegedly power-hungry McBride. Phahlane was creating fake news, and the parliamentarians were buying it. Either that or perhaps the parliamentarians were banking on a future police chief who would protect them from corruption charges in a bizarre quid pro quo.

McBride kept a clear head during Phahlane's media attacks, sticking to the facts while Phahlane raged. McBride revealed that Phahlane had already spent R900 000 in a bid to have the search warrant on his house ruled invalid:[112] McBride told the Police Portfolio Committee in Parliament that:

> *Phahlane sits with a big litigation budget, he sits with Crime Intelligence, he sits with a unit from the Northwest which counter investigates us, which interferes with our witnesses, and he launches a civil claim against us. We have a small litigation budget. We*

111 SABC News, Public spat between Phahlane, McBride under spotlight, Youtube, 16 May 2017, https://www.youtube.com/watch?v=BZR_Y-fymZQ

112 SABC News, McBride accuses Phahlane of waging a war against IPID, Youtube, 4 May 2017, https://www.youtube.com/watch?v=Tjb9t-boOS4

have three people in legal services. We have to deal with that. If the honourable members and the public expect us to make an impact, we have to stop a war raging against us by those abusing their power, like Acting Commissioner Phahlane.

IPID OFFICERS ARRESTED

Phahlane went one step further when the IPID investigators we accompanied to the Sable Hills estate were charged along with Trent and me. Mandlakayise Mahlangu and Temane Abram Binang's names were added to the charge sheet.[113] If this wasn't a case of defeating the ends of justice, then I didn't know what was. How could the IPID officers who were investigating Phahlane be charged for investigating him? It made no sense and completely undermined the reason for IPID's existence – an independent body to investigate wrongdoing in the police, free from interference.

And yet, there were Mahlangu and Binang summonsed to appear in the Pretoria Magistrate's Court alongside myself and Trent, charged with threatening witnesses and making misrepresentations that myself and Trent were IPID investigators so that we could gain access to certain places or information. It was a load of rubbish. Magistrate Aubrey Mphahlele ordered that the IPID investigators have no further contact with the seven witnesses, effectively killing the investigation into Phahlane.

What followed were months of going backwards and forwards to court, only to have the case postponed again and again for the corrupt State to conduct 'further investigations'. We were desperate for the trial to go ahead because we knew we had done nothing wrong and wanted to clear our names.

---

113 Virginia Keppler, IPID members added to O'Sullivan, Trent charge sheet, The Citizen, 31 May 2017, https://citizen.co.za/news/south-africa/1529019/ipid-members-added-to-osullivan-trent-charge-sheet/

When we arrived at court in November, instead of being handed a copy of the docket like we had been promised, we were handed a four-page letter containing thirty-four additional charges that the State said it intended to add to the case. The prosecutor also said that they wanted to add more accused. We would later discover that the other person they intended to charge was McBride himself. The false charges included contraventions of the Prevention of Organised Crime Act, racketeering, managing a criminal enterprise, intimidation, attempted extortion, and contravention of the Prevention and Combating of Corrupt Activities Act, among others. It was ridiculous, and after hours of arguing, the Magistrate agreed and struck the case from the roll.

Adding to this abuse of power, IPID's attorney's offices in Garsfontein were raided the night before on the orders of a name we now recognised – Brigadier Pharasa Ncube, the Northwest Head of Commercial Crimes Investigations.[114] Mabula's dirty Northwest team was hard at work, it seemed.

FIKILE MBALULA ENTERS THE PICTURE

In one of the many cabinet reshuffles that President Zuma orchestrated in the final months of his Presidency, Zuma, in a surprising move, removed Police Minister Nathi Nhleko from his portfolio and placed Fikile Mbalula in his place.[115]

I cannot describe how happy I was to hear this. Nhleko had been instrumental in seeing Ntlemeza, Mokotedi and Phahlane being unlawfully placed in their high-ranking positions. Aside from being irregular and illegal, the appointments were a complete disaster for the

114 Marianne Thamm, IPID vs SAPS: Robert McBride approaches court to stop Northwest unit interfering with investigations, Daily Maverick, 15 November 2017, https://www.dailymaverick.co.za/article/2017-11-15-ipid-vs-saps-robert-mcbride-approaches-court-to-stop-north-west-unit-interfering-with-investigations/

115 ANA Reporter, Police union welcomes 'energetic young minister' Mbalula, IOL, 31 March 2017, https://www.iol.co.za/news/politics/police-union-welcomes-energetic-young-minister-mbalula-8433216

police. Nhleko was the head under which the capture of the criminal justice sector had been fulfilled. In one fell swoop, the three stooges lost their political support base. Finally, things could start turning around.

Mbalula didn't have time to acquaint himself with his new job. He had to act quickly. Soon after his appointment, the courts had declared Ntlemeza unfit for the position of Head of the Hawks, and Ntlemeza was trying to delay being chucked out of the position by launching appeals against the court's decision. Mbalula put a stop to this and told Ntlemeza to leave. Following that, he quickly moved to replace and suspend Phahlane. Just one month after taking office, Mbalula appointed Lieutenant-General Lesetja Mothiba as the Acting Police Commissioner. Phahlane's days were over, and so too were Ntlemeza's. The future was certainly looking brighter. In a statement, Mbalula said:

> *There are clearly serious allegations of misconduct on the part of Lieutenant General Phahlane, which also impacts on his fitness to hold office as the Acting National Police Commissioner. The allegations against Lieutenant General Phahlane raise questions of conduct that would be inconsistent with expectations that attend those who hold leadership in our police service, the South African Police Service. I am duty-bound to make it clear that Lieutenant General Phahlane has a right to be presumed innocent until proven otherwise.116*

Phahlane was furious, but there was nothing he could do. Instead, he focussed on continuing his fight with IPID.

IPID FIGHTS FOR INDEPENDENCE

McBride knew he had to secure IPID's independence from attacks like those launched against them by Mabula's dirty Northwest team. The only way to do this was through the courts. McBride wanted

116 Samkelo Maseko, Phahlane must be given space to clear his name: Mbalula, JacarandaFM, 1 June 2017, https://www.jacarandafm.com/news/news/phahlane-must-be-give-space-clear-his-name-mbalula/

to stop the Northwest team from investigating IPID's officials. In November 2017, he filed an application in the Pretoria High Court seeking to urgently interdict SAPS members implicated in IPID investigations from investigating IPID's officers.

By then, we had discovered that the contents of Trent's phone had indeed been illegally downloaded and that Phahlane was using her WhatsApp messages in his fight-back campaign. IPID discovered that the same Northwest team was attempting to lay a new charge, this time against IPID officer Mantsha Raphesu for passing personal IPID information to non-IPID members in a WhatsApp group – information the IPID team had discussed with Trent as part of the Phahlane investigation.

Although she was an attorney, I had personally trained Sarah-Jane Trent in the art of intelligence and counterintelligence, and she had become masterful at obtaining and analysing crime intelligence data and joining the dots. Since IPID was woefully short of such skills due to budgetary constraints, I provided these services to them at no cost for several years, except during the time in which McBride was suspended. Since I was providing the service free of charge, there was no need for any procurement process, and I simply saw it as an extension of the work of Forensics for Justice. We collaborated with decent cops in a similar way for many years without anyone complaining, except for the criminals, of course. Now that IPID had a secret weapon like Forensics for Justice, it allowed them to focus on other aspects of the investigations. This was problematic for Phahlane and his crooked accomplices, and they decided, as part of a coordinated strategy, to drive a wedge between ourselves and IPID by charging Raphesu. It was a big mistake that only served to close our ranks and have us digging deeper for evidence.

Raphesu was involved in an investigation against Ncube, Dawood and Kgorane, related to the unlawful arrest, kidnapping and intimidation of myself and Trent. It was clear that Phahlane's plan was to completely neutralise not only myself and Trent but the whole of IPID.

In the court application, IPID asked the new Acting Police Commissioner to ensure that the SAPS investigation against IPID's Phahlane team – Mandlakayise Mahlangu, Temane Binang and Mantsha Raphesu – not be carried out by the officers from the Northwest team. The urgent application launched by McBride argued that there was a real conflict of interest in the SAPS investigations against them.

McBride touched on the persistent obstructions the IPID team had faced during their investigation into Phahlane. The arrest and charges against me, Trent, Mahlangu and Binang were also mentioned. The new charges against Raphesu alleged that he "provided information which was supposed to be kept confidential, to Trent who is not a member of IPID, thereby aiding Sarah-Jane Trent, Paul O'Sullivan, Mandlakayise Mahlangu and Robert McBride to commit corruption".[117]

In his affidavit, McBride said that one of the main concerns was that members of the Northwest team – including Mabula, Northwest Head of Commercial Crimes Brigadier Daniel Ncube, Northwest Commander of the Special Crimes Unit Lieutenant Colonel Ismail Dawood, and Organised Crime Brigadier Clifford Kgorane – were also being investigated by the same IPID officials they were investigating. He said it was an untenable situation that was escalating. He added that of grave concern was that Brigadier Daniel Ncube, the officer who was charging Raphesu, was the subject of an investigation by Raphesu.

McBride also revealed that two Deputy Directors of Public Prosecution had recommended prosecution against Ncube and other team members. Attached to the court papers was a memorandum by a

---

117 Angelique Serrao, IPID's ongoing battle with Northwest SAPS over Phahlane heats up, News24, 15 November 2017, https://www.news24.com/news24/SouthAfrica/News/ipids-ongoing-battle-with-north-west-saps-over-phahlane-heats-up-20171115

deputy director of public prosecutions and a senior state advocate that found evidence of unlawful arrest, kidnapping, fraud and defeating the ends of justice related to my arrest. The prosecution's office concluded that "prosecution must be instituted" against the SAPS members for their unlawful kidnapping of myself and Trent.

We later found that despite the recommended prosecution, captured friends of Nomgcobo Jiba in the NPA had managed to block all the charges against the Northwest team relating to our kidnapping. In his statement, McBride said:

> *The position adopted by the SAPS seriously compromises the independence of IPID. The result is that IPID's investigators cannot function effectively and independently without fear of reprisal and retaliatory investigation by the SAPS officers they are required to investigate.*

He also said the current situation was making it impossible for them to finalise the investigation into Phahlane.

I am determined to see the crooked cops from the Northwest face hard prison time and will run a private prosecution if necessary.

The court turned down the application for urgency and set the case down for a further date but ordered that any case that was to be investigated against the three IPID officers had to go through the National Director of Public Prosecutions. The case would sit in the court system for years to come, but, in getting the interim order, the team from the Northwest was not able to do as they pleased. They now had to get permission from the NPA every time they wanted to move forward in their illegal investigations. While it partially stopped them in their tracks, their accomplices in the NPA ensured that Shaun (The Sheep) Abrahams declined to prosecute them for their own crimes. It had become a stalemate.

While the cases between Phahlane, the SAPS and IPID filled the court rolls, IPID's investigators were following leads about Phahlane's cars. Why would a car dealership overpay such large amounts of money for Phahlane and his wife's vehicles? What did the dealer have to gain?

The information that emerged would reveal the far-reaching depths of corruption in SAPS' Procurement division.

CHAPTER 20

DISHONEST WITNESSES, NO EVIDENCE AND THE POLICE'S CRIMINAL CONDUCT

BACK TO COURT

In between investigating and exposing Phahlane, Ntlemeza, Mokotedi, Montana, Myeni and others – and my subsequent arrest by the Northwest 'hit squad' Phahlane had recruited – I still had to travel to Kempton Park every few weeks to attend court for the trumped-up charges in the passport case.

The fake charges were a drain on my time and my financial resources, and I was growing increasingly frustrated by the way it was dragging on. By now, the trial was well underway, and I sat and watched Barry Roux make short work of the dirty police officers who were the State's witnesses. While I enjoyed watching them squirm on the stand, I was also aware of what a phenomenal waste of time the whole thing was. The case was a disgraceful abuse of my human rights, from my illegal arrest, detention, and torture to the stringent bail conditions and the seemingly never-ending court appearances. But I had no choice but to sit there and watch the State embarrass itself each time I appeared in court. And embarrass themselves they all did.

Always straightforward, clear and eloquent, Barry Roux never faltered in putting forward my case that not only was I unaware of the alleged illegality of my actions in using my Irish passport (because nobody else in the country had ever been charged with the crime) but also that I had only used my Irish passport when entering and leaving the country to avoid the very real threats on my life posed by Radovan Krejcir, who himself had many high-ranking dirty cops on his payroll.

One by one, the State's witnesses were torn apart on the witness stand revealing, despite their best efforts not to, that I had obviously been arrested to stop me from exposing to the world the extent of the corruption of Zuma and his allies. Like a broken record – and despite the case falling apart in front of him – Prosecutor Jabulani Mlotshwa kept unlawfully postponing the court dates. He knew that it was the only case that's stringent bail conditions allowed the State some form of control over me. They relished forcing me to bring an application every time I had to leave the country, which they vigorously opposed every time. When I was found not guilty, as I inevitably would be, this control would end.

By June 2017, more than a year after the trial had begun, I had had enough. Roux put forward a section 174 application to have the case discharged from the court. In his judgement, Magistrate Wynand Nel was brutal about the State's case, stating that it was beyond his understanding why I had been taken to Pretoria Police Station, adding, "But only the police who arrested him would know why".

Nel listed the police officers and Home Affairs employee who had taken the witness stand and stated that Advocate Roux had "literally wiped the floor with these witnesses" and that his impression of them as poor witnesses had not changed during the trial.

During my previous appearance, the court had ordered that the police return my passports, but instead, the crooked policeman holding my passports had quickly walked out of the court with them, at Mokotedi's instance, intending not to give them to me. In his judgement, Magistrate Nel said that their actions bordered on contempt of court:

> *At this point, I would also like to mention that the behaviour of the witnesses and the demeanour of them was also a matter of concern for the court. Furthermore also the conduct of the investigating officer and other police officials that were involved, especially with reference to the last appearance of the accused in this court when their conduct bordered on an act of contempt of court and, in that regard, I refer to the issue surrounding the handing over of Mr O'Sullivan's passports.*

Nel said that my defence that I was trying to protect myself from Krejcir was justified because Krejcir was already convicted on several serious charges:

> *May I add to it that he [Krejcir] is for the last couple of years a frequent visitor to our specific court here in Kempton Park in criminal matters as well as a long drawn out extradition hearing that has been going on for quite a number of years now. For each and every occasion, the courts are to be swept by the bomb squad, and arrangement has to be made for extra armed security supplied by the police force because of the security risk that his appearance posed to the courts and its personnel when he appears.*
>
> *In this regard, I would say the arguments forwarded by the defence is not something that should be disregarded as not serious or as a poor excuse and that the accused, in light of the seriousness of what this person's threat posed, had to take steps to protect himself.*
>
> *In Advocate Mlotshwa's argument, he argued passionately, opposing the request by the defence for the dismissal of the accused. What is, however, disturbing to the court was his argument that there was an evidential burden on the accused to adduce evidence that he did not have the intention to contravene the legislation.*

I must say this there is no burden on the accused or any accused to prove anything. The burden of proof is always on the State to prove their case beyond reasonable doubt on criminal matters.

Magistrate Nel concluded that the evidence led by the State was of a very poor quality "by lack of a better word by the court". The case was then dismissed.

As soon as Magistrate Nel delivered his judgement, a furious Mlotshwa jumped out of his seat and said the State intended appealing the case's dismissal. I walked out of the court free of this case, passports in hand and the freedom to enter and leave the country as I pleased. Needless to say, Mlotshwa never bothered to launch an appeal, proving to me that he was all hot air and lies.

While I felt triumphant, free of the burden this case had on my life for more than a year, I was furious. I intended to sue the State and all those who had been involved in my illegal arrest, detention, and torture.

When I walked out of the on the morning of the 2nd of June 2017, surrounded by cameras and the media jostling for a comment, I wanted to make it clear to the world that this case had been nothing more than the State Capture gang's attempt to silence my investigations against them.

It was about time I dealt with Mlotshwa.

THE ROT AT THE NPA

Although my financial resources had been badly eroded, my information war chest was growing by the day. No matter where I looked, I found proof of criminality in every one of the crooks investigating me. It wasn't just the police. By then, it had become clear that the National Prosecuting Authority was badly compromised, from top to midway.

In my *Joining the Dots Report* published in 2016 and updated again in June 2017, I made this crystal clear. By 2013, the process of capturing the police, Hawks, NPA and SARS was well underway, but it was only in 2015 that the capture process was fully completed. The underworld had had two years to run the criminal justice system by then, and the wheels of equal and fair justice had clearly fallen off. Our research at Forensics for Justice showed that, by March 2015, all the key appointments for the state capture roles had been completed. Major General Ntlemeza was at the Hawks, Lieutenant General Phahlane was Acting Commissioner of Police, the National Prosecuting Authority was being influenced by Zuma's lawyer Michael Hulley – who had head-hunted and unlawfully appointed Shaun (The Sheep) Abrahams, and Zuma's relative Tom Moyane was ensconced at SARS. It appeared that the whole of the NPA's specialised Priority Crimes Litigation Unit was populated with criminals.

During 2016, every criminal docket opened against Zuma and his connected underworld, including every tax case and every prosecution that may have been underway before this point, had been quietly killed or simply vanished into thin air.

Between 2015 and 2019, we opened no fewer than thirty criminal dockets implicating Zuma and his cohorts in serious crimes, including the cases against Phahlane, Ntlemeza, Moonoo, Mdluli, Jen Chi Huang, Yusuf Kajee, Dudu Myeni, Mokotedi, Jiba, Mrwebi, Maema, Mlotshwa, Montana, the Bhana family, and Krejcir.

The capture of the criminal justice system included not only dirty cops and prosecutors but also several members of the judiciary who had found a way of getting to the trough. In late 2016, one of Radovan Krejcir's lawyers, Eric Bryer, wrote to the Director of Public Prosecutions in Gauteng, requesting a deal for Radovan Krejcir. In return, he offered that Krejcir would testify against Lieutenant General Moonoo, Lieutenant General Mdluli, Major General Mabasa and Magistrate Stephen Holzen, with whom Krejcir claimed to have a corrupt relationship.

Regarding Magistrate Holzen, I already had a sworn statement that set out in detail how Krejcir's evil was unleashed on South Africa purely as a result of bribes allegedly paid to Holzen. During the Krejcir investigations, I had been to Cyprus to track down George Louca, a.k.a. George Smith, after he was framed by both Mabasa and Krejcir for the murder of Lolly Jackson, a notorious strip club owner from the wrong side of the tracks. Louca and Krejcir had met in prison, where Louca was languishing awaiting trial for theft of a container load of imported footwear.

Of course, I had known all along that Louca did not shoot Lolly Jackson. That was Krejcir's handiwork. Both Krejcir and Jackson had been involved in money laundering. By the time the wheels came off, Krejcir had scammed Jackson to the tune of R5-million. This led to heated discussions, which eventually resulted in Krejcir fatally shooting Jackson in Louca's rented Kempton Park house. According to Louca's subsequent sworn statements, Louca knew the inner workings of Krejcir's syndicate up to the time of Jackson's murder.

After playing cat and mouse with the authorities in South Africa for several years, Louca was eventually extradited to South Africa, based on admissions he allegedly made to Krejcir and Mabasa, who (mysteriously) were first on the scene of the Jackson murder and later pronounced key witnesses in the murder. I already knew by then that Mabasa was on Krejcir's payroll, along with Moonoo and Mdluli. However, I did not know about Holzen's alleged involvement. This only emerged after I paid an attorney to act for Louca in obtaining Section 204 statements and trying to cut a deal with the State.

According to Louca's sworn statement, a young girl approached him in the exercise yard at Kempton Park's holding cells and asked if he knew Krejcir. She then handed him a note through the fence, instructing that it be passed to Krejcir. According to Louca, the note was in Czech but of such a quality that it had been translated from English using an online translator.

The note was sent to Krejcir, not by Magistrate Holzen, but by someone connected to him. I later found out that this woman was Holzen's girlfriend. I suspected that the girl delivering the note may have been the girlfriend's daughter.

Louca obtained a cellular phone and began communicating with Magistrate Holzen's girlfriend via that phone. The alleged arrangement was that Krejcir would have to make an upfront payment of R1-million to show good faith and a further R3-million after he had been released on bail. To be certain that he wasn't being stung by an opportunistic fraudster, Krejcir devised a scheme whereby Magistrate Holzen would personally give Krejcir a 'signal' to indicate that he was in on the scheme. This signal would entail Holzen dropping his pen on the floor three times – and retrieving it each time – while Krejcir was in his courtroom at Kempton Park. Which is exactly what happened.

An arrangement was made to drop off the initial deposit of R1-million, which Louca supervised along with a certain Petronella Englebrecht, the sister of a friend of Krejcir from the Seychelles. Engelbrecht and Louca, who by now was out on bail, delivered the R1-million to Holzen's girlfriend at a predetermined spot on the R21 freeway. I traced Petronella Engelbrecht to a beauty parlour in Pretoria, but she said she was too scared to get involved in the matter by giving evidence. No one in the justice system ever bothered to follow it up.

Although Holzen's price was R4-million, he only ever got the first instalment of R1-million. This was because Krejcir met with him after his release from jail, threatened him, and agreed to only pay him a further half a million rand. That money was never paid. The State Prosecutor called for the recusal of Magistrate Holzen from carrying out the extradition hearing. Holzen refused to recuse himself and went ahead and heard the extradition matter before dismissing the application for extradition. The State fought back and took Holzen's refusal to recuse himself on review at the High Court and not only had the magistrate recused, but also had Holzen's dismissal of the extradition application set aside.

When I joined AfriForum at a media conference in December 2016, we named and shamed various parties, including Generals Moonoo, Mdluli and Mabasa, and Magistrate Holzen, for having a corrupt relationship with Radovan Krejcir. We did not hear from Moonoo, Mdluli or Mabasa, but Holzen sent a letter of demand through his attorney Charles Coetzee demanding an apology and payment of R10-million. I decided to simply ignore the demand, and nothing was ever heard again, proving that I had hit the proverbial nail right on the head. If Holzen were clean, he would have definitely sued me.

In the thirteen years that Radovan Krejcir had been in South Africa, he was directly connected to thirteen murders and more than five attempted murders, as well as countless cases of conspiracy to commit murder. The price he paid for entering into and staying in the country was a paltry R1-million, thanks to the corrupt conduct of a single magistrate. The financial cost of Krejcir's stay in the country to South Africa has already topped R100-million, most of which has been spent on expensive multi-disciplinary team police escorts for all of his court appearances.

But just like every other case, the State never followed through on Krejcir's admittance to corrupting Holzen, Moonoo, Mabasa and Mdluli. Between the NPA and the Police, they managed to squash almost every single case I had opened. The only reason any investigation on Phahlane was taking place was that IPID, under McBride, had managed to unshackle itself from the state capture brigade. This, too, would not last long, and they too would once again be targeted.

The NPA seemed to be only capable of targeting genuine corruption fighters, and I felt it was time to shine the limelight on what was really happening there.

THE CASE AGAINST MLOTSHWA GROWS

I had already laid a complaint against (the fake) Advocate Jabulani Mlotshwa with the NPA in 2016 after he dishonestly tried to have Magistrate Nel recuse himself in the trumped-up passport case. His conduct had been fraudulent, and I asked the NPA to investigate the matter. Not only did they ignore my complaint, but they allowed Mlotshwa to continue laying new fake charges against me.

But just like an apple that's core is decaying, Mlotshwa's rotten behaviour would soon come to the fore.

Initially, it was Vlok's bumbling investigation skills that revealed both his and Mlotshwa's criminal schemes. Lynn Fliess had, by then, seen the transcripts of the recorded conversation between her attorneys and Vlok, where Vlok asked that she allow her ex-husband to see her child and that, in return, he would drop the fake firearm and racketeering charges against her. In the conversation, Vlok revealed that he and Mlotshwa had sat together planning the charges against her. Fliess opened a criminal docket against Vlok, her ex-husband, and Mlotshwa for extortion, intimidation, defeating the ends of justice, and corruption.

I took Fliess' docket and laid a complaint against Mlotshwa at the General Council of the Bar in September 2016. I attached my complaint to the NPA to make them aware of it. In my letter to the NPA, I made it clear that Mlotshwa had completely abandoned his oath of office in terms of the Constitution and the NPA Act, that he acted without regard for the NPA code of conduct, that he intentionally and unlawfully lied to the Kempton Park Magistrate's Court during the Magistrate's recusal application, and that he had aided and abetted the giving of false testimony under oath by dishonest police officials. I made it clear that Mlotshwa's conduct was part of a continued strategy within the NPA and the Hawks, aimed at suppressing public participation in the fight against the scourge of corruption in South Africa. I was fully aware by then that they knew they would never get a conviction against me on any of their many fake charges and that their sole intention was to tie me up in legal costs, destroy me financially and stop me from exposing further corruption.

In my complaint, I wrote:

> *It is no coincidence that, despite Advocate Mlotshwa's office (the so-called Priority Crime Litigation Unit or PCLU) being manned by only four advocates, it is this very same office, previously acting under (the now disgraced and suspended) Ms Nomgcobo Jiba, that were leading the attack on corruption busters such as General Booysen, General Dramat, General Sibiya, Robert McBride, and many others. I would not be surprised if they have not fallen under the control of Jiba and copied her example.*

In further complaints, I attached the 12 April 2016 memorandum from the National Director of Public Prosecutions, Shaun Abrahams, instructing the Priority Crimes Litigation Unit to manage all the investigations and prosecutions of myself. I also asked how it was that Mlotshwa had been made responsible – under law – for *all* aspects regarding my prosecution. In my complaint to the NPA's George Baloyi, I asked:

I am entitled to know how such a person could ever be assigned to harass and intimidate me and commit fraud against me and violate my Constitutional rights in the way he has done.

> *It also means he is responsible for the criminal conduct of Vlok, either in that they acted with a common purpose or he was an accessory before or after the fact.*

It means he was also responsible for the facts that have already come out in court:

No investigation was carried out, no search for inculpatory or exculpatory evidence took place, which means that he is liable in law, and so too are the NPA, for the criminal conduct, not only of himself but also of Vlok.

What lay behind the decision to write the memorandum (Shaun Abraham's memo of 2016-04-12) in the first place? Who requested the memorandum be written? Why was a decision made to refer all matters to the Political Crimes Litigation Unit when there are many, many competent prosecutors out there at court level? Is it because the court-level prosecutors could not be controlled to carry out political directives?

There were endless questions about their conduct, but no answers were forthcoming. In a damning indictment of their culpability, every single email I sent went unanswered.

I asked to see the same memorandum that had no doubt been made available in the cases against Julius Malema, Dramat, Sibiya, Gordhan, McBride, Booysen, and Glynnis Breytenbach, where this same unit had been tasked with prosecuting them. If any proof was needed that the NPA had embarked on politically inspired prosecutions in breach of the Constitution, the proof would be in these memorandums. I jokingly re-named the PCLU the Political Crimes Litigation Unit since corrupt politicians were directing it in the same manner that a marionette is directed by a puppeteer.

Not only was the NPA carrying out illegal prosecutions, but they were also deliberately ignoring genuine high-profile cases that needed prosecutions to take place. Mine and Sarah-Jane Trent's illegal arrests in February 2017 were a case in point. We had opened cases against police members from the Northwest involved in our arrests, and we had learnt that two senior prosecutors recommended that they all be prosecuted for kidnapping in respect of Sarah-Jane and kidnapping and contempt of court in my case. Instead of acting on this, the NPA decided that these two prosecutors could not be part of the decision-making process, and the docket was sent off somewhere else.

After months of pushing for a decision to be made in the cases we had opened concerning our kidnappings by dirty cops, I received a letter stating that the NPA had decided not to prosecute. It was a travesty of justice and further proof that the NPA had been fully captured.

PUBLIC LETTER

I made sure I made as many public statements about the corrupt PCLU Unit as possible. This hit-squad within the NPA needed to be exposed to public scrutiny. I openly cc'd Deputy President Cyril Ramaphosa (now President) into all my emails to the NPA. I also wrote an open letter to him, which was published on *Biznews*.[118]

In the letter, I made it clear that the recipients of all my emails had remained silent on the serious allegations I had made against them, which I believed was an admission of guilt.[2]

I explained how the PCLU had become Abraham's weapon of choice – along with his accomplice Michael Hulley – to go after myself and a number of other politically important people. The only thing we had in common is that we had all, in one way or another, been involved in exposing the dark underbelly of institutionalised corruption in South Africa.

I went on to say that during 2017 it emerged that, despite ample prima facie evidence of criminal wrongdoing, decisions were being taken, at the instruction of Abrahams, not to prosecute certain persons where a prosecution was warranted.

118 Jackie Cameron, Dear Cyril: Warning! Shaun Abrahams has personal 'hit squad' – Paul O'Sullivan, Biznews, 18 January 2018, https://www.biznews.com/thought-leaders/2018/01/18/shaun-abrahams-has-personal-hit-squad

Four years later, we witnessed the real effects of this damage. Why had there been there no high-profile state capture prosecutions? The damage to the NPA was so severe that the institution was disembowelled of any high-level expertise, allowing crime to flourish.

But there were some, like me, who kept on fighting and refusing to give up. The response was always that of silence, but I didn't stop barking at their door.

NOT AN ADVOCATE

For months, I heard nothing back from my complaints about Mlotshwa. In April 2017, I received a reply from the Law Society of the Northern Provinces that stated they had a record of a JJ Mlotshwa being struck from the Roll of Attorneys in February 2000. They gave me a case number and said the case would have been heard in the North Gauteng High Court. I further learnt that Mlotshwa's wife had also been struck off the roll of attorneys in 2005 for misappropriation of trust money, having stolen clients' funds.

Mlotshwa had been in court purporting to be an Advocate when he was nothing of the kind and had even been struck off the attorney's roll years before. The information was shocking. Not only had he somehow become a prosecutor after this, but he had become a deputy director, which in itself was non-compliant. To be a deputy director, one had to have the right to appear in the High Court. Mlotshwa did not have this right when he was promoted by Advocate Xolisile Khanyile, his cousin at the NPA, who was the Director of Public Prosecutions in the Free State at the time. Khanyile left the NPA a year later to take up a senior position at the Financial Intelligence Centre.

I made it clear to the NPA that Mlotshwa was a fraud, but they did nothing about it. Instead, Mlotshwa ramped up his attacks on me in an act of revenge. In one of my appearances in the Randburg Magistrates Court during the fake Alice Johnston case, Mlotshwa flagrantly lied to the court. When the magistrate asked him why he had not advised the court of the complaint before the trial started, Mlotshwa claimed he had not been aware of the case I had opened against him before the trial had started.

Not only had I sent the complaint to him before the start of the trial, but Mlotshwa had, in fact, provided an answering affidavit to the allegations I had made against him. It was clear that there was not an honest bone in that man's body. Furthermore, despite the illegality in doing so, he seemed to accuse all white people of being racist – an act of racism in itself.

Soon after I exposed Mlotshwa for being a fake advocate, he issued me with a summons in the Neil Diamond matter to say he was charging Melissa Naidu and me in the case. This was nothing more than another fake malicious prosecution, and I requested that my legal team launch an urgent application to set aside the summons.

A picture I doctored and posted on the walls at Randburg Magistrates Court to shame Mlotshwa.

EXPOSED FOR ALL TO SEE

The truth was, the summons was the last kicks of a dying horse. Mlotshwa had been exposed. I had found the truth behind his charade and was revealing it openly. With all the cases he had charged me with, he couldn't avoid me. I suspect he would have loved to have slunk away and avoided me at all costs. Instead, he had to meet me face-to-face in court every time I appeared.

A few weeks after making my complaint and revealing his fraud, I met Mlotshwa once more. This time it was for the fake Cora van der Merwe case, which was also being held in the Randburg Magistrates Court.

I was on the stand, and Mlotshwa was cross-examining me. He was grasping at straws – he knew the case against me had all but collapsed. He asked me in reference to Ronald Bobroff:

> *Mr O'Sullivan, is it not true that your client was struck off the roll of attorneys for dishonesty?*

My response was as quick as it was factual:

> *I believe it is true, but then, you were also struck off the roll of attorneys – and so was your wife – for stealing client funds. And here you are, working as a prosecutor.*

Needless to say, the fake advocate abruptly ended his cross-examination with no further questions and retreated to his chair. To say that the Magistrate looked shocked would have been an understatement. A deathly silence descended over the proceedings while she gathered herself together.

I made sure I emailed Abrahams to tell him about my day in court:

> *I wish you and the team were in court today and yesterday to see what a true circus looks like. The star performer was the criminal with a gown, JJ Mlotshwa. How on earth did he rise up the ranks to become a Deputy Director? It can only be corruption.*

I asked how the NPA could justify having such a tainted individual prosecuting people and asked that all his cases be reviewed. I also laid out evidence proving that in acting as an Advocate when he wasn't one, Mlotshwa was committing fraud.

Mlotshwa had been signing off all his documents as Counsel for the State. He had used this title previously when he launched the illegal application to have Magistrate Nel recuse himself, but the word 'Counsel' can only be used lawfully by a real Advocate. In court, and on numerous other occasions, Mlotshwa allowed himself to be called "Advocate" by other (real) advocates and judges, including during the so-called Cato Manor Death Squad trial, without ever correcting anyone of their mistake. After I outed him, he stopped appearing in the High Court on the Cato Manor matter because he knew he would face honesty questions.

Sello Maema, Mlotshwa's captured colleague at the Political Crimes Litigation Unit – as I liked to call it – had also referred to Mlotshwa as a Senior State Advocate in a sworn statement. I could not understand why they would refer to a fraud as a Senior State Advocate. Then it dawned on me that Mlotshwa had not only lied to me and the courts, but he was also lying to all of his accomplices.

In my email to Abrahams, I added:

> *Why would Maema perpetuate such a lie? Was it perhaps to do with Maema's perjuriously criminal support of Jiba? Perhaps it's just because Maema is part of the captured crew at PCLU. General Booysen soon picked up on it and opened a case against Maema in Silverton. Another one of those many cases gathering dust in the dark underbelly of the NPA.*
>
> *The NPA is hell-bent on 'punishing' all those exposing corruption whilst protecting the corrupt. I say again what I said to Selebi, Agliotti, Mdluli, Mabasa, Krejcir, Phahlane, Ntlemeza:*
>
> *'NEVER p!$$ in an Irishman's beer and expect him to roll over. It just doesn't happen. As of today, I am officially going all-out for justice, and NOTHING or no one will stop me.*

THE ADVOCATE'S NEW CLOTHES

As with all the complaints that had gone before, I never received a single response to any of my emails to Abrahams. He had exercised his constitutional right to remain silent to avoid incriminating himself.

There had been one noticeable reaction to it all, though. – Mlotshwa was wearing a new gown. At my next court appearance on the 6th of October 2017, instead of his usual Advocate's gown, he now wore a brand new standard prosecutor's gown as worn by those who were not advocates.

I decided to rub the fact into what was obviously a raw wound by emailing Mlotshwa (and all his bosses) that afternoon when coming back from court to say that I was glad he had ceased committing a criminal offence by wearing an advocate's gown. I was now the cat playing with the mouse I had caught stealing the cheese.

> *That kind of proves to me, and the rest of the world, that he has made an admission of guilt. If he was right to wear an Advocate's gown all along, he would still be wearing it. That's three years of crime, with repeated offences at every court appearance. I reckon we could be looking at a sentence of 200 years, assuming he works two days a week, which is about right.*
>
> *He, therefore, admits guilt and hopes that by currently complying with the law, his past criminal conduct will be overlooked by the management of the NPA. A bit like someone who stops robbing banks and expects the previous bank robberies to be ignored.*
>
> *Will his crimes be condoned, or will he be prosecuted? Does the NPA act without fear, favour or prejudice? Or does it protect criminals in its ranks?'*

I told Mlotshwa that I would not stop pursuing him and that the charges would be extortion, fraud, racketeering and defeating the ends of justice.

> *The fake advocate stuff is peanuts compared to the case I am building on you. By the way, how much did you and your wife steal from client funds, and why has no one ever been prosecuted for that?*
>
> *Perhaps when we meet in court next week, you can tell me. Or would you prefer it if I tell you? Perhaps you can also explain all the debt judgements against you? Or do debt judgments just make you more flexible as a prosecutor, along with your crooked past? Debt-ridden prosecutors are, in my humble opinion, open to corruption and should not pass muster at the NPA. Especially when they have a hidden past and are married to a thief.*
>
> *Perhaps if you tell me who put you up to these heinous crimes against the State, I will be lenient with you. Heck, I may even ask for indemnity for you? Would that work for you?*
>
> *You should know by now; I am the one who will send you to prison, not the other way around. It's lucky for you that you have no assets, like a house or anything, or you would lose that when I'm done.*

I'm still waiting for Mlotshwa's response to my final taunt in that email:

Stop me if you can.

CHAPTER 21

THE HOUSE OF CARDS COLLAPSES

COURT CASES CRUMBLE

Now that the illegal passport case and the fake charges opened by Phahlane had been resolved, I had four more cases before court to deal with. These were the cases opened by the convicted fraudster and attempted murderer, Alice Johnston, her friend and fellow thief, Cora van der Merwe, the SAA case opened by the corrupt Dudu Myeni and finally, the revenge case launched by Mlotshwa involving allegedly corrupt ANC counsellor Neil Diamond. The common denominator between all these people was the fake advocate Jabulani Mlotshwa, the dirty cop Jacobus Vlok, his boss, a crooked General called Mokotedi and a dishonest journalist by the name of Anthony Beamish.

Every single case was a flimsily constructed set of lies with zero evidence (or substance), but Mlotshwa – and the shady set of characters who were conspiring with him – insisted they go ahead. Any decent police officer or prosecutor would have refused to have proceeded with an investigation or prosecution in the first place, but, as the court cases unfolded, it became increasingly clear that decency was in short supply when it came to these characters.

Watching the spectacle unfold, I was torn between exasperation, amusement at Mlotshwa's bungling, and fury. It felt like this interminable time in the middle of 2017 would never end.

During the same period, my investigations into all these state capture cronies were finally bearing some real fruit. I had also obtained a copy of the Gupta Leak emails, and I was able to verify their authenticity. The Zuma state capture network had left the country ravaged and teetering on the edge of economic and moral descent. It needed to be stopped yesterday if any State institutions were to be left standing. With the leak of the Gupta emails and the upcoming ANC conference, Zuma and his cronies were acutely aware that the last months of 2017 would be their last hoorah. They rushed through projects to empty what was left of the State's coffers. The spy networks within the SSA and Crime Intelligence, which had already wrought their destruction across institutions like SARS and the Hawks, went into overdrive in an attempt to ensure Zuma's political ascension after his presidency through his ex-wife, Nkosazana Dlamini-Zuma.

It was a critical time, and I wanted to spend every minute of my day working to stop this criminal enterprise from securing any more of the South African taxpayer's hard-earned money. I also had to waste my time in court, throwing my money at top-class attorneys while Mlotshwa's accomplice's 'witnesses' squirmed on the stand with tears pouring down their cheeks as their lies were exposed during cross-examination. Mlotshwa's theatre became ever more dramatic as he came up with increasingly inventive excuses to get the magistrates to postpone the trial days, so that he could delay each case for as long as possible. Sitting in court, I gnashed my teeth as I watched each case die a long-winded death. Every minute gone was a lost opportunity to stop the rampant plundering which was taking place. This had been their intention, tie me up in knots, while they plundered the country.

THE ALICE JOHNSTON TRIAL

The best example of Mlotshwa's fraudulent time-wasting tactics was on display during the Alice Johnston trial in July of 2017. As explained earlier, Johnston alleged that I had committed fraud by claiming I had told her that if she confessed to committing conspiracy to commit murder, I would get her a suspended sentence for her role in the near-fatal shooting of her employer, James Murray, after he opened various cases of fraud against her. She falsely claimed I had intimidated her during an interview, not knowing that the entire interview had been video recorded.

Instead of a speedy trial, Mlotshwa's handling of the matter was so incompetent that I kept notes of his actions and emailed them to Shaun (The Sheep) Abrahams in another written complaint, which was, not surprisingly, ignored. Mlotshwa consistently arrived late for court. One day, in particular, stood out. It was a Monday, and Randburg Regional Court Magistrate Gayle Pretorius had asked us to start promptly at 9 a.m. Mlotshwa only arrived at 9:25 a.m., with a pathetic sheepish grin on his face. It was the day of Alice Johnston's cross-examination, and my counsel ripped her to shreds. Mlotshwa's case was so feeble that Johnston was his only witness. It didn't take long for my legal team to tear holes into her version of events. As soon as her lies were exposed, Johnston caved in.

Johnston began to cry, and the court had to adjourn. When we came back into court, Johnston clearly had had a change of heart. She suddenly testified truthfully, and her evidence distinctly contradicted her previous testimony under oath. At one point, Mlotshwa jumped up and asked the court to warn the witness that she was committing perjury. Magistrate Pretorius refused to enter the fray and rebuked Mlotshwa for asking her to do so. Johnston then made a stunning admission, stating that she felt she had overreacted when she opened the docket and that she now realised she should not have done so. She apologised to the court for all the time she had wasted.

A furious Mlotshwa again accused Johnston of perjury and threatened to have her declared a hostile witness. How could a prosecutor possibly call the only witness in his case hostile? It was beyond reason and clearly demonstrated the lengths he would go to to keep running a case with no steam left in the engine.

My counsel then announced his intention to play audio recordings and a video of the meeting we had held with Johnston. It was incontrovertible proof that Johnston had not been intimidated in any way. Johnston had already accepted the correctness of the transcripts from the video, but Mlotshwa opposed the entering of the audio and video, saying it had been tampered with and that the police's forensic people had told him this.

My counsel then had to read into the record a written application for the admission of the video material into the court record. It was not even lunchtime when Mlotshwa said he needed a postponement so that he could draft a head of argument against the application. We adjourned for the remainder of the day. More intentional wasted costs for me.

On Tuesday, Mlotshwa announced that he had changed his mind and no longer objected to the video material. It was then played to the court, and the witness admitted to its authenticity. After watching the video, Johnston said that she felt at the time that I had been shouting at her while interviewing her, but the video showed I was not shouting, only confrontational and firm.

Mlotshwa said he objected to both the transcript and the video being introduced as evidence in my defence and said he needed another postponement so that police forensics could issue a report on it. My counsel had supplied Mlotshwa with the video in September 2016, so there was no reason why he did not have this report already.

At teatime, Mlotshwa advised the court that he would not be able to commence with the re-examination of the witness because he first needed to apply for and obtain the transcript to prepare for the cross-examination. We already had the transcript. At my own expense – and to stop Mlotshwa from using it as another delay tactic – I had another copy printed, and my counsel handed it to him. Since we had finished the cross-examination, we fully expected Mlotshwa to spend the next two to three hours re-examining Johnston. Instead, he brought an application for a postponement, saying the transcript had only been handed to him a few minutes earlier and that he needed some time to study it.

We lost the remainder of the day. More intentional wasted costs, thanks to Mlotshwa's dishonesty.

On Wednesday, Mlotshwa arrived late for court again. When Magistrate Gayle Pretorius walked in, my team had to say that he was not there. She left and asked to be called up for his arrival, which took place just after 9:30 a.m.

Mlotshwa immediately addressed the court and said that he needed to postpone the case because he had been instructed by Shaun Abrahams to immediately return to the office to attend to a complaint laid against him by me.[119] My counsel and I were taken completely by surprise, and the court was forced to adjourn for ten minutes for me to instruct counsel. I made it clear that my constitutional rights had been breached more than once by Mlotshwa and that I was entitled to a fair trial and a speedy conclusion. We elected to oppose his application for an adjournment. The court then instructed Mlotshwa to provide evidence of his claim that he needed to leave immediately.

The matter was stood down for a whole hour, after which Mlotshwa delivered a three or four line email from Shaun Abraham's secretary, which did not say anything useful at all, merely that he must attend to dealing with my complaints against him as soon as possible.

119 Angelique Serrao, Shaun Abrahams calls prosecutor in court to answer a complaint, News24, 27 July 2017. https://www.news24.com/SouthAfrica/News/shaun-abrahams-calls-prosecutor-in-court-to-answer-a-complaint-20170727

Mlotshwa's application was dismissed, and he was instructed by the court to continue with his re-examination.

Mlotshwa then said he needed a postponement to obtain a report on the video from the police. The court denied his application, saying that his only witness had verified the authenticity of the video – and the contents of the transcript – and that his application would not take the matter anywhere.

HOSTILE WITNESS

Mlotshwa began the re-examination by asking several peculiar questions that went far beyond re-examination. In fact, it amounted to aggressive cross-examination, which brought Johnston to tears in an attempt to get her to incriminate herself (for perjury). My counsel objected and asked the court to instruct Mlotshwa not to conduct himself in such a manner. The court intervened, and Mlotshwa received another rap on the knuckles.

Mlotshwa then brought an oral application in terms of Section 190 of the Criminal Procedures Act to have his only witness declared a hostile witness. My counsel, Advocate Zirk Pansegrouw, opposed this absurdity and Mlotshwa's application was dismissed. Mlotshwa was then instructed by the court to continue with his re-examination. Instead, Mlotshwa suddenly announced that he needed to see Magistrate Pretorius in chambers, together with my counsel. After three or four minutes, they all re-emerged.

Magistrate Pretorius announced that Mlotshwa had asked her something in chambers but that she had cut him short and asked that he ask her the question in open court. Mlotshwa then accused the magistrate of being hostile towards him and asked her to recuse herself. She instructed him to bring a written application and then stood the matter down for two hours.

At 2 p.m., the circus continued, with Mlotshwa handing over his written argument for recusal.[120] It was uncannily similar in many respects to the argument he presented at Kempton Park court a year earlier when he attempted to fraudulently have Magistrate Nel recuse himself. After thirty minutes of dishonest argument by Mlotshwa and twenty minutes by my counsel opposing his application, Magistrate Pretorius gave a lengthy judgement dismissing his application.

In my affidavit opposing Mlotshwa's application to have Magistrate Pretorius recuse herself, I noted that this was the second time Mlotshwa had called for a magistrate to recuse themselves in a case against me and that he seemed to believe a recusal application was an acceptable method to derail a criminal matter that was not going according to his dictates. Clearly, this case, as with all the other fake cases, was not going well for him.

Magistrate Pretorius seemed to agree when she said:

> *The court can't please everyone. A criminal trial is not a game. The court has tried its best to be fair to all, and that includes to the witness. The court can't make a ruling that suits all parties. You can't be like a naughty child whose sweets were taken away.*

She then instructed Mlotshwa to continue with his re-examination. Mlotshwa refused and said he was taking her decision not to recuse herself on review.

During oral argument on one of Mlotshwa's many time-wasting and dishonest interlocutory applications, he alluded to the fact that he was only continuing with the trial because he had been instructed to do so. It also seemed that he brought the application in terms of Section 190 of the Criminal Procedures Act and the recusal application as a result of instructions from above, whatever that meant.

---

120 Amanda Watson, Paul O'Sullivan magistrate refuses to recuse herself, The Citizen, 16 March 2018, https://citizen.co.za/news/south-africa/1857905/paul-osullivan-magistrate-refuses-to-recuse-herself/

The alluding to instructions from somewhere else caught the attention of the Magistrate, and she asked him who was 'instructing' him. It is perfectly clear in law that every prosecutor must act independently and without fear, favour, or prejudice. Mlotshwa then stumbled over his words, saying he alone had decided to continue, thereby contradicting his earlier statement that he had received 'instructions from above'.

The court stood down for a month to allow Mlotshwa to review the Magistrate's decision – which he never did – and so the case dragged on. More intentional wasted costs for me.

Meanwhile, in October 2017, Johnston was found guilty of the fraud and theft case her former boss James Murray had brought against her. She was sentenced to seven years in jail, suspended for five years, and had to pay back the R380 000 she had stolen. Mlotshwa's only witness was not only found to be a liar but also a convicted fraudster and thief. His case was obviously collapsing around him.

Yet, somehow, Mlotshwa managed to drag the case on, postponing it time and again, until June 2018 when a review application by the State saw the case finally withdrawn on the instructions of the National Director of Public Prosecutions after they realised the boiler had run out of steam.

On the 29th of June 29 2018, I was acquitted after wasting two years facing fake charges for something I did not do. The time and money I poured down the drain is something I will be sure to make Mlotshwa – and all the crooks who were working with him – pay for.

THE CORA VAN DER MERWE TRIAL

The second case I had to attend in the Randburg Magistrate's Court was the false kidnapping, intimidation, and extortion charge opened by Cora van der Merwe, involving personal injury lawyer Ronald Bobroff, who had asked me to investigate theft of documents from his office. This was years before information emerged that Bobroff had allegedly been overcharging some of his clients.

Just to recap, I had interviewed van der Merwe on the theft from her office in October 2014. During the interview, she admitted stealing files and sending them to *Carte Blanche* journalist Anthony Beamish. Running out of time and knowing I had a doctor's appointment to get to, I asked that we continue the interview later at my office. Van der Merwe came willingly to my office, but after taking a call from her lawyer, she stopped cooperating, and I told Melissa Naidu to take van der Merwe back to her office. I later established that the reason she stopped cooperating was that she had sent a text message to Beamish's friend, attorney Anthony Millar, saying she was on her way to my office and that I had evidence she had stolen documents and sent them to him. Millar quickly responded to say *"...sign nothing – you need to get away from them ASAP"*.

Mlotshwa, the fake advocate, was once again the prosecutor, and the fake kidnapping charges were being torn apart in court. I always disputed that van der Merwe had made a protected disclosure when she gave information on Ronald and Darren Bobroff to Beamish but had instead committed theft by sending confidential work emails and proprietary information to the journalist.[121] In one instance, Beamish had secretly met and advised a client of the Bobroffs, Des Steenkamp, to contact Bobroff's rival attorney, Anthony Millar of Norman Berger and Partners, about Bobroff's overcharging. Beamish knew about Steenkamp's case because van der Merwe had sent the file with the client's information to him via email. Millar then used the information to institute a claim against Bobroff on behalf of Steenkamp. Another example of the result of her conduct was an affidavit from a Mr Mthunzi, who alleged he had received an unsolicited call from Beamish

121 Antoinette Slabbert, It was theft, not a protected disclosure, says O'Sullivan, The Citizen, 14 September 2017, https://citizen.co.za/business/business-news/1653187/it-was-theft-not-a-protected-disclosure-says-osullivan/

requesting a meeting about his wife's Road Accident claim. Mthunzi met with Beamish at Maxi's Restaurant in Alberton sometime in 2014 and Beamish had tried to persuade Mr Mthunzi that his wife would be better off firing Bobroff and handing the claim over to Anthony Millar, as he would get more money out of the claim. The only way Beamish could possibly have Mthunzi's number, to call him, was if Cora van der Merwe had given it to him. It was an elaborate triangle of deceit and also amounted to touting on the part of Millar and Beamish.

This was clearly not your normal run-of-the-mill whistle-blower working-with-a-journalist scenario since proprietary information on the Bobroffs was being used against them to harm their business and not simply to uncover alleged wrongdoing. By way of example, Bobroff had instructed senior counsel to prepare an application against Millar to have him struck off the roll of attorneys for alleged 'touting' over the practice of sending ambulance chasers to hospitals to acquire road accident cases. Cora van der Merwe went onto her employer's server, to which she had access via her work computer, lifted the instructions to counsel, and sent them to Beamish, who in turn gave them to Millar. I'm not saying the Bobroffs were angels – a couple of years later, they were accused of fraud – but the manner in which Cora van der Merwe worked with a journalist and lawyer amounted to nothing short of theft.

Just like in the Johnston case, it was easy for me to prove that Melissa Naidu and I had not kidnapped van der Merwe, nor had we intimidated her in any way because we had the audio and video footage of the interviews to prove it. The court agreed.

After months of postponements and a stop-and-start trial, which included Mlotshwa scraping the barrel to use case law from the 1800s,[122] I was acquitted on the 19th of January 2018 – nearly two

122 Amanda Watson, Court rejects 103-year-old law to try Paul O'Sullivan, The Citizen, 14 July 2017, https://www.security.co.za/news/34876

years after being falsely charged for a kidnapping, that had allegedly taken place four years earlier. Magistrate Ndivhuwo Sethusha said the state had 'dismally failed' to prove our guilt on all counts.

Magistrate Sethusha began her judgement by noting that that case had taken too long to be investigated and placed on the court roll:

> *I am stating that the incident occurred on 14 October 2014. The complainant's statement was only filed with the police in May 2016. Accused persons were only summoned to court on 19 August 2016 for the incident that took place in October 2014.*

The Magistrate, just like Nel before her, said the case was badly investigated. She noted that it was surprising that none of van der Merwe's colleagues from Bobroff's office had been called as witnesses in the supposed kidnapping incident. I knew that the reason for this was that no colleague would be able to truthfully corroborate van der Merve's version of events because she had made them up. Mlotshwa knew this too and said:

> *I do not hesitate to state that the State, in proving its case, is relying mainly on the evidence of the complainant. The law in terms of section 209 of the Criminal Procedure Act permits the court to convict an accused person on the evidence of a single competent witness provided the evidence is consistent and reliable in all material aspects.*

Sethusha warned that the evidence must be approached with caution:

> *Her testimony, under evidence in chief as well as under cross-examination, in which she was subjected over several days by advocate Pansegrouw, I do not hesitate to state that it was not persuasive. She is found to have been inconsistent and evasive in answering questions from the defence.*

The Magistrate said van der Merwe "did not play open cards with the court", that she changed her story under cross-examination, and that a journalist was not the relevant authority to deal with protective disclosures. Her judgement read as follows:

> *I, therefore, found that her actions in sending office information without the consent or knowledge of her office, tantamount to malicious actions and it is unlawful. Further, the complainant is found to have contradicted herself in most material aspects to an extent that it raises a concern about the reliability and honesty of her story.*

Sethusha did not accept van der Merwe's version that she was afraid when she accompanied us to my office as the video showed her entering and leaving unescorted:

> *To me, I found it to be a relaxed environment. It further came from the complainant's testimony that she cried during the interview. Throughout the video that we observed, that was not depicted. I must comment that when she testified in court, I observed that she was very emotional about the incident that occurred in 2014. Yet surprisingly, the video does not depict her crying, considering that at the time, the incident was fresher than when testifying in court.*

Sethusha also commented on the fact that the video showed that when van der Merwe arrived at our offices, she was asked if she would like tea or coffee, to which she jokingly replied, "wine". Hardly the conduct of a kidnap victim.

In summary, Magistrate Sethusha said:

> *I found that the State has dismally failed to prove the guilt of the accused persons beyond reasonable doubt in all the counts. I arrived at the following conclusion. The accused are found not guilty and discharged on all the counts.*

The verdict was no surprise. As I walked out of another court, free of the lies that had been used against me, I vowed once again that I would not rest until I saw the perpetrators of these illegal acts facing justice for what they had done, including Abrahams, Tori Pretorius, Mlotshwa, Mokatedi, Hoosen, Vlok, and lying witnesses like Cora van der Merwe.

LETTER TO SHAUN ABRAHAMS

The afternoon after the judgement was delivered, I sat in my office and thought about what these crooks had put me through. I wrote an open letter to Shaun Abrahams, the still missing-in-action National Director of Public Prosecutions.[3] I told him that we were tired of watching the mafia running the NPA and that it had to stop.

I noted that in her judgement, Magistrate Sethusha referred to Mlotshwa as "Advocate" numerous times. Instead of standing up and correcting her understandable error, Mlotshwa sat there playing with his phone. Finally, I told Abrahams that Mlotshwa was a criminal with a gown and that the NPA was now a circus where the clowns wore gowns and had red faces instead of red noses.

CHAPTER 22

UNDETERRED

MORE CASES COLLAPSE

Cora van der Merwe, Alice Johnston, and the passport case were the only three of the six cases with which I had been formally charged to go through the full court process. The others were eventually withdrawn after dragging on for years.

One of these was the SAA case, opened by Dudu Myeni. I first appeared in court a few days after my first arrest in April 2016. The case was postponed numerous times over a year and a half before being withdrawn. It never reached trial. My second appearance in court was in June 2016, my third appearance in August, the fourth in September, the fifth in January of 2017, and so on, until I finally appeared on the 12th of January 2018, to be told the case had been withdrawn. Written representations had been sitting in Shaun Abraham's office for well over a year with no movement on the case, and the court finally decided to strike it from the roll since it was clear no decision would be forthcoming.

Obviously, the case was so weak that even Mlotshwa could not pretend he had something concrete to present to the court. Either that or he had been so embarrassed by the cases that had left before deciding to give up the fight. I would have loved to have seen this case continue so that we could put the corrupt Dudu Myeni on the witness stand. Putting Barry Roux up against Dudu Myeni would have been something to see.

THE NEIL DIAMOND CASE

By the middle of 2018, only one case remained before the courts – the false Neil Diamond extortion case. In another travesty of justice, I discovered that the original case opened by myself and Melissa Naidu against Diamond, which involved fraud and theft from a deceased estate, had mysteriously disappeared.

A docket opened by Vlok (Mokatedi's sidekick) – and another by Diamond – against me as a smokescreen for the charges we laid against Diamond on behalf of a widow who had more than R5-million allegedly stolen by Diamond, had also disappeared. When asked to respond to Vlok's false allegations, I simply copied my original docket, which was full of prima facie evidence, and attached it to Diamond's false sworn statement against me. At the beginning of my statement, I wrote that his case was an abuse of process and that Diamond was the one who should be on trial.

It would soon emerge that both dockets had been 'stolen' by Vlok. The only reason for Vlok to have done this is if there was clear evidence against Diamond contained in either docket and exculpatory evidence in my favour. Vlok and Mlotshwa would not want this emerging as they intended using Diamond's complaint against me. It was the last card they had left to play.

I obtained three affidavits that revealed the 'stolen' dockets were actually in Vlok's hands. The first came from seasoned investigator Hennie Els, who deposed an affidavit stating that Vlok had told him that he (Vlok) was in possession of my docket. Vlok even told Els that it contained nine sworn statements. Despite only being a warrant officer, Vlok told Hennie Els he was a captain, threatening Els with arrest if he did not provide him with some evidence against me. Hennie Els is now a witness against Vlok, but more about that later.

Police officers from the Alberton Detective Unit also provided sworn statements confirming that a 'Captain' Vlok had taken the fake docket Diamond had opened against me from their storeroom where it had been filed and had refused to sign for it. When they insisted he sign for it, Vlok told them they should speak to Phahlane, as he was there on Phahlane's instructions. The officers also revealed that the docket had already been sent to the NPA for a decision and which, surprise, surprise, they had declined to prosecute me. The Police had already prepared the docket for closure and filed it in the storeroom when Vlok came by to collect it.

I opened a case of theft against Vlok and Mlotshwa and, although the Police actually investigated this case, it gathered dust at the NPA with no one deciding on it. I later arranged for IPID to pick it up, and Vlok is now awaiting trial, having been charged with fraud, extortion, perjury, and defeating the ends of justice.

Meanwhile, I had to attend the Palm Ridge Magistrates Court for the false charges brought against me by Diamond. In my first appearance in October 2017, I was told the court file was incomplete, and the case was postponed. The second court date saw another postponement because Mlotshwa had failed to secure a date for the matter to be moved to a regional court. On my third court appearance in November, the matter was moved to the Regional Court. At my fourth appearance in February 2018, the case was postponed. Finally, at my fifth appearance in August 2018, the case was unceremoniously withdrawn. The corrupt police/ National Prosecuting Authority train had finally run out of steam. There was not a single case left against me.

FREE BUT NOT FORGOTTEN

The Neil Diamond saga was the last tangible case I had been charged with. I was finally free of the malicious prosecutions which had tormented my life for almost three years and cost me more than one hundred and thirty days in lost productivity and an absolute fortune on lawyers.

I will never forget what I had been put through. I was determined to hold all of those who had tormented me to account. In the letter I wrote to Shaun Abrahams, I reminded him that everything Mlotshwa had done had been under his watch and his instructions:

> *I've got a simple message for both of you and Vlok:*
>
> *'Criminals don't send me to prison – I send them to prison!*
>
> *Ask Selebi, ask Krejcir.*
>
> *I will see to it that for every day I spent in court in these fake cases, someone will do a year in prison. For every day I was unlawfully detained, someone will do ten years in prison, and for every million I spent on legal fees, someone will do ten years in prison.*
>
> *For your information, that adds up to well over 200 years in prison. I think we can share it out amongst the lot of you and include Phahlane and Ntlemeza. There's enough to go around to keep 20 of you out of trouble for ten or more years.'*

It was a threat I still promise to make good on.

MY INVESTIGATIONS CONTINUE

Despite the wasted time and money spent in court, I never lost focus on my investigations into Ntlemeza, Phahlane and Mokotedi, amongst others. Their criminal plans to distract me had failed. If anything, it had made me even more resolute to stop them in their tracks.

The crooks in uniforms were becoming ever more desperate and were upping the ante to get rid of me. I had people on the inside feeding me information on what was happening behind the scenes, and I discovered that the Northwest team was going all out to try and silence me. Frustrated that their illegal charges against Sarah-Jane and me had fizzled away in court, the Northwest team (headed by Mabula) had moved up to Pretoria, where the focus was solely on destroying us. They had sent the cellphone they stole from Sarah-Jane (without a search warrant) to Israel to download all its contents.

My informers kept me up to date on meetings being held by Ntlemeza (who had, by now, been removed from his duties), Phahlane (who was suspended), Mdluli (who was suspended) and Mabula (who was still in office). They had met at Nhleko's house in Pretoria to come up with a plan to get rid of McBride and me. I believe that the Northwest team weren't above having us murdered, and I knew it was a dangerous time for all of us to be alive. Certain members of the Northwest team had been implicated in kidnapping and murders, so their ability to commit crimes was definitely on the cards.

CROOKED CAR DEALERSHIPS – EVIDENCE AGAINST PHAHLANE MOUNTS

Undeterred, we carried on. By then, we had discovered the link between the car dealer who had sponsored Phahlane's cars and that of a major Police Forensics supplier.[123] Phahlane had accepted the cars as a part of his concealed kickbacks to secure tenders within the Forensics Division, where he had been the Divisional Commissioner before being promoted to Acting Police Commissioner.

We had acquired evidence that showed that the director of a police supplier had paid large amounts of money into car dealer Durand

---

123 Barry Bateman, Exclusive. Phahlane's luxury cars: IPID finds new evidence of money trail, EWN, 1 November 2017, https://webcache.googleusercontent.com/search?q=cache:AyhQLfeaGf0J:https://ewn.co.za/2017/11/01/exclusive-phahlane-luxury-cars-probe-ipid-finds-new-evidence-of-money-trail+&cd=18&hl=en&ct=clnk&gl=be

Snyman's Namibian bank account. We had the bank statements, which showed that a man called Keith Keating, an ex-police officer who owned a company called Forensic Data Analysts (FDA), had paid R1 820 000 into Snyman's foreign bank account between January and March of 2016. Snyman transferred the money to various South African bank accounts – and other car dealers. The vehicles purchased were registered in the names of Phahlane, his wife Beauty, his sister Josephine, and a Colonel Johann Potgieter, who worked in a SAPS division known as TMS.

The banking records showed that the first sum of money, R275 000, was paid on the 4th of March 2016 under the name of Keating. It was used to buy a Ford Ranger bakkie and given to Josephine Phahlane, Phahlane's sister. A Toyota Hilux 3.0 4x4 Single Cab bakkie was purchased for R377 000, given to Phahlane, and registered in his name. The transactions also showed that a VW Polo was purchased for Phahlane's wife, Beauty (a Brigadier in the TMS division), for R230 000. A Hyundai i20 was purchased for R229 000. The Polo and the i20 were invoiced under the name "John Doe".

Phahlane insisted there was nothing untoward about the cars he had received from Snyman, claiming he played no part in the awarding of tenders. But our evidence was mounting, and it was showing something quite different. Money laundering and racketeering are serious crimes, especially when used to conceal corruption.

FISCAL DUMPING - SITA AND SAPS

By linking Phahlane to Keating, we had unwittingly stumbled upon the criminal justice sector's key state capture project. Keating's companies were linked to numerous tenders both within the SAPS and another state department, State Information Technology Agency

(SITA). The tenders we traced went as far back as 2010.[124] While we estimated their value to be in the region of R5-billion, forensic reports later revealed the true amount to be in the region of R11-billion. The figures were astronomical and put the alleged looting that had taken place under Phahlane (and other top police management) at the same level as the state capture theft at SAA, PRASA and Eskom.

FDA, along with two other companies belonging to Keating – Grid Control Technologies and Investigative Software Solutions – had merged with listed company subsidiary EOH Abantu in November 2015. Keating, Desmond van Rooyen, Vhonani Mufamadi (the brother of former Minister of Safety and Security, Sydney Mufamadi), John William King, and Adri Els were listed as the directors of Grid Control Technologies and Investigative Software Solutions. Competition Commission documents showed that Grid Control Technologies supplied water and electricity meters. FDA provided forensic software and hardware solutions, including evidence management, firearm management, and forensic hardware equipment. Investigative Software Solutions provided analytical software solutions.

We would soon discover just how extensive the range of products was that these three companies had supplied to the SAPS. Between the three companies, they controlled most of the police's critical software systems.

IPID discovered one contract in particular that raised numerous red flags – the supply and maintenance of one hundred and sixty-nine Rofin light sources.[125] While our investigation helped expose many suspicious transactions, this one was by far one of the biggest, with FDA's contracts for this product alone amounting to around R1-billion.

---

124 Angelique Serrao, R5bn in contracts allegedly paid to company accused of buying Phahlane's cars, News24, 7 November 2017, https://www.news24.com/SouthAfrica/News/r5bn-in-contracts-allegedly-paid-to-company-accused-of-buying-phahlane-cars-20171107

125 Marianne Thamm, Scorpio : SAPS forensic torch contract: a R1bn gift that keeps in giving, Daily Maverick, 8 November 2017, https://www.dailymaverick.co.za/article/2017-11-08-scorpio-saps-forensic-torch-contract-a-r1bn-gift-that-keeps-on-giving/

These specialised forensic torches, of which FDA was the sole supplier, should never have cost R300 000 each, but this was what the police paid Forensic Data Analysts. While other companies offered significantly cheaper alternatives, Phahlane's Forensics Division did not appear interested in sourcing anything else. The tender for the torches also came with an annual maintenance and support contract for a product that should have been maintenance-free. The contract had been in place since 2010 but was apparently 'evergreen' and rolled over repeatedly.

In a letter to Police Commissioner Khehla Sitole, McBride detailed how a purchase order for the one hundred and sixty-nine light sources (valued at R52.9-million) was generated at 4:57 p.m. on the 31st of March 2016. While it was three minutes before the close of business that day, it was also the last day of SAPS's 2015/2016 financial year. FDA's invoice was submitted to SAPS Information Technology Services, a division of SAPS Technology Management Services, which just so happened to be where Phahlane's wife, Beauty Phahlane, worked.

Anyone who has ever supplied products or services to the State would know how laboriously slow the State can be when making payments. Payment for the Rofin lights sources, however, was made on the same day. How was it possible that an invoice could be submitted and paid within three minutes? It was a miracle indeed.

What happened, in this case, is known as fiscal dumping. The budget allocated to SAPS to spend on crime-fighting equipment within the 2015/2016 financial year was underspent. To avoid losing the money to Treasury, SAPS had to quickly spend it before the financial year closed. Money that should – and could – have been spent to help in the fight against crime was instead set aside to purchase these criminally over-priced torches.

THE CAPTURE OF SITA

Our investigations revealed that the irregular tenders going through SAPS were just the tip of the iceberg. The real money was disappearing through SITA, a state department that often went under the radar. Billions of rands flowed through the agency but, because they procured (expensive) technology for numerous state departments, it often managed to avoid scrutiny. It seemed that some of these tenders were evergreen, which meant that anyone looking to see what tenders were being handed out at any one time would not find them easily. We soon discovered that this created a loophole that was being exploited by corrupt tenderers like FDA and EOH.

The scale of what had been happening required a deep forensic investigation into the money that was being spent through SITA. Audit firms Bowmans, Grant Thornton, and Sizwe Ntsaluba Gobodo all conducted forensic investigations. Bowman's report titled *SITA – SAPD Capture* looked specifically at FDA (and all its related companies) and the contracts they had been rewarded. The report discovered spending of R6.1-billion for contracts involving IT hardware and software, forensic equipment and consumables from Keating's companies. This was just the beginning of the looting. Over the next three years, the auditors also uncovered planned expenditure valued at R11.2-billion for police technology.

The media had caught wind of the story, and the *Daily Maverick* and *News24,* in particular, wrote numerous exposés on what was happening. As the news started unfolding, SITA came forward and admitted that there had indeed been irregularities linked to SAPS tenders, particularly related to the procurement of forensic light sources.[126] SITA spokesperson Lucky Mochalibane said that several

126 Angelique Serrao, SITA admits there was irregularity in SAPS tender allegedly linked to Phahlane, News24, 8 November 2017, https://www.news24.com/SouthAfrica/News/sita-admits-there-was-irregularity-in-saps-tender-allegedly-linked-to-phahlane-20171108

employees at SITA had been suspended after an investigation and that criminal cases had been opened against those involved.

Mochalibane said that while their investigation did not focus on a single entity, it did, however, reveal that the procurement of specialised forensic goods and services – and in particular the forensic light sources for SAPS, which was facilitated and maintained by SITA – was irregular and had possibly resulted in large scale fruitless and wasteful expenditure. In other words, theft!

During these revelations, Keating came out fighting instead of hiding in shame – much like Phahlane. He denied wrongdoing, stating that all the contracts FDA had been engaged in with SAPS had taken place through an open tender process. He was lying through his teeth.

The planned theft of R11-billion needed to be stopped. Keating and Phahlane could bluster all they wanted, but McBride was making sure that the capture of SITA was revealed in Parliament. The forensic reports were presented to the Standing Committee on Public Accounts (SCOPA), exposing numerous instances of overspending where Keating's companies were involved.[127]

SCOPA REVELATIONS

The extent of the corruption was vast. In one instance, it was revealed that SAPS received funds from the Department of Justice and Correctional Services specifically aimed at improvements towards an integrated justice system. Because Phahlane had already wasted his own budget, he quickly saw to it that there were fewer controls in place and diverted SAPS's share towards day-to-day procurement. A consolidated summary of this single budget revealed that FDA was paid over R229-million, a R106-million overshoot of the original budget. It was looting on a grand scale.

---

127 Jan Gerber, Scopa instructs SITA to end corrupt R900m deal, News24, 30 November 2017, https://www.news24.com/SouthAfrica/News/scopa-instructs-sita-to-end-corrupt-r900m-deal-20171130

In one meeting between SCOPA, SAPS, SITA and IPID, where the irregular, fruitless and wasteful expenditure was discussed, SCOPA took the bull by the horns and instructed SAPS and SITA to terminate all contracts with FDA. This, it turned out, would have a huge effect on critical police systems, including the maintenance and support of the firearm permit system and the supply of forensic equipment. FDA also held the keys to the SAPS Property Control and Exhibit Management System, known as PCEM, which meant that if FDA's contracts were ever cancelled, the firearms and exhibit systems would be in jeopardy. The corruption that had taken place had placed the country's national security at risk.

Throughout the entire parliamentary briefing, Keating sat there, directly in the line of sight of the police and SITA officials. His presence was viewed as a form of intimidation, and SCOPA chairperson Themba Godi called him out on it:

> *For the first time in this Parliament, the person who is alleged to the irregular procurement came and sat throughout the meeting – Mr Keating – without any hint of shame or embarrassment. We deplore and condemn that kind of stuff.*

The revelations of what had been going on were nothing short of astonishing.[128] Twenty-two police officers were implicated in the corruption, including Phahlane, SAPS CFO Lieutenant-General Avhashoni Ramikosi, Lieutenant-General Stefanus Schutte and Deputy National Commissioner of Management Intervention, Lieutenant-General Lungiswa Shezi.

IPID's Head of Investigations, Matthews Sesoko, told parliament that there was a "clear manipulation of the procurement system", that the system was "rigged" to favour FDA, and that there was "a corrupt relationship" between the company and the police.

---

128 Marianne Thamm, Analysis: SITA/SAPS capture – Scopa hearing marks a turning point as massive fraud uncovered, Daily Maverick, 30 November 2017, https://www.dailymaverick.co.za/article/2017-11-30-analysis-sitasaps-capture-scopa-hearing-marks-a-turning-point-as-massive-fraud-uncovered/

McBride said the investigation into Phahlane and FDA was expected to reach a climax before Christmas when IPID would hand the matter over to the NPA. However, McBride told SCOPA there were criminal elements in the NPA harassing IPID officials. SITA CEO Setumo Mohapi also said that he and his management team had received death threats. Advocate Michael Mashuga, for example, had seen fit to collaborate with the criminals with badges from the Northwest in bringing fake charges against myself and Sarah-Jane. Mashuga subsequently added senior IPID members to the charge sheet and made it clear that McBride's name would also make it onto the list of names. Shaun (The Sheep) Abrahams, as we would later discover, fully endorsed the criminal conduct of Mashuga and the corrupt Northwest team.

THE ESKOM MAFIA - LAWYERS THAT GLADLY RECEIVE THE PROCEEDS OF CRIME

In the first half of 2019, after a year of investigation, I opened a criminal docket against Antonio Trindade, for his bribing of senior ESKOM officials. The case was watertight and Trindade's only response to my demands for him to pay back the money he'd stolen, was to use the proceeds of crime to pay lawyers to bring an anti-harassment application against me.

Some lawyers will do anything for money. Robert Kanarak and Laurance Hodes tried their best to keep Trindade out of prison and to suppress my investigations into him. They took their attacks on me personally and would stand outside court and swear at and insult me, taking turns to use the crudest of language. Lying to the court, was another trait of Hodes, in his desperation to get me off Trindade's back, in a trumped-up anti-harassment application. He ranted and raved in the court, until the magistrate shut him up and told him to sit down. He was really peeved, because I defended myself and accused him of living off the proceeds of crime. Outside the court, Kanarak continued the rant and even screamed after me up the street. I turned on him and told him to shut up, or I would put him on my keyring. I told him that like Napoleon, little men often have superiority complexes, and he was no different.

Our year of investigations revealed the depth of the corruption at ESKOM, including the inability of banks, like ABSA, to recognise their contributory role in greasing the wheels of corruption, by allowing an ESKOM employee to withdraw massive amounts of cash, running to as much as five million rands in a single day.

Through his company, Tubular Construction Projects, Trindade had paid millions in bribes to senior ESKOM manager, Mangope Frans Hlakudi. Initially, the bribes were bags of cash, which then became direct transfers. Later still, Hlakudi received the bribes after issuing dummy invoices to Tubular, from his company, Hlakudi CC. It was easy to see through the invoices because, as time went on, both Hlakudi and Trindade became lazy and made shocking mistakes, which left a clear audit trail. In return, Hlakudi unlawfully awarded a seven hundred million Rand contract to Tubular, and then issued increase orders over the next few years raising the total to almost two billion Rand. It was theft on a major scale. Worse still, the work done by Trindade was sub-standard and resulted in delays to the project and subsequent rolling black-outs because the electricity grid could not cope with the demand. Hlakudi had to share his bribes with other Eskom officials and we were keen to identify them. One of the biggest beneficiaries of Hlakudi's largess was ESKOM's Group Executive for Procurement, Abram Masango, who had to be in on the theft, or he would have red-flagged Hlakudi's signoffs.

I had managed to get a Tubular whistle-blower to hand over the incriminating details of Trindade's accounting system, including copies of all the invoices and spreadsheets detailing the payments. At the same time, ex ESKOM CEO Matshela Koko, keen to nail Hlakudi for his own agenda, dropped me an envelope containing Hlakudi's bank statements, which clearly showed money laundering running to over one hundred million Rand, as well as thousands of pages of other useful documents.

After opening the criminal docket against Hlakudi, I made up a couple of memory sticks with the thousands of pages of evidence on and handed it over to the investigating officer and to the Special Investigations Unit, who had been on Trindade's trail for quite some time.

During the anti-harassment process, launched by Kanarak and Hodes on behalf of Trindade, the lawyers tried every trick in the book including bringing an application for contempt of court, because I refused to hand over the thousands of pages of evidence against their corrupt client. Like pretty much everything else Hodes does for his criminal clients, his contempt application failed, and he never got his hands on the evidence in my possession.

I also flew to London and met with ex Tubular employee, Mike Lomas, who gave me a damning sworn statement implicating Trindade in paying bribes to Hlakudi through Lomas' personal bank account, a clear case of money laundering. As Lomas was in his 70's and suffering from ill health, I wanted to help him become a state witness, in return for a non-custodial sentence. He gave us a special power of attorney to obtain all his bank statements from his personal bankers and we got the years of account statements that proved he had channelled money to Hlakudi through his personal account. However, a few weeks later, after Trindade found out I had met with Lomas in London, Lomas withdrew his cooperation and blocked me on his e-mails and telephone. I assume that Trindade had got to him.

A few weeks later Trindade was arrested and charged, along with Hlakudi and Masango and other suspects. A warrant of arrest was also issued for Lomas, who by now had gone rogue. Despite his ill health and age, Lomas knew what he was doing at all material times and, if he was not prepared to assist the prosecution, he ought to face the music.

Perhaps one day, Kanarak and Hodes will be forced to hand back the stolen ESKOM money they received from Trindade.

TRANSNET MAFIA & THE ITALIAN JOB

In late 2018, Forensics for Justice published a report, "Any Port in a Storm", which was a forerunner to criminal dockets we opened against a company called CMI Emtateni and its directors, for fraud and corruption. Our investigation was predicated by the receipt of a copy of a High Court application initiated by a disgruntled losing bidder (WBHO) in a seven billion Rand tender to lengthen and deepen one of the docks in the Durban Port.

Our investigations found prima facie evidence of tender rigging and outright fraud on the part of the winning bidder and its Italian partner, a public company in Italy, known as CMC di Ravenna. In short time we discovered that CMC di Ravenna was technically insolvent. Its local partner CMI Infrastructures had been formed a few days before the tender was advertised, as it was clearly set up solely for that purpose. The main directors in the fraudulent joint venture were Italian national Paulo Porcelli and Zuma benefactor Philane Mavundla. The same Mavundla who had allegedly paid off Jacob Zuma's tax arrears a year or two earlier.

Despite both the local company and the Italian company being insolvent, they were awarded the tender and soon picked up an advance payment of over seventy million Rand.

We met with Transnet's then chair, Popo Molefe and director Ed Kieswetter. A few weeks later, the CMI Emtateni contract was nullified.

Our investigations took us further afield and we discovered that administrators had been appointed to oversea CMC di Ravenna in

Italy, after they defaulted on bond repayments. They produced a set of accounts, intended to make it look like they just had a temporary cash-flow problem. However, when we investigated some of the declared work in progress, we found that some of the contracts did not exist. One claimed contract in progress was a massive project in the port in Poland. In discussion with the Polish authorities, we found that the contract had been cancelled after corruption allegations. We supplied the Kenyan authorities with all our files, after finding out that Kenya had been fleeced out of more than a hundred million Euros by CMC di Ravenna. In mid-2019, Kenya's Director of Public Prosecutions, issued an arrest warrant for Paulo Porcelli, who by then had fled to Italy.

CHAPTER 23
MORE CORRUPTION UNCOVERED

THE RAIDS

In the first week of December 2017, with Phahlane's diversions having been neutralised, IPID decided it was the perfect time to pounce on Keating and Phahlane.[129] In a joint operation between the honest cops in the Hawks and IPID, search warrants were obtained from the different courts, and seven properties connected to Keating and Phahlane were raided – including Phahlane's mansion in Sable Hills and his sister's house. FDA's offices were also searched, as well as Keating's home, car dealer Snyman's office and home, and TMS Colonel Johann Potgieter's house. A vehicle was seized from Phahlane's sister's house. SAPS Local Criminal Record Centre equipment was found at Keating's offices, and a truck load of documents was seized from Keating's house and offices. Radio-frequency identification tags for which SAPS had paid R374-million were found hidden at a construction site under Keating's control. They had never even been used, and no one could explain why they were not in SAPS' possession.

129 Angelique Serrao, IPID, Hawks raid 7 properties in case against Phahlane contractor, News24, 6 December 2017, https://www.news24.com/SouthAfrica/News/ipid-hawks-raid-7-properties-in-case-against-phahlane-saps-contractor-20171206

Documents that showed Phahlane's involvement in the cases against IPID investigators, myself, Trent, and McBride were also found at Phahlane's house, proving what we had always known – that our arrests were nothing more than a revenge tactic used by a corrupt Chief of Police who was misusing his position to stop an investigation into his misdeeds.

Keating and Snyman retaliated immediately through the courts by launching an application to have the search warrant overturned.[130] They wanted all their documents and equipment, as well as mirror copies of computers, laptops, cell phones, and electronic storage devices, sealed and returned.

In the court application, Keating denied that he had paid Snyman to buy cars for Phahlane, claiming that the Namibian payments were related to shares he purchased in a farming operation in Namibia in excess of R17-million. He said the money paid to Snyman was for wild animals, a tractor and a trailer. The lies were queuing up to jump from his tongue.

McBride responded by making it clear that the items seized provided them with plenty of incriminating evidence against Phahlane. Boxes of State goods seized at FDA's offices were found to contain boxes of Rofin light sources with web numbers on them, indicating that SITA had already taken control of them and that they should have been in the State's possession.

IPID showed the allegations were serious and involved large-scale corruption in the police at the highest levels. The search warrant made it clear this was an investigation into fraud, theft, corruption, racketeering and money laundering from 2014 to 2018. It specifically stated that three of the applicants supplied private vehicles to police officials either free of charge or at inflated trade-in prices.

130 Angelique Serrao, Police supplier attempts to have search warrant reversed, News24, 24 January 2018, https://www.news24.com/SouthAfrica/News/police-supplier-attempts-to-have-search-warrant-reversed-20180124

Keating's court bid eventually failed with Judge Jody Kollapen ruling that the warrants were indeed valid.[131] Keating took it on appeal to the Supreme Court of Appeal and lost. He then took it on appeal to the Constitutional Court and lost again. While completing this book, the NPA's new Investigative Directorate under Advocate Hermione Cronje are putting the finishing touches on the indictment that will hopefully see Keating spending the rest of his life behind bars, along with Phahlane and all the others involved in the gravy train of corruption at the police service.

EOH TAKES A HIT

During the week in which the raids took place, EOH saw their share price plummet, plunging by over thirty percent in several trading sessions. EOH publicly stated they had agreed with the former shareholders of FDA, Grid Control Technologies, and Investigative Software Solutions to unwind their transactions. EOH paid R385-million for the unwinding. They said the drop in share price was triggered by the forced sale of shares by financial institutions against equity financed transactions to various individual shareholders. It seemed they were trying to distance themselves from the police supplier scandal.

Stories later emerged that John King, the Chief Financial Officer of EOH, was a non-executive director of the three companies between March 2016 and October 2017.[132] EOH CEO Asher Bohbot was a non-executive director of the companies from March 2016, as was EOH's company secretary Adri Els. Questions were being asked about whether these directors knew what Keating had been up to. They

131 Jenni Evans, Challenge to Phahlane-linked warrants failed News24, 4 August 2018, https://www.news24.com/SouthAfrica/News/challenge-to-phahlane-linked-warrants-falls-20180804

132 Gareth van Zyl, EOH mess: CFO John King, Asher Bohbot were directors of dodgy Keating firms, Biznews, 10 December 2017, https://www.biznews.com/undictated/2017/12/10/eoh-cfo-john-king-asher-bohbot-were-directors-of-keating-firms

denied knowing anything, but the suspicion refused to die down, and the share price continued to nosedive, triggered by insiders dumping shares as quickly as they could.

Later still, EOH were embroiled in further corruption scandals that nearly wiped them out altogether, when it was found they were corruptly ripping off the governments departments, including defence and the National Prosecution Authority.

Keating, in the meantime, claimed that the allegations against him were part of a hostile takeover of his business, but his claims lacked detail.

FINALLY, PHAHLANE IS CHARGED

Phahlane's game was up. The raids had revealed enough incriminating evidence to see him charged for the cars he received from Snyman. In February 2018, IPID obtained arrest warrants and Phahlane, his wife Beauty, and Snyman were asked to hand themselves over to IPID to be charged with corruption.[133] The three appeared in the Specialised Commercial Crimes Court in Pretoria on a Thursday morning.[134] They were granted R10 000 bail, and the case was postponed several times over the next few months. I sat behind the 'accused' in court, much to the chagrin of him and his wife.

---

133 Angelique Serrao, Phahlane due to be charged with corruption, News24, 7 February 2018, https://www.news24.com/SouthAfrica/News/phahlane-due-to-be-charged-with-corruption-20180207

134 Angelique Serrao, Phahlane, wife, car dealer appear in court for corruption, News24, 8 February 2018, https://www.news24.com/SouthAfrica/News/phahlane-wife-car-dealer-appear-in-court-for-corruption-20180208

Phahlane, his wife and co-accused in the dock, Commercial Crimes Court in Pretoria, March 2017.

IPID's case was airtight, but because so much was being uncovered in relation to Keating, prosecutors asked (in June 2018) for a three-month postponement to finish their investigations. They wanted to charge more people in the case. Magistrate Nicola Setshoege disagreed, saying it would prejudice the accused. In a travesty of justice, the State provisionally withdrew the matter against the three, and it was removed from the roll.[135] I am still waiting for its reinstatement.

Later, at the State Capture Inquiry, McBride and IPID's National Head of Investigations, Matthews Sesoko, revealed how reluctant the NPA was to prosecute high-ranking police officials while Shaun Abrahams was in office.[136] This, while the cases against myself had

135 News24, Corruption charges withdrawn against former top cop Khomotso Phahlane, Politicsweb, 7 June 2018, https://www.politicsweb.co.za/news-and-analysis/corruption-charges-withdrawn-against-former-top-co

136 Canny Maphanga, State Capture: NPA was unwilling to deal with probes involving top cops – IPID investigations head, News24, 25 September 2019, https://www.news24.com/SouthAfrica/News/state-capture-npa-was-unwilling-to-deal-with-probes-involving-top-cops-ipid-investigations-head-20190925

been so eagerly pursued. By way of example, Shaun Abrahams issued a letter to IPID stating that he concurred with NPA's George Baloyi's decision *not* to prosecute certain senior police officers, despite the fact that deputy directors below Baloyi had stated in writing that the suspects had a case to answer. Abrahams also issued an unlawful instruction that *all* decisions relating to the prosecution of senior SAPS members had to first be endorsed by his office. He used this instruction to keep dirty cops and prosecutors out of jail.

Instead of fighting back, IPID regrouped. They had more than enough information to launch other cases against Phahlane. It seemed that whatever Phahlane touched was corrupt.

A THREAT TO STATE SECURITY

Keating's companies were so adept at capturing SAPS and SITA that they had become the sole supplier of police systems vital for the performance of criminal investigations, evidence control and firearm registration. Without them, SAPS would cease to function. How was it possible, I wondered, that police officials like Phahlane had lost all sense of decency, allowing their own personal gain to override serious state security issues? Corruption had allowed them to hand over numerous indispensable police systems on a golden platter to just a few companies, all of them interrelated. Looking at the bigger picture of what had happened, it became clear that one man, Keating, essentially controlled most of SAPS's computer systems.

Keating was well aware of this and, when backed into a corner, he decided to unleash the power he held over the State by threatening to switch the systems off.[137] A supplier holding the entire functioning of the criminal justice system to ransom was indeed an unprecedented phenomenon. Keating sent out press releases to the country's media in

137 Marianne Thamm, SAPS/SITA Capture: FDA holds South Africa to ransom, threatens to 'collapse criminal justice system', Daily Maverick, 5 April 2018, https://www.dailymaverick.co.za/article/2018-04-05-sapssita-capture-fda-holds-south-africa-to-ransom-threatens-to-collapse-criminal-justice-system/

April 2018, marked "Urgent", and addressed "To all public stakeholders and the media", stating that if his company was not paid by midnight, he would flick the switch[138]. The press release was headed: *SAPS AND SITA SOC LIMITED INDIFFERENT TO IMMINENT COLLAPSE OF CRIMINAL JUSTICE SYSTEM* and read as follows:

> *...on Wednesday, 4 April 2018, at midnight, use of and access to proprietary licensed software and ancillary support services in respect of PCEM (Property Control and Exhibit Management) and FPS (Firearm Permit System) will unfortunately be suspended by FDA unless an appropriate agreement could be reached with SAPS before system shutdown. The Minister, SAPS and other stakeholders have been duly warned about the risks involved but had acquiesced regardless of the impacts.*

Keating claimed he had not been paid for three months. He demanded a meeting with National Police Commissioner General Khehla Sitole, failing which the State would face "dire consequences". These consequences would be that police officers would not be able to check in and out of duty, that they might be unable to lawfully possess or use firearms, that firearms and ammunition in possession of SAPS might not be accounted for, and that police officers might not be able to access and manage evidence in the Forensic Science Laboratory. He added that the NPA might also be unable to remove evidence to be used in court proceedings and that South Africa would be in breach of certain international treaties involving Interpol and the United Nations.

SAPS, refusing to give in to Keating's threats, paid over nothing. The systems were promptly switched off. There were rumours that some of the systems were faulty and that the switch-off could have revealed that this was indeed the case. Instead of alarm bells ringing

138 Jan Gerber, FDA threatens to 'collapse criminal justice system', Mail & Guardian, 5 April 2018, https://mg.co.za/article/2018-04-05-justice-system-threatened-if-police-didnt-pay-up/

over the collapse of the criminal justice system, the public heard nothing but absolute silence.

Police officers still went off to crime scenes with their firearms, the courts continued with their cases, and things just went on. Whether this was because the state had made contingency plans or whether the fancy billion-rand systems had never worked properly in the first case wasn't clear at the time. Police said they had made contingency plans within days of the shutdown. In various press conferences, Mohapi said that four days after FDA had switched the systems off, SAPS had them up and running again. SAPS managed to access the systems and switched them back on without any input from FDA or ISS.

FDA BOEREMAG LINK

Keating's threats had backfired, it appeared, and by mid-May 2018, the FDA's offices in Wapadrand, Pretoria, closed their doors.[139]

In the meantime, McBride told SCOPA that their investigations into the company revealed an even more sinister side than the racketeering and corruption IPID had already uncovered. It was that SITA and FDA employees were linked to the right-wing terrorist group, the Boeremag.[140]

McBride told SCOPA that he had alerted previous police commissioners (i.e. Phahlane) about this and that nothing had been done. Instead, IPID was met with resistance. McBride stated:

> *The question needs to be asked whether SAPS had been used as a vehicle to fund a white supremacist, non-constitutional organisation whose sole aim is to undo, to destroy with violence the constitutional order.*

139 Angelique Serrao, Police supplier's offices closing but business still running, News24, 16 May 2018, https://www.news24.com/SouthAfrica/News/police-suppliers-offices-closing-but-business-still-running-20180516

140 Jan Gerber, Boeremag link to State IT company and dodgy police supplier, News24, 2 May 2018, https://www.news24.com/SouthAfrica/News/boeremag-link-to-state-it-company-and-dodgy-police-supplier-20180502

DA MP Tim Brauteseth mentioned the names of Barnie Venter, Rachel Venter, Christo de Bruyn and Yolanda Potgieter. He said they worked – or had worked – at SITA, which SITA CEO Setumo Mohapi confirmed. Brauteseth then mentioned the name of Boeremag member Andre du Toit, who was serving a jail sentence for treason.

"I remember him well," said Khehla Sitole, the new Police Chief appointed after Phahlane had been suspended.

Brauteseth said the Boeremag-connected SITA people were in correspondence with du Toit and were supporting him financially. Mohapi admitted that the employees used SITA's laptops and networks in their dealings with du Toit.

"So, we have someone sitting in prison, who is a convicted terrorist, sending emails to SITA?" asked Brauteseth.

ANC MP Vincent Smith said there were more people at SITA involved than those that Brauteseth mentioned. However, Vincent Smith himself had been accused of corruption.

"Do we have a problem in SITA with a cabal that has taken over SITA?" Smith asked. "Are they still in place and still assisting people like the Boeremag?"

Mohapi said they were "actively working against the cabal itself". He said that, of those identified, five had resigned, five had been suspended, and three had been dismissed.

ANC MP Nyami Booi said SITA "is running a counterrevolutionary structure" and that Parliament *"must take over"*.

"It is a national threat to us," Booi said. "The safety of our country is not in capable hands. Have you told anybody of the Boeremag?"

Sitole said he was aware of "up to 80%" of what was revealed at the meeting, saying, the Boeremag issue is a bigger national security investigation".

Even after these astonishing revelations, Keating remained cocksure of himself. He sent a statement to the media denying the allegations and saying that the suggestion that FDA's software services were being run from a prison cell was a "completely unfounded quantum leap".

In his statement, Keating claimed that FDA was approached two earlier by former SITA employees who demanded the company give away a significant portion of their shares. Keating said FDA refused to comply and had reported the matter to SITA, adding:

> *This damaging campaign against FDA, ending in a mythical Boeremag takeover plot, has meant that FDA has not been paid since October 2017, resulting in the retrenchment of 62 hard-working and dedicated staff members.*

Keating declared that he would be taking SAPS and SITA to court.

COURT BATTLES

When Keating switched off the systems, SAPS had written to FDA and ISS to say that in barring police from accessing the Firearm Permit system, the Property Control and the Exhibit Management (PCEM) system, and the Analytical Capabilities and Visualisation system (VA-Amis), the companies were acting unlawfully.[141]

The Firearm Permit system marked, identified, issued, and tracked firearms and enabled the storage of information relating to the ballistic characteristics of those firearms. SAPS said they had been granted a permanent, non-expiring licence for the system and were advised to make copies for backup purposes. According to SAPS' statement, SAPS had paid a once-off licence fee of R11.6-million for the license.

The PCEM system, which was used for logging and tracking evidence (ensuring the chain of evidence was not broken), was governed by a written agreement concluded between SAPS and Unysis Africa in 2010. According to SAPS' statement, SAPS had paid a once-off fee of R35-million for the licence.

---

141 Angelique Serrao, Battle between police and IT supplier heads to court, News24, 12 April 2018, https://www.news24.com/SouthAfrica/News/battle-between-police-and-it-supplier-heads-to-court-20180412

The VA-Amis contract was governed by a written agreement between SITA and ISS that saw SITA remunerate R80-million to ISS. According to SAPS' statement, this amount was paid in full.

Keating replied, claiming that SITA and SAPS had switched back on the firearms control and PCEM system illegally. Without the system being on, the police would be unable to electronically locate evidence to be used in criminal cases or issue firearm licences.

SITA, meanwhile, vowed that FDA and Keating would never be allowed near their systems again.[142] They had completely locked them out. SITA intended to go to the courts to recuperate some of the money they had spent on corrupt contracts with FDA where they had found proof of irregularities.

The battle lines had been drawn on all fronts, and the courts would be the place where the State and Keating's companies would fight it out.

SITA and SAPS approached the Gauteng High Court in Pretoria on an urgent basis to obtain an order for FDA to reactivate the systems. SITA was successful in getting FDA to reactivate their system. However, FDA brought a counter application to interdict the use of the software.

A massive legal battle raged over whether SAPS really did own the original source codes for the systems they thought they had paid for years before.[143] The *Daily Maverick* revealed that another legal wrangle, this time in the civil courts, was underway over a fourth system involving fingerprint tracking. A company called FACTT had sold their FPS licence to FDA in 2005, and the question about whether FACTT was allowed to sell the license in the first place was before the court. Essentially, Keating's company was dishonestly claiming ownership of something it did not own.

142 Alex Mitchley, FDA will not switch off police systems again – SITA, News24, 11 May 2018, https://www.news24.com/SouthAfrica/News/fda-will-not-switch-off-police-systems-again-sita-20180511

143 Marianne Thamm, SAPS/SITA Capture: The continuing mess around fireamrs and exhibit control systems a threat to South Africa, Daily Maverick, 16 May 2019, https://www.dailymaverick.co.za/article/2019-05-16-saps-sita-capture-the-continuing-mess-around-firearms-and-exhibit-control-systems-a-systemic-threat-to-south-africa/

National Police Commissioner, General Khehla Sitole, said that Keating had approached his office asking if SAPS would like to purchase the intellectual property from FDA. Divisional Commissioner of Legal and Policy Services, Lieutenant General A Khan, wrote that SAPS faced the risk that FDA could block access to the system.

When SCOPA instructed SITA to stop paying FDA, FACTT withdrew its licence agreement, which led to the ownership of the original patent and codes being under question. Like a tangled ball of yarn, none of it made sense. Who owned the software for the systems? Who had paid what for them? What was working and what was not? It was as clear as mud and probably deliberately so. The real object of what had been going on was to bleed state coffers as dry as possible. It was certainly not to improve the SAPS systems so that police officers on the ground could fight crime. It was the perfect example of state capture. The more confusion reigned, the easier it was to plunder the state cookie jar.

Keating claimed SAPS and SITA had been using FDA's software illegally for more than eighteen months and refusing to pay for it. In an interview with *News24,* Keating said SITA owed his company R11-million.[144]

> *I was accused of holding South Africa to ransom when in fact, SITA and the police refused to discuss or negotiate a settlement with FDA even after* [standing committee on public accounts] *gave permission to the police to negotiate and settle the matter in October 2018.*

In January 2019, the Pretoria High Court ruled in favour of FDA but suspended their ruling for sixty days to allow SITA and the

---

144 Jeanette Chabalala, Will FDA now switch off police systems again after SCA ruling, News24, 26 June 2019, https://www.news24.com/SouthAfrica/News/will-fda-now-switch-off-police-systems-again-after-sca-ruling-20190626

police to find an alternative system.[145] In his judgment, Acting Judge Swanepoel stated that:

> [*The*] *SAPS and SITA have been using the FPS system unlawfully for more than a year. They clearly have every intention of continuing to do so, thereby prolonging their unlawful conduct. A court cannot simply sit by and allow the state to continue acting in contravention of the law...*

The court said that neither SAPS nor SITA had a perpetual license to use the system and that FDA should therefore be compensated for its use. The High Court also ruled that despite being warned that their conduct was "reprehensible", SITA and SAPS continued to put up a "frivolous defence". The court also interdicted SAPS and SITA from infringing on FDA's copyright of the firearm permit system's software.

SITA appealed the High Court ruling, while SAPS withdrew its application and agreed to abide by the ruling. When the case was later dismissed in the same court, SITA petitioned the Supreme Court of Appeal but fell short again.

In March 2019, SAPS met with FDA and agreed to set out its position regarding the outstanding invoices. SITA insisted that SAPS be subjected to a technical and financial due diligence process and that FDA should direct all future offers to National Treasury and not SAPS.

SAPS' internal legal department either negligently or deliberately botched the litigation so that FDA would win. Of course, this played directly into Keating's hands. Keating launched an anonymous social media campaign aimed at maligning the new leadership of the police. But the media wasn't buying it – except for *Carte Blanche,* which in my opinion, places sensationalism over truth in its desire to rake in advertising revenue during prime-time viewing on a Sunday evening.

---

145 Jeanette Chabalala, Will FDA now switch off police systems again after SCA ruling, News24, 26 June 2019, https://www.news24.com/SouthAfrica/News/will-fda-now-switch-off-police-systems-again-after-sca-ruling-20190626

In August 2021, I wrote and told Khehla Sitole that his legal department had been captured and had been leading him down the garden path on many matters. Not only in terms of the FDA botch-up but also with regard to other high-profile matters. I also met with Sithole at the Inanda Club and spent two hours going through the challenges he faced within his own ranks. However, Sitole's indecisions led to calls for him to be fired. It was a great shame because one thing about Sithole was that he was *not* corrupt. If he got fired, we might be back to square one again.

MORE REVELATIONS

While the State and Keating sat in various courts, SITA, IPID, and SAPS continued their forensic investigations, revealing an endless quagmire of tender irregularities and corruption. The more they looked, the more rot they discovered. Some of this was revealed to the public through SCOPA.[146]

The parliamentary body heard more about how SAPS' top management had colluded with SITA employees to siphon hundreds of millions from the budget of the criminal justice system to favour FDA – and they did this by bypassing Treasury completely. For two decades, the SAPS SITA cabal drained billions from the State's coffers.

A year and a half later, the investigations found a total of forty cases involving twenty-five employees within SITA and more than twenty within SAPS.[147] At SITA, twelve employees had been dismissed, and twenty-one had resigned. There were three final written warnings and three disciplinary hearings. In some cases, SITA found that senior

146 Marianne Thamm, Scopa hears how SAPS illegally siphoned off R100m from criminal justice system budget, Daily Maverick, 2 November 2018, https://webcache.googleusercontent.com/search?q=cache:y_UjCavTdB4J:https://www.dailymaverick.co.za/article/2018-11-02-scopa-hears-how-saps-illegally-siphoned-off-r100m-from-criminal-justice-system-budget/+&cd=4&hl=en&ct=clnk&gl=be

147 Marianne Thamm, Key state technology agency was captured lock stock and secret codes, Daily Maverick, 28 August 2018, https://www.dailymaverick.co.za/article/2018-08-28-key-state-technology-agency-was-captured-lock-stock-and-secret-codes/

supply chain management employees were linked to companies but had not declared it. These employees were using SITA's offices and equipment to conduct their business.

SITA CEO Setumo Mohapi admitted that SITA personnel who were meant to be looking after technical equipment had limited knowledge of how the system was configured or even where the server was located:

> *There was a dangerous and unhealthy reliance on Forensic Data Analysts. Documents, when we found them, were out of date and unusable. We also found that Forensic Data Analysts personnel had superuser rights and could do anything and everything with the system. Nobody in the state system had the right codes.*

SITA had essentially outsourced their duties.

SITA sent Restriction of Trade letters involving five companies and their directors who had been involved in the capture to Treasury.

McBride told SCOPA that even though the top management who had been involved had been suspended, IPID investigators were still having trouble extracting information from SAPS because they had unlawfully classified key tender documents as secret. This was just the start of a new tactic used by the police to halt IPID's investigations. McBride made it clear that it was nothing more than a deliberate attempt to sabotage their team. McBride subsequently went to the Inspector General of Intelligence to have the documents declassified, but it was going to be a long fight, and McBride would be forced to leave IPID before the issue was resolved. I will deal with the reasons later.

McBride had, however, won an important victory in the courts in his case against the Northwest (Mabula) team. The North Gauteng High Court ruled in IPID's favour, saying that SAPS members with personal interests in cases were prevented from investigating IPID members who were investigating them. The judge in the case suggested the ruling should be included in new legislation on IPID that was working its way through Parliament.

McBride made a fundamental change to the way IPID was run, ensuring its independence and finding ways to stop the interference that had plagued our investigations into Phahlane. McBride was making long-term changes that would benefit the organisation and the country for years to come.

The result of our investigations into Phahlane had ended up achieving far more than I originally hoped. It broke up a state capture cabal and saw numerous corrupt employees who had allowed the capture to take place lose their jobs. It revealed a serious state security risk and put a stop to Keating's companies doing business with the State.

The alleged leaders of the crime syndicates, like Phahlane and Keating, were, however, still roaming free. But IPID was determined to see them charged for some of the harm they had done. It remains to be seen whether the newly appointed head of IPID has the gravitas to see the game to the finish line. I somehow doubt it, as she has already taken steps to neutralise some of the good work done by McBride.

CHAPTER 24

THE ROLE OF THE MEDIA

INQUIRY INTO MEDIA CREDIBILITY AND ETHICS

In 2019, the South African National Editors' Forum (SANEF) launched its much-hyped-up inquiry into media credibility and ethics. The need for the inquiry came about after the *Sunday Times* was forced to publish several apologies over mistakes it made by publishing stories that helped launch the capture of the criminal justice sector and SARS – including the (fake) Cato Manor death squad stories, the Zimbabwean Renditions stories, and the SARS Rogue Spy Unit articles. SANEF indicated it was time for the media to seriously introspect and review their editorial systems and practices as the media industry had not been immune from being drawn into manipulative practices and collusions. The organisation said it believed it was an important moment for the industry to examine ethics breaches in terms of the capture of journalists across the industry by the State and corporations.

The inquiry was led by a panel of commissioners headed by retired Judge Kathleen Satchwell and included panellists Nikiwe Bikitsha and Rich Mkhondo.[148]

---

148 Sanef, Sanef's media credibility and ethics inquiry looks to review editorial systems, practices, BizCommunity, 13 August 2019, https://www.bizcommunity.com/Article/196/15/194245.html

The organisation called on all interested parties to send the panel written submissions. I didn't hesitate to send in a detailed submission.

I have a longstanding and professional relationship with various journalists and media houses. While there are strong, independent journalists who refuse to bow down to societal and political pressures, many others should never be allowed to work in the industry again. Unfortunately, I have witnessed journalists whose behaviour is criminal – behaviour that should see them being sent to prison – yet they are supported by the media houses they work for.

The truth is that certain elements in the media, just like the management of the NPA and SAPS, have a lot to answer for when it comes to the capture of the criminal justice sector during Zuma's corrupt rule. Its capture was predicated by the capture of certain media, most notably the *Sunday Times,* and later, Gupta-owned media outlets that ran false stories supporting the state capture cabal.

One of the first journalists I came across – who, in my opinion, was as unethical as they come – was De Wet Potgieter. He first worked at the *Sunday Independent* and then moved on to the *Saturday Star* when Krejcir was at the height of his criminal empire. He later moved to Gupta-owned *The New Age.* Potgieter got up close with Krejcir and would often be the only journalist the mobster would give interviews to. Potgieter was invited into Krejcir's home and even took portrait shots of Krejcir and his family.[149] His stories about me were very defamatory, falsely claiming I had assaulted suspects and that I was leading the Hawks against Krejcir, a lie similar to the one later propagated by Vlok and Phahlane.[150] With the latter two, I was supposed to be controlling IPID. These stories didn't just come out of nowhere. Some of my sources revealed that Potgieter was

149 De Wet Potgieter, At home with Radovan Krejcir, Sunday Independent, 11 April 2011, https://www.iol.co.za/sundayindependent/at-home-with-radovan-krecjir-1055061

150 De Wet Potgieter, Crime-fighter accused of assault, IOL, 26 March 2011, https://www.iol.co.za/news/south-africa/crime-fighter-accused-of-assault-1047580

being "encouraged" to write his articles. In an interview with Milosh Potiska, one of Krejcir's connections in Prague, he revealed to me that he (Potiska) had personally paid for a holiday for Potgieter worth R15 000. Cash had been given to Potiska by Krejcir for this express purpose.

Potgieter stopped writing about me after I invited him to take a polygraph to disprove allegations of kickbacks he had allegedly received from Krejcir.

Potgieter has the dubious credit of being fired from *The New Age*. After his ignominious departure, Potgieter published an article in the *Daily Maverick* on al-Qaeda being alive and well in South Africa in 2013, which was quickly debunked. The *Daily Maverick* retracted the article and apologised.[151] To right his name, Potgieter wrote a book titled *Black Widow, White Widow* to prove his hypothesis. But the book was met with poor reviews, suggesting that, if anything, Potgieter, like certain other dodgy journalists, did not let the truth get in the way of a good story. [152,153]

Potgieter then found his way to the *Lowvelder*, a local newspaper in Mpumalanga, where he is the editor today. In my opinion, a journalist like Potgieter should never be allowed to work in a newsroom again, let alone secure the position of editor.

When told that the journalists who work for them have acted unethically, I have seen a pattern of media houses protecting their own and being reluctant to do anything about it. This has led to the journalists involved holding onto senior positions and continuing

---

151 GroundUp, The Daily Maverick and the Dockrats: Is Al-Qaeda really 'alive and well' in SA?, Africa Check, 8 June 2013, https://africacheck.org/2013/06/18/daily-maverick-and-the-dockrats-where-is-the-al-qaeda-link/?fbclid=IwAR1Og1ZktQQO7mkMY7Pe5SL9gPgDqG6EBHfNVe7QLF7jYKwyykmYDWao d6E

152 Neels Blom, No sense of present danger, Business Day, 25 November 2014, https://www.pressreader.com/south-africa/business-day/20141125/281736972762401

153 Christopher Merrett, Poor editing and repetition spoil a potential illuminating expose, The Witness, 15 September 2014, https://www.pressreader.com/south-africa/the-witness/20140915/281840051871211

to do real damage to the country. Criticism of dirty journalists is often quickly defended by the South African National Editors Forum, SANEF.

Like the sources who told me about the alleged payments to Potgieter, the reason why damaging stories were written by investigative journalists at the *Sunday Times* was allegedly also for money. These stories helped bring about the capture of the Hawks and the Revenue Service, getting rid of hard-working, ethical employees like Johan Booysen, Anwa Dramat, Shadrack Sibiya, and the entire criminal investigative capacity at SARS.

In 2012, Colonel Kobus Roelofse's investigative report (which was subsequently made public as Annexure FA1 to the Freedom Under Law Application) revealed that Major General Solomon Lazarus, the Chief Financial Officer of the SSA (Crime Intelligence), allegedly paid journalists at the *Sunday Times* to publish a story on the Zimbabwe Renditions. I tried to do something about it back then by calling Yusuf Abramjee, who was then the Head of News and Current Affairs at Primedia Broadcasting, the Head of Crime Line, and the chairperson of the Pretoria Press Club. A day later, I followed up with an email to Abramjee and the *Sunday Times* asking that they investigate these allegations and put the journalists who wrote the story under investigation, including a polygraph test. Abramjee penned an article under the Pretoria Press Club calling for an urgent investigation into whether Crime Intelligence had paid journalists to write reports which discredited other officers.[154]

Unfortunately, that was as far as the complaint went. My calls for an investigation were ignored for the next seven years. Speculation still lingers about what happened at that time.

154 Yusuf Abramjee, Did Crime Intelligence bribe journalists? – NPC, National Press Club, 17 May 2012, https://www.politicsweb.co.za/documents/did-crime-intelligence-bribe-journalists--npc

In October 2018, after I threatened to attack the income base of the *Sunday Times,* editor Bongani Siqoko retracted the stories and apologised for having published them. He said they had made mistakes *"and allowed ourselves to be manipulated by those with ulterior motives"*. Former *Sunday Times* editor Ray Hartley published his response to the paper's decision to apologise for the articles published under his editorship on *News24.*[155] Hartley wrote:

> *It sickens me to think that those intent on abusing state power for corrupt purposes used articles published by the Sunday Times on irregular police killings and the rendition of suspects to Zimbabwe for their nefarious ends.*
>
> *This was also the case with the lamentable reporting on the SARS rogue unit. But I was not editor at the time the SARS "rogue unit" stories were published, and it does not follow that because errors were made there, they must have occurred in all preceding stories.*

Hartley went on to defend the Cato Death Squad and Zimbabwe Rendition stories, saying that he and his journalists spent a year investigating them. The stories were utter rubbish – Hartley knew it but would never admit it.

I responded to Hartley's article by sending *News24* editor Adriaan Basson a letter pointing out the faults in Hartley's argument:

> *What Mr Hartley obviously fails to understand is that the dark forces from the SAPS' Crime Intelligence Unit 'cut their teeth' on the Cato Manor and Zimbabwe Rendition fake news threads. Having perfected their modus operandi, they then rolled it out to the 'SARS Rogue Unit'. If Mr Hartley and his journalists had conducted themselves with a little more circumspection in 2012, South Africa might have been saved from the horrors of state capture. One thing is for certain, Mr Hartley cannot deny that the dark cloud of suspicion was already*

155 Ray Hartley, READ: Former Sunday Times editor Ray Hartley's blistering response to 'death squad' criticism, News24, 21 October 2018, https://www.news24.com/SouthAfrica/News/read-former-sunday-times-editor-ray-hartleys-blistering-response-to-death-squad-criticism-20181021

hanging over Biermann Avenue, long before the SARS Rogue Unit catchphrase was 'invented' by the same journalists that 'invented' the catchphrase "Cato Manor" and "Zimbabwe Renditions".

What Mr Hartley has forgotten is that the fake Zimbabwe Rendition was created by the Sunday Times, who then became the ONLY visible accuser, not another person or state institution.156 The word 'alleged' is therefore not appropriate when you are manufacturing and publishing your own news for and on behalf of a criminal syndicate, which is the case in all three narratives falsely run by the Sunday Times. The real reason the word 'alleged' was missing is because the journalists and editor (not to mention the puppeteer/s that were controlling them) wanted the whole country to believe the lies they were pedalling in pursuit of a much more sinister agenda. This is one of those times when the people were tried and convicted in the court of public opinion by the very same people that were behind all three stories.

In the same way that General Booysen can dismantle the Cato Manor story, Generals Dramat and Sibiya can dismantle the fake Zimbabwe Rendition stories, and the SARS three can dismantle the fake Rogue Unit stories. I have looked into all of them and can dismantle all three of them. I can also prove that there is a causal link between three fake narratives the Sunday Times printed between 2012 and 2015 and the capture of the criminal justice systems and SARS. The only thing I cannot (yet) prove is the controlling hand. I could prove the controlling hand if the journalists would come clean and privately name their sources. However, they won't do this as this would prove their own culpability in nearly bringing this country to its knees and possibly even lay them open to very serious criminal charges.

The dark cloud of mistrust in journalism that these stories rendered still hangs over the profession today and could have been cleared if the investigation Abramjee and I called for had taken place in 2012.

156 Ray Hartley, Claims against the Sunday Times a smear – Ray Hartley, Politicsweb, 17 May 2012, http://www.politicsweb.co.za/sitemap/claims-against-the-sunday-times-a-smear--ray-hartl

The journalists involved – Stephan Hofstatter, Mzilikazi wa Afrika and Piet Rampedi, all eventually left the *Sunday Times*. Hofstatter and wa Afrika only left in 2018 after the release of Hofstatter's book on Eskom, *Licence to Loot*, caused a stir after it was met with anger by ex-members of SARS who protested at his book launch and asked him to explain the role he played in the SARS Rogue Unit saga.[157]

Wa Afrika and Rampedi found a new home at the *Sunday Independent*, one of the newspapers in the Independent Newspaper stable, where they have been publishing stories that appeared to favour Zuma and tarnish President Cyril Ramaphosa.[158] However, their attempts at State Capture Version 2 have lit no fires because their names have been so discredited already that few readers take them seriously.

The *Sunday Times*, *Sunday Independent*, and (former) Gupta-owned *The New Age* were not the only media that played a role in state capture.

I am pleased to say that at the time of writing this book, the *Sunday Times* is now under new ethical leadership and on course for a positive future.

CARTE BLANCHE AND TONY BEAMISH

Tony Beamish and the role he played in the Bobroff story – as well as his attacks on me – needed to be thoroughly investigated. I did just that, and what I uncovered beggars belief.

The reason why I investigated Cora van der Merwe was that she had been allegedly stealing information from the law firm of Ronald and Darren Bobroff to pass on to Tony Beamish. Beamish allegedly used some of the documents to write numerous stories on the Bobroffs for *Moneyweb*. Then he attacked the Bobroffs on Carte Blanche and

157 Citizen Reporter, Journalist slammed as 'state capture crony' at launch of anti-corruption book, The Citizen, 21 September 2018, https://citizen.co.za/news/south-africa/2012514/journalist-slammed-as-state-capture-crony-at-launch-of-anti-corruption-book/

158 Marianne Thamm, Discredited Sunday Times journalists find new home at Iqbal Surve's media empire, Daily Maverick, 30 April 2019, https://www.dailymaverick.co.za/article/2019-04-30-discredited-sunday-times-journalists-find-new-home-at-iqbal-surves-media-empire/

had his girlfriend make false allegations that I had kidnapped her. Beamish also supplied the stolen documents to Bobroff's rival, Anthony Millar. I was supplied evidence that Beamish had secret meetings with Bobroffs' clients named in the stolen files he had received from van der Merwe and attempted to persuade them to fire Bobroff and go over to Anthony Millar. He did not always succeed, which left a trail of failed attempts with witnesses willing to talk.

Despite what I consider appallingly unethical behaviour, Beamish subsequently won a Webber Wentzel legal journalist of the year award for the stories he wrote on the Bobroffs.

During my first court appearances, Beamish was always present, lurking at the back of the room, watching what was happening and gloating. Much like an arsonist has to hang around and see the fruits of his crime. He even surreptitiously videotaped some of the court proceedings, in itself illegal. I later learnt that his role in my charges was more sinister than simply that of a journalist reporting on what was happening. He and Cora van der Merwe were alleged lovers, and it was clear that she had stolen the documents from the Bobroffs to give her boyfriend something to write about. It was all deeply unethical, and Beamish's reporting on the matter was highly questionable, as he failed to disclose that his 'source' was his lover. I am certain Beamish would not have won the Webber Wentzel award had he disclosed that he was engaged in an affair with van der Merwe and that he had manipulated her into stealing and sending him the files upon which his stories were based.

I later learned that Beamish and van der Merwe had become friends with Vlok and that Beamish had instructed van der Merwe to open the false charges against me so that he would have a story to write about. A fraud his gullible bosses at Carte Blanche were happy to go along with. I learnt all of this from van der Merwe's daughter, Michelle, who had deposed to all this information in an affidavit which, in 2019, was placed before a court. Michelle van der Merwe had applied for a protection order against Beamish after he allegedly sexually assaulted her. In her affidavits, she described a man who was allegedly deeply disturbed and an alcoholic who was controlling her mother.

Michelle's account of what happened to her was chilling. The young woman lived at home with her mother and could not escape Beamish, who stayed over at their house more often than not. In her affidavit, she described how an allegedly drunk Beamish entered her room while she was sleeping and how she woke up to find him with his hand down her panties and touching her privates. She said that Beamish repeatedly goaded her after the incident, deliberately doing things to make her angry and then filming her as she angrily shouted at him. He threatened to send those videos to her employer to have her fired.

Beamish had, in the meantime, moved from *Moneyweb* to *Carte Blanche* as a so-called senior journalist and was using his position there to try to run a false story on me as far back as 2015. During 2016 and 2017, I also discovered that Beamish was using pseudonyms and false email accounts to send 'press releases' accusing me of being a crook to ethical journalists who had been reporting fairly on my cases. He also used his anonymous email account to write to AfriForum in an attempt to disrupt the anti-corruption work we were jointly doing. However, when AfriForum invited the e-mail sender to a meeting, he went quiet on them. A face-to-face meeting would have exposed his true identity. Beamish was showing all the signs of a psychopath. He also took it upon himself to send anonymous e-mails to my children. How sick can one get I thought.

Amazingly, his employers chose not to see through the man they had hired and went along with his 'story ideas'. I was first contacted in March 2015 by Wynand Grobler, the Managing Editor at *Carte Blanche*, asking for my input on a story they were planning to run on van der Merwe's claims of being kidnapped by me. I told Grobler that the allegations came from Beamish, and I invited him to come and look at the video footage of the meeting we had with Cora van der Merwe, which clearly showed her jokingly asking for a glass of wine to drink and stepping outside to take a phone call. These were not exactly the actions of a woman who was in the midst of a kidnapping situation. I warned Grobler that *Carte Blanche* was being used in the furtherance of a criminal agenda. I also suggested he put van der Merwe through a polygraph test and even suggested questions to be put to her to prove her lies.

I did not hear back from him until a year later, when he came forward with the same allegations as before. Again, I invited him to come and look at the video, and again, he went quiet. In my opinion, *Carte Blanche* is a programme that *sometimes* refuses to let the truth stand in the way of a good story. After all, it's their sensational "exposés" that bring in the advertising revenue each Sunday during prime time when *Carte Blanche* is being aired.

I emailed Grobler and chastised him:

> *I did not expect to see a reputable organisation like Carte Blanche being duped into believing the lies of persons responsible for the theft and receiving of stolen property. If that is going to be the attitude of the media, to bolster criminal conduct and destroy the reputation of someone that has made such sacrifices, then the country will not have people stepping forward to take the extreme risk at stopping the rot because they will know that they will get kicked in the teeth for wanting SA to be a better country.*
>
> *Over the years I have been in South Africa, my actions have led to the break-up of many crime syndicates, and many persons have been sent to prison. Others have had their criminal actions curtailed. It would be disappointing now to see Carte Blanche being used as a rallying point for the many disgruntled people out there that have*

been on the receiving end of my attempts to make this a better country for all, however misguided they might be.

I would later learn, through Michelle van der Merwe, that *Carte Blanche* had given Beamish a formal warning over some of his actions. Curiously, Grobler did not even reply to my email and, when I later sent him damning evidence of Beamish's fraudulent conduct, he brushed it off, preferring to keep a fraudster on his payroll than admit *Carte Blanche* had unwittingly – or not – become part of the state capture project. Michelle van der Merwe opened a criminal case against Beamish, for sexual assault. The State again failed her, like it does many female victims of sexual assault and rape. Without carrying out any investigation, the NPA declined to prosecute. Michelle van der Merwe then started a private prosecution. Beamish then wrote to the Legal Practice Council and made false allegations against Michelle van der Merwe, which were subsequently dismissed. Her then employer terminated her employment contract after receiving anonymous e-mails about her. Following continuous unlawful harassment by Beamish which led to her trying to take her own life, she was advised by her doctor to pull out of the prosecution, to avoid further stress.

It was not only Carte Blanche's attack on me that led me into believing they were culpable in their role with state capture. They had also run a damning false story on the SARS 'Rogue Unit' on the 22nd of February 2015. In a letter to Parliament, former SARS spokesman Adrian Lackay stated that the show made *"untrue and slanderous allegations against Johann van Loggerenberg and others"*.[159]

To this very day, *Carte Blanche* has never apologised for airing the show. Nor have they retracted these false stories. They have, however, removed any reference to it from their website. There is no doubt in my mind that *Carte Blanche* was prepared to run scandalous but false

159 Adrian Lackay, SARS: This is the inside story – Adrian Lackay, PoliticsWeb, 23 April 2015, https://www.politicsweb.co.za/news-and-analysis/sars-this-is-the-inside-story--adrian-lackay

stories to garner lucrative advertising revenue while becoming a part of the state capture arsenal to be used by criminals for nefarious purposes. They certainly piled the pressure on me with their false insinuations that I had kidnapped their employee's mistress. It is clear that they allowed themselves to be used, which reminded me of the French quislings who collaborated with the fascists during World War II.

Carte Blanche has never been held to account for their actions. The fact that Beamish was still employed there is a huge blemish on their reputation – particularly since I made them aware of Michelle van der Merwe's allegations against him, as well as another case against Beamish launched by a man called Paul Mullon. Mullon, a web developer and information governance consultant, also turned to the courts to protect himself from Beamish. Mullon, who had been mandated by the Bobroffs to register two websites for them, had become another one of Beamish's many targets in his bitter and twisted pursuit of the Bobroffs. After discovering Mullon's name under the domain listings of the two websites, Beamish called Mullon at 3:30 a.m. to tell him to remove content (that Beamish wasn't happy about) from the websites. Mullon explained that he had simply been paid to set up the domains and had no say over the content on the websites. That did not cut it for Beamish.

In what can only be described as outright fraud, Beamish then contacted credit reporting agency TransUnion and fraudulently told them that Mullon was a bad debtor and owed Beamish R850 000. Transunion immediately logged a negative bad debt on Mullon's credit profile. Beamish also contacted Mullon's personal banker at ABSA by e-mail and said there was an adverse credit listing against Mullon. According to Mullon, this was all fabricated by Beamish, who had also turned to Twitter to tell the world that Mullon had conspired with the Bobroffs.

Mullon's attorneys sent Beamish letters saying that what he was doing was tantamount to extortion and defamation. TransUnion cancelled the adverse credit rating, and Beamish, probably fearful of losing his job at *Carte Blanche,* settled with Mullon out of court. But what he could not do was remove the evidence of his acts of psychopathic fraud intended to harass and extort Mullon.

Once I had this information, I contacted *Carte Blanche* to alert them to what Beamish had been up to. I also contacted Webber Wentzel because I believed Beamish's award for his coverage of the Bobroffs should be withdrawn. Again, Grobler chose to ignore my information. He protected the criminal on his payroll and kept him on.

Still, *Carte Blanche* did not respond to my allegations. I again wrote to Grobler and told him that *Carte Blanche's* day of reckoning was fast approaching:

> *You've had so many chances to engage, but arrogance and low ethics seem to have prevented you from doing so. Perhaps being outed for what you are will change your mindset?*

I often wonder how anyone can really trust the stories coming out of *Carte Blanche* when they have a fraudulent senior journalist like Beamish working there? The damage this does to their credibility is immense.

By 2015, my forensic practice was earning in the region of R10-million in fees each year and employed an array of well qualified and highly professional Certified Fraud Examiners, forensic specialists, and a lawyer. One of our recurring clients was the law firm Webber Wentzel. I was pleased to be associated with them as they had taken a strong stand against state capture by allocating around one percent of their six hundred employees and another one percent of their R4-billion annual income towards taking the fight back to the likes of Nhleko, Ntlemeza, and the corrupt government.

I was shocked when I found that Dario Milo, a well-known media lawyer and partner at Webber Wentzel, took a denying yet sabre-rattling approach to my exposing the rot at Carte Blanche. I was even more shocked when, in late 2017, the work that my practice was carrying out for Webber Wentzel was summarily terminated. No reason was given. Ironically, the termination came a few days after Dario Milo fired a shot across my bows on behalf of *Carte Blanche*, threatening me with legal action. Bit silly really, as I do not cower to threats of legal action, when I know I am on firm ground.

It showed me that even good law firms that had nailed their flag to the mast in exposing corruption were prepared to run with the foxes and hunt with the hounds. I guess *Carte Blanche's* fee income was a bridge too far, and Webber Wentzel chose fee income from those engaged in state capture, alongside *pro bono* work. Fighting against state capture while earning fees from those supporting it seemed a strange mix, but then I don't run a four billion rand a year law firm.

To further demonstrate their complicity *Carte Blanche gave a platform to* infamous state capture player Keith Keating. Despite being fully aware that Keating had been accused of paying substantial bribes to then Acting Chief of Police, Phahlane, Carte Blanche's Derek Watts unwittingly gave Keating and FDA a clean bill of health while criticising the leadership of the SAPS. Once again, *Carte Blanche* demonstrated that they would not let the truth stand in the way of a good story. While being protected by Webber Wentzel's Dario Milo, Carte Blanche had repeatedly engaged in activity that, in my opinion, is treasonous. They were actively engaged in publicly assisting the criminals who were busy with the national project known as "State Capture".

I repeatedly wrote to Carte Blanche and accused them of assisting in the state capture project. On the 24th of March 2021, I once again wrote to *Carte Blanche's* Wynand Grobler.[4] Needless to say, Grobler, who had previously been desperate to run a fake story alleging I had kidnapped his employee's mistress, did not even bother to respond to my email.

To make sure *Carte Blanche* fully understood the hole they were digging for themselves, I wrote to them again the following day, the 25th March, to reinforce my accusations.

At the time of writing this book, *Carte Blanche* continued to ignore me. I plan to send a copy of this book to every company that spends money advertising on DSTV's Channel 101 between 7 p.m. and 8 p.m. on Sunday evenings, requesting that they boycott Carte Blanche advertising.

WHY WE CANNOT ALLOW THE MICE TO GUARD THE CHEESE

The South African National Editors' Forum, SANEF, the self-appointed guardian of media ethics, has, in my experience, failed its mandate. In some instances, it has done a fair amount to in fact protect dirty journalists. Not long after the *Sunday Times* retracted its stories and made a public apology, SANEF awarded itself the role of appointing an 'independent' panel to investigate the shocking state of dirty journalism in South Africa. SANEF hand-picked the panel and paid them for their work.

I did not expect much to come from SANEF's inquiry into media ethics. In my opinion, the final product was nothing more than a whitewash of the single-most-important burning issue – South Africa's sordid media. When SANEF published its report, it misrepresented the role of Forensics for Justice. SANEF falsely claimed that we had requested to make a submission but had not got back to them – which was completely untrue. They deliberately kept me away from the so-called panel, because they knew what I had to say would expose the rot in the media, something they had been protecting.

In my submission, I made it clear that without the media's help in removing key players in the criminal justice system, the levels of crime and corruption that had taken place in the past decade would never have been possible. State capture would probably have failed because good cops and prosecutors would have been there to stop it – the same good cops and prosecutors who were unlawfully removed from their posts, along with the SARS High-Risk Unit members.

Over the years that I faced false prosecutions, at least a dozen journalists regularly published knowingly false stories, seeking to impugn my character and the characters of others. Their editors either did nothing, helped with the process, or defended their conduct after the event. Journalists working for *The New Age* and *ANN7* repeatedly made false and defamatory comments against me and many others who exposed corruption. It was clear, even to a blind man, the agenda they were pushing.

In my submission to SANEF, I wrote about the shocking state of affairs at the *Sunday Times* at the time. In October 2018, I gave the *Sunday Times* a seven-day ultimatum to come clean or face the music. I attacked the dishonesty of one of their journalists for deliberately lying to the public through their latest story intended to prop up state capture. The journalist accused me of being a 'spy' for IPID and/or controlling IPID and implied that Phahlane was a 'victim' of my illegal activity. This narrative unlawfully and intentionally assisted Phahlane with his corrupt practices. It also helped Phahlane's senior police accomplices from the Northwest to continue their criminal conduct against Forensics for Justice and IPID.

It was clear that the false allegations against me were being peddled by criminal cops, again, when the *Sunday Times* happily walked into the trap set for them and published selectively chosen WhatsApp messages unlawfully downloaded from Sarah-Jane Trent's stolen phone after she was 'kidnapped' at gunpoint by dirty cops. Instead of questioning how the 'source' managed to hand him WhatsApps from a kidnap victim's stolen phone, the 'flexible' journalist, Poloko Tau, became part of the state capture machinery. The other journalists in question, Mzilikazi wa Afrika and Stefaan Hofstatter, were possibly played or paid.

(In recent times, Arena Holdings, the *Sunday Times'* new owners, have seen the light and have taken steps to restore the newspaper – and its ethics – to its former glory.) It's hard to restore the virtue of a prostitute, as both SANEF and Sunday Times should know, but I wish Arena Holdings well in their task.

More recently, Sizwe Yende, a journalist from the *City Press*, saw fit to support a criminal syndicate that obtained a multi-billion rand tender from Transnet by trying to turn the tide against me for exposing it, by accusing me of having a hidden agenda against the crime syndicate involved. Shortly after Yende turned on me, a warrant for the arrest for the head of the crime syndicate was issued in Kenya, yet Yende did not seem to find this newsworthy. He ignored the story because it did not appear to fit his false narrative.

When the forces of state capture repeatedly arrested me and dragged me off to court on trumped-up charges, the media were all over it. Yet, when the last of the cases was thrown out of court, and I launched a claim against the State, the incident received little coverage. Anybody that does not know me would, by googling my name, think I am an outright criminal because the media have not updated their online stories (with footnotes) to set the record straight – something that should be obligatory. This failure to update stories led to two overseas banks wanting to close my accounts because of the adverse media coverage – I had to engage expensive lawyers to stop them. I was now considered a PEP (Politically Exposed Person) along with criminals and global money launderers. Notwithstanding this, one of the banks unilaterally closed the account and froze over R7-million in cash for more than three months. The media coverage also led to a lost property deal in the UK when the prospective investor got cold feet after receiving a negative due diligence report on me.

This is part of the price I have paid for helping clean up South Africa, over and above the massive personal and financial cost to myself, my family and my staff. And this is largely due to the fact that some media are intentionally slack at fixing out-of-date online stories that portray me as a criminal. It's a narrative that only benefits the corrupt and those peddling fake news to protect the corrupt.

When I threatened to expose or sue Poloko Tau, SANEF unilaterally issued a statement accusing me of 'threatening' a journalist without clearly defining the nature of the 'threat'. This was gleefully lapped up by the many pro-Zuma journalists who, like SANEF, did not consult me for my version of events before publicly defaming me – a basic requirement of the Press Council's code of conduct.

I wrote a scathing e-mail to SANEF's CEO, Kate Skinner, in October 2018 after they unilaterally and publicly defamed me. Needless to say, SANEF continued with what I perceive is arrogance in the belief that *only* SANEF has the right to call out dishonest journalists.

In my submission to SANEF's inquiry, I made it clear that SANEF undeservingly claimed the high moral ground and publicly attacked me (without first picking up the phone and talking to me) for calling out the *Sunday Times* journalist who unlawfully propped up a crime syndicate that was trying to bring the country to its knees. According to SANEF, I should have complained to the Press Council. Been there, done that, it does not serve the purpose – especially since membership of the Press Council is voluntary and the baddies choose not to belong. The Press Council is for bad, negligent, or incompetent reporting. It is not for journalists playing the tune of the underworld in the media.

Throughout the whole period of state capture, SANEF has, in the main, remained silent about the role of criminal elements in the media in assisting state capture. To put it bluntly, I believe they fiddled whilst Rome burned. Yet, they have now unilaterally assigned themselves the role of investigating what went wrong at the media houses of South Africa that led to the creation of an enabling environment for the crime syndicates that brought South Africa to its knees. Again, it's a bit like asking the mice to guard the cheese. Now is the time for SANEF to do some inner soul searching and for its members to ask themselves what they could have done differently to stop the rot.

If SANEF really wants to make a difference, they need to team up with the Press Council and see to it that every chequebook journalist who sides with criminals is never employed by the media again. Journalists who have been dumb enough to have been played by subversive agents should have a choice – either name and shame the source or stop being a journalist. If, on the other hand, the journalist was paid and not played, they should never put pen to paper again.

SANEF later recruited Kathleen Satchwell to carry out an inquiry into what went wrong in the media. After I sent through my submission, Satchwell acknowledged receipt and said she would be in touch with me. After months of silence, I was invited to present my story. I was only given three days notice but was overseas at the time and could not attend. I offered to present the following week, but Satchwell did not respond.

SANEF, upon releasing their report, then falsely represented my involvement in exposing dirty journalists without even bothering to apply the principle of *audi alteram partem* (allowing the accused to be heard) before publicly defaming them.

When I saw the lies in the so-called report, I immediately launched a scathing attack on their integrity, laying out all the 'mistakes' in their report.

It is my opinion that if journalists cannot police themselves – which they sometimes appear to be unable to do – it is up to the public to stop supporting them. The reality is that unless the media holds to account those within its ranks who clearly aided and abetted state capture, the public's trust in the media's important role in society will never be fully restored.

I am adamant that SANEF stood by and watched for years while a handful of dirty journalists corruptly assisted the state capture project and did nothing – a sad state of affairs but, in my opinion, true. To subsequently issue a false report exonerating themselves and the dirty journalists means they were part of the problem, not part of the solution. Sadly, there are people and organisations that financially support the conduct of SANEF, blissfully unaware of their lack of integrity and ignorant complicity with the criminal State Capture project.

In 2019, when I issued a summons against the State for damages, I did not include George van Niekerk or ENS Africa. As time went on, however, I decided to add ENS Africa for George van Niekerk's role in assisting Dudu Myeni to open a fake docket against me. Before adding ENS Africa as defendants, I became involved in pre-summons settlement discussions with them. These discussions resulted in a mediated settlement, in terms of which, without accepting liability, they agreed to pay me damages of three and a half million rands. It was an amicable settlement, and there was no need for ENS to admit any culpability. By mutual agreement, the settlement was to remain confidential.

Daily Maverick's Pauli van Wyk later maliciously and publicly accused me of selling out when she tweeted: *"R3.5 million to forget your gripe, your ethics and your crusade against corruption. Such upstanding citizens."* At a loss as to why the *Daily Maverick* was publicly attacking me, I called for an apology. When none was forthcoming, I decided to investigate the *Daily Maverick* to see if I could uncover any underlying problems. The dubious historical connections I uncovered were shocking. Since a picture paints a thousand words, I decided to publish an organisational chart on Forensics for Justice's website showing the *Daily Maverick's* historical links to the underworld and state capture.

I made it clear in the posting that the *Daily Maverick's* director and co-founder, Branislav (Branko) Brkic, had previously published a magazine called *Maverick* under Business Century Publishing (Pty) Limited, a company he ran at the time. Brkic's co-director was a certain Marcus Steyn, who (at the time) was also a director of Gupta criminal enterprise Sahara Holdings (Pty) Limited – the same Sahara Holdings used by the Guptas for money laundering. Business Century Publishing (Pty) Limited, which had received an almost R4-million loan from the Industrial Development Corporation, subsequently crashed and burned, leaving the taxpayer to foot the bill for the unpaid loan from the IDC.

When Branko Brkic formed his new company, the *Daily Maverick*, from the ashes of *Maverick Magazine*, his new partner was Stylianos (Styli) Charalambous. Charalambous was at the time deeply involved in Card Owner Location Verification (Pty) Limited, a company owned by Gavin Varejes, a businessman infamous for his connections to the underworld. I thought it appropriate that Charalambous's historical connection to the criminal underworld should be made public. Charalambous was also a director of another company, Friedshelf 748 (Pty) limited, and had infamous Gupta lieutenant Mark Pamensky as his co-director.

After publishing my explosive exposé about the *Daily Maverick*[160] – and despite executive Pieter Louis Myburgh telling me that he did not care what I published about them – their lawyers sent me a threatening letter that same day. I made it clear that I would stand my ground and would not be threatened by the lawyers of a media house with dubious connections. I feel sorry for Myburgh – he was one of the best journalists I knew – but allowing himself to be dragged into a dispute that had nothing to do with him left me with negative feelings

160 Daily Maverick's Links to State Capture and the Underworld, Forensics for Justice, 15 November 2021, https://www.forensicsforjustice.org/portfolio-posts/daily-mavericks-secret-links-to-state-capture-and-the-underworld/

about his ability to be impartial, one of the tenets of a good journalist. In a WhatsApp he sent me, he told me to "Fuck off" and accused me of being part of an unlawful attack on the daily maverick. In turn, I took him off my Christmas card list.

I was subsequently subject to a disinformation campaign by other journalists whom I previously thought to be at the top of their game, which just goes to show that journalists and media houses stick together. Or at least they do in certain circumstances. While it is critical to have good journalists to rely on to ensure the public is kept informed of corruption findings, I never thought these same journalists would be so fickle as to turn against me for refusing to turn a blind eye to an apparent lack of media ethics. Today, as in the past Brkic is ultra-secretive about his cash flows and the millions he is allegedly getting paid by wealthy South African ex-pats.

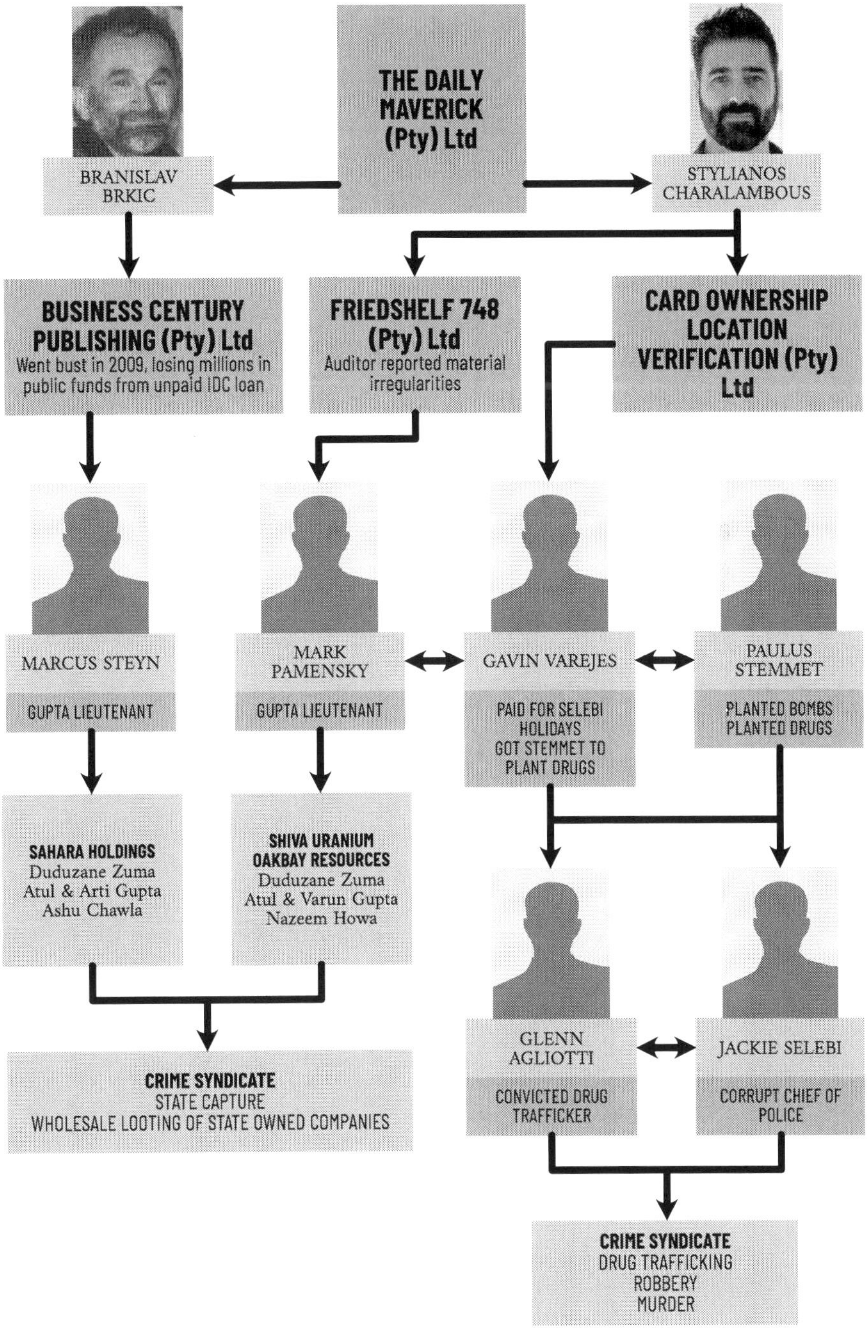
THE DAILY MAVERICK (Pty) Ltd
BRANISLAV BRKIC
STYLIANOS CHARALAMBOUS
BUSINESS CENTURY PUBLISHING (Pty) Ltd
Went bust in 2009, losing millions in public funds from unpaid IDC loan
FRIEDSHELF 748 (Pty) Ltd
Auditor reported material irregularities
CARD OWNERSHIP LOCATION VERIFICATION (Pty) Ltd
MARCUS STEYN
GUPTA LIEUTENANT
MARK PAMENSKY
GUPTA LIEUTENANT
GAVIN VAREJES
PAID FOR SELEBI HOLIDAYS
GOT STEMMET TO PLANT DRUGS
PAULUS STEMMET
PLANTED BOMBS
PLANTED DRUGS
SAHARA HOLDINGS
Duduzane Zuma
Atul & Arti Gupta
Ashu Chawla
SHIVA URANIUM
OAKBAY RESOURCES
Duduzane Zuma
Atul & Varun Gupta
Nazeem Howa
GLENN AGLIOTTI
CONVICTED DRUG TRAFFICKER
JACKIE SELEBI
CORRUPT CHIEF OF POLICE
CRIME SYNDICATE
STATE CAPTURE
WHOLESALE LOOTING OF STATE OWNED COMPANIES
CRIME SYNDICATE
DRUG TRAFFICKING
ROBBERY
MURDER

There have been many journalists who have intentionally played down Forensics for Justice's role in exposing corruption, and I can make peace with that, but I take umbrage at those who are quick to criticise when the message we put out is unpalatable or does not suit their self-acclaiming narrative.

CHAPTER 25

A CHANGE IN LEADERSHIP BRINGS NEW HOPE

A NEW DAWN - CYRIL RAMAPHOSA

In February 2018, a new ruler entered government. Cyril Ramaphosa, who defeated Nkosazana Dlamini Zuma at the ANC's National Conference at Nasrec in December 2017, became the fifth President of a democratised South Africa.

He was a breath of fresh air, who seemed determined to change the instilled culture of corruption that had decayed State institutions under Jacob Zuma's rule. Unfortunately, the damage done by Zuma (and those he placed in positions of power) was so extensive that it would take a lot more than a moral leader with good intentions to clean up the mess.

Ramaphosa was hampered by Zuma acolytes who still held positions of power in numerous institutions. Right underneath him sat the Deputy President, David Mabuza, whose cat-like reputation for having endless lives and dodging all his enemies was well earned. He was dangerous and appeared to be just as (if not more) corrupt as Zuma. Alongside Ramaphosa sat Ace Magashula, the Secretary-

General of the ANC who, like Mabuza, seemed to have risen through the ranks using fear and the theft of state funds.

Having two such men around Ramaphosa was like having the captain doing his best to steer his ship through a violent storm at sea while keeping an eye on nefarious pirates who had thoughts of mutiny clouding their eyes and whose swords were ready to be drawn at any second. Ramaphosa was clearly surrounded by evil hyenas.

Even if Ramaphosa manages to conquer the tempest and safely steer the ship into port when the time comes to pass on the captain's hat, he may be handing it to one of the pirates, and the looting will likely continue.

In 2019, before the ugly reality emerged of the damage that state capture had done to the country – the rapid economic decline, the load-shedding woes and the few reserves available for the catastrophic coronavirus lockdown – South Africa entered its wonderful Ramaphoria phase, with renewed optimism, if only he could shake off the hyenas around him.

TIME TO PAY BACK THE MONEY

I, too, was optimistic. Finally, some justice was being served for the injustices perpetrated – on me, on others, and on the country as a whole. I was not going to allow the Mokotedi team, the captured NPA, Dudu Myeni and Phahlane (with his Northwest goons) to get away with what they had done to me. Aside from my investigations and pursuing criminal charges against the group of corrupt crooks, I planned to hit them where it would hurt the most – in their pockets. Besides the emotional, physical and financial trauma associated with the last five years, I planned to sue them for every single cent they had cost me, including the emotional toll my family had suffered in the process, along with the long periods I spent without being able (or allowed) to see my family. I would not only be making a claim against the State but would also hold every single one of the criminals in badges and gowns liable in their personal capacity.

In June 2017, after one of my numerous court appearances, I told *News24*:

> *So, we will sequestrate them, take their homes and cars so their family can go hungry because of their conduct.*

I planned to launch several different claims and, in December 2018, I filed my first papers.[161] I was suing the State for more than R150-million. I demanded R22.6-million for loss of income and R164.8-million for an estimated loss of future income, R5-million for pain and suffering, and millions of rands in legal fees. Fighting the fifty or more illegal charges in court cost me more than R8-million in legal fees alone.

The first papers I served made it clear that my business had suffered from the criminal defamation of character the spiteful criminal pursuit of me had caused. Before the State launched their unlawful campaign against me, I was earning R10-million a year, with forensic work growing at 18% annually. After my arrest in 2016, those earnings dropped to R4-million. By 2017, my earnings had dropped to R2-million. My company's growth had dramatically shrunk, and I was forced to lay off good staff.

VICTORY AT LAST – PHAHLANE GOES DOWN

By February 2019, nine months had gone by since the charges against Phahlane, his wife Beauty, and Durand Snyman were provisionally withdrawn. While Phahlane must have thought he was a free man, IPID had been quietly and steadily gathering more evidence against him.

---

161 Graeme Hosken, Forensic investigator Paul O'Sullivan to sue state for R193 million, Timeslive, 8 December 2017, https://www.timeslive.co.za/news/south-africa/2017-12-08-forensic-investigator-paul-osullivan-to-sue-state-for-r193-million/

Their investigation linked Phahlane to a 2016 tender awarded to a company called Instrumentation Traffic Law Enforcement, owned by millionaire Vimpie Manthata.[162] The contract, worth R86-million, was to supply and install blue lights, sirens and radios in SAPS vehicles. The investigation uncovered that Manthata allegedly supplied fraudulent tax clearance certificates to SAPS in his tender documents.

The investigation found that the SAPS members involved with the awarding of the contract failed to take the necessary steps to disqualify Instrumentation Traffic Law Enforcement for this and that they misrepresented to the accounting officer of the SAPS and Treasury that the company was tax compliant, which it clearly was not.

In 2011, *The Star* reported that the 'blue light prince', Manthata, who also called himself "His Royal Highness Prince Vimpie Phineas Manthata of the Royal Kingdom of Batlokwa Pietersburg", travelled around with his own blue light escort from the Johannesburg Metro Police Department (JMPD).[163] Manthata denied this, saying he had an arrangement with the JMPD that they would provide him with an escort when he hosted foreign dignitaries. Such utter rubbish was easy to see through, especially when it became known that the foreign 'dignitaries' were police chiefs from neighbouring African states who were being looked after, allegedly in exchange for buying from Manthata's business.

In 2018, IPID arrested former Gauteng Police Commissioner Deliwe de Lange, National Divisional Commissioner in charge of SAPS Supply Chain Management, Lieutenant General Ramahlapi Mokwena, Brigadier James Ramajalum, and Gauteng Deputy Police

---

162 Mandy Weiner, Jeanette Chabalala and Kyle Cowan, Phahlane arrested on new charges linked to R86m blue lights tender, News24, 1 March 2019, https://www.news24.com/SouthAfrica/News/breaking-phahlane-arrested-on-new-charges-linked-to-r86m-blue-lights-tender-20190301

163 Thabiso Thakali, Blue light 'prince', IOL, 23 July 2011, https://www.iol.co.za/news/south-africa/gauteng/blue-light-prince-1104572

Commissioner Nombhuruza Napo, on charges of corruption, fraud, forgery, and uttering on the case.

One year later, in February 2019, Phahlane and Major General Ravichandran Pillay, the Head of SAPS Supply Chain Management, were arrested as part of the same case. Pillay had previously been linked to controversial Durban businessman Thoshan Panday. Panday was eventually charged for corruption in 2021 and is yet to be tried. He should have been charged years ago but was protected by dirty cops and prosecutors. The Zuptoids in the police and NPA went after General Booysen, who was managing the case against Panday, instead. They appeared in the Johannesburg Commercial Crimes Court shortly afterwards and were released on R20 000 bail each.

Phahlane's lawyer, Piet du Plessis, who appears to earn massive fees from the proceeds of crime, told the court that Phahlane had received an email from me at 7:05 a.m. that Friday, just a few hours before Phahlane's court appearance. He was right – I had done just that.

In the email, I told him that *"you will rue the day you chose to send dirty cops on me"* and that *"prison will be your reward, and your dishonest paid liars will not be there to help you"*. I was referring to the R100 000 a month tax payers spent on dishonest spin-doctors to publish his lies, throwing their own ethics down the drain in the process. I meant every word.

Generals Phahlane and Pillay in the the dock in Johannesburg, February 2019. Source Abigail Javier / Eyewitness News

Phahlane, in his usual style, did his normal public blustering performance after his arrest, attacking IPID for setting him up.[164] He repeatedly waived his right to remain silent by making absurd claims in public – and with 'owned' journalists – to portray himself as the good guy when nothing could be further from the truth. During his bail application, he claimed that his arrest was timed to one day after Parliament refused to renew McBride's contract as Head of IPID. He said his arrest had been sensationalised. In his affidavit, he said:

> *The matter reeks of ulterior motives and an attempt at point scoring by McBride and IPID as well as their cohorts frantically trying to bolster his efforts to be reappointed as chief executive officer by building his image as crusader in chief against corruption while he personally had been tainted by numerous parties of being corrupt himself.*

164 Nomahlubi Jordaan, Former top cop Khomotso Phahlane fuming after 'sensationalised' arrest, Timeslive, 1 March 2019, https://www.timeslive.co.za/news/south-africa/2019-03-01-former-top-cop-khomotso-phahlane-fuming-after-sensationalised-arrest/

Phahlane's arrest had come following careful investigation and evidence of his involvement in the questionable tender process. It had nothing to do with making McBride look good. Phahlane's corrupt ways had simply caught up with him. And despite his attempts at throwing me off his tail, I had persisted in assisting IPID, and Sarah-Jane had provided very useful evidence.

Phahlane raged on. He told *Independent Newspapers* that he had earned almost R4-million sitting at home since his suspension on the 1st of June 2017, adding:[165]

> *I am the most senior lieutenant-general within the SAPS today, and it has been painful to sit at home and watch the crime situation get out of hand. But I will be back in the service to do my work.*

Although I doubted he would ever be back at SAPS, Phahlane did have a point about earning a salary while being on suspension. The SAPS needed to dismiss him once and for all and stop spending State money on an out-and-out criminal. It was a disgrace that the man should brag about his unlawful gain from being at home while the paralysis within SAPS did nothing to get rid of him. One thing I was able to guarantee was that neither Phahlane nor his wife would *ever* return to work – not while I was alive anyway.

I wrote strongly-worded emails to General Sitole demanding action against Phahlane. In July 2020, Phahlane was finally dismissed.

PRINCE MOKOTEDI GETS SHIFTED

As for Prince Mokotedi, he was quietly moved out of the Hawks in January 2019 and redeployed to the Management Intervention

165 Khaya Koko, Suspended ex top-cop Phahlane earns R4m while on paid holiday, IOL, 12 December 2019, https://www.iol.co.za/the-star/news/suspended-ex-top-cop-phahlane-earns-r4m-while-on-paid-holiday-39116542

Unit at SAPS headquarters.[166] Again, a complete breach of the law since his appointment was to the DPCI (Hawks). He could not just be conveniently moved. He should have been in the departure lounge, but instead, he was getting a job for life as a reward for his crimes.

Mokotedi, along with his counterparts in KwaZulu Natal and the Western Cape who were unlawfully appointed by Ntlemeza and Nhleko, were moved out of their top positions. It wasn't clear what Mokotedi was doing at the SAPS head office, but it was no doubt a demotion. Instead of being the Head of the Hawks in Gauteng, he now had a desk job. It was a sickening waste of public funds.

Mokotedi wasn't exactly happy with his redeployment. He decided to go to the Labour Court in an attempt to be reinstated as the Head of the Hawks in Gauteng. He told them the move was irregular, unlawful, and amounted to unfair dismissal. He said he had been told to "oblige and complain later".

He was later booked off on extended sick leave, further draining the public purse.

Nothing more was heard of Mokotedi until 2020 when, all of a sudden, he decided to make an appearance on Twitter. He claimed state capture was a fabrication of the white minority who were trying to take over the country. He attacked me, and he attacked professional journalists, claiming he would reveal everything he knew about me in a book he would publish when his name was cleared.

I think I got there first, Mokotedi. As you can see, I have enough information on you and your gang of crooks to fill all these pages.

Mokotedi dug himself into another hole on social media with prize tweets like these:

> *"Their first salvo at me was that I told lies at the Selebi trial. They got Barry Bateman to say that I stole documents and gave them to Selebi.*

166 Marianne Thamm, Gauteng Hawk's head Prince Mokotedi 'redeployed' to head office, Daily Maverick, 7 December 2018, https://www.dailymaverick.co.za/article/2018-12-07-gauteng-hawks-head-prince-mokotedi-redeployed-to-head-office/

He ran a story for a while on 702 and the story just died. Then they got Scorpions to investigate me on numerous cases, all fell flat."

"I am probably the only public servant against whom they opened cases against as a co-accused with two successive Presidents, Thabo Mbeki and Jacob Zuma. Those two cases never saw the light of day."

"They came hard on me after I opened and investigated a case against Glynnis Breytenbach for allegedly receiving $1 million from a billionaire whose case she was prosecuting. The billionaire continued to Sponsor her through FW de Klerk Foundation. I was labeled a Zuma man and corrupt!"

"When one takes a different view from the likes of @AdriaanBasson and @pierredevos on policy matters they quickly label u as corrupt or state capturer. I'll never be afraid to raise a view because they will shame me! Their strategy is wicked and unbefitting of academics and journalists."

"I forgive @MarianneThamm and @dailymaverick for ever attempting to shame, demonize and dehumanize me. I do understand from your book @MarianneThamm that you struggle to outgrow the sins of your father. I believe you will overcome that. Live in peace!"

"I have had my fair share of being shamed, demonized, vilified and brutalized by other public officials, media, pseudo analysts, DA etc. I voiced my support and sympathy to @AdvBMkhwebane before. I respect her for she goes where eagles dare!"

"The white minority's plan to come back to power is timed and connected to the stages of post colonial revolution which are Euphoria (Mandela stage), Embarkment (Mbeki period), Eclipse (Zuma term 1), Erosion (Zuma term2) and the Explosion (Current period)."

WMC introduced the Corruption and state capture narrative was during stage 2 in order to break the camels back. However, it did not go far enough to dislodge power totally from the movement - but succeeded to draw a wedge and to factionalize it.

> *Lastly, the Erosion stage was meant to totally obliterate the movement. The intention was to isolate and silence them through the electoral process, commissions, courts and media. There was some victory, but that arose the sleeping giant, and that's where we are at - Explosion!"*

In my opinion, Moktedi was nothing more than a criminal. When it came to me, he wasted no time spewing his vitriol.

> *He sends me zillions of emails and I warned him to stop. He is vengeful and bitter 'cause I took him to court few times. Soon I will tell nation who this man really is and why he is doing what he is doing. My hands are tight (sic) because I am cop. As soon as I leave he will be my project.*

Interestingly, in one of his tweets, he said he was on a renewable contract of ten years and that he would be retired when it ended.

After being sent the tweets, I emailed Mokotedi's bosses, the Head of the Hawks General Godfrey Lebeya, and Police Commissioner General Kehle Sitole, asking them to investigate.[5]

I received a reply from General Lebeya, saying that he would forward my email to Mokotedi's immediate supervisor. Soon afterwards, a furious Mokotedi deactivated his Twitter account. I am certain he was instructed to do so. He emailed me to say that he thought I was not worth writing about in his 'book':

> *You will be relegated to a footnote in my story. You do not deserve to be mentioned in any good to tell inspirational book. I have been a villain in too many books Paul, go ahead and make my brand.*

I will, as always, be watching to see that something is done about his actions. A few months later, whilst waiting in the 'departure lounge', Mokotedi was found guilty at an internal hearing and was fired from the police. I knew the wheel would eventually turn on him.

I only have one message for Mokotedi now: "Real justice is coming for you soon. ***Stop me if you can!***"

THE TABLES TURN ON VLOK

Phahlane was not the only one to see his day in court. The charges I had laid against Warrant Officer Vlok had eventually landed on fertile ground. IPID investigated and, in June 2019, the Gauteng Director of Public Prosecutions decided to charge Vlok for his crimes.[167]

Vlok appeared in the Randburg Magistrate's Court in July 2019. His illegal actions had come full circle. He had to appear as an accused in the same court where I had spent years during the fake Cora van der Merwe and Alice Johnston cases. The charge sheet listed a total of five charges against him – an extortion charge and two counts of defeating the course of justice related to his attempt to intimidate Lynn Fliess when he threatened to arrest her for racketeering unless she gave evidence against me and granted her ex-husband access to their minor child. The third count of defeating the ends of justice related to his unlawful removal of the Neil Diamond docket. Vlok had deposed an affidavit saying the docket had been stolen so that he could open a duplicate docket containing missing exculpatory evidence. He was also facing a fourth charge of defeating the ends of justice for obtaining a statement from the state witness in the Dave Sheer Guns' case. The witness was testifying before the court when Vlok obtained a contradictory statement that he handed to the defence lawyers, assisting them in discrediting the witness.

Vlok wasn't only facing criminal charges. He was also being charged for misconduct at work and had to attend disciplinary hearings.

In another twist of fate, Captain Boitumelo Ramahlaha, the police officer who had been targeted by Ntlemeza, had by now had his suspension revoked and was placed at police headquarters. Vlok was

---

167 Marianne Thamm, Hawks officer who dragged investigator Paul O;Sullivan off plane to be charged, Daily Maverick, 26 June 2019, https://www.dailymaverick.co.za/article/2019-06-26-hawks-officer-who-dragged-investigator-paul-osullivan-off-plane-to-be-charged/

required to collect the paperwork listing the disciplinary charges he faced from Ramahlaha. It was true poetic justice.

Vlok was facing three disciplinary charges. The first was for his threats to Lynn Fliess. The second was for his attempts to get police officer warrant officer Gysbert Coetzee and Warrant Officer Stella Ngwenya from the South African National Defence Force Military Police Division to depose affidavits against me. If they didn't, Vlok threatened to arrest them. The third charge was that Vlok had conducted himself in an improper, disgraceful, and unacceptable manner when he failed to comply with the South Gauteng High Court order that he should return the contents of my computer to me and destroy all copies made when he illegally conducted a search of my office in 2015.

The years had rolled by. It was a long battle, but I was finally seeing (some of) the results of my hard work.

MYENI GETS A SURPRISE

In 2020, Dudu Myeni was finally held to account for some of her criminal activity. OUTA and the SAA Pilot's Association had brought an application before the Pretoria High Court to declare Myeni a delinquent director in terms of the Companies Act. The application was based on her shocking conduct while chairperson of the SAA board between December 2012 and October 2017. It was the first application brought to declare a director of a state-owned entity as a delinquent director, and if granted, would mean she would be barred from serving as a director, as a senior executive, or appear on the board of organisations in South Africa for seven years or more.

It was the least Myeni deserved. Her mismanagement and the resultant corruption at SAA had caused the airline to virtually collapse with little hope of recovery without a massive injection of public funds. Personally, I think what she really deserves is to see the inside of a prison cell – and I will do what I can to make sure she gets there. The 'delinquent director' judgment, when it comes, will be a costly and hollow victory. With her track record, no one in their right mind would give her a job as a company director.

Myeni tried for months to avoid appearing in court, even claiming that she did not have the money to pay for the transport to Pretoria. But as much as she tried to duck and dive, her day in court had finally arrived. I was just sorry that she wasn't facing up to Barry Roux. I even offered to pay her bus fare.

I had helped OUTA with some of the case details and witnesses, and I was watching what happened very carefully. I had been trying to serve a summons on Myeni as part of my claim against the State since December 2017, but the Sheriff of the Court had never been able to pin her down.[168] The Sheriff and his team went to her house in Richards Bay countless times and, even though the lights were on, nobody answered the door. They even saw the curtains move. By February 2020, however, we knew exactly where she was – it was the perfect time to pounce.

My lawyers had applied for and been given permission by Judge Ronel Tolmay at from the High Court in Pretoria to serve the summons, and, during a break in proceedings, the papers – the legal proceedings I had launched against her and nine other people, including the Ministers of Police, Justice and members of SAPS and NPA – were served on Myeni.[169] I laid out how Myeni had maliciously collaborated with dirty cops, including Moonoo, to lay the false charges against me for extortion, intimidation, fraud, and forgery, which ultimately led to my arrest on the passport case. I asked that Myeni, the Police Minister

168 Carin Smith and Phumi Ramalepe, Paul O'Sullivan says he has served summons on former SAA chair Dudu Myeni, Fin24m 25 February 2020, https://www.fin24.com/Companies/Industrial/paul-osullivan-says-he-has-served-summons-on-former-saa-chair-dudu-myeni-20200225

169 Greg Nicolson, Legal action mounts as Dudu Myeni stuck in bizarro world, Daily Maverick, 25 February 2020, https://www.dailymaverick.co.za/article/2020-02-25-legal-action-mounts-as-dudu-myeni-stuck-in-bizarro-world/

and Justice Minister pay millions, with interest, for my false arrest, detention and prosecution.

Not being able to serve the papers on Myeni had delayed my civil claim. Now that she had them, Myeni would have to plead to the claim, and I could eventually set the matter down for trial. The OUTA case would not be the only time Myeni would see the inside of a courtroom.

I was told that Myeni was so surprised by the papers being served on her that it left her flustered and wrong-footed in court. That day, OUTA's lawyers tore into her. As expected, Myeni was evasive and illogical during cross-examination. She would never be able to prove that she acted judiciously during her tenure at SAA. I am certain she called Jacob Zuma as soon as she could to pour out her tales of woe.

Finally, in May 2020, OUTA and the SAA Pilot's Association's court battle with Myeni ended in victory. Myeni was declared a delinquent director for life and had to pay OUTA's legal fees. Judge Ronel Tolmay didn't mince her words in the judgement when she said that Myeni was "a director gone rogue" who "did not have the slightest consideration for her fiduciary duty to SAA", adding:

> *To serve on a Board of an SOE (State Owned Enterprise) should not be a privilege of the politically connected. Whoever serves on the Board of an SOE should ultimately be a servant of the people, and whoever is appointed as such has a sacred duty to society and should ensure that state resources are not squandered, or the economy placed at risk.*

Myeni's actions were described as "dishonest, reckless, and grossly negligent". Judge Tolmay said that Myeni had breached her fiduciary duty. She said that her judgement and the evidence from the case would be referred to the NPA for their consideration and to determine whether an investigation regarding possible criminal conduct should follow, adding:

> *This constitutes reprehensible conduct and is sufficient reason for a punitive costs order. Her actions caused SAA and the country immense harm, and it was of the utmost importance that she be brought before a court to answer for her deeds.*

OUTA's Chief Legal Officer Stefanie Fick said they were pleased to see justice meted out in a matter related to state capture, but they believed that it was the duty of all boards to do the work of instituting charges against previous directors who mismanaged the funds and assets of their organisations. In a press release, OUTA stated that it was a sad reality that, far too often, those who perform this extremely necessary work to civil society are left in the difficult position of bringing these challenges at great cost to themselves. Unfortunately, it doesn't look as if this will change any time soon. Organisations like OUTA, Forensics for Justice, Freedom Under Law, and the Helen Suzman Foundation have become the last bastions in the battle against state malfeasance and corruption.

Of course, SAA was not the only organisation that Myeni managed to get her grubby hands into. In December 2017, when former Eskom chairman Zola Tsotsi testified before Parliament that Jacob Zuma as well as Myeni and Jacob Zuma's son, Thalente Myeni, were in the room when Myeni instructed Tsotsi to toe the line at Eskom by suspending three officials or be dismissed himself, Tsotsi revealed the first strong link to Zuma and state capture. Aside from the fact that Tsotsi's revelations on Myeni, who had absolutely nothing to do with Eskom, were astonishing, this was the first time in all these investigations that Zuma himself was directly involved in what happened. It was a watershed moment indeed.

Myeni and Zuma helped bring the country's largest entity, Eskom, to its knees. In the process, Zuma and the Gupta family made billions of rands from substandard coal that was taken from a mine, paid for by taxpayers, and then sold at twice the normal cost.

Forensics for Justice used Tsotsi's testimony to supplement our original docket opened against Myeni, but, once again, nothing happened with the criminal charges we laid.

As soon as Tolmay's judgement was made, I immediately followed up on what was, to me, the most important finding – that the NPA looked at the case to see if criminal proceedings could follow from it. I emailed new NPA Head Shamila Batohi, asking that she take note of certain parts of the judgement, as well as the dockets I had opened against Myeni and the entire SAA board. I also asked Batohi to take note of the role Myeni played in everything that happened to me. I included a paragraph from one of the dockets I opened against Myeni where I stated that it could not be a coincidence that the first docket I opened against her set in motion a chain of criminal events that saw me arrested, subjected to four days of unlawful detention and torture, followed by two and a half years of facing false charges.

During the trial on the trumped-up charges in terms of Section 26B of the South African Citizenship Act, one of Mokotedi's accomplices admitted that the arrest had been expedited because I had 'threatened' the chairman of SAA, Dudu Myeni. It subsequently came to my attention that Nick Linnell (who worked as an advisor for Myeni) was paid handsomely by SAA to orchestrate my arrest, billing SAA hundreds of thousands of rands for such 'work'.[170]

Despite opening countless dockets against Myeni and providing copious amounts of *prima facie* evidence, she has been left to her own devices and was 'allowed' (or encouraged) to eviscerate a once great airline and put thousands of people out of work while irrevocably damaging our country's economy.

---

170 Susan Comrie, SAA's R167K a month advisor, 9 August 2015, City Press, https://city-press.news24.com/News/SAAs-R167K-a-month-adviser-20150809

I told Batohi that it pained me to record that more than four years had passed since I opened the original case against the board of SAA and that more than two years had passed since I opened the docket against Myeni and Zuma related to the capture of Eskom. It is my belief that the reason no steps have been taken to bring the suspects to justice is solely because the criminal justice system was captured and remains captured to this very day. I believe that these dockets and the Tolmay judgement will provide enough evidence for Myeni to be arrested and charged, along with her accomplices, when the NPA finally shakes off the shackles of state capture and turns its attention to her.

I pledged the assistance of Forensics for Justice to bring these people to book. I just hope that this time, something will actually be done. If not, I will have to go the route of private prosecution. Either way, every dog has its day, and in Myeni's case, the days ahead will be dark indeed. I cannot wait to meet her in court and finally see her held liable for her actions. During the discovery process, I will demand the bank accounts of the Jacob Zuma Foundation, which I know were used for money laundering.

Can you imagine what we will discover there?

CHAPTER 26

STATE CAPTURE VERSION 2

THE CROOKS FIGHT BACK

Unfortunately, the crooks in the system were not prepared to give up without a fight. Just when it looked as if the tide against evil in the country was slowly turning a corner, a Zuptoid fight-back campaign was taking hold. One of the targets of their vendetta was McBride.

Aside from his investigations into Phahlane and Ntlemeza – both of whom ensured a big dent in the state capture machinery – McBride uncovered irregular police activity that had taken place during the ANC's elective conference at Nasrec in December 2017.

By stopping a tender for a phone signal grabber that would be used to intercept cell-phone communications on the eve of the conference, McBride likely prevented the buying of candidates, which could have led to a very different outcome for the country's presidency. McBride found that the purchase price of the grabber – which was set at R45-million – was intentionally inflated so that surplus cash could be delivered to the conference venue to buy off delegates.

Many high-profile names had been linked to the case, including Police Commissioner General Kehle Sitole, former Minister of Police Fikile Mbalula's advisor Bo Mbindwane, Acting Intelligence

Head General King Bhoyi Ngcobo, Deputy National Commissioner of Crime Detection, former Provincial Commissioner of the Free State, Lieutenant-General Lebeoana Tsumane, and Deputy National Commissioner of Management Advisory Services Major-General Francinah Ntombenhle Vuma.[171] They were all filmed at a secret meeting held at the Courtyard Hotel in Arcadia, Pretoria, on the 13th of December, 2017, three days before the ANC's conference.

McBride was determined to hold those behind the plot to account. He had been trying to get Sitole to declassify certain 'secret' documents related to the attempted fraudulent purchase of the phone signal grabber. SAPS refused to declassify the documents, claiming it would threaten national security. McBride did everything he could to fight it. Sitole cancelled the deal after IPID contacted him about the illegality of the procurement.

Instead of being praised for the sterling work he was doing in uncovering criminality in SAPS and within the ANC, McBride was viewed as a troublemaker. It was decided that he needed to be removed from his position at IPID. Clearly, he was getting too close to the truth, a truth that would involve too many high-profile names being uncovered in wrongdoing.

After McBride's departure from IPID, the Supreme Court of Appeal overturned the 'secret' classification and ordered the documents to be released.

THE PROBLEMATIC PUBLIC PROTECTOR

Conveniently, and just when this group of criminals needed it the most, a complaint against McBride came up that was grabbed onto and used against him. Instead of disappearing into obscurity, the underhanded IPID investigator, Cedrick Nkabinde – the same

171 Marianne Thamm, Zondo, SAPS, McBride and the anatomy of the capture of South Africa's law enforcement cluster, Daily Maverick, 8 April 2019, https://www.dailymaverick.co.za/article/2019-04-08-zondo-saps-mcbride-and-the-anatomy-of-the-capture-of-south-africas-law-enforcement-cluster/

man who had been used as a spy for Mokotedi and spun lies about my December get-together at Krejcir's old house in Bedfordview – emerged again. His mission was to get rid of McBride. Nkabinde's complaints had grown ever more fantastic, and he had taken them to the Public Protector Busisiwe Mkhwebane.

Aside from losing every single court case her reports were challenged on, with judges making clear that her legal understanding in them was "irrational", it was widely believed that Public Protector Mkhwebane was a well-placed Zuptoid who chose the cases she investigated for political reasons. Many believed she was in her position to give the Zuma fight-back campaign some clout and destroy the impressive work her predecessor, Thuli Madonsela, had done in taking a limp Chapter 9 institution and giving it real teeth. Mkhwebane, it would seem, was deliberately eroding the office of the Public Protector.

Mkhwebane will probably threaten me with legal action just for pointing out this widespread opinion, but there is a section of the Public Protector Act that outlaws the act of insulting the Public Protector. Mkhwebane has used this section to try to stop any criticism of her office. This needs to be challenged in court – and the sooner, the better.

I referred to Mkhwebane in one of my many emails to the criminals with badges. Her lawyer later tried to claim that by calling her a "Zuptoid appointee", I was committing the offence of "contempt of court". I later found that the same threat had been made to many journalists, but no action was ever taken. They were clearly on shaky ground trying to balance the protection of their boss with the constitutional right to freedom of expression and had probably decided not to venture into that arena.

Like Madonsela had achieved with the Office of the Public Protector, McBride was trying to build IPID into an organisation independent of interference and one that was tackling state capture head-on. His mission was to take on the onerous task of tackling corruption within the leadership of the police, and he was being met with resistance every step of the way.

The capture of the criminal justice system was the central element of the state capture project. It was crucial for the crooks involved to have a compliant police force and prosecuting authority that allowed them to continue looting state coffers on the scale they had been unhindered. That is why the few people who were doing everything possible to stop this – people like McBride, Booysen, Sibiya, and me – were being targeted so vehemently. They needed to stop us from succeeding, no matter what it took.

Nkabinde claimed McBride had paid himself R100 000 for unused leave credits without approval, that he had raised his salary without complying with the Performance Management Policy and undergoing a performance assessment, that he had made irregular staff appointments and transfers, and that he oversaw irregular procurement processes for buying guns and surveillance devices. Nowhere, of course, did Nkabinde mention that he was offered a cushy police job as a Brigadier as a reward for the untruths he levelled against McBride and me. I wrote to Nkabinde and told him what I thought of him. He is now unemployed, and if I get but a sniff of him being reappointed into the police, I will bring an urgent application to prevent it.

The Public Protector, in the meantime, issued her report. It was the eve of McBride testifying before the Zondo Commission on State Capture. Of course, she found in favour of Nkabinde's claim that McBride had meddled in procurement processes.

McBride and other senior officials at IPID applied to the Pretoria High Court for an interdict of the report's absurd findings, listing at least eighteen grounds for it to be overturned.[172] One of the grounds

172 Business Day, McBride and IPID officials want Public Protector's report overturned on 18 grounds – report, News24, 9 October 2019, https://www.news24.com/SouthAfrica/News/mcbride-and-ipid-officials-want-public-protectors-report-overturned-on-18-grounds-report-20191009

mentioned was that Mkhwebane had ignored critical evidence IPID officials had given. Another was that she had failed to take into consideration that most of her report dealt with a complaint that was previously investigated by the Public Service Commission and found to be unsubstantiated. McBride also pointed out that the report's timing was suspicious and was likely intended to discredit his evidence at the Zondo Commission.

"It is clear that the intention is to disrupt the functioning of IPID," he said.

MCBRIDE'S CLASH WITH CELE

One of President Ramaphosa's first ministerial appointments was appointing Bheki Cele as Police Minister. Cele had a chequered past. He replaced Jackie Selebi as Commissioner of the Police in 2009 but was suspended in 2012 on the back of allegations of corruption relating to two police lease deals signed with business tycoon Roux Shabangu. With a history like that, there was always going to be conflict between Cele and McBride. Cele also had his people in the police from his Chief of Police days, whom he considered loyal to him. He was intent on exercising executive control over the police, especially when it came to high-level appointments.

As *amaBhungane* pointed out, the heart of the clash between Cele and McBride was a war for the soul of the ANC and the gangsters, cops, and politicians all had a big stake in the outcome.[173]

While both Cele and McBride had fought against Zuma and everything he stood for in their different ways, McBride, in investigating the phone signal grabber deal – and the abuse of secret funds at Crime Intelligence – was naming too many high-profile people within the police's leadership. If he went further with his investigations, he

173 Sam Sole and Caryn Dolley, SAPS Wars Part 3: Bhei Cele, Robert McBride and the mysterious Mr Marimuthu, AmaBhungane, 8 April 2019, https://www.news24.com/SouthAfrica/News/saps-wars-part-3-bheki-cele-robert-mcbride-and-the-mysterious-mr-marimuthu-20190408

could bring down the entire top structure of the police's leadership, interrupting Cele's command and control plans.

Cedrick Nkabinde's complaint was being used as the proverbial manna from heaven by the grouping of politically powerful cops who did not want to see McBride succeed. Unfortunately, Cele had taken up the mantle of his predecessors in trying to get rid of McBride, but for different reasons. He had timing on his side because McBride's first term contract was up for renewal. Cele used Nkabinde's complaint and the Public Protector's investigation to stop the renewal of McBride's contract. In a submission to parliament, Cele claimed it would be "irrational" to appoint McBride at IPID for another five years because of the serious allegations of misconduct he was facing:[174]

> *In my view, it would be irrational for the [Police] Portfolio Committee to renew McBride's appointment as Executive Director. Serious allegations of misconduct have been levelled against McBride, and these allegations undermine his fitness to hold office. At a minimum, the incumbent must be suitably qualified and fit and proper.*

In January, Cele wrote to McBride, informing him that his contract would not be renewed or extended when it expired at the end of February. In response, McBride filed an urgent application to the High Court in Pretoria, asking that Cele's decision be declared unconstitutional, unlawful, and invalid. The court ruled that Cele's decision was preliminary and needed to be confirmed or rejected by the Police Portfolio Committee in Parliament. The Helen Suzman Foundation and Corruption Watch filed an application with the Constitutional Court to appeal the High Court order.

The Foundation said that in terms of the IPID Act, the Head of IPID serves a term of five years, which is renewable for one additional term, without mentioning who is required to make the decision regarding

---

174 Nico Gous, It would be 'irrational' to reappoint McBride as IPID boss: Cele, Timelive, 20 February 2019, https://www.timeslive.co.za/politics/2019-02-20-it-would-irrational-to-reappoint-mcbride-as-ipid-boss-cele/

such a renewal. Unsurprisingly, Parliament's (ANC-controlled) Police Committee endorsed Cele's decision.[175]

ANC members in support of Cele argued that the relationship between Cele and McBride had clearly broken down and that McBride did not have the legal right to an automatic extension or renewal of his contract. MPs from the DA were outraged, criticising the committee's decision, boycotting the session in which the report was adopted and calling the decision a sham.[176] DA MP Zakhele Mbhele was quoted as saying:

> *The fact is that there are no compelling, substantive reasons not to renew McBride's contract. All that the Minister gave to the committee in his submission of reasons were allegations that are, as yet, untested and unproved. Nor can anything else that has surfaced be assessed as being egregious enough to warrant nonrenewal.*

Mbhele said the IPID Act was defective in providing for a renewable term of the IPID Executive Director:

> *Given the need for the independence of the IPID, identical to that for the Hawks, it is now clear that the term of the IPID Head should be similarly non-renewable and lengthened so that any incumbent can fulfil their responsibilities without fear of career consequences from a seemingly vindictive minister.*

Whereas Cele claimed that McBride's contract should not be renewed due to a breakdown in trust between him and McBride and that McBride had failed to meet performance assessments, the DA said that McBride's track record was *exactly* why his contract should

175 Bekezela Phakathi, Police committee agrees on not renewing Robert McBride's contract as IPID boss, Timeslive, 28 February 2019, https://www.timeslive.co.za/politics/2019-02-28-police-committee-agrees-on-not-renewing-robert-mcbrides-contract-as-ipid-boss/

176 Kamva Somdyala, No compelling reasons not to renew McBride's contract – DA, News24, 1 March 2019, https://www.news24.com/SouthAfrica/News/no-compelling-reasons-not-to-renew-mcbrides-contract-da-20190301

be renewed.[177] The party stated that losing McBride was a blow to the State's capacity to fight corruption – in the same way the decision to disband the Scorpions was.

Victor Senna was announced as IPID's Acting Executive Director. I was outraged. After everything he had done, the last thing McBride deserved was to be treated this way. No other head of IPID had tackled police corruption as he had. He was the only person who was getting real results, and he had been targeted to stop him from uncovering more.

I emailed Cele, Nkabinde, and members of the ANC Portfolio Committee. I told Cele that he was not part of the solution in South Africa – he was a part of the problem. I then attached key parts of the Public Protector's report – which has, interestingly, since been removed from the current Public Protector's website – into the allegedly corrupt leasing deals Cele had been a part of:[178]

> *How you can suggest that McBride has a case to answer from the Public Protector is an absolute joke. Although we all know that the current Public Protector is a Zuptoid and does the bidding of the Zuptas, the previous Public Protector had some choice things to say about you, which should render you unfit for anything except PRISON.*
>
> *I have no knowledge of what McBride has or has not done during his term of office, other than the good things he has done, but I am pretty certain he has not tried to shaft the taxpayer out of hundreds of millions of Rand on corrupt leases. In case you have forgotten, let me refresh your memory.*
>
> *I believe you want McBride gone with your lies because you fear that IPID will eventually send you to prison for what you did as a*

177 Zakhele Mbhele, ANC decision on McBride renewal is Scorpions 2.0, Politicsweb, 28 February 2019, https://www.politicsweb.co.za/opinion/anc-decision-on-mcbride-renewal-is-scorpions-saga-

178 Public Protector's report, Against The Rule Too, Creamermedia, 14 July 2011, http://us-cdn.creamermedia.co.za/assets/articles/attachments/34110_public_protectors_report.pdf

> *corrupt policeman. Putting you in charge of the police is like putting mice in charge of the cheese. Also, like putting Fraser in charge of the BOSASA investigation, seriously meant to be nothing more, or less, than 'STATE CAPTURE #2' or 'State Capture #1 COVER UP'.*
>
> *We have been looking into you, Cele, and you should expect a lot more to come. Silencing McBride and cutting him off from getting you in jail where you belong will NOT save you because you cannot stop me in the same way. Unlike McBride, I don't report to Parliament; Parliament reports to me and all the other citizens that pay their salaries.*
>
> *I'm coming for you Cele, be ready. My starting point will be to force the State to take action against you for the corruption you engaged in whilst a dirty cop, which the (uncaptured) Public Protector so readily identified. We are currently seeking out the docket – if Abrahams didn't torch it.*

I then addressed the Parliamentary Portfolio on Police, asking them not to be willing participants in State Capture #2 left by Zuma's sleeper cells:

> *It's clear that what Cele has sent you is part of a well-orchestrated criminal plot between Cele, Nkabinde and Phahlane, designed to keep them all out of prison.*
>
> *If McBride was supposed to have a term of office of FIVE years, then he is still due another 18 months, being the time the current crooked minister's crooked predecessor had him sitting at home, so that state capture could continue uninterrupted and criminals like Zuma, Ntlemeza and Phahlane could bring SA to its knees.*
>
> *If you neutralise him, you will go down in history as having put a stop to the clean-up that is now well underway in the police.*

Public Prosecutor Busisiwe Mkhwebane subsequently used my email to try to threaten me with criminal charges for having given my honest opinion of her, using the erroneous section of the Public Protector's Act, which states her offices cannot be insulted.

MP's LAUNCH A CASE AGAINST ME

I sent Francois Beukman, the chairman of the Parliamentary Portfolio Committee, a few more emails in which I revealed that McBride had started to look into Cele's 2011 leasing deals. The docket had been opened by the DA's Wilmot James all those years ago but was never investigated by IPID. The system simply showed the case to be 'Closed/Withdrawn'. Wondering what the quid pro quo was, I said:

> *This leads to the inevitable conclusion that Cele is being protected by one or more generals in the police.*

If anything, it provided further proof that IPID needed to remain completely independent if the criminal justice system was to remain uncaptured. I also stated that, since people like Cele and Nkabinde guided the Parliamentary Portfolio Committee, I thought Forensics for Justice should conduct detailed forensic investigations into every committee member, the results of which I would publish on our website:

> *Please advise your committee members that this is not the end; this is just the beginning. Our country just deserves better after years of the Zupta led rampage, and it now seems we were wrong to trust Parliament to lead us out of the darkness.*
>
> *I shall be raising this continued unlawful conduct aimed at State Capture #2 at the Zondo Commission.*

I then received a phone call from a too-friendly Captain Naicker at the Dieprivier Detectives Unit, who had been put in charge of yet another trumped-up investigation against me. The ANC MPs in the Parliamentary Portfolio Committee and Cele had opened a case against me because of my emails, falsely claiming that I had contravened the Powers, Privileges and Immunities Act of Parliament. Captain Naicker had been asked to drop everything to pursue me. This was not exactly the sign of an "open" Parliamentary committee. Clearly, their members were not open to personal forensic investigation. I wonder why?

Naicker emailed me asking me to provide a warning statement on the matter. I ran rings around him in my responses, asking him to point out which sentence or what portion of the emails was alleged to be an offence.

"It's refreshing to see such diligence in the police, as all of the dockets I have opened against connected criminals just sit and gather dust," I told him, adding:

> *I will NEVER be silenced by criminals in Parliament or the captured elements within; State Attorney's office, DPCI, SAPS, NPA, SSA or anyone for that matter. Far too many good people suffered over decades and decades at the hands of oppression to secure the Freedom of Speech we have today.*
>
> *Criminals with badges and gowns will NEVER take away those freedoms. They might try and suppress the right, but they will NEVER stop me from speaking out against corruption whilst I am breathing. They've arrested me, tortured me, kidnapped me, raided my office. I don't know how many times. They've tried to kill me many times over the last few years, yet I am still alive, so I will carry on speaking out against corruption.*

I told Naicker that they should not be wasting their time investigating false complaints, nor should they be using the criminal justice system to intimidate those exposing corruption, particularly when real crimes are being committed out there:

> *The Constitution quite clearly states that* ***"Everyone is equal before the law and has the right to equal protection and benefit of the law."*** *Yes, it actually says that, believe it or not.*
>
> *It does not say that* ***"Every ANC Member of Parliament shall have the right to jump the queue in opening criminal cases in order to silence those that are speaking out against the corrupt and criminal conduct of said MP's whilst totally ignoring the serious corruption cases that have been opened against said ANC MP's and their accomplices over seven years."***

I reminded Naicker that telling a member of Parliament that he is engaged in unlawful conduct is not an offence, no matter how much the criminals wanted it to be. I pointed out that I was allowed to look into public documents (like MP's declarations of interest). I said I had already found that when Cele stated in his declaration that he had resigned from three companies he had interests in, that he had lied – the CIPC records clearly showed he still had interests in the companies.

In closing, I told Captain Naicker that if he continued to harass me, I would instruct my attorneys to apply for yet another interdict against the 'Minister of Crime'. I copied Cele into the email and sent it off.

THE MINISTER AND HIS JEWEL-LOVING SPOKESMAN

In my email to Captain Naicker, I also pointed out that Cele had employed a criminal.

> *Since our Minister of Crime even hires an illegal immigrant, convicted of using a fake ID, as his Chief of Staff after the prior Minister fired him, I really wonder what is going on over here?*

I was referring to Leon Abednigo Mbangwa, who had somehow found himself back at the top position in the police ministry despite being publicly exposed for having faked his South African ID. This convicted criminal clearly had nine lives, or perhaps it was just that our police ministers enjoyed spending their time with people of like minds. This certainly seemed to be the case, as Cele had also hired a criminal as his spokesperson. The spokesman, Vuyo Babalo Mkhize, also happened to be Cele's business partner. This appointment could be viewed as a gratification because Cele never declared this conflict of interest.

In March 2019, my forensic practice was mandated by a man from Thailand, Agopyan Hovig Ohanes, to investigate a case of fraud, theft, possession of stolen property, and smuggling committed by Mkhize. Agopyan told us how Mkhize had unlawfully taken possession of a necklace, a ring, and earrings worth US$190 000 – valued at almost R3-million – from Agopyan's company, Jacob's Jewellery. In a docket we opened against Mkhize, we laid out how Mkhize had committed fraud against Agopyan by acquiring the jewellery and then smuggling it into South Africa in contravention of the Customs and Excise Act. Moreover, he had not paid the approximately R400 000 in Excise Duty, which would have been payable had he declared it at customs, as he was legally obliged to do.

In May 2008, Mkhize was first introduced to Agopyan as being part of an official South African delegation to businesspeople from Thailand. In September 2016, Mkhize contacted Agopyan to assist him with his travels to Thailand. Before leaving for Thailand, Mkhize told Agopyan that he was in a financial position to buy expensive jewellery from him. Mkhize claimed he was buying a present for his fiancée, who was also a business partner. Agopyan had no idea Mkhize was already married to someone else. His 'fiancée' was also married to someone else.

Mkhize was also nine months in arrears with his credit loans, owing approximately R836 000 to his creditors. It is highly unlikely, therefore, that he was in any financial position to afford jewellery worth US$190 000. This implied that Mkhize had intended to travel to Thailand to commit fraud and theft against Agopyan, pretending to be engaged and needing new jewellery for his fiancée. Once Mkhize had acquired the jewellery, he told Agopyn he would make payment into Jacob's Jewellery's bank account before leaving Thailand. He never made the payment and, when Agopyn tried to organise for Mkhize to drop the jewellery off at a business associate of his at the SA Diamond Centre in downtown Johannesburg, Mkhize never delivered the jewellery.

In the docket we opened against Mkhize, I pointed out:

> *Mkhize has a reputation in South Africa for being a renowned spin doctor, who are generally charismatic individuals who use speech to persuade people towards a specific viewpoint.*

Mkhize was now wanted by the authorities in Thailand.

Not long after sending the email, Mkhize contacted me and denied the allegations. He said he had hired BDK Attorneys to deal with the matter and that he would contact the Thai police to have the case closed. It was clear that Captain Naicker had either tipped Mkhize off or shared the revelations with the Minister – either way, an offence on his part.

Mkhize said he had registered a business with Cele in 2013, but Cele had resigned as a director of the company in 2014; therefore, the question of Cele giving him a job as a gratification did not arise. I told Mkhize that I had opened a docket against him and had given a copy of it to the criminal investigation team at SARS. We were satisfied that he had stolen the jewellery, smuggled it into South Africa and that there was prima facie evidence proving this.

I will continue to push for justice on behalf of my client in this case.

DECLINE TO PROSECUTE

In June 2019, I received an email from Advocate Rodney de Kok, the Director of Public Prosecutions in the Western Cape, saying that, after careful consideration of the docket opened by the ANC members of the Portfolio Committee, he had declined to prosecute me. Clearly, unlike the Political Crimes Litigation Unit and its corrupt attack dog, Mlotshwa, the NPA in the Western Cape was, at that stage, uncaptured.

McBride had, in the meantime, approached the court again, requesting that they review the decision by the Portfolio Committee, citing five instances that proved the Committee had been biased in taking its decision not to renew his contract. The five instances in question were that the Committee did not have an open mind and were acting under political dictation; that the committee did not act in compliance with its constitutional duty to protect the independence of IPID; that the decision by the Committee was not substantively rational, and that the decision was procedurally unfair because McBride was not allowed an opportunity to deal with evidence.

Since the wheels of justice take time to turn and the case will probably only be heard in a year's time, it is entirely possible that McBride will be back at IPID at some point in the future. In the meantime, he has been placed as the Head of a new Ethics Unit in the Department of Public Service and Administration, where he is fighting corruption within Government.

In McBride's absence, untold damage is being wrought on IPID. Acting Head Patrick Setshedi almost immediately suspended several senior managers, including National Head of Investigations Matthews Sesoko. Concern was raised that these suspensions would be used to scupper the Blue Lights investigation into Phahlane and the other senior police officers involved.[179] The case involved massive corruption, with many senior officers taking kickbacks from a supplier of blue lights and sirens for police vehicles. Serious attempts were being made to derail the case. To date, all attempts have failed, but to me, it remains a stark reminder to be vigilant at all times.

MANDLA IS ASSASSINATED

In the early hours of Tuesday the 10th of March 2020, one of the worst things that could have possibly happened, did. Mandlakayise Mahlangu, the IPID investigator who had led the initial investigation

---

179 Daneel Knoetze, IPID investigations aim to thwart police corruption investigations, say former officials, GroundUp, 11 March 2020, https://www.groundup.org.za/article/ipid-suspensions-aim-thwart-police-corruption-investigations-say-former-officials/

into Phahlane, was shot dead on his Jakkalsdans plot.[180] At around 3:30 a.m., a group of men entered Mandla's property, which was not far from Cullinan, and held him and a worker at gunpoint. They shot Mandla and fled in his Nissan Hardbody NP 300 bakkie with a fridge. It was an apparent house robbery, but I was sure it was a hit, and the 'robbery' was merely a smokescreen – a line they used because it suited them. A blind man could see through this ruse.

Mandla had been the target of the death threats sent by Phahlane's goons, and he had stood beside me in the dock on the false charges laid by Phahlane. He was an excellent investigator – the type of man there are too few of – incorruptible, decent, ethical, determined and honest. During everything we went through together, we had become more than just associates – we had become friends. The loss of his life was an enormous blow to both myself and Sarah-Jane.

I was convinced that people close to Phahlane were behind the murder. I wrote to him and the other co-conspirators who had targeted me over the past four years:

> *Hello criminal with a badge and thief of tax-payer funds.*
>
> *A good man died yesterday. A much better man than a crook like you could ever be.*
>
> *The same man that your criminal associates threatened to kill (along with me) three years ago when he knew I had uncovered and exposed your crooked ways.*
>
> *Whilst you and your crooked family members that have been living off the proceeds of crime and that bunch of thugs with badges in the Northwest may think this is going to be of great help to you, I've got news for you all:*

180 Shaun Smillie, IOID investigator probing former police chief shot dead, Daily Maverick, 11 March 2020, https://www.dailymaverick.co.za/article/2020-03-11-ipid-investigator-probing-former-police-chief-shot-dead/

It won't help you at all. Not a bit. Not even an iota of help.

If the State does not finish what I have started, I will finish what I have started. I will NEVER rest until Mandla's murderers have been brought to justice, and the dockets I opened against you and your accomplices have been prosecuted to the full, and those that belong in prison are in prison.

I'm going to have my lawyers put the state on terms to prosecute you and those criminals with badges from the Northwest, along with that lying driver that helped you carry the bags of cash around.

If they don't hurry up and finish the job off, I will launch a private prosecution against the whole sordid lot of you.

Not you, not your paid liars, not anyone can stop me from sending you and your accomplices to prison where you all belong.

I repeat what I said years ago, that your crooked Mulaudzi deliberately lied about after that corrupt thug Mokotedi and his crooked accomplice Hoosen had me yanked off the plane:

"If you are sending anyone to kill me, let them bring their own body bags because I will send them to hell – along with those that sent them".

STOP ME IF YOU CAN! Go ahead, make my day.

Sarah-Jane put out a reward poster asking for any information on Mandla's murder. The reward we were offering was R250 000, but if the information led back to any of these thugs with badges, the reward would go up to R500 000.

A few weeks later, surprisingly, police made arrests in the case, and it emerged the hitman was singing like a bird. He revealed exactly what I believed – that Mandla's assassination had been ordered and paid for by a known police officer.[181] The hitman and three of his accomplices had been paid R50 000 each.

Mandla's murder certainly wasn't the end for his family. The assassins came back to the farm. Mandla's nephew Xolani told *City Press* that two men entered the property by jumping over the fence. The family was living in fear, believing the assassins were returning to kill any witnesses. Is this what they deserved for Mandla's fighting the scourge of state capture? Mandla should have been offered a state funeral and his family honoured for the brave work he did for this country. Instead, they were cowering in fear. It was a disgrace.

Weeks later, information emerged indicating that Mandla's murder was related to his work at IPID. GroundUp reported that two IPID officials were recalled from a special task team probing corruption allegations against top police officials, including Phahlane and his relationship with Keating. They were told to hand over their dockets to IPID's head office.

It also emerged that Mandla was about to testify in a disciplinary hearing against Crime Intelligence officer Tlou Kgomo when he was murdered. It was Kgomo who allegedly offered Mandla a brigadier position in the police if he turned on IPID management and implicated them in wrongdoing. Mandla recorded the phone call where the offer was made.

But something made Mandla, a man who was not normally scared, back out of testifying. According to Viewfinder, in a handwritten statement made shortly before he died, he said that *"due to my security concerns and even those of my family, I have decided not to continue with my testimony as it is posing a risk on me"*.[182]

---

181 Abram Mashego, Family of murdered investigator in fear for their lives as intruders return, City Press, 11 May 2020, https://city-press.news24.com/News/family-of-murdered-investigator-in-fear-for-their-lives-as-intruders-return-20200511

182 Daneel Knoetze,Police watchdog pulls investigators from State Capture probe, Daily Maverick, 28 May 2020, https://www.dailymaverick.co.za/article/2020-05-28-police-watchdog-pulls-investigators-from-state-capture-probe/#gsc.tab=0

Despite this, Mandla was subpoenaed to testify at the disciplinary hearing. He was shot before he could testify.

The two investigators recalled from the special corruption task team had been assigned the Phahlane probe in Mandla's place. It appeared that Phahlane and a new team of state capturers were determined to hold onto their positions by any means possible. Instead of getting some rest after all my years spent fighting corruption – and the threats and intimidation that came with it – I would have to renew my efforts into stopping the scourge of greed and criminality that lay at the heart of our beautiful country, once and for all.

As a result of what I saw going on at IPID, I carried out a detailed investigation into the Executive Director of IPID, Dikeledi Ntlatseng. I discovered her appointment had been unlawful, as she could not have obtained the requisite security clearance, due to serious mismanagement of her own financial affairs. I also found that she was living well beyond her means and moonlighting on government tenders. I called for Ntlatseng's dismissal and an investigation into how she got appointed in the first place, as the whole thing wreaked of fraud and corruption.

CHAPTER 27

DAYS OF ZONDO

ANGELO AGRIZZI

I often have whistle-blowers contacting me. Many of them are scared, not knowing where to turn. One of the most damaging results of the capture of the criminal justice system is the destruction of the public's trust in the police. Without a single conviction for state capture, why would anyone go to the police with sensitive information?

The only high-profile arrests that have taken place in the police for corruption has been Phahlane and his accomplices. The public is well aware that the sole reason they faced a court of law is because of the work IPID and my team put into the casework, which didn't come without a personal cost. In Mandla Mahlangu's case, it cost him his life. His family lost a husband, a father, a son, and a brother.

Forensics for Justice is often one of the only institutions a whistle-blower can approach when they need help. I listen to them; I take down their information, secure it, legalise it (by helping them put it into affidavit format), make sure it reaches the right ears, and help in any other way I can, to the best of my ability. Of course, we are not always able to help. We are inundated with on-the-record and anonymous information through our tip-off line 0800 118 118, a service run by the twenty-four-hour tip-off call centre, Be Heard, which provides the service at no cost to Forensics for Justice as part of their contribution to building a better South Africa. Some of the tip-offs we get are not capable of being worked due to a lack of resources. Others may be petty squabbles between employee and employer in the police or other parts of the criminal justice system.

Before taking on any case, we, therefore, have to determine if it is of potential national importance, i.e. does it reveal evidence of serious corruption that would have the effect of undermining our social democracy?

On the 18th of October 2017, one such whistle-blower made his first contact with me. His name was Angelo Agrizzi, a name that became well known after his dramatic testimony in January 2019 at the Judicial Commission of Inquiry into Allegations of State Capture chaired by Deputy Chief Justice Raymond Zondo. The subject line of his email to me was *"Potential corruption case Watson's Bosasa ACSA and politicians."*

Agrizzi, who was the chief operating officer of Bosasa (the name was later changed to African Global Operations – no doubt to try to escape the historical stigma), a company whose business dealings were tainted with the bribing of officials and politicians to secure massively inflated government contracts, mainly to supply security for organisations like the Department of Correctional Services. Agrizzi shocked the country when he revealed that Bosasa paid officials like Dudu Myeni on a monthly basis. He said that Myeni was regularly paid in cash, under the guise of donations to the Jacob Zuma Foundation. On one occasion, R300 000 was placed in a Louis Vuitton handbag – a special gift just for her. Another standout allegation Agrizzi made was against Environmental Affairs Minister Nomvula Mokonyane, whom he said received R50 000 in monthly bribes. Bosasa also allegedly did home renovations for her and bought her "groceries", including expensive liquor, braai packs, frozen chicken and cold drinks. Agrizzi also fingered Vincent Smith, Deputy Minister of Correctional Services.

Agrizzi had worked for Bosasa for nineteen years. He knew where the bribes were paid, he knew the names of those involved, and he had the proof to back everything up. He had been in the muck, wallowing in the dirt of it all, and he wanted to come clean, revealing the extent of Bosasa CEO Gavin Watson's crooked company model – and outing politicians like Dudu Myeni and Nomvula Mokonyane while he was at it.

When Agrizzi sent me that first email in 2017 asking me to contact him, nobody really knew who he was. I was out of the country at the time, and Agrizzi was advised of this. In his response, he said:

> *May I suggest we get together when you return to South Africa? The matter is extremely sensitive. It includes a myriad of politicians corrupted by the Watsons as well as high-level BEE fronting via a company called BOSASA or African Global, as well as widespread planned corruption at ACSA that includes Jason Tshabalala ACS Bongi, the Procurement Mohammed Bashir and various other state-owned enterprises.*
>
> *You are also looking at approximately R200,000,000.00 tax fraud and misappropriation in "Cash for tenders", where sums of cash were fraudulently claimed as expenses on a monthly basis and paid out to high ranking officials.*
>
> *If you do a Google search on Gavin Watson BOSASA corruption, you should have enough reading material.*
>
> *My reason for the disclosure is due to the fact that I've had 20 years working as the Chief Operations Officer for the group. During my tenure, numerous incidents occurred where I raised my discontent, ultimately resulting in Gavin Watson negotiating an exit for me, and hence, due to my agreements in place, we would have to ensure my anonymity in the process.*

> *There are also numerous ex and current employees who will offer testimony to the corruption that took place, which they were forced to participate in.*
>
> *I trust you will keep the information confidential. Both Carte Blanche's Nicky Troll and News24's Adriaan Basson are aware of the situation at this stage and have agreed to stand back until I have consulted with yourself.*

Several meetings followed this initial reaching out, and Agrizzi handed Forensics for Justice several sworn affidavits. We placed these affidavits before the Special Investigating Unit (SIU) and the Hawks. We opened a criminal docket against Bosasa's Watson and Vincent Smith in the middle of 2018.

We had so much information on Bosasa that we could have opened numerous dockets, but I know from years of experience that you will tie up investigators for years if you do that. It is better to make a case out that is crystal clear for the police – one that is crisp and easy to prove so that justice is done.[183] We focussed on the payments to Vincent Smith, who had been the Deputy Minister of Correctional Services at the time and opened a case of corruption and racketeering.

In the docket, we described how Gavin Watson paid Vincent Smith large amounts of money – R100 000 a month in cash. Payments were made at a Mugg & Bean in a mall in the West Rand. Smith's daughter was a student at Aberystwyth University in Wales, and Bosasa was paying for her tuition. We were handed the receipts.

The docket followed on from a September 2018 article in *City Press* that alleged a corrupt relationship between Smith and Bosasa. Smith, by then, was SCOPA's chairperson and an ANC MP.[184] The bribes were paid so that Smith could organise for Bosasa to be granted

183 Gareth van Zyl, Paul O'Sullivan: 'Cyril Ramaphosa son NOT corrupt', Bizews, 14 December 2018, https://www.biznews.com/interviews/2018/12/14/paul-osullivan-cyril-ramaphosa-son-not-corrupt

184 Kyle Cowan, Bosasa paid top ANC MP, News24, 1 September 2018, https://www.news24.com/SouthAfrica/News/bosasa-paid-top-anc-mp-20180901

inflated contracts at the Department of Correctional Services. It was also alleged that when Smith moved to Parliament, he would use his position to attack Bosasa's competitors who were tendering for the same contracts. Our prior and then-current investigations corroborated this information.

During the PRASA investigation, I had taken evidence from a Mr Greyling from a company called SA Fence and Gate. Greyling said at the time that he felt his firm was being 'targeted' by SCOPA. He said that one of their projects at the Department of Correctional Services was the subject of numerous Auditor General reports, a Parliamentary Portfolio Committee inquiry, and a treasury-led investigation. According to a statement by SA Fence and Gate, Smith was involved in the solicitation of a R5-million bribe. When SA Fence and Gate refused to pay him the money, he turned to Bosasa.

Our investigation also discovered that Bosasa was paying for the infamous former SABC Chief Operating Officer Hlaudi Motsoeneng's legal fees. A payment of R1 187 656.82 was made into the account of his lawyers, Majavu Incorporated. Smith just happened to be Chairperson of the Parliamentary Ad Hoc Committee on the SABC board in 2017.

Agrizzi provided us with evidence that showed that Watson provided either cash, goods, or services to:

- *Nomvula Mokonyane – a high-end security system and monthly cash payments of R50 000.*
- *Gwede Mantashe (Chairperson of the African National Congress) – security systems worth R300 000.*
- *Dudu Myeni – security systems worth R250 000.*
- *Richmond Mti (previous National Commissioner of Correctional Services) – security systems worth R350 000.*
- *Vincent Smith – security systems worth R200 000.*

- *Thabang Makgwetla (previous Deputy Minister of Justice and Correctional Services) - security systems worth R350 000.*

Angelo Aggrizzi (right) with corruption accused BOSASA chief, Gavin Watson.

ANDILE RAMAPHOSA

One of the affidavits provided to us was from an accountant, Petrus Venter, who had previously worked for Bosasa and subsequently left.[185] This accountant said that Watson had instructed him to pay R500 000 to the Andile Ramaphosa Foundation.

Venter said in his affidavit that Watson instructed one of their employees to pay R3-million from Watson's personal bank account into the account of a liquidated company, Miotto Trading and Advisory Holdings (Pty) Ltd. Of that money, R2.5-million was used to purchase a residential property. In a separate deal, Venter was told to send

185 Kyle Cowan, Bosasa scandal 2: Top ANC MP Vincent Smith got cash, CCTV, City Press, 2 September 2018, https://www.biznews.com/interviews/2019/06/13/paul-osullivan-ramaphosa-verdict

R500 000 to an ABSA bank account that Watson said belonged to the Andile Ramaphosa Foundation.

"I found this strange but wouldn't dare question Gavin Watson," Venter said.

Andile is the son of the current President of the country, Cyril Ramaphosa. I have known Ramaphosa for a long time, more than twenty years. When still at school, his son, Andile, would play tenpin bowling with two of my daughters at the then Randburg Waterfront. Today those daughters are a doctor and a space scientist. The Ramaphosa I knew was not someone who engaged in unethical activity, so I was shocked when I saw this accusation.

Personal affiliations aside, Forensics for Justice is apolitical. I did what I do with any information provided to us by a whistle-blower – I forensically investigated the claims. One of the first things I established was that there was no Andile Ramaphosa Foundation and that Andile did not bank with ABSA. We concluded that while Venter's statement was partially true, the bank account he had been given was, in fact, a fundraising account for Cyril Ramaphosa's ANC presidential campaign bid, known as CR17. Watson had deceived Venter into thinking the money was for Andile. I believe Watson did this to conceal where the money was truly being paid.

The money was being laundered through a liquidated company that should not even have had a functioning bank account. The money was then paid into the collection trust account for the CR17 Campaign for Ramaphosa to be elected as the President of the ANC. These bank details were publicly available, and Watson paid the money over, duping Venter because he did not want the Campaign to know where the funds originated. Why Watson paid the money to the campaign is unclear. Ramaphosa had no idea where the money came from. I later discovered that Watson was trying to slip in through the back door by hedging his bets in case Zuma's appointee did not win the ANC's presidential race due to take place at NASREC later that year.

The problem with corrupt people is they believe that everyone else is like them, as do most criminals and psychopaths. Watson obviously thought that if he had paid R500 000 to Ramaphosa's campaign fund, he would later be able to get up close and personal if Ramaphosa beat Zuma's nominated successor.

Leaving out all names, I contacted one of Ramaphosa's special advisors and said I wanted to know what was going on. Andile then contacted me and revealed that he had, in fact, entered into a consulting contract with Bosasa but that it had nothing to do with the R500 000 payment. We later had several meetings to clear the air. I wanted to satisfy myself that there was no link between Bosasa and Cyril Ramaphosa that might later lead to a State Capture version 2.

Andile explained that, through his company Blue Crane Capital, he had been in contact with a man called Trevor Mathenjwa from African Global Operations (Pty) Ltd (AGO). He said he was first introduced to AGO around mid-2017. He had been in contact with a Chinese company called Dahua, specialists in electronic security integration. Andile said he wanted to roll out an integrated product offering of Dahua's in East African countries and asked if they had any South African or East African business associates. He was then introduced to Mathenjwa, who was the director of a company called Global Technology Services, an operating division of AGO. Blue Crane Capital then entered three months of sporadic discussions, which culminated in a consulting agreement, styled as an 'Advisory Mandate' between AGO, Blue Crane, and another company called Offtake. In terms of the mandate, Blue Crane and Offtake were to provide "Strategic Advisory and Financial Advisory Services" to AGO on a monthly retainer basis for a fee of R150 000 per month plus VAT. We noted that Blue Crane's banking account (to which AGO paid the invoices) was an FNB account and not the ABSA account into which Watson paid the R500 000 (via Miotto) in October 2017.

After studying all the documentation involved in the contracts and interviewing Andile for hours, we were satisfied that there was a genuine commercial relationship between Blue Crane Capital and AGO and that the invoices were issued in the normal course of business. I did, of course, advise Andile that Watson was as corrupt as they come and that any further association with him could be seen as poor judgement, at the least.

Andile also told us that when Ramaphosa took over as President of the ANC, he called all his family together and said he wanted to know about all their business interests because he did not want any accusations made about anyone in his family. He asked them all to implement an anti-bribery and anti-corruption policy with all their business associates. Andile did this with AGO. They signed an anti-bribery and corruption policy, and we were furnished with a copy. We were also furnished with a comprehensive deal-flow spreadsheet, which clearly indicated that there were significant deals in East Africa flowing as a result of the advisory mandate between Blue Crane and Global Technology Solutions.

The irony was not lost on us that Watson chose to sign such a policy document at a time when he was engaged in activities that were in contravention of the said policy, albeit not with Blue Crane Capital, but with others. I have no doubt that Gavin Watson would try later to score something out of the transaction, but Andile had gone into the business dealings completely innocent.

POLITICAL FOOTBALL

In the meantime, the accusation linking Andile to the R500 000 emerged publicly. Although Agrizzi had initially approached us in October 2017, he had subsequently made a U-turn and had entered into a settlement agreement with Watson, where he was the recipient of large monthly 'hush' payments until he chose to resign from Bosasa and become a whistle-blower. Questions were asked in Parliament, and Mmusi Maimane, the then leader of the DA, laid a complaint with the Public Protector. Any link with Bosasa was being used by the DA to score political points.

Andile Ramaphosa wanted his father to pay the R500 000 back, but I advised him not to because this money was likely the proceeds of crime. I recommended that they rather pay the monies into their lawyer's trust account and keep it there until the authorities decided whether they wanted to attach it. The deposit slips were supplied to SAPS and the NPA in this regard.

When the matter was raised in Parliament, the President wrongly assumed the question referred to payments received by his son's company through his mandate with AGO. So Ramaphosa told the National Assembly that he had spoken with Andile and that he was certain the payments were above board. He had no idea at that stage that Bosasa had paid money to the CR17 campaign.

Ramaphosa's response to the DA was a genuine error. One of his special advisors called him to one side immediately after the parliamentary questions to explain the discussions between ourselves and Andile and what we had uncovered. When Ramaphosa was told that the money had, in fact, been paid into the trust account for his campaign, he immediately corrected his mistake by sending a letter to Speaker Baleka Mbete stating that he did not have all the information at hand when he responded to the question. The opposition parties immediately rallied together, accusing Ramaphosa of lying to Parliament.

I had put a lot of work into the case and knew that Cyril and his son did not have a corrupt relationship with AGO. In fact, Cyril had no relationship with the company at all and was completely at arm's length to the campaign's fundraising efforts. I then did something that I do not normally do – I put out a statement and an affidavit showing why I believed that neither Andile nor his father was guilty of corruption in this case.

I felt the country needed to know. After eight years of Zuma rule, confidence in the country's leadership was so low that many people automatically believed any ANC leader was corrupt. But, in this case, it simply wasn't true. The accusations were damaging our already fraught economy, and I felt that I should issue a certificate of good health. I felt like I should stand by a President whom I believed was clean then – and that I still believe to be clean today. The DA were having none of it and their outspoken leader, who always shoots from the hip, accused me of being partisan. It backfired on him, and he was later exposed as being one of the main reasons for the DA's fall in voter support. His arrogance had lost the DA voters it badly needed.

BOSASA CRIME SYNDICATE

As Agrizzi's testimony at the Zondo Commission continued to shed light on the extent of state capture on the country's leaders, I found myself becoming frustrated with the lack of prosecutions. Not one of them was being held to account for their treasonous crimes. Of those who bothered to respond to Agrizzi's accusations, they, without fail, denied any wrongdoing. It was as easy as that. They provided no proof and gave no details to show why they were innocent. I publicly called upon them to come forward and take a free polygraph test to clear their names:

> *If they REFUSE to step forward, we are saying that this amounts to a public statement that they are afraid of what the results might yield.*

In particular, we call upon:

- *Jacob Zuma*
- *Dudu Myeni*
- *Nomvula Mokonyane*
- *Nomgcobo Jiba [and]*
- *Lawrence Mrwebi*

...to step forward for a free polygraph test if they have nothing to hide.

We asked Mokonyane to make a transparent disclosure about who was paying for her daughter's university education in China, her daughter's luxury apartment, and her daughter's pocket money. I also called for a forensic audit of the Jacob Zuma Foundation, which was, no doubt, used for money laundering under Myeni's control. I also called upon the Hawks and the NPA to prosecute Watson and Smith through the docket Forensics for Justice had opened in which we had set out a handful of simple charges. These charges were what I describe as the low-hanging fruit – charges that would be quick and easy to prove.

For reasons best known to the dilly-dallying or corrupt incompetents in the criminal justice system, there seems to be a belief that a corruption investigation should take years and should include every single act of corruption along the way. Of course, this is utter nonsense. I had learnt many years ago that a handful of crisp charges that are easy to prove quickly meets the 'interests of justice' rule because it will put the criminal behind bars quickly and thereby set an example to others.

While working in the Fraud Unit at Johannesburg Central Police station in the 1990s, I put a substantial docket together against a serial fraudster by the name of Andre Bouwer. The charge sheet ran into almost two thousand counts, and the trial took three years. At the conclusion of the trial, Bouwer was found guilty of almost one thousand counts and sentenced to more than three hundred and sixty years in prison. However, due to the summing up rules, he would only serve an effective fifteen years, cut to ten for good behaviour, which meant he would be eligible for parole after five years. The Regional Court magistrate later remarked to me that if Bouwer had only been charged with ten counts, the sentence could still have been fifteen years, and the trial would have only been a few weeks at the most.

When I was in the police, the next big fraud investigation I was involved in was The State v Vito Assante, a rogue bank manager from the NBS Bank at Kempton Park who had swiped R375-million by receiving depositor cheques and pushing them through a crooked lawyer's trust account. Although Assante had committed over a thousand offences, he was charged with only a handful of crisp charges that were easy to prove. Realising he was on the ropes, Assante pleaded guilty to the specimen charges and was sentenced to twenty years. There was no trial, and Assante was sent to prison.

Forensics for Justice carried out some crude calculations and came to the conclusion that if every criminal involved in state capture were to be prosecuted for every crime they committed, it would tie up between ten and fifteen prosecution teams for more than thirty-five years. Since the institutional memory in both the police and the NPA would not last as long as that, most of these criminals would simply get off the hook.

Our suggestion was (and is), therefore, simple: select four or five crisp and easy to prove charges against each of the suspects, charge them, try them, and send them to prison. It could all be done and dusted within five to six years, instead of more than a generation. So what if some of them only get ten years instead of fifteen years? They would be out of government and in prison, and the example would have been set for future would-be state capturers.

Not long after all this muck slithered into the public consciousness, the entire Bosasa investigation opened a whole new can of worms when Gavin Watson died in a supposed car accident outside the airport. Alone and driving an old company car instead of one of his luxury vehicles, Watson's death had all the markings of a murder mystery reminiscent of an old-fashioned crime novel.[186] It was early in the morning. Where was Watson going at such an hour? Was he already dead when his car crashed into a barrier on the side of the highway? Where was his cell-phone? There were more questions than answers related to his death and, despite the numerous investigations launched, I wonder if any answers will ever really emerge.

A SILENT COUP

Three months after Agrizzi dropped his Bosasa bombshells at what had now commonly come to be known as the Zondo Commission on State Capture, Robert McBride entered the witness box for four days in April 2019.

Like Agrizzi, his testimony was much anticipated. As an ANC member and Head of IPID, McBride was one of the few people who fully understood the bigger picture of the capture of the criminal justice sector. His testimony described how he, Dramat, Sibiya, top SARS investigators, and I were targeted for the various investigations we were conducting. We were getting too close, uncovering the links between politicians, high-ranking police officers, and their business connections.

McBride went deeper. He showed the modus operandi behind what happened: how the police, Hawks, and NPA – and other state

186 Azarrah Karrim and Mandy Weiner, Gavi Watson's death: 5 holes in the investigation, News24, 22 September 2019, https://www.news24.com/SouthAfrica/News/gavin-watsons-death-5-holes-in-the-investigation-20190922

bodies that were meant to tackle corruption – had been systematically weakened since 2010 when Zuma came to power, to the point that they could not perform their functions sufficiently.

The debilitating evisceration of law enforcement was the winning ingredient of the criminals involved in the capture and looting of state institutions like SAA, PRASA, and Eskom. If the Hawks, police, Crime Intelligence and the NPA had all been functioning the way they should have, the looting by the Guptas and other corrupters would have been quickly stopped. In a properly functioning country, there would have been quick and harsh punishment for those who plundered state resources, especially on such a large scale. Instead, like a badly written farce, investigations bumbled along, dockets were ignored, and Crime Intelligence busied themselves fighting petty battles among themselves and spying on leaders for political gain. If by some small chance, any investigation did happen to take place, it stopped dead at the National Prosecuting Authority, where the files piled up on a shelf and gathered dust.

I have been told that Shaun Abrahams had an office there specifically for this purpose – a special place where justice was sent to die. The very same resources were then used by the crime syndicates to go after corruption fighters. Sarah-Jane Trent and I were just two of many who were singled out in their attacks. Others that we know of were Lieutenant General Anwar Dramat, Major General Shadrack Sibiya, and Major General Johan Booysen from the Hawks. From the NPA, it was Advocate Glynnis Breytenbach. From IPID, there was Mandla Mahlangu, Robert McBride, Temane Binang as well as Matthews Sesoko and Innocent Khuba. From SARS, there was "The SARS Three" – Ivan Pillay, Johann van Loggerenberg, and Pravin Gordhan. There are many others.

The corrupt were being protected both actively and passively through non-prosecution. There were unjustified withdrawals of criminal cases linked to politically associated individuals.

Between 2010 and 2018, the only high-level investigations that seemed to be taking place were against crime fighters like McBride and those of us who were trying to do something to turn the tide against institutionalised corruption.

The capture of the criminal justice system began with the destruction of the Scorpions. In an address to the Commission before McBride's testimony, Advocate Paul Joseph Pretorius, the Zondo Commission's legal team head, described how the Scorpions had had a conviction rate of 94%. He pointedly asked if any other law enforcement agency since 2009 had been able to match that statistic. By comparison, the Anti-Corruption Task Team has only ever had one conviction, and the Special Investigating Unit (SIU), which had sent six hundred and eighty-six cases to the NPA between 2013 and 2018, secured not even one successful prosecution. The figures make one question the real purpose behind disbanding the Scorpions in the first place.

Journalist Marianne Thamm pointed out in the *Daily Maverick* that what Pretorius did in his address was to set out just how many institutions in South Africa were aimed at combatting corruption.[187] There are the SAPS, the Hawks, the SIU, the NPA, the State Security Agency, the Asset Forfeiture Unit, the Ministry of Justice, the Ministry of Police, IPID, the Inspector General of Intelligence, SARS, the Auditor General's office, the Department of Public Administration, the Public Service Commission, the Public Protector's office, the State Attorney's office, the Financial Intelligence Centre, Treasury, and Parliament. It is astonishing to look at that list and realise that despite the existence of

---

187 Marianne Thamm, Wake up and smell the McBride: How the state capture project corroded essential law enforcement cogs and wheels, Daily Maverick, 12 April 2019,https://www.dailymaverick.co.za/article/2019-04-12-wake-up-and-smell-the-mcbride-how-the-state-capture-project-corroded-essential-law-enforcement-cogs-and-wheels/

so many institutions aimed at stopping and providing oversight over bodies that fight corruption, state capture still happened.

McBride's testimony gave us a glimpse into how this came about. He described how the Crime Intelligence component of South Africa's law enforcement network was primarily used to frustrate IPID's work. McBride said that the very nature of IPID, which was established to provide oversight over the police, would naturally be met with resistance from within the police service. It was up to the person heading it up to either succumb to the external pressures or fight for its independence.

McBride said a pattern became clear to him: IPID was not facing resistance against all its cases – it only happened to cases related to investigations into procurement maladministration and criminality within the police's leadership. He said this was a fight against what he and some of his colleagues called a 'silent coup', which now has come to be known as 'state capture'.

McBride said the attack on anti-corruption bodies would follow a certain methodology: upright leaders were removed from positions of authority using transfers, by arrest, disciplinary processes, and the use of 'flexible' journalists, in a compliant media to discredit them. They would then be replaced by people who did not deserve the promotion, sometimes through nepotism. The new leadership would not carry out their tasks diligently. What they were really doing was advancing an agenda outside of the institutions they were running.

A message would then be communicated that, since the removal of the previous leader, the institution was performing much better, which was often a lie. In IPID's case, McBride's successor, Israel Kgamanyane, told Parliament that IPID was performing better under his watch. What really happened is that bizarre transfers took place where people with specialised skills were redeployed – such as a financial management specialist who was redeployed to head up investigations, in which they had no experience – rendering the institution dysfunctional.

McBride detailed the resistance he met when conducting investigations. He described how the Secret Service Account at Crime Intelligence was looted and how, when IPID attempted to investigate, documents related to procurement would be classified, leading to a point where no prosecution relating to criminality at Crime Intelligence had ever taken place.

He set out the patronage system within the police, where relentless plots, schemes, and conspiracies took place to drive him out of IPID.[188]

"It is the same tactic that they used when they are dealing with criminal syndicates," he said. "If they are doing their work properly, they will disrupt, and they will tie them up in litigation," adding that this tactic had delayed the work of the IPID.

McBride explained that, during his suspension, two officers were transferred from SAPS Crime Intelligence to IPID, which included Tlou Kgomo, who was appointed to head investigations. The Commission was played an audio clip where Kgomo was heard offering IPID investigator Mandla Mahlangu, the same investigator who was killed a year later, a promotion if he cooperated to bring McBride down.

McBride went into the Phahlane investigation and Phahlane's hit squad, the Northwest team, which was used as a weapon to stop IPID from digging any further. He described our illegal arrests and how we were targeted to stop our investigation.

His testimony was followed by that of (former) Hawks boss Johan Booysen, whose arrest and villainous prosecution displayed the extent to which criminal elements within the police and NPA would go in shutting down investigations into politically connected individuals.

---

188 Makhosandile Zulu, SAPS runs on a patronage system – McBride tells Zondo Commission, The Citizen, 16 April 2019, https://citizen.co.za/news/south-africa/state-capture/2119014/saps-runs-on-a-patronage-system-mcbride-tells-zondo-commission/

MY ZONDO AFFIDAVIT

Before writing this book, I prepared to testify before the Zondo Commission. I prepared an affidavit to reveal some of what I have revealed here – how I was attacked to stop my investigations into Khomotso Phahlane, Berning Ntlemeza, Dudu Myeni, Vineshkumar Moonoo, the Mpisi Group, Lucky Montana, Jacob Zuma and many others.

In my submission, I identified how the criminal justice system and large state-owned companies had been captured by politically corrupt individuals who served unconstitutional agendas. Instead of upholding the law, enforcement bodies spent their time protecting the underworld connected to Zuma and his family from corruption charges. They were assisting in the cover-up of serious fraud and corruption by blocking any attempts at prosecution.

This was a high-level conspiracy whose purpose was three-fold:

- To protect criminals who were near and dear to President Jacob Zuma.
- To protect corrupt police and prosecution service officials who were already engaged in criminal conduct outside of state capture.
- To use the captured criminal justice system to silence and punish anyone attempting to expose the dark underbelly of state capture. My evidence showed how criminals within the criminal justice system were unlawfully placed into senior positions to achieve this.

All of this resulted in the near destruction of fundamental institutions in the country. It created a situation where the criminal justice system was rendered impotent and is now overwhelmed with a massive backlog in cases. The clean-up will take years, if not a whole generation, to turn around.

The politicisation and management takeover by criminals resulted in a situation where the morale of good men and women in the criminal justice system was (and still is) at an all-time low. It is no good having brave men and women with hearts of lions protecting their citizens when the lions are being led by corrupt donkeys.

While I found many of the Zondo Commission witnesses admirable, I believe they should have come forward earlier. If they had stepped up three years ago with sworn affidavits, we might have been able to stop state capture in its tracks. By remaining in their positions and simply carrying on, many witnesses found themselves complicit in the state capture project. Had they spoken out sooner, we might not have suffered in the way we did. Their silence was an enabler of state capture.

On the other side of the coin, there are those who stood up against the wide-scale looting and were determined to stop it.

However, from the treatment meted out, it felt like I was state capture enemy number one. Multiple arrests, raids on my offices, and the bringing of more than six trials on more than fifty false charges against me, with police making (or leaking for publication) false allegations that I was involved in treason, tax fraud, money laundering, and a plot to overthrow the government. I tried to figure out why I was singled out for special treatment and concluded that everyone else who had been targeted was targeted for doing their jobs. They were either police officials, prosecutors, or IPID members. I was a quandary for them since I could, within the law, say and do what I wanted to expose corruption. If a prosecutor or police officer is suspended from duty or dismissed, that marks the end of that person's official role in crime-fighting. Suspension, of course, is the best weapon because it effectively silences that person. But they could not silence me. Every time they tried, I fought back – and hard. I sent them emails telling them I would send them to prison. I taunted them with photos of their ill-gotten gains and dared them to "Stop Me if You Can".

The only way they could deal with their fear of me was to get rid of me permanently. That is why the multiple arrests, detentions, and raids were closely matched with a conspiracy to have me murdered.

Aside from those whose human rights were abused, there was the part of the media that independently reported on what was happening. There were non-governmental organisations that would not bow to political pressure – organisations like Forensics for Justice, the Helen Suzman Foundation, Freedom Under Law, and AfriForum. Their role cannot be underestimated. Together we proved to be democracy's last line of defence.

I planned to give evidence on the veracity of the Gupta Leak emails. I had analysed many of them and could prove they were genuine. It would consume approximately 30 000 man-hours to analyse the sheer volume of evidence contained on various hard drives – equal to tying up twelve people, full time for two years. I explained how we had placed the database on a special server located in a secret place and that we were able to give the Commission access to this web-based e-discovery system at no cost to reduce the number of hours spent analysing the emails and documents.

My submission at the Zondo Commission also detailed how I opened a multitude of criminal cases against high-profile individuals like Vineshkumar Moonoo, Berning Ntlemeza, Khomotso Phahlane, General Riah Phiyega, Nomgcobo Jiba, Jen Chi Huang, Khulubuse Zuma, Edward Zuma, Yusuf Kajee, Lucky Montana, Jacob Zuma and Dudu Myeni. I explained how, despite providing *prima facie* evidence, all the dockets were hidden away in dark rooms, and no steps were taken to investigate any of them. Instead, as this book has shown, I became the target of false criminal investigations propagated by criminals working in conspiracy with those that I exposed to scrutiny.

For the Commission, I explained how I had gone through the cases opened against me and their eventual outcome and said that I would detail the role played by the Priority Crimes Litigation Unit and the Hawks in all of it. I also said that I would point out that the PCLU was used as the 'hit squad' for Shaun Abrahams, Nomgcobo Jiba and Jacob Zuma.

I stated that the cornerstone of our criminal justice system is that those vested with power must exercise their power without fear, favour or prejudice. Yet, at its hands, I endured the arbitrary deprivation of my freedom and have been on the receiving end of inhumane and degrading treatment by the police. I have been tortured, my character publicly tarnished, and numerous attempts have been made on my life. Our Constitution means nothing if ordinary citizens cannot be protected, and it means even less if they cannot be protected from those who are supposed to protect them.

DO SOMETHING

I stated that we could not allow this situation to continue unabated, that we must clean up and remove all the unlawful appointees that were made. We do not even know all of them. A process needed to be carried out that quickly identifies and removes the 'plants' or 'sleepers' who have been positioned to protect criminals in future.

I would ask the Commission to obtain documentation and to subpoena the criminals that were protected during this state capture process, including the Zumas, Dudu Myeni and the Jacob Zuma Foundation, the Gupta cabal, Michael Hulley, Yusuf Kajee, Jen Chi Huang, Lucky Montana, Roy Moodley, and the Bhanas.

I said that Myeni should be made to bring the bank accounts and ledgers of the Jacob Zuma Foundation, which I believe was used as a piggybank for propping up an illegal regime. Myeni should also bring a detailed list of her income and expenditure for the last six years and be made to explain how she managed to live such a high life.

The books of SAA should also be brought, so we could see how much money Myeni siphoned off for her own use. A detailed explanation of the aborted Emirates Airline code-share agreement should also be included since we were reliably informed it was aborted because Emirates refused to make a significant donation to the Jacob Zuma Foundation.

The current Police Commissioner should additionally bring through documentation, including the details of all spending and instructions to law firm Hogan Lovells to conduct internal police disciplinary enquiries as well as the details of all the unlawful appointments made by Phahlane while he was Acting Commissioner.

I would ask that all the memoranda Abrahams addressed to the PCLU be obtained as I was certain it would provide prima facie evidence that Abrahams used the PCLU to help capture the criminal justice system.

In closing, I stated that I had taken a principled stand against state-sponsored corruption and crime for more than twenty years. Along with a few other principled people like McBride and the investigators from IPID and SARS, we have exposed senior employees of state-owned companies and organs of state who were involved in the capture of the State. For this, we have been attacked, harassed, and maligned. Sadly, it cost Mandla Mahlangu his life. While I prevailed, fought back, exposed, and had some of the criminals removed – mostly with the help of the Helen Suzman Foundation and IPID – the remaining Zuma loyal foot soldiers remained in their unlawfully appointed positions. Unless steps are taken to root them all out, the ingredients are there for a re-run of state capture when the enabling environment is once again created by the underworld. We need to make sure that never happens.

Unfortunately, the Zondo Commission either mis-read, or misunderstood its mandate to investigate and report on State Capture, as far as the criminal justice system was concerned. Having spent more than R200 million looking into high-level corruption within the criminal justice system and despite Forensics for Justice having spent more than two years preparing hard facts and evidence for them, the Commission unceremoniously announced in October 2021, that they would no longer report on the capture of the law enforcement agencies.

I was gob smacked. Without the capture of the criminal justice system, all the other crimes committed by the corrupt government officials and corrupt people, like the Gupta's, would just not have been possible.

If the police and NPA were doing their jobs, instead of protecting the criminals and targeting whistle-blowers, there would have been no need for Forensics for Justice, or the Zondo Commission and the economy of South Africa today, would be booming.

This meant that 20% of the Zondo Commission budget and time was totally wasted and failed to get to the reality that, without the criminal justice system being captured, there could not have been any other state capture.

CHAPTER 28

STATE CAPTURE – THE OUTCOME

HOLDING STATE CAPTURERS TO ACCOUNT

More needs to be done to hold those accountable for their role in enabling state capture. Aside from the looters and their beneficiaries, there were large companies – particularly lawyers, transaction advisors, and accountants – which acted as the glue that held the whole state capture project together. They dotted the i's and crossed the t's, legalising the illegal transfer of money and victimising anti-corruption watchdogs, honest cops and activist citizens like myself.

When a house is built, the ceilings will fall without the support of central load-bearing walls. With state capture, the professional consultants were these key pillars of strength. They were the ones who helped criminals create and maintain the enabling environment necessary for state capture to get off the ground.

Apart from KPMG, which had, to some extent, come clean for the role they played in state capture, other companies needed to be held to account – companies like Hogan Lovells, Bain, and McKinsey. As a victim of the capture of the criminal justice system, I focussed my attention on international law firm Hogan Lovells, which played a huge part in defending corrupt leaders, thereby keeping them in office to wreak havoc. Hogan Lovells were the law firm of choice for the capturers of the criminal justice system. Their clients included the Minister of Police, Nkosinathi Nhleko, unlawfully appointed Head of the Hawks, Lieutenant General Ntlemeza, and SARS Commissioner Tom Moyane. Notwithstanding the absolute devastation the actions of Nhleko, Ntlemeza and Moyane caused the country to suffer, Hogan Lovells worked with these criminals to target those fighting crime and corruption.

If it weren't for firms like Hogan Lovells, which benefitted from public funds to keep criminals and their accomplices in their positions, many of the events that enabled the capture of the criminal justice sector would not have taken place. Dramat, Sibiya and Booysen would not have been suspended. Neither would have McBride. The unlawful charges against Minister Pravin Gordhan – whose real aim was to unblock the illicit flow of funds to Dudu Myeni via SAA and free up Treasury for the wholesale raid of the Guptas and their accomplices – would not have taken place. The criminal charges would not have been brought against me, and Sarah-Jane Trent and I would not have been arrested or tortured but for Hogan Lovells keeping Ntlemeza at the helm and Sibiya off the ship.

Hogan Lovells, and other firms that worked for other parts of the state, helped support criminal structures and undermined our constitutional democracy. The fight against state capture would have been over in two years had it not been for so-called professional firms propping up an illegitimate regime. At all material times, they knew what they were doing, and their appetite for unlawfully earned fees kept them doing it.

In January 2018, I wrote to Susan Bright at Hogan Lovells to bring all of this to her attention. I was determined that they be held accountable for what they had done.

I had also provided information to a good friend of mine, British peer Lord Peter Hain. He had referred Hogan Lovells to the UK's Solicitors Regulation Authority, an independent body that regulates solicitors and law firms in England and Wales. Lord Hain asked them to withdraw Hogan Lovell's authorisation as a recognised body. In a speech in the House of Lords, Lord Hain mentioned Hogan Lovells' involvement in South Africa. He had been championing a money-laundering bill there and often spoke about the South African state capture project and how British-based financial institutions were used as a conduit for the laundering of looted state money. We assisted Peter Hain by providing him with factual evidence to prop up his hard-hitting speeches. Needless to say, no sanction was received by Hogan Lovells in the UK because the Solicitors Regulation Authority has no jurisdiction over what UK law firms do in South Africa.

Hogan Lovells' response was that I did not know how the South African legal system worked. Of course, partly thanks to their defence of the corrupt police leadership at the time, I had a particularly good understanding of how it worked, having spent years in and out of court defending myself from illegal charges laid against me. Furthermore, I had studied law in London many years ago, so I knew the system well. I had also spent many years as a senior lecturer at the Police Training Centre lecturing in Criminal Law, A, Criminal B, and Police Administration.

Lavery Modise, the chairperson of Hogan Lovells South Africa, told *Fin24* that, while I was a passionate anti-corruption campaigner, my attempt to lay the "genuine suffering of our country at [their] doorstep [was] incorrect and not well-founded".[189]

My battle against them had taken root. Just over a year after Modise made this glib statement, Hogan Lovells in South Africa had begun

189 Jan Cronje, O'Sullivan doesn't understand SA's legal system – Hogan Lovells, Fin24, 31 January 2018, https://www.fin24.com/Economy/osullivan-doesnt-understand-sas-legal-system-hogan-lovells-20180131

fragmenting.[190] The firm had shrunk to a quarter of its former size, their office building in Sandton that they shared with McKinsey was closing, and seventy-one lawyers were going off into other independent operations. The firm would possibly disappear into obscurity, but I warned Modise that I would always follow him. I told *BizNews* that I was going to be like the proverbial hyena behind the kudu: "Every time he thinks he's shaken them off and slows down, ten minutes later he looks behind him, and we're on his tail.

MAHLOBO'S SECRET SPY NETWORK

The more we dug into Zuma's 'lost eight years', the more information came to light on how vehemently I, and other active citizens, had been targeted by his corrupt regime. In 2018, a disillusioned ex-spy came forward and revealed that he had been part of a secret 'off-the-books' agent network run by ex-Minister of Intelligence, David Mahlobo. This illegal, parallel intelligence structure was breathtaking, and one of its many illicit activities was to wiretap ourselves and many others.

The agent, codenamed 'Prophet' and 'Whiskey', was no longer being paid by Mahlobo, and he came to me to spill the beans. He put everything he knew of the network into an affidavit. He described how money was paid into his girlfriend's bank account and that phone signal grabbers were installed in houses in Whiteriver and Hazyview in Mpumalanga before being moved to Mahlobo's house in Waterkloof, Pretoria. The grabbers were allegedly provided by the Russians, who were allegedly aiming to have Mahlobo take over from Zuma.

The agent's job was to listen and transcribe the tapes, which had thirty-eight high-profile people under illegal surveillance.[191] Those

190 Alec Hogg, Paul O'Sullivan draws Hogan Lovell's blood: 'I'm a hyena onto your kudu', Biznews, 8 August 2019, https://www.biznews.com/interviews/2019/08/08/paul-osullivan-hogan-lovells-hyena-kudu

191 Alec Hogg, SSA insider spills beans, names those tapped, exposes Mahlobo, Biznews, 11 March 2019, https://www.biznews.com/undictated/2019/03/11/ssa-insider-spills-beans-names-those-tapped-exposes-mahlobo

who were being spied on between 2015 and 2018 included me, cabinet ministers, heads of non-governmental organisations, trade unions, judges, and others.[192]

The agent named those who were under surveillance: former Minister Malusi Gigaba, Chief Justice Mogoeng Mogoeng, journalism professor Anton Harber, CEO of Sygnia Group Magda Wierzycka, Executive Director of Freedom Under Law Nicole Fritz, Finance Minister Tito Mboweni, ex-Public Protector Advocate Thuli Madonsela, Constitutional Court Justice Edwin Cameron, former Finance Minister Pravin Gordhan, AngloGold chairman Sipho Pityana, Gauteng ANC Chair Paul Mashatile, Minister of Energy Jeff Radebe, Economic Affairs Minister Ebrahim Patel, and Foreign Affairs Minister Lindiwe Sisulu.

I handed the agent's revelations over to President Ramaphosa so that he could be aware of the threat. I also opened a criminal docket with the Hawks and called for Mahlobo to be hauled before the Zondo Commission so that he, too, could spill his secrets as Angelo Agrizzi did.

I am certain that as time goes on, even more will be revealed. Perhaps only then will we get the full picture of just how badly our human rights were abused during the state capture years.

STATE CAPTURE: ITS PHYSICAL EFFECTS

The truth is that despite three years (at the time of going to print) having passed since the Gupta Leaks emerged and the subsequent unravelling of the Zuma patronage network, there has been zero accountability for the corruption that took place in government services at state-owned companies, and the decimation of the criminal justice sector. By now, it cannot be claimed that there is no prima facie

192 Nicola Miltz, Respected editor angry on finding out he was spied on by government, South African Jewish Report, 22 March 2019, https://www.sajr.co.za/extras/test/2019/03/22/respected-editor-angry-on-finding-he-was-spied-on-by-government

evidence to prosecute at least one high-profile case. I have provided enough evidence to prosecute countless corruptors. Investigations, if there have been any, are just gathering dust.

Corruption has become a progressive disease in South Africa, a cancer that has permeated all levels of the state. South Africa is sick from corruption, which is stealing the country's future and hope. And yet, the beneficiaries of corruption are an exceedingly small percentage of the South African population who have unlawfully reaped untold wealth, all of which negatively affects the poorest of the poor.

"If you can't beat them, join them" has become the attitude of many connected people of South Africa. To have a job, food, education and clothes, you must either obey or carry out the unlawful bidding of the corrupt – or both. Comply or be fired – or worse still, be a target.

We are all suffering the symptoms of this. The thriving economy that was expanding year on year before Zuma and his gang of looters were handed the country's reigns in 2009 has dried up. So much so that when a real crisis like COVID-19 swept across the world, we had next to nothing left in the piggy bank to buffer us from its onslaught.

Cyril Ramaphosa is trying his best. But we all know he was handed a poisoned chalice. The looting of the country by the Zuptas was so severe that the current leadership has been left with nothing but bare bones to work with.

I have tried to do my part – as any employed and financially stable South African should – by handing out food parcels to the poor in my local community. But two deliveries of one hundred food parcels was already pushing the limit for our small company. The truth is that the lines of poor people waiting for food aid are a shame on all of us. Individuals like you and I can only do so much. It is Government that needs to step in during times like this to help the people who voted them into power. They need to take care of the most vulnerable. The high number of homeless people and people living below the poverty line can be directly attributed to Zuma's regime, yet Zuma lives like a fat cat while running rings around the justice system with taxpayer-funded teams of lawyers.

Unemployment is simply getting worse and critical sectors like health, education and social development are not receiving the investment boost a developing country like ours needs to lift its population out of poverty. The problems to our electricity supply, due to massive looting at Eskom, have already become obvious. Rolling blackouts will be with us for years, hampering growth and diminishing our overall quality of life. Other sectors have been neglected. Pollution, water infrastructure and sewage works – which have been given little attention in the public psyche but have come to the fore as the climate crisis comes into focus across the world – have shown us that when public money is stolen, all parts of the system suffers.

South African Airways, after eighty-six years of existence, will suffer financially for years. I am furious about what has happened to SAA. When Zuma promoted his alleged mistress to the helm, she singlehandedly stripped its asset value. Not only will its strategic and brand value be lost if it closes – with competitors quickly hiking up their prices – but eight thousand people will in all likelihood lose their jobs. I am not a supporter of closing the airline down. If every state-owned enterprise bled dry by the Guptas and their friends were to close their doors, we would have to say goodbye to Eskom, PRASA, Transnet, Denel, the water boards and many more municipalities too.

I was so angered by the news of SAA that I wrote an open letter to Pravin Gordhan in April 2020.[193] While I defended him when he was being targeted unfairly by Ntlemeza for his time as SARS Commissioner, I believe that he had questions to answer about his work between 2015 and 2017 when he appeared to do nothing to

193 Jackie Cameron, Paul O'Sullivan: Gordhan must be SCALPED, with Zuma, Myeni for crooked mess at SAA, Biznews, 15 April 2020, https://www.biznews.com/thought-leaders/2020/04/15/paul-osullivan-gordhan-zuma-myeni-saa

stop the rot taking place under his very nose. Gordhan was quick to go to the Zondo Commission in March 2019 to speak about Moyane and Zuma, but he remained silent about why he did nothing about it. In my letter, I said Gordhan should be asked why he never opened criminal dockets for the fraud and corruption he witnessed – and why he kept Myeni and Moyane in their jobs.

I'd asked him a similar question many years earlier, in July 2016, during a presentation he gave to the Institute of Directors at EY's Sandton head office.[194] When I asked him when he was going to fire Dudu Myeni and stop the corruption, he shot me a dirty look and stated that he was in the process of changing the whole board and that we would have to wait and see. Instead, he chose to keep Myeni in place for a further sixteen months, which was all the time she needed to inject the final kiss of death to SAA and clean up her audit trail.

In my 2020 open letter to Gordhan, I wrote:

> *The inconvenient truth is that Gordhan must shoulder joint and several liability along with Myeni, Zuma and the whole cabinet and NEC of the ruling party for the crooked mess created at SAA.*
>
> *If Gordhan had put his foot down and fired Zuma's mistress when the opportunities presented themselves (and there were many of them), we would not have been in the mess we are in today. Now he wants to claim the Q-dos for stopping the bleeding when, in fact, he was part of the cause of it and will simply cause hundreds of thousands of job losses in the tourism industry.*

What corruption has done to South Africa is unforgivable. Small towns and municipalities have been forsaken. Their neglect is more than just an eye-sore. They are an in-your-face reminder of the malaise corruption has wrought on our land. Their neglect threatens another critical section of our society – the farms and our still-strong food

194 Fin24, SAA requires a whole new Board – Gordhan, Politicsweb, 26 July 2016, https://www.politicsweb.co.za/documents/saa-requires-a-whole-new-board--gordhan

supply. Our broken small towns need to be fixed up and cannot simply be allowed to be forgotten, to become nothing more than dustbowls of once-fertile communities.

The economic decay has already come to pass. Rating agencies have moved South Africa to junk status and, with the whole world in depression due to COVID-19 lockdowns, foreign investment will likely be hard to come by. This will lead to further delays in growth, a lack of development, and even more poverty. The reality is that many of our people will starve, and crime will likely increase. The level of raw sewage flowing into the streets will rise. These are just the obvious physical effects state capture has wrought upon our country.

There are also the many sociological aspects that the malaise of corruption has bestowed on us. Distrust in the police is just one. The capture of the criminal justice system saw human rights violations aimed at those of us who spoke out against corruption. Security services were used to settle political scores, and whistle-blowers were targeted for speaking out. All of this moved us closer towards a police state. Even though we have moved back slightly from the precipice with the removal of people like Ntlemeza, Mdluli and Phahlane, we are still dangerously close to the edge. There are far too many 'sleeper' cells planted by people like Ntlemeza, Phahlane, Mdluli and Nhleko, who are serving the previous regime. No one has the will or ability to drive them out.

Another symptom we are seeing in our society is a general lack of respect for government or any figure of authority for that matter. The torching of schools is just one such causality. People have started to lose faith in the system. It is probable that fewer people will vote in the future, enabling the possibility of even worse corrupt leaders to come. Those who were part of Zuma's cabinet were all dirty rotten scoundrels, and many belong in prison, but sadly it is becoming clearer that they are immune from sanctions at the hands of the impotent and captured Hawks, SAPS and NPA.

Unfortunately, the Zondo Commission – as we knew it – was effectively killed off by COVID-19. The hearings were reduced to 'witnesses', many of whom were actually suspects, sitting behind closed doors in their lawyer's offices and giving the middle finger to the so-called evidence leaders, some of whom had completely ignored relevant evidence because it did not fit a particular agenda.

SOLUTION

I have a simple solution: hold the current government accountable for ruining an almost ninety-year-old airline, along with their crimes at PRASA, Eskom, Transnet, Denel, and most of the city councils and water boards. Hold them accountable by putting those responsible in prison for an exceedingly long time. Fix the state-owned companies and get this country back on top. If the only way to do this is to fire the whole government, then so be it. Let the voters decide.

A clean up *must* proceed from the valuable work of the Zondo Commission. Multiple prosecutions should also flow, even on one or two specimen charges, so that each and every one of the criminals who were part of the state capture project is sent to prison, if only for a year or two. The list of those I would prosecute includes – but is not limited to – Dudu Myeni, Lucky Montana, Khomotso Phahlane, Prince Mokotedi, Berning Ntlemeza, Nomgcobo Jiba, Lawrence Mrwebi, Jabulani Mlotshwa, Ntebo Mabula, Phumlani Ncube, Clifford Kgorane and last, but by no means least, Jacob Zuma himself.

I wait with bated breath. I am ready to start a process of private prosecutions with others who will join me if the paralysed National Prosecuting Authority does not rise to the challenge. It's not my function to be the gatekeeper of the country's moral fibre. It's not my function to investigate crime and corruption by public officials. It's certainly not my job to prosecute the same corrupt officials. However, the vacuum that has been left by state capture will see them all get away with their evil crimes if I take my foot off the gas now.

I am not someone who dwells in negativity. Negativity can paralyse a person, and that helps no one. I am someone who acts, and even though I am just one person, I am surrounded by others who feel the same way – people who have helped me in my fight against a corrupt regime and people who stand for what is right, no matter the personal cost.

People like Sarah-Jane Trent, Robert McBride, Colonel Candice Coetzee, military policewoman Stella Ngwenya, Captain Boitumelo Ramahlaha, Brigadier Sandragasen Moonsamy, General Johan Booysen, General Shadrack Sibiya, Johan van Loggerenberg, Glynnis Breytenbach, Freedom Under Law, the Helen Suzman Foundation, AfriForum, and the brave men and women at IPID. People like Mandla Mahlangu who gave the ultimate sacrifice – his life. We all owe them our gratitude for going the distance.

But there are not enough of us who have stood up and said, enough is enough.

DOMINOES START TO FALL

The latter part of 2020 and early 2021 brought good winds to South Africa as the wheels of justice started to turn again.

Ace Magashula, wannabe president of the country, was charged with corruption. Dudu Myeni was grilled at the Zondo Commission and chose to answer each question with, "*Chairperson, may I not answer that question in case I might incriminate myself?*" Phahlane tried desperately to stall his criminal trials by launching an application to have the matter withdrawn. He failed. Keith Keating lost his battle at the apex court to have the search warrants executed by IPID declared unlawful. When Keating desperately attempted to demand a further R540-million from the police by 'persuading' a dishonest MP, Tina

Joemat-Pettersson, to unlawfully 'order' the police to pay Keating's company and become owners of the disputed FDA Software, General Sitole flatly refused to comply with the unlawful instruction.

NOT ON MY WATCH

Too many good people suffered so that South Africa could prosper under a constitutional democracy. Some of them, like Steve Biko and Ahmed Timol, made the supreme sacrifice. Many others languished in prison under the Apartheid regime and lost the best years of their lives. These sacrifices meant nothing if those who followed robbed the poorest of the poor by stealing a sizeable chunk of the collected taxes so that there would be nothing left to uplift our desperate communities. When one considers that these criminals have set the country back more than a decade, if not longer, their conduct of these criminals is nothing more than a crime against humanity.

If the state does not rise to the challenge, I will do what must be done and send these people to prison, where they belong.

Many of these criminals with badges and gowns think that the COVID-19 pandemic will save them, that it will distract society, and we will forget what they did. How wrong they are. I will never forget what they did, and I will make them pay for it – as true as Bob.

How many South Africans will die and lose their jobs because of COVID-19? The ability to respond efficiently to the pandemic was greatly reduced due to the corruption epidemic that plagued South Africa for a decade before the pandemic came along. The shortage of hospital beds and equipment can be laid at the doorsteps of those who were engaged in state capture and the dirty cops and prosecutors who created the enabling environment for state capture to flourish. The final death toll from the lack of preparedness for COVID-19, the death toll from abject poverty, contaminated water – and all the other ailments that follow poverty – is a direct result of Zuma, his illegal immigrant Gupta friends, and all the dirty cops and prosecutors who aided and abetted them. I will *not* allow them to get away with what they have done.

Because the Zondo Commission decided not to report on the failings in the criminal justice system, I shall be calling for a judicial review of the role of corrupt cops and prosecutors in enabling State Capture by looking the other way and then attacking those, like me and my colleagues, in order to prevent us from exposing the dark underbelly. Don't get me wrong, the Zondo Commission did some great work, they just missed the most important point, i.e., that without a captured police and prosecution service, other forms of capture would not have gone un-checked.

I will not rest until justice has been done. I owe that to people like Mandla Mahlangu, and Babita Deokoran who both made the ultimate sacrifice whilst trying to expose corruption in our country. Their murders will not be forgotten. I also owe it to people like Cynthia Stympel and countless others who did the right thing, by speaking out, and paid for it with their livelihoods.

To the crooks who know I am coming after them, as they surely must, I will repeat what I said to Khomotso Phahlane, Vineshkumar Moonoo, Dudu Myeni, Berning Ntlemeza, and their paid liar Hangwani Mulaudzi on the 15th of March 2016:

STOP ME IF YOU CAN!

A SHORT AFTERWORD

At 8 a.m. on the 22nd of September 2021, which just so happened to coincide with the day I finished writing this book, I checked in on flight SA 317, South African Airways' inaugural flight, departing for Cape Town from OR Tambo International Airport at 8:05 a.m. on the 23rd of September 2021.

Rising from the ashes of Dudu Myeni's term of corruption, SAA took to the skies again, proving that something can be done about corruption and that South Africa can – and will – rise again.

South Africa remains, in my view anyway, one of the greatest countries on earth. If we all work together to rid it of the scourge of corruption, we can restore the country's credibility to the halcyon days of the mid to late 90s when the Rainbow Nation was at its best.

HOW CAN YOU HELP?

We are not journalists; we are not lawyers – we are forensics experts. Unethical journalists hate us because we expose them. Some journalists don't understand us as they don't believe we actually do what we do without being paid. We will keep doing what we do, whether people like it or not, until we no longer have a function – because South Africa will be back to normal.

Unlike some NPOs we do not receive any significant funding and I, Paul O'Sullivan, have covered 90% of the costs of what we do. To those who have supported us financially, however small, we are grateful.

Anyone who hates corruption and wants to support the work of Paul O'Sullivan and Forensics for Justice is welcome to contribute to our war chest by visiting:

www.forensicsforjustice.org

APPENDIX: EMAILS AND OPEN LETTERS

1 MY 21 NOVEMBER 2016 EMAIL TO PHAHLANE

I note that the SMS expresses an intention to kill me and the investigator (it says he can die with me) if he does not stop with his investigations. I understand why you want me dead, but you should not threaten senior investigators of IPID with such things. That's only likely to cause more trouble for you.

In fact, I know you are behind it, and I will state now why I know.

Firstly in order to create a red-herring, you suggest that I am in cahoots with various people and include yourself in that list. You know full well I am not in cahoots with you. You know I want you in prison for the good of SA. However, you include yourself so that we will think it could not have come from you. A really unintelligent double-bluff that had failed.

Next, you have this person, Tsholofelo Mogale, whom I have traced the cellular number to, let you use her phone to send the message, and then the phone is switched off. It's still off.

The same message that is sent to Mandla Mahlangu is copied to me but is meant to intimidate Mandla Mahlangu of IPID.

Your motive for the threats:

My only association with Mandla Mahlangu is that I am helping him with an IPID docket I opened against you following intensive investigations which began last year. The docket pertains to your corrupt relationship with the owners of a supplier to SAPS Forensics Division, which you used to head, and still control. To launder the money that was paid to you in carrier bags, you used the same cash to build an 803 square metre mansion at Sable Hills Waterfront Estate. I know this, and now we (the "we" being myself and IPID investigators) can prove this.

I traced the builder of the house by using old-fashioned detective work and shoe leather on the floor. Mandla and a colleague were with me when I did it, as we were chasing a paper trail, and I was assisting them since I knew what you'd been up to. We then went and had a short meeting with this guy. His name is Frikkie Terblanche. Frikkie very quickly made startling admissions. He admitted he was paid in cash for the whole construction project. His discussions with us were recorded and transcribed, and this is precisely what he said.

There are a lot more admissions concerning how the house was paid for. But the above should serve to show you, you have a big problem, and you know it. Hence the threats.

Frikkie was warned not to communicate with you. I guess he was worried, and his (betrayal of you) feelings got the better of him, as last Wednesday he called you and told you what he had done, with all the detail. But he did not tell you his discussions with us were recorded, as he did not know, until last Friday afternoon when Mandla called him and told him. There is no doubt that he then called you again and told you what Mandla had said to him concerning the recording of his initial discussions, where he admitted you paid him in cash. Since Mandla had left his business card with Frikkie, with his telephone number on it and since he had my telephone number as well, he clearly supplied that information to you. In doing what he did, he broke the law, and the offence is known as defeating the ends of justice.

And what did you do? You picked up the phone last Wednesday and called the estate manager at Sable Hills Waterfront Estate. You told him, in no uncertain terms, that he was not to cooperate with the guys from IPID, and he was NOT to give anything pertaining to you or your house to IPID. That conduct makes you guilty of the same offence as Frikkie, i.e. Defeating the Ends of Justice.

And what did you do after Frikkie called you on Friday afternoon and told you that Mandla had called him and told him that the call with him had been recorded? You had a sleepless night Friday and Saturday. On Sunday, you asked Tsholofelo Mogale to let you use her phone, and you sent a crude message to Mandla and copied me.

In that SMS, you tell Mandla that he can die with me or stop working with me. It can only have been you, as no one else had the knowledge that I was assisting the IPID, Mandla in particular, to obtain crucial evidence against you.

That was a big mistake and will not only speed up your entry to prison. It will see that you get a longer time in prison.

Of course, your criminal conduct does not just extend to the house built with cash kickbacks from a supplier to the police. There are a lot of other areas where you have been found wanting, and I have no doubt that in the fullness of time, you will face the music for all of it.

One of these things is my unlawful arrest and torture at the hands of your accomplice, Mokotedi. I've only now joined the dots on that one ...

I told this to Selebi 15 years ago, and I'm telling this to you now.

PREPARE YOURSELF FOR PRISON. I am sending you there.

By copy to the Deputy President, I am requesting you to be relieved of your duties NOW.

Don't even dream of threatening me again, or you will wake up and suffer the consequences.

2 A SNIPPET OF MY OPEN LETTER TO DEPUTY-PRESIDENT CYRIL RHAMAPHOSA EXPLAINING WHY SHAUN ABRAHAMS SHOULD BE REMOVED FROM THE NPA

Under Shaun Abrahams, certain senior members of the NPA have become a part of the largest crime syndicate this country has ever seen since the dawn of democracy. Between Abrahams and the incumbent President of the Republic, we have seen countless appointments at the level of Director of Public Prosecutions. Without exception, each and every one of those appointments is questionable and stand to be reviewed as soon as Abrahams has been removed from office.

As a case in point, it emerged during attempts by IPID to obtain agreement to charge certain police officials for serious offences that there was a general instruction that had come down from Abrahams office, that in all 'high-profile' cases, the decision to prosecute had been removed from the normal management line to his office, resulting in a back-log of awaiting decisions. Upon Abrahams receiving the request for a decision, he would then delegate that work to people under his control, who have been appointed during his watch, with an off the record instruction to decline to prosecute.

By this method, he has effectively stymied all prosecutions of high-profile persons, including, but not limited to, Myeni, Lucky Montana, Phahlane, Ntlemeza, Jen Chi Huang, Moonoo, Yusuf Kajee, Mdluli, and many others.

It is, therefore, my contention that Abrahams stands to be charged with various serious offences of obstructing justice and breaching section 32 of the NPA Act. Furthermore, since his conduct was deliberately calculated to protect the largest crime syndicate this country has ever seen, he should also be charged with Racketeering.

I, therefore, hope that you will not only remove Abrahams from his post as NDPP but that you will cause an investigation into every single decision taken by him during his time as NDPP. In addition, the investigation needs to look into the vast sums of out-of-budget spend he has made on senior advocates in private practice to attempt to prop up his unlawful conduct.

I also request that you disband the so-called PCLU, which has been completely bastardised and reform it with people that can be trusted and review each and every politically motivated prosecution they have commenced and hold those persons accountable.

It goes without saying that Abrahams is not a fit and proper person to act as a prosecutor in any sphere and should NOT be returned to his previous position, but should be suspended from work altogether, pending the outcome of the necessary investigations. Every day that Abrahams remains in office is a day too long. It may take decades for the NPA to recover from the damage he and Hulley have done.

3 MY LETTER TO SHAUN ABRAHAMS

The unlawful conduct of the NPA leadership facilitates serious crime in South Africa. I can and will prove it. You and your accomplices Torie Pretorius, Sello Maema and JJ Mlotshwa are living proof of all that is wrong at the NPA.

The Magistrate dissed the State so badly, Shaun, that your ears must have been burning. She made it clear that I had never acted unlawfully, and the State had failed to bring a proper case, and their only witness, the complainant, was a very poor witness and repeatedly contradicted herself and had, in fact, acted unlawfully herself. She also made it clear that the State had not carried out any investigation and queried why certain witnesses were not called.

Well, I can tell her the answer as to why certain witnesses were not called: it is because they would have provided exculpatory evidence, and Mlotshwa, in breach of his oath of office, but in compliance with the unlawful game-plan being run by you and Torie Pretorius, wanted to keep exculpatory evidence away from the court. As proof of this allegation, he tried desperately hard, not only in this case but in the other cases he had maliciously brought against me, to exclude exculpatory evidence in my possession, but failed.

4 MY 24 MARCH 2021 LETTER TO CARTE BLANCHE'S WYNAND GROBLER

The false FDA narrative you ran on 2021-03-21 refers.

It is now clear that you have turned a once fine investigative media programme into a propaganda machine for criminals.

I am extremely disappointed that, notwithstanding Carte Blanche's previous role in aiding and abetting state capture by:

Publishing a false narrative concerning the so-called SARS Rogue Spy Unit, thereby assisting in the evisceration and Capture of SARS;

Encouraging one of your crooked staff and his mistress to run a story that I had kidnapped the said mistress of the said crooked employee, thereby assisting in criminal attempts at shutting down the activities of Forensics for Justice;

Allowing convicted fraudster and state capture accomplice Mike Bolhuis to promote himself as a good guy on Carte Blanche, thereby bolstering the ongoing criminal conduct of Bolhuis;

... you have now seen fit to promote the dishonest narrative of members of a crime syndicate. A member of that syndicate was partly responsible for the capture of the criminal justice system, Keith Keating of FDA, who have stolen hundreds of millions from the fiscus, having first corrupted the senior management of SAPS Forensics Division.

Put simply, you have promoted the lies of FDA, whose corrupt activities were instrumental in bringing the SAPS Forensics Division to a grinding halt. Yet, you allow them to publicly blame others for their crimes, which led to the destruction of the forensic capacity of the police.

And you make money out of their criminal activity. How low can one stoop?

Only a week before you gave airtime to those corrupt criminals, we succeeded in putting a stop to a R540m payment to FDA, thereby saving the taxpayer the same amount. Yet Carte Blanche, who seems to relish the role of serial quislings, gladly promote the dishonest lies of criminals.

It is no coincidence that in recent weeks, one of your employees, the fraudster Beamish, has been working hand-in-glove on social media with his own anonymous Twitter handles and the anonymous Twitter handles of Keith Keating in garnering public support for their criminal lies.

You are, of course, afforded the opportunity to correct your treachery by revisiting the lies of FDA within 14 days.

If you maintain your treacherous position, it seems to me the country should be warned of the fact that Carte Blanche are serial offenders in the realm of assisting state capture and helped bring this country to its knees.

Accordingly, if the false narrative that you have advanced on behalf of FDA continues after 14 days, we will start a process to widely publish the fact that Carte Blanche is a state capture enabler and has been for many years.

You might enjoy employing criminals and advancing fake narratives of criminals, but I take a very dim view of the fact that the criminals you support were part of the machinery that was used to bring this country to its knees. Not to mention my repeated arrests, unlawful detention, torture, multiple raids by dirty cops on my offices and the kidnapping and detention of my legal counsel. For your information, the IPID investigating officer of the Keith Keating led criminal enterprise was murdered just a few weeks before Keating was to be arrested, and his colleagues were arraigned on trumped-up charges intended to disrupt the investigations against FDA and other members of the crime syndicate.

Does Carte Blanche have blood on its hands? Is Carte Blanche partly to blame for this country being brought to its knees? I certainly think so. If I think so and believe it's in the public interest to inform the rest of South Africa as to how low you stoop, I am constitutionally entitled to expose your conduct to public scrutiny.

You have a lot to answer for, and your sheer arrogance in the face of overwhelming evidence of your complicity with the underworld will be your undoing.

However, since the media in South Africa sometimes protect each other, and it is therefore extremely unlikely that any of your media associates will expose you for what you are, it is then up to me to finish what you have started with your unlawful conduct.

You have 14 days to reverse the damage you have done by promoting corrupt criminals from FDA.

You guys made a big mistake when you chose to let your crooked employee publish false narratives concerning me, to prop up the criminal conduct of him and his mistress, in stealing files from the Bobroff's and passing them on to Millar, so he could turn their clients into his clients and be forewarned of a touting charge he was facing.

Your unlawful conduct against me and the assistance you have repeatedly given to criminals is a mistake you have yet to pay for.

ALL RIGHTS RESERVED

5 MY EMAIL TO MOKOTEDI'S BOSSES, GENERAL GODFREY LEBEYA AND GENERAL KEHLE SITOLE ASKING THAT THEY INVESTIGATE MOKOTEDI'S TWEETS

...I've copied a selection below of his public rantings and support of the Bell Pottinger (Gupta Agents) terms WMC (white Minority Capital) and RET (Radical Economic Transformation).

Does that mean that the DPCI actually condone the use of such racist terms by a Major General in the police? If that is the case, are you aware that it breaches the constitution for a major general to be behaving like this and stoking racial hatred amongst the citizens of our country?

Has Mokotedi gone rogue, or is he just a law unto himself?

What's of more interest is that he claims to be ***"on a renewable ten-year contract with the Hawks, my transfer to the SAPS notwithstanding."*** *Clearly, that cannot be correct, as he was unlawfully hired as a Provincial Head of DPCI, with no security clearance. If he was unlawfully hired into the Hawks, how can he be 'lawfully' transferred into the SAPS and then allowed to stoke racial hatred against whites and hatred against me on*

Twitter and to propagate his threats and defamatory comments against me? I note he also viciously attacks respected journalists, surely not the policy of SAPS?

It is clear that Mokotedi has NEVER been a fit and proper person. It is equally clear that his appointment was unlawful. How then can it be justified that he is transferred to the SAPS on a renewable ten-year contract?

As you know, I am currently suing the state for in excess of ZAR150m. If the State continue to support such a bigot as this, I will be left no alternative than to issue a further summons for damages.

I therefore hereby ***DEMAND*** *that urgent steps are taken to silence this racist charlatan with a uniform, who led the charge (he claims at the instance of Ntlemeza) to have me subjected to brutal infringements of my constitutional rights, to protect those near and dear to Zuma.*

Since he makes it clear that he is in the DPCI notwithstanding his transfer to the SAPS, I am copying General Sitole so that perhaps the two of you can have a chat and make a decision that avoids the need for me to launch an application in the High Court, to put a stop to this ongoing abuse of my rights.

Printed in Great Britain
by Amazon

14757944R00331